Second Edition

Gateway to Early American History

Mark Jarrett, Ph.D. ▪ Robert Yahng, J.D.

Florida Transformative Education

Florida Transformative Education
10 Folin Lane
Lafayette, CA 94549
Tel: (925) 906-9742 Fax: (925) 939-6557 www.floridasocialstudies.com

Printed in the United States of America

Our books are printed on long-lasting acid-free paper. When it is available, we choose paper that has been manufactured by environmentally responsible processes. These may include using trees grown in sustainable forests, incorporating recycled paper, minimizing chlorine in bleaching, or recycling the energy produced at the paper mill.

ISBN 978-0-9976835-2-3

Second Edition

22 21 20 19 18 17 10 9 8 7 6 5 4 3 2

About the Authors

Mark Jarrett studied at Columbia University (B.A.), the London School of Economics (M.A. in international history), Stanford University (Ph.D. in history), and the University of California at Berkeley, where he received a law degree with honors (Order of the Coif). He was an editor of the school's law review and received the American Jurisprudence Award for Comparative Legal History. He studied constitutional law with Robert Post, now dean of the Yale Law School. Mark has taught at Hofstra University, at the Mander Portman School in London, and in the New York City Public Schools. He has served as a test writer for the New York State Board of Regents, and practiced law at Baker & McKenzie, the world's largest law firm. He is the co-author of more than thirty test preparation books and textbooks. James Sheehan, past President of the American Historical Association, describes Mark's recent book, *The Congress of Vienna and its Legacy* (London: I. B. Tauris, 2013), as "beautifully written" and providing "a fine sense of political structures without losing the human element," while Robert Jervis, past president of the American Political Science Association, calls his book a "model treatment."

Robert Yahng has taught Honors U.S. Government and Honors Micro and Macroeconomics at Salesian High School in Richmond, California, for the past sixteen years. He has been the school's Chairman of the Board of Directors from 2003 to 2013. Robert earned a B.A. in History at Berea College in Kentucky, the South's first interracial college, where his grandfather, father and mother were professors. He received his Juris Doctor degree from the University of Kentucky School of Law. Robert was a partner in the law firm of Baker & McKenzie for twenty-one years. He was the Managing Partner of its San Francisco and Palo Alto offices in the 1990s, and also founded its Taipei office. From 1999 to 2002, he served as a Public Governor on the Board of Governors of the Pacific Stock Exchange. He has been a member of the Board of Trustees of Berea College since 2003. From 1997 to 2014, he has been Chairman of American Bridge Company, which constructed the Bob Graham Sunshine Skyway Bridge, and the new Bay Bridge in San Francisco, as well as many other national landmarks, including the Chrysler Building in New York City. From 1967 to 1972, Robert served in the USAF and was honorably discharged with the rank of captain.

The Cover

Washington Crossing the Delaware (1851), painting by Emanuel Leutze

Contents

	Special Features of this Book	iv
Part 1	Before and When Americans were Colonists	
Chapter 1	Two Worlds Collide: Europe and the Americas	1
Chapter 2	Strangers in a Strange Land: How the English Colonies Began	21
Chapter 3	Life in the Thirteen British Colonies	49
Chapter 4	The Road to Revolution	75
Chapter 5	"The Times that Try Men's Souls": The Story of the American Revolution	101
Part 2	When Americans Established a New Republic	
Chapter 6	The Critical Period: America under the Articles of Confederation	133
Chapter 7	The "Miracle at Philadelphia": The Story of Our Constitution	153
Chapter 8	Launching the Ship of State: The Presidency of George Washington	185
Chapter 9	The Young Republic: America under Presidents Adams and Jefferson	207
Chapter 10	The War of 1812 and the "Era of Good Feelings"	229
Part 3	When Americans Expanded, Prospered, and Divided	
Chapter 11	Andrew Jackson and the Age of Reform	257
Chapter 12	An Expanding America: Manifest Destiny and the West	291
Chapter 13	The Industrial Revolution and its Consequences: North and South	317
Chapter 14	A House Divided: The Story of the Civil War	351
Chapter 15	The Reconstruction Era	383
	Index	I-1

Dedications

To Małgorzata, Alexander, and Julia, and to my mother, Beverly

—Mark Jarrett

To Tina, Christopher, and Kacie

—Robert Yahng

Acknowledgments

The authors wish to thank the following individuals for their generous help and advice: First and foremost, Ms. Jackie Viana, District Social Studies Supervisor of Miami-Dade County Public Schools, for her expert guidance as a reviewer and consultant. We thank her for her encouragement, suggestions and tireless devotion to the needs of the teachers and students of her district. We would also like to thank Ms. Angela Miller, former Social Studies Supervisor of Houston Independent School District (HISD), for reviewing parts of the book, and Ms. Małgorzata Jarrett, Mr. Alex Jarrett, Ms. Julia Jarrett, Mr. Malcolm Wyatt-Mair, and Ms. KrisAnne Nuguid for a multitude of services from finding images and typing to writing initial drafts of study cards and initial layout of some of the special features of the book. We would like to thank Ms. Nina Tyksinski for her excellent work as proofreader, Ms. Helen Stirling for her superb maps, and Ms. Jerianne Van Dijk for her delightful original drawings. Finally, we would like to thank Mr. Jonathan Peck and Ms. Joan Keyes of Dovetail Publishing Services for their creativity in the design and layout of this book.

The illustrated unit openers in this edition are based on the work of Genevieve Foster (1893–1979), whose books, such as *George Washington's World*, inspired Dr. Jarrett's love of history during his own middle school years.

These acknowledgments are not to be taken as an endorsement of this product by any of these individuals. In fact, in some cases we were not able to follow all of their recommendations. Any remaining errors are therefore our own.

Special Features of This Book

This book is designed especially for sixth graders in Florida who will be studying civics in seventh grade. Several features of the book will help them not only learn early American history but also to lay a firm foundation in civics. Highlighted text shows information that is required for middle school civics as well as for early American history. Special pop-ups in yellow draw connections between history and civics. Every chapter opens with an advanced organizer telling students which standards they are covering, identifying important vocabulary, and providing an overview of the chapter in the Florida "Keys" to Learning. At the end of every chapter, students will find a concept map, study cards, and review questions based on the format of the released items for the EOC in civics. We hope you enjoy this book.

Part 1
Before and When Americans were Colonists

Some Events that Took Place between 1492 and 1783

Columbus sailed west and united two hemispheres.

Spain failed to invade England in 1588.

English colonists inherited political traditions including rights from Magna Carta.

Captain John Smith saved the English colony at Jamestown.

Captured Africans were taken across the Atlantic by force and sold into slavery.

Britain defeated France in the French and Indian War

SAMUEL ADAMS

Samuel Adams organized the colonists against the Stamp Act and other taxes

Colonists threw chests of British tea into Boston Harbor.

Colonists fought the British in the American Revolution and declared their independence.

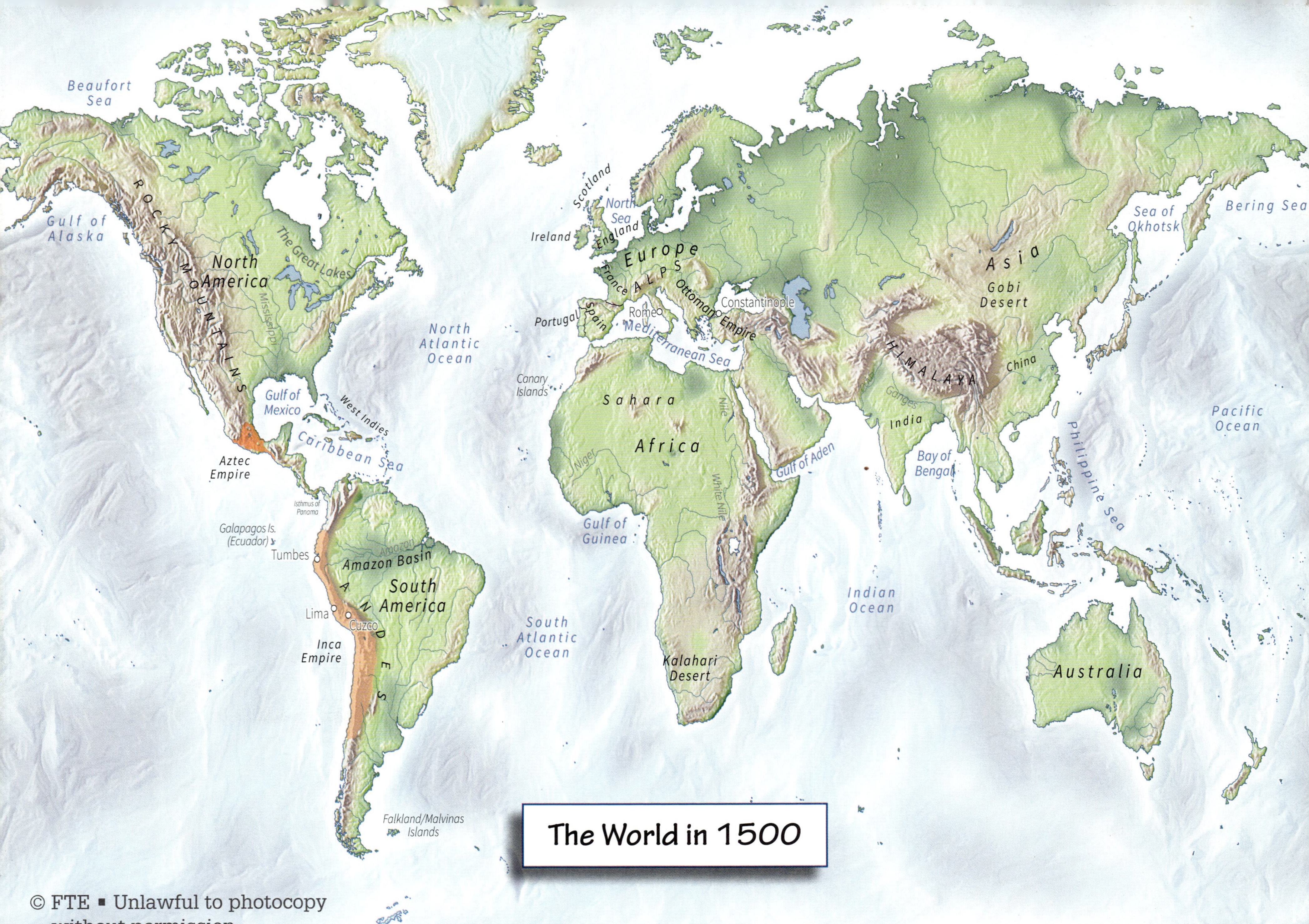
The World in 1500
Beaufort Sea
Gulf of Alaska
ROCKY MOUNTAINS
North America
The Great Lakes
Mississippi
Gulf of Mexico
West Indies
Caribbean Sea
Aztec Empire
Isthmus of Panama
Galapagos Is. (Ecuador)
Tumbes
Amazon
Amazon Basin
South America
ANDES
Lima
Cuzco
Inca Empire
Falkland/Malvinas Islands
North Atlantic Ocean
Canary Islands
South Atlantic Ocean
Scotland
North Sea
Ireland
England
Europe
France
ALPS
Portugal
Spain
Rome
Mediterranean Sea
Ottoman Empire
Constantinople
Sahara
Nile
Africa
Niger
White Nile
Gulf of Guinea
Kalahari Desert
Gulf of Aden
Asia
Gobi Desert
HIMALAYA
China
Ganges
India
Bay of Bengal
Indian Ocean
Sea of Okhotsk
Bering Sea
Pacific Ocean
Philippine Sea
Australia

CHAPTER 1 Two Worlds Collide: Europe and the Americas

SS.6.A.2.1 Compare the relationships among the British, French, Spanish, and Dutch in their struggle for colonization of North America.

SS.6.A.2.5 Discuss the impact of colonial settlement on Native American populations.

Names and Terms You Should Know

Eastern Hemisphere
Silk Road
Western Hemisphere
Americas
Descendants
Encounter
Columbian Exchange
Colonies
Catholic Church
Pope
Martin Luther
Protestants
Netherlands
Northwest Passage
New France
Competition
Religious Competition
Political Competition
Economic Competition
Cultural Competition

Florida "Keys" to Learning

1. Five hundred years ago, the peoples of the Eastern and Western Hemispheres had no knowledge of one another.

2. Europeans used a trade route known as the "Silk Road" to trade with Asia. Europeans were fond of Asian spices, silks and porcelains.

3. European explorers tried to find new routes to East Asia, especially after the Ottoman Turks conquered Constantinople.

4. Christopher Columbus believed he could reach Asia by sailing west. With the support of Queen Isabella of Spain, Columbus sailed west across the Atlantic and landed in the Americas in 1492. He thought he had landed in Asia.

5. Columbus' voyage led to an exchange of plants, animals, technology, culture and diseases known as the Columbian Exchange. Europeans brought the first horses, dogs, sheep, chickens, wheat, rice and other crops to the Americas. Native Americans introduced Europeans to corn, tomatoes, potatoes, squash, chocolate, tobacco and other crops. Europeans also brought new technologies and new diseases. Native Americans had no immunity to smallpox, measles and other European diseases. Many died in epidemics.

6. Spain set up colonies in the Americas, starting in the Caribbean Islands. Hernán Cortés conquered the Aztecs in 1521. Spanish soldiers enslaved the Indians and built themselves large estates.

7. In 1530, Francisco Pizarro conquered the Inca Empire of Peru. Mexico and Peru provided large amounts of gold to Spain.

8. Disagreements between Catholics and Protestants led to religious wars in Europe. Other European rulers worried about Spain's riches from the Americas. They began to send their own explorers to make their own claims.

9. French explorer Samuel Champlain started the French settlement at Quebec in 1608. Champlain was also the first European to reach the Great Lakes.

10. Fifty years after Champlain, French explorer Robert de La Salle sailed down the Mississippi River and claimed the territory around it for France. He named it Louisiana after French King Louis XIV. French settlements in the New World never attracted large numbers of colonists and mainly served as fur trading outposts.

11. The Netherlands hired English navigator Henry Hudson to explore the Americas. In 1609, Hudson entered New York Harbor and sailed up the Hudson River. Later he was the first European to reach Hudson Bay. His explorations became the basis for the Dutch claims in the New World.

12. The Dutch established a colony, which they called New Netherland. Control over the colony was given to the Dutch West India Company. The Dutch encouraged settlers and welcomed all people from all parts of the world leading to a great diversity of religious beliefs.

Two Worlds Apart

The World as it was understood in 1490: Europe, Africa, and Asia

What was it like to live 500 years ago?

Travel was slow compared to today. There were no airplanes, cars, or even trains. To travel on land, people could only walk, ride on a horse or donkey, or sit in a horse-drawn cart or carriage. To travel by water, they had to sail on wooden ships. Ships were powered by oars or the wind. Travel was so difficult that most people spent their entire lives in their own village without ever going anywhere at all.

While travel was limited, people in Europe, Asia, and Africa used the resources they had to create complex lifestyles. They developed mathematics, science, religion, philosophy, medicine, and the arts. They learned to grow different crops, such as wheat and rice. They raised pigs, cattle, and sheep. Although most people lived in the countryside, many lived in towns and cities. These became centers of craftsmanship and trade. People developed skills, such as making metal armor, that were useful in war. Builders were able to construct large structures, from the pyramids of ancient Egypt to the towering stone Gothic cathedrals of medieval Europe.

The Eastern Hemisphere

By 1492, Europe was divided into separate kingdoms. To the east, powerful emperors ruled China. The Middle East was united under the Ottoman Turks. South of the Sahara Desert, Africans were divided into kingdoms and tribes.

Europeans, Africans, and Asians shared a few giant land masses. The people of the **Eastern Hemisphere** traded goods and ideas with one another. Europeans loved the spices, silks, and porcelains of East Asia. These goods were traded along the "Silk Road"—an overland route across Central Asia that has existed since Roman times. After the Turkish capture of the city of Constantinople in 1453, it became more difficult for Europeans to reach the Silk Road.

A depiction of traders on the Silk Road

Sometimes trade and other contacts between peoples led to trouble. In the 1340s, merchant ships from Asia brought the Black Death to Europe. This disease killed as much as one third of Europe's population.

People suffering from the Black Death

The Western Hemisphere—The Americas

Unknown to the people of the Eastern Hemisphere, millions of people also lived on the other side of the Earth—in the **Western Hemisphere**. More than fifteen thousand years ago, hunters and their families crossed a land bridge that once connected northeastern Asia and Alaska. From there, their **descendants** (*children and later generations*) spread across the Americas. They discovered how to plant corn and other crops. In some places, such as central Mexico, they built large cities.

The peoples of the Eastern Hemisphere (Europe, Africa, and Asia) and of the Western Hemisphere (the Americas) lived completely apart for thousands of years. Separated by the oceans, they had no idea at all of each other's existence. But that was about to change.

Columbus and the Great Encounter

The Voyages of Columbus

Christopher Columbus was an experienced sailor from the Italian city of Genoa. Most Europeans already knew that the world was round. Columbus mistakenly believed it was smaller than it actually is. By using the trade winds, he thought he could reach Asia by sailing west. Travel to the east by land had become more difficult after the Turkish conquest of Constantinople, making Asian spices and other goods even more valuable. New inventions, such as the magnetic compass and ships with moveable rudders, seemed to make such a voyage possible. However, Columbus lacked the money he

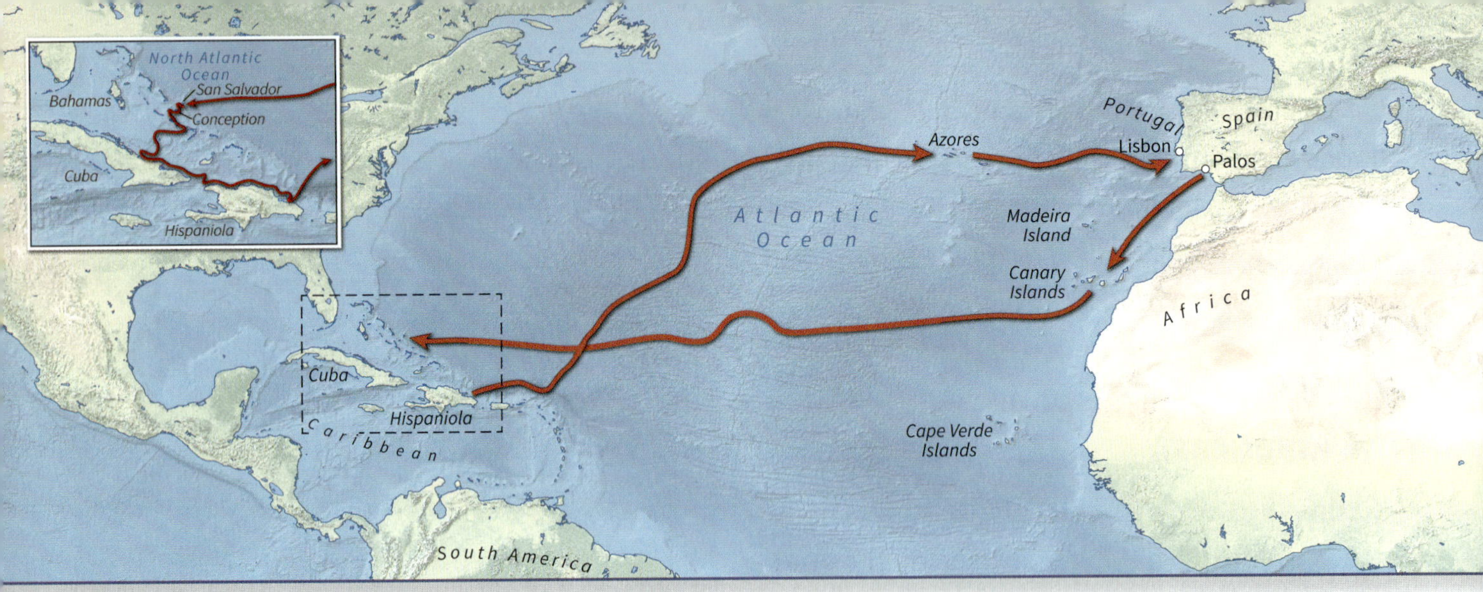

Columbus' Route to the Western Hemisphere: the First Voyage

needed to make this journey. He needed ships, men, and supplies.

Columbus tried to persuade the King of Portugal to support his expedition. He failed. Finally, Queen Isabella of Spain agreed to help. Columbus set sail from Spain with three ships in early August 1492. He stopped at the Canary Islands in September. Then he sailed west into the open ocean for five weeks before reaching land in early October. Columbus landed on the

The Historian's Apprentice

Imagine that you are Christopher Columbus. Write a letter to Ferdinand and Isabella describing your voyage and discoveries. You can use the paragraph frame below or write your own letter.

Your Majesties,

Thanks to your great generosity, I was able to hire _____ ships. We set sail on __________

The weather was ___________. First we stopped at _________________. Then we were on the open sea with no sight of land for many weeks. I became afraid that ______________________. The crew ____________________________. Finally, we arrived on land. Your Majesties have never seen such a beautiful place. ___________. The people of Asia are very strange and not at all what I expected. ______________

Your very devoted subject,
Christopher Columbus

island of San Salvador. He thought, however, that he had landed in Japan. He then sailed to Cuba and the island of Hispaniola (Haiti and the Dominican Republic). Columbus made three other voyages to the Americas. He forced native peoples to search for gold and was later accused of treating them cruelly. But he was still a great explorer. Because of Columbus, the two worlds of the Eastern and Western Hemispheres finally came into contact with one another.

The Columbian Exchange

The **encounter** (*meeting*) between the Old and New Worlds brought new plants and animals to each hemisphere. This is known as the **Columbian Exchange**. Native Americans grew corn, tomatoes, potatoes, sweet potatoes, chocolate, squash, green beans, lima beans, peanuts, vanilla, and tobacco. These crops were all unknown in Europe at the time. European explorers brought with them horses, dogs, sheep, chickens, cows, goats, rats, wheat, rice, sugar, oats, onions, oranges, apples, bananas, and coffee. None of these had ever been seen in the Americas until the explorers arrived. Europeans also brought new products that they made, such as large ships, cannons, glass, and steel. Finally, the Columbian Exchange brought new diseases to the Americas. Native American peoples had no **immunity** against these diseases.

The Columbian Exchange

Europeans called the Americas the "New World." Of course this area wasn't really new at all. It had existed for millions of years. Native Americans had been living there for thousands of years. But for Europeans, the lands discovered by Columbus were new. The idea that there was a whole other previously unknown continent came as a great surprise.

Europeans Divide the New World

Soon after Columbus' first voyage, the **Pope** (*the head of the Catholic Church*) divided the Americas between Spain and Portugal. The Pope gave Portugal the territory of present-day Brazil, where people still speak Portuguese. He gave the rest of the New World to Spain. France, Holland, and Great Britain—all countries on the Atlantic—did not accept this division. They sent new explorers across the Atlantic Ocean to make their own claims on the lands of the New World.

Europeans looked down on the native peoples of the Americas. They saw them as savage and uncivilized. They thought of the Americas as their own. European rulers competed to make claims in the New World. They hoped to gain new territories, obtain enormous riches, and convert the peoples of the Americas to Christianity.

The Spanish Conquest of Mexico and Peru

The Conquest of Mexico

The Spanish set up their first **colonies** in the Caribbean Islands.

> A **colony** is a settlement that a country makes in a different place. It sends colonists who bring their own language, traditions and ways of doing things.

From the Caribbean, Spanish explorers went to the mainland. **Hernán Cortés** landed with a force of only five hundred men in Mexico. He burned his ships and marched into the interior. He became a guest of the powerful Aztec Emperor in his capital city of Tenochtitlan. This large city was built on many islands. Impressed by its riches, Cortés made plans to conquer the Aztecs. Cortés actually took Emperor Montezuma as his prisoner while still in the capital. Later, Montezuma was killed and the Spaniards fled. They allied with enemies of the Aztecs. Then they returned and conquered the Aztec capital in 1521. Cortés and his men

Hernán Cortés

An Aztec temple: Human sacrifices to the sun god were once made at the top of the temple.

The Historian's Apprentice

How did a handful of Spaniards conquer the entire Aztec empire? Write a paragraph explaining how this happened in your journal or on a separate sheet of paper. Illustrate your paragraph with your own picture.

had cannons, horses, dogs, and Indian allies. The Aztecs were suffering from an epidemic of smallpox at the time of the attack.

Mexico under Spanish Rule

The Spanish conquerors tore down the giant Aztec temple used for human sacrifices and for worshipping the sun. They used its stones to build a great Catholic cathedral, which still stands in the center of Mexico City today. The Spanish also set up a new government. A **viceroy** (*deputy*) of the King of Spain became the governor of Mexico. Spanish became Mexico's official language. The Catholic Church started converting the Indians to Christianity.

Mexico had vast amounts of gold and silver. These were seized by the Spanish conquerors and sent back to Europe. Indians were forced to work in Mexico's gold and silver mines. The King of Spain received one-fifth of all the gold and silver that was taken.

Cortés rewarded his soldiers with large pieces of land in Mexico. Indians were handed over to Spanish landowners to work in their mines and on their farms. Millions of Indians died from overwork and from the spread of smallpox, measles, and other diseases that the Spanish had brought from the Old World.

The Conquest of Peru

Francisco Pizarro, a second "**conquistador**" (*conqueror*), was the mayor of the capital of the Spanish colony of Panama. Learning of Cortés' success, Pizarro dreamed of conquering the **Inca Empire** in Peru. In 1530, he received the support of the King of Spain for his plans. Pizarro sailed to Peru. With just two hundred men and four cannons, Pizarro faced an army of several thousand Inca warriors. The Inca Emperor Atahualpa went to greet Pizarro with only unarmed nobles. Pizarro surprised the Incas by attacking and capturing their Emperor. Pizarro then demanded that an entire room be filled with gold and silver for Atahualpa's release. Even though the Incas provided the gold and silver that Pizarro demanded, Pizarro had Atahualpa killed anyway. Pizarro next conquered the Inca capital of Cuzco. He turned Peru into a Spanish colony and founded its new capital at Lima.

Religious Conflict in Europe

While Spaniards were conquering the Americas, the people of Western Europe fell into a sharp disagreement. For centuries, they had been united by the **Catholic Church**. The Catholic Church was led by the Pope in Rome. Some Christians now openly questioned the Pope's authority. It all began when **Martin Luther**, a German monk, nailed a list of 95 complaints onto his church door. Luther believed that people should read the Bible for themselves. Luther and his followers no longer accepted the Pope as God's representative on Earth. Because Luther and other reformers protested against the Catholic Church, they became known as **Protestants**.

These disagreements over religion led to a series of bloody wars. For more than a hundred years, Protestants and Catholics fought one another. The rulers of Spain used much of their wealth from the Americas to pay soldiers to fight in these wars.

Both England and the **Netherlands** (Holland) became Protestant. Their leaders feared the growing power of Spain. They especially did not want to see all the riches of the New World go to this Catholic country. France remained Catholic, but its rulers also feared the power of Spain. Each of these other countries therefore decided to establish its own colony in the Americas.

New France

The French sent explorers to find a **Northwest Passage**—a way to reach Asia by sailing north of the American land mass. In fact, there is no practical water route above North America, but no one knew that at the time.

Champlain

One of these explorers, **Samuel Champlain**, landed in Canada in 1608. Champlain sailed up the **St. Lawrence River**. He started a French settlement at **Quebec**. Champlain was also the first European to reach the Great Lakes. Champlain was appointed Governor of "New France" and promoted the fur trade with the Indians. French traders gave European goods to the Indians, including guns, to obtain furs they could sell in Europe.

Samuel Champlain and his original map of the entrance to the St. Lawrence River

La Salle

Fifty years after Champlain's voyages, **Robert de La Salle** sailed south from Canada. He became the first European to enter the Ohio River. La Salle sailed down the Mississippi River and claimed all the lands surrounding it for France. He named the territory "**Louisiana**" after the French King Louis XIV. On another expedition, La Salle tried to find the mouth of the Mississippi River. He landed instead on the coast of Texas. La Salle lost a ship to pirates and two others to storms. He was eventually killed by his own men.

Based on the "discoveries" of these explorers, France claimed control of the very center of the North American continent. French claims stretched from the St. Lawrence River to the Great Lakes, and down the Mississippi River to where it enters the Gulf of Mexico.

French settlements in North America never attracted many colonists. They mainly served as trading posts for the valuable fur trade. Furs, especially beaver pelts, were highly prized in Europe for making hats.

An early map of La Salle's exploration from Canada to the Gulf of Mexico

New Netherland

The **Netherlands** (or Holland) is a small country in Western Europe. It is next to the Atlantic Ocean just north of France. At one time, the Netherlands had been ruled by Catholic Spain. When the **Dutch** (*the people of the Netherlands*) became Protestants, they successfully fought for their independence.

Henry Hudson

For centuries, the Dutch were known for their skills at sea and successful trade. Dutch merchants hoped to be the first to find the Northwest Passage. They hired an English sea captain named **Henry Hudson** to explore for them. In 1609, Hudson crossed the Atlantic and entered New York Harbor. He sailed up the **Hudson River** (named after him). On another voyage, he discovered Hudson Bay. His crew members finally tired of his exploring and rebelled. They put Hudson and his son on a small boat in the middle of Hudson Bay in freezing weather. No one ever heard from them again.

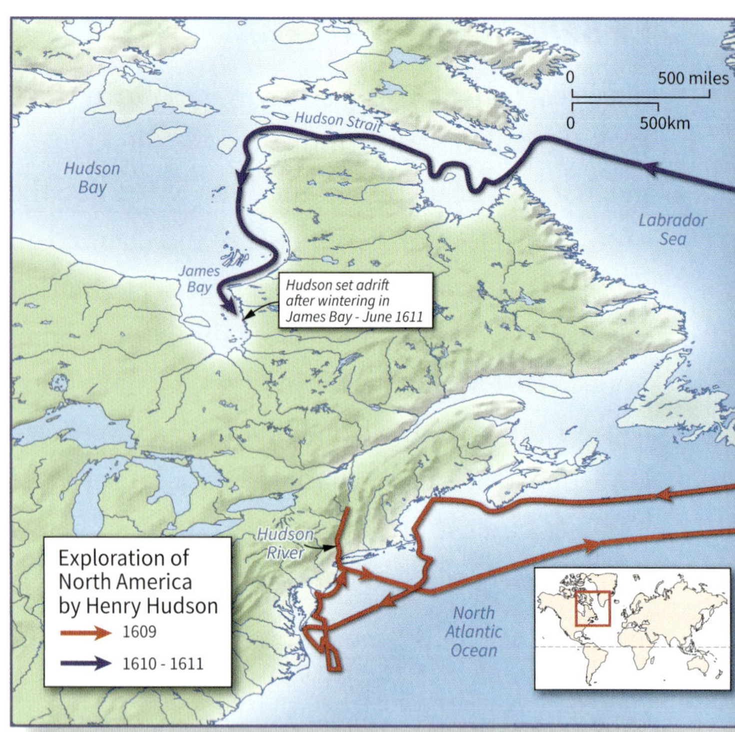

Henry Hudson's voyages in 1609 and 1610

Hudson's voyages became the basis for Dutch claims in the New World. The Dutch established a colony in present-day New York. They called it **New Netherland**. Control over the colony was given to the **Dutch West India Company**, a company of Dutch merchants. The company established two towns—Fort Orange on the Hudson River and **New Amsterdam**, where the Hudson River empties into the Atlantic Ocean. To encourage settlement of the colony, the Dutch West India Company offered land to any rich investor, known as a **patroon**, who could bring fifty new settlers to the colony.

The Dutch welcomed people from all parts of the world to their colony, including those of different faiths. There was greater **diversity** (*differences*) of religious beliefs in New Netherland than in any other colony in North America. The Dutch were also active in the slave trade. They brought African captives to New Netherland as early as 1625.

The Historian's Apprentice

Countries **compete** when they try to win an advantage over one another. It is like trying to win a contest. Competition between European powers took several forms:

- Competition between the European powers was political: Each country hoped to increase its power and influence.
- Competition between the European powers was religious: Catholic and Protestant countries were at war with each other. Each hoped to spread its religious beliefs.
- Competition between the European powers was economic: Each power hoped to gain riches from the New World—either from gold or trade.
- Competition between the European powers was cultural: Each power hoped to spread its language and way of life.

Choose one of the forms of competition above. Then make your own poster, chart, or cartoon to illustrate it. Use information you learned in this chapter to help make your illustration.

Find where these words are used in the chapter. Then make one sentence of your own using each word.

	Page number	Your sentence
continent		
descendants		
colony		
immunity		
conquest		
diversity		

Name______________________________

Complete the following chart by describing the Spanish, French and Dutch colonial empires in North America.

European Colonial Empires in North America

Areas of Settlement	Characteristics
Spanish colonies	
French colonies	
Dutch colonies	

Chapter Review Cards

Background to the Exploration of the Americas

- Five hundred years ago, the peoples of the Eastern and Western Hemispheres had no knowledge of each other.
- European merchants traded with Asia. They used the "Silk Road," a land route that linked Europe and Asia. Europeans were especially fond of spices, silks and porcelains from East Asia.
- Trading along the Silk Road had many problems. Europeans began to search for an all-water route to Asia. The Portuguese started sailing along the coast of Africa.

Columbus Sails to the Americas

- Christopher Columbus believed he could reach Asia by sailing west. In 1492, Queen Isabella of Spain agreed to sponsor Columbus' voyage.
- Columbus sailed west across the Atlantic and landed in the Americas.
- Thinking he had landed in Asia, Columbus was quick to enslave native peoples in order to search for gold.

The Columbian Exchange

- An exchange of plants, animals, technology, culture and diseases took place between Europeans and Native Americans. This is known as the Columbian Exchange.
- Native Americans introduced Europeans to corn, tomatoes, potatoes, sweet potatoes, squash, chocolate, tobacco and other new foods.
- European explorers brought horses, dogs, sheep, chickens, wheat, rice, sugar and other crops unknown to Native Americans at that time.
- Europeans also brought new technologies to the Native Americans, such as ships and cannons.
- They also brought new diseases against which Native Americans had no resistance, such as smallpox and measles. These led to epidemics that killed most Native Americans.

The "New World"

- The Europeans called the Americas the "New World," even though the area had existed for millions of years.
- Europeans viewed Native American peoples as uncivilized, and often treated them cruelly.
- The Pope divided the Americas between Spain and Portugal. Portugal received present-day Brazil while Spain was given the rest of the "New World."
- France, Holland and England did not accept this division. They sent explorers to claim their own territories.

The Spanish Conquest of the Americas

- Spain was the first European country to set up colonies in the Americas. Hernán Cortés marched through Mexico and conquered the great Aztec Empire in 1521. The Aztecs were suffering from a widespread epidemic of smallpox. Cortés had horses, dogs, guns, armor and Indian allies. The Spaniards enslaved the Aztecs. They introduced Christianity, the Spanish language and Spanish laws.
- In 1530, another Spanish "conquistador," Francisco Pizarro, conquered the Inca Empire. He turned Peru into a Spanish colony with a new capital at Lima.
- Spain was enriched by gold and silver taken from the Aztec and Inca Empires.

Religious Conflicts in Europe

- During the Reformation, Christians in Europe divided into Catholics and Protestants. Protestant countries like England and the Netherlands started competing with Spain to obtain riches in the Americas.

New France

- France sent its own explorers to the Americas. Samuel Champlain landed in Canada in 1608 and started the French settlement at Quebec. Champlain was also the first European to reach the Great Lakes. He became a governor of "New France." He promoted the fur trade with the Indians.
- French explorer Robert de La Salle sailed down the Mississippi River and claimed the territory around it for France. He named the area Louisiana after French King Louis XIV.
- French settlements in North America never attracted large numbers of colonists and mainly served as trading posts for the fur trade.

New Netherland

- The Netherlands hired Henry Hudson to explore the Americas. In 1609, Hudson entered New York Harbor and sailed up the Hudson River. Later he discovered Hudson Bay. His explorations were the basis for Dutch claims in the New World.
- The Dutch established the colony of New Netherland. They built settlements at New Amsterdam and Fort Orange. The Dutch West India Company had control over the colony. The Dutch encouraged settlers and investors by offering large acres of lands to patroons. They also welcomed people from all parts of the world and tolerated those of different faiths.

Two Worlds Collide: Europe and the Americas

World was divided in two parts
- Eastern Hemisphere: Europe, Asia, Africa
- Western Hemisphere: The Americas
- Neither side had knowledge of the other

Columbus and the Great Encounter
- Columbus received support from the rulers of Spain
- In 1492, Columbus sailed west to reach Asia
- Columbus reached the Americas

The Columbian Exchange
- Europeans and Native Americans gave new plants, animals, products and diseases to each other
- Americans: corn, potatoes, tomatoes, sweet potatoes, peanuts, tobacco, chocolate
- Europeans: horses, dogs, sheep, cows, wheat, rice, sugar, oranges, apples, smallpox, measles

Spanish Conquest of Mexico and Peru
- The Pope divided the "New World" between Spain and Portugal
- Spain set up its first colonies in the Caribbean

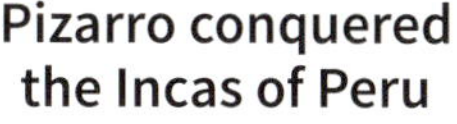

Pizarro conquered the Incas of Peru

Cortés conquered Aztecs of Mexico; replaced Aztec temples with churches
- Gave his soldiers large properties
- Aztecs forced to work for Spaniards
- Many Aztecs died from smallpox epidemic

Religious Conflicts in Europe
- Protestants challenged Catholic Church
- England and Netherlands became Protestant
- Catholics and Protestants fought each other
- Other European rulers wanted colonies

New France
- Based their claims on the explorations of Champlain and La Salle
- Established control over the St. Lawrence River, Great Lakes and Mississippi River
- French colonists focused on the fur trade with Indians

New Netherland
- Based their claims on the explorations of Henry Hudson
- Established settlements at New Amsterdam and Fort Orange
- Dutch West India Company allowed diversity

What do you know?

SS.6.A.2.1

1. The map below shows North America.

Which conclusion about European territorial claims can be drawn from this map?

A. The Netherlands and Spain had conflicting claims.

B. Spanish claims included all land surrounding the Gulf of Mexico.

C. Western European nations claimed ownership of North America.

D. The British and Spanish fought over land in the Mississippi River Valley.

SS.6.A.2.1

2. Which reason for seeking colonies was shared by Spanish, French and Dutch rulers?

A. to gain wealth and power

B. to discover new farming methods

C. to spread the Catholic religion

D. to avoid political conflict in Europe

SS.6.A.2.1

3. What advantage did Spain have over other European powers in establishing overseas colonies?

A. Its colonists were immune to local diseases.

B. Its explorers had reached the Americas first.

C. Its colonists were more used to American conditions.

D. Native Americans preferred Spaniards to other Europeans.

SS.6.A.2.1

4. How did the Columbian Exchange affect the lives of Europeans?
   A. New foods and exploration promoted economic growth.
   B. Millions of Europeans died from new American diseases.
   C. Native Americans moved to Europe to compete with Europeans for jobs.
   D. New Native American religions competed with the Roman Catholic Church.

SS.6.A.2.1

5. How did religious competition affect the colonization of North America?
   A. Most colonists converted to Native American religions.
   B. The Pope encouraged Protestant rulers to start their own colonies.
   C. Dutch officials persecuted colonists with different religious beliefs.
   D. France and Spain sent priests to convert Native Americans to Catholicism.

SS.6.A.2.5

6. The passage below was written by Bartolemé de Las Casas, a Spanish friar, in 1542.

> *The Indies were discovered in the year 1492. In the following year a great many Spaniards went . . . [to this] large and most happy isle called Hispaniola . . . Once so populous (having a native population that I estimated to be more than three million), [it] has now a population of barely two hundred people.*

   Which conclusion can be drawn from this passage?
   A. The Spanish conquest of Hispaniola led to the deaths of millions of native islanders.
   B. Conflicts between Britain and Spain for control of Hispaniola led to the deaths of millions.
   C. The Spanish forced native peoples to move to other islands so that they could control Hispaniola.
   D. Spanish conquerors executed the native peoples of Hispaniola because they were not Roman Catholic.

SS.6.A.2.5

7. Which belongs in a list of reasons for conflict between Native Americans and Europeans?
   A. Europeans refused to share their farming methods.
   B. Europeans took over lands used by Native Americans.
   C. Native Americans refused to learn European languages.
   D. Europeans forced Native Americans to adopt Christianity.

SS.6.A.2.1

8. What was an important economic incentive for the European colonization of North America?

   A. Europeans discovered gold in parts of North America.

   B. Europeans were able to find a Northwest Passage to Asia.

   C. Europeans wished to convert the Native Americans to Christianity.

   D. Europeans found more advanced technologies in North America.

SS.6.A.2.1

9. Which statement describes the Spanish colonization of North America?

   A. Its colonists were families facing persecution in Europe for their religious beliefs.

   B. Its colonists settled along the Hudson River and permitted different religious groups.

   C. Its colonists established ranches, farms and mines in the Caribbean and Mexico and shipped gold back to Europe.

   D. It colonists established trading posts along the St. Lawrence River and Great Lakes to obtain furs from Native American trappers.

SS.6.A.2.1

10. Which European power established settlements along the Hudson River to grow crops and trade with the Native Americans?

    A. Spain

    B. France

    C. Holland

    D. England

SS.6.A.2.5

11. The picture below is from a handwritten book completed in 1569. It was put together by Spanish missionaries to show Aztec life at the time the Spanish arrived in Mexico. This book was written in both the Aztec and Spanish languages. The artists were probably Aztec indians.

Which conclusion can be drawn from this illustration?

A. The Aztecs copied the ancient Greeks for their styles of clothing

B. The Aztecs were a very peaceful people before the arrival of Europeans.

C. The Aztecs benefited greatly from the arrival of European explorers in Mexico.

D. The Aztecs had developed their own advanced culture with musical instruments and woven cloth.

CHAPTER 2 Strangers in a Strange Land: How the English Colonies Began

SS.6.A.2.1 Compare the relationships among the British, French, Spanish, and Dutch in their struggle for colonization of North America.

SS.6.A.2.2 Compare the characteristics of the New England, Middle, and Southern colonies.

SS.6.A.2.3 Differentiate economic systems of New England, Middle and Southern colonies including indentured servants and slaves as labor sources.

SS.6.A.2.4 Identify the impact of key colonial figures on the economic, political, and social development of the colonies.

SS.6.A.2.5 Discuss the impact of colonial settlement on Native American populations.

SS.6.A.2.7 Describe the contributions of key groups (Africans, Native Americans, women, and children) to the society and culture of colonial America.

SS.6.C.1.4 Identify the evolving forms of civic and political participation from the colonial period through Reconstruction.

Alignment to Grade 7 Civics Standards

SS.7.C.1.2 Trace the impact that the Magna Carta, English Bill of Rights, Mayflower Compact and Thomas Paine's *Common Sense* had on colonists' views of government.

Names and Terms You Should Know

House of Burgesses
Separatists
Mayflower
Pilgrims
Mayflower Compact
Puritans
General Court
Religious toleration
Fundamental Orders of Connecticut
William Penn
Frame of Government
Lord Baltimore
Debtors
Exclusive ownership
King Philip's War

Florida "Keys" to Learning

1. In the 1580s, the English sent settlers to Roanoke to start their first colony in North America, but it failed.

2. In 1607, the first permanent English colony in North America was started at Jamestown by English investors. The investors hoped to make money.

3. Half the colonists died before a second group arrived in 1608. Captain John Smith saved the colony by establishing friendly relations with the Indians and by insisting all colonists work. John Rolfe began growing tobacco in 1612 and brought success to the colony. In 1619, women from England and Africans arrived, and the colony also established the House of Burgesses.

4. Pilgrims and Puritans came to America for religious reasons. The Pilgrims were Separatists who wanted to separate from the Church of England. The Pilgrims landed in Plymouth. Before they left their ship, the men signed the **Mayflower Compact** in which they pledged to form their own community and obey its laws.

5. In 1630, the Puritans landed in Massachusetts Bay. The Puritans wanted to "purify" the Church of England. John Winthrop and other leaders saw their colony as a "City upon a Hill" setting a shining example for the world. The colony was governed by officials elected to the General Court.

6. Other English colonies were also established:

Rhode Island. Roger Williams was forced to leave Massachusetts and established the colony of Rhode Island based on religious toleration: its colonists could worship freely in their own way. Anne Hutchinson joined Williams.

Connecticut. Thomas Hooker started this colony. The Fundamental Orders of Connecticut served as a written plan for its government.

New Hampshire. A group of investors in England started this colony.

Pennsylvania. The Quakers were Protestants who supported non-violence. William Penn was given land in America to create a land for Quakers.

Maryland. George Calvert, known as Lord Baltimore, started the colony of Maryland as a home for England's Catholics.

North and South Carolina. King Charles II gave eight nobles land for a new colony. They established Carolina. The colony divided into North and South Carolina in 1712.

New York, Delaware, and New Jersey. In 1664, England took over the Dutch colony of New Netherland and divided it into the colonies of New York, Delaware and New Jersey.

Georgia. James Oglethorpe founded Georgia as a colony for debtors in English prisons.

7. English settlements had harmful effects on Native Americans. English settlers took the land and pushed the Indian tribes westward. The introduction of guns and new weapons made warfare more dangerous. Many Indians died from European diseases.

Imagine spending months crossing the Atlantic Ocean in a small wooden ship. At the end of your voyage, you land in a wilderness without houses, electricity, or plumbing. There are no stores to buy things. Everything you need—water, food, shelter, firewood, and clothes—you must take from nature or make for yourself. And this is not all. Angry people who speak a different language and have different customs may attack you. Finally, you will face extremes of weather and dangerous diseases. Would you make such a journey? In this chapter, you will learn about people who did: the first English colonists in North America.

Events Leading to the First English Colonies

What conditions led the first English colonists to be willing to make such sacrifices? To answer this question, we need to know more about what was going on in the world at the time.

England becomes Protestant

Like the rest of Western Europe, England was once a Catholic country. However, in the 1530s, King Henry VIII of England suddenly became Protestant. He declared himself to be the head of England's Protestant Church, which he called the Church of England. Then he grabbed the rich lands of the Catholic Church for himself.

After Henry's death, England turned from Protestant to Catholic and back again. In 1588, the King of Spain, a Catholic, tried to overthrow England's Protestant ruler, Queen Elizabeth. He sent a great naval fleet of 130 ships. Spanish ships covered the sea as far as the eye could see. But the commanders of the English navy and stormy weather destroyed this fleet, saving England from invasion.

The threat from Catholic Spain led England's rulers to seek colonies of their own.

The Spanish fleet

The Lost Colony

Only three years before Spain's attempted invasion, **Sir Walter Raleigh** had established the first English colony in North America. In 1585, Raleigh had sent a hundred colonists to its shores. They landed on **Roanoke**, a small island in the Outer Banks of North Carolina. The colonists remained a year and then returned to England. A second expedition of colonists was sent to Roanoke in 1587. John White, the leader of the colony, sailed back to England to get more supplies. White's mission was delayed by the Spanish attempt to invade England. It took three years before White could return to Roanoke. When he finally returned, the settlement had mysteriously disappeared. No one was there. Now known as the "Lost Colony," the English settlement at Roanoke did not survive.

1585 map by John White of the coastline of North America from Chesapeake Bay to Cape Lookout

The Historian's Apprentice

What do you think happened to the members of the Lost Colony?

Jamestown, the First Permanent British Colony

The first permanent English colony in North America was established twenty years later at **Jamestown**. The **London Company** was formed by English investors who wanted to start a colony. The goal of these investors was to make money. King James approved their plan because he wanted England to have its own colonies.

The London Company sent three ships across the Atlantic in 1607. They carried just over a hundred colonists. The expedition landed in present-day Virginia (named after Queen Elizabeth). The colonists chose to settle on a marshy place on the James River (named after King James). The river was narrow enough there to defend against any future attack by Spanish ships. The area was also full of mosquitoes that sometimes carried diseases like malaria.

The Historian's Apprentice

If you had been in charge of this expedition in 1607, would you have picked the same location? Or do you think you might have chosen a different one? Which factors would you have considered in selecting your location?

Check all of the following that you think would apply. Then rank them in order of importance. Put the number "1" in front of the factor you think is the most important. Compare your rankings with a partner and discuss where you agree and disagree.

- ☐ Good natural harbor for landing the ship
- ☐ Plenty of fresh water from rivers, streams, or lakes
- ☐ Possible gold and other precious minerals
- ☐ Trees for building cabins and fences
- ☐ Good weather in summer and winter
- ☐ Good soil for farming
- ☐ Plenty of wild animals for hunting
- ☐ Ability to sail back and forth to England
- ☐ Ability to defend against hostile Indians
- ☐ Ability to defend against Spanish or French attacks

Now look back at the map showing the location of Jamestown. See if you and your partner can pick any better location for England's first permanent settlement in North America.

The colonists at Jamestown built simple cabins. They surrounded their settlement with a stockade of sharpened tree trunks to protect themselves from animals and Native American attacks. The settlement was built in the shape of a triangle. As members of the Church of England, the colonists brought a minister to lead their worship.

Half the newcomers at Jamestown were "gentlemen" who had no intention of working. Instead, they spent their time searching for gold—even where there was none to be found. Soon the settlers started running out of food. Others became sick. More than half of the colonists died before a second group of settlers arrived in 1608.

Courtesy of National Park Service, Colonial National Historical Park

Captain John Smith (1580–1631) was only twenty-seven years old when he was placed in charge of the colony at Jamestown. He had previously fought against the Turks in Europe, where he had been captured and enslaved. He escaped and returned to England in 1604. The Virginia Company named Smith as one of seven leaders of the new colony. Smith saved the settlers by enforcing a simple slogan: "He that will not work, shall not eat." In December 1607, Smith was captured by the Powhatan Indians. Smith wrote that he was saved from execution by the chief's daughter, Pocahontas. Some historians question Smith's account.

Captain John Smith saved the colony by establishing friendly relations with the local Indians and insisting that all the colonists help in growing crops. Only those who worked would receive food. However, Smith was injured and had to return to England. In the terrible winter of 1609–1610, many of the colonists at Jamestown died from hunger. In their desperation, they even ate the bodies of those who had already died. Only 60 of the 214 settlers survived this "Starving Time."

Despite these losses, the colony survived. New colonists from England kept coming. One colonist, **John Rolfe**, planted tobacco seeds in 1612 and began growing tobacco. Conditions in Virginia were perfect for this crop, which was

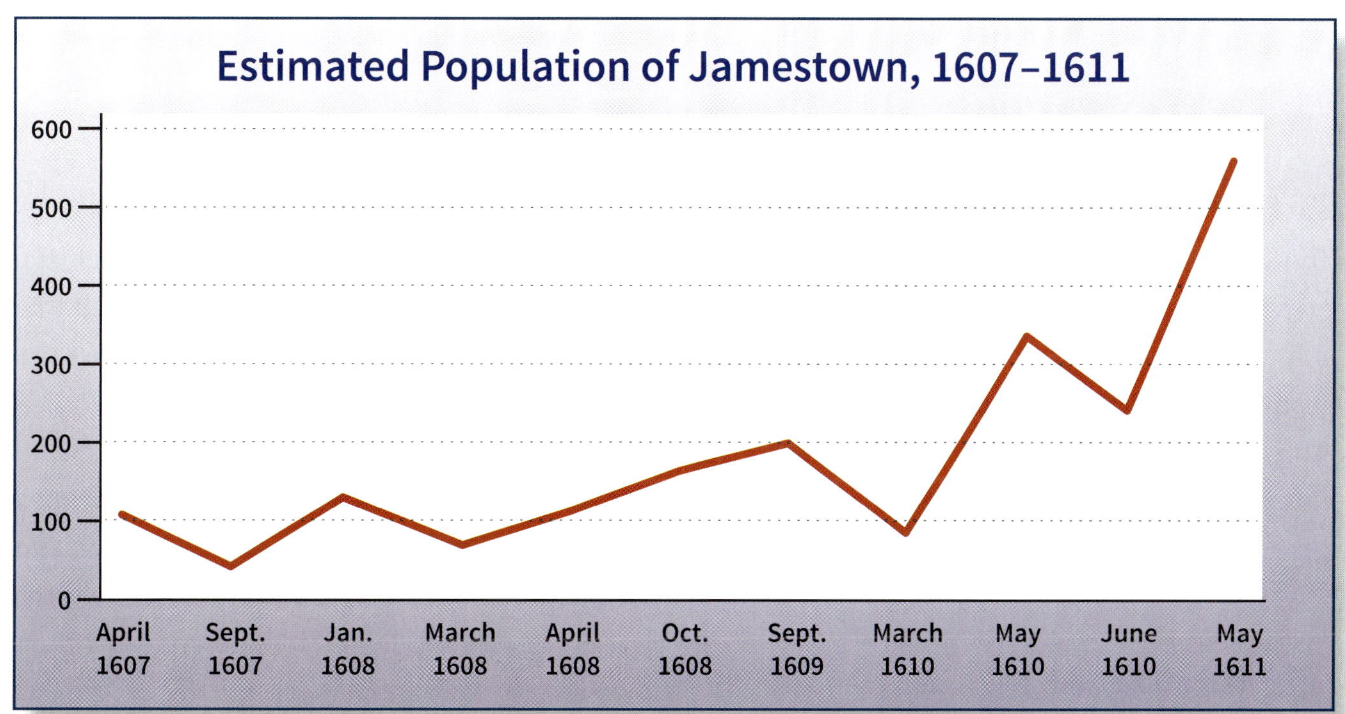

1585
Sir Walter Raleigh promotes establishment of an English colony at Roanoke

1588
Spanish Armada threatens England

1607
Jamestown founded

1585 | 1600 | 1610

1586–1587
Colony started at Roanoke but mysteriously disappears

1603
Death of Queen Elizabeth I; James I becomes King

1609–1610 (Winter)
"Starving Time" in Jamestown

already in great demand in Europe. By growing and selling tobacco, the colonists at Jamestown soon prospered.

In 1614, Rolfe married Pocahontas, the daughter of the local Indian chief. This began a period of friendly relations between the colonists and Indians. In 1619, women from England and the first Africans arrived in Jamestown. That same year, the colony established its own representative assembly, the **House of Burgesses**. Each district of the colony sent two representatives. The colony at Jamestown was clearly there to stay.

John Rolfe and Pocahontas

Pilgrims and Puritans

The colony at Jamestown was established by private investors who hoped to make money. Its colonists were also seeking wealth. The next two groups of English colonists to arrive in North America came for a very different reason: to worship God in their own way.

The Pilgrims at Plymouth

The **Separatists** were Protestants who lived in northern England. They disagreed with the teachings of the Church of England—the official Protestant church. The Separatists believed that the Church of England could not be reformed, so they wished to **separate** from it.

To worship God in their own way, the Separatists moved to Holland. They became unhappy when their children began learning Dutch and losing touch with English ways. Their church leaders decided to leave Holland and start their own colony in North America.

1612
John Rolfe plants tobacco

1619
English women and Africans arrive in Jamestown; House of Burgesses founded

1630
Puritans start Massachusetts Bay Colony

1615

1630

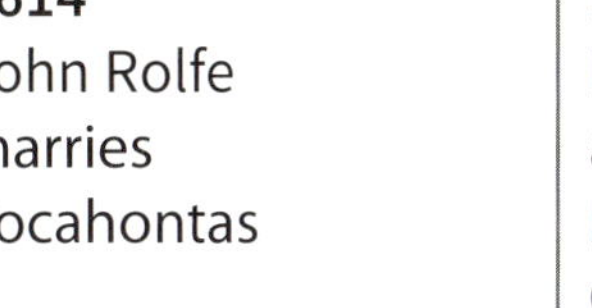

1614
John Rolfe marries Pocahontas

1620
Pilgrims land at Plymouth; Mayflower Compact

This was the birth of self-government and an example of a direct democracy.

A company in England obtained a charter for them from King James. About fifty Separatists then sailed from Holland to England. There they boarded the ship known as the **Mayflower**. The Separatists were joined by an equal number of other colonists eager to move to the New World. **William Bradford**, one of the leaders of the group, called the colonists "**Pilgrims**." A pilgrim is a person who makes a journey for religious reasons.

Unlike the colonists who first went to Jamestown, the passengers on the Mayflower included men, women, and children. It took them two months to cross the Atlantic. The Pilgrims planned to settle in Virginia but landed hundreds of miles to the north at **Plymouth** (in present-day Massachusetts). They arrived in late November during chilly weather.

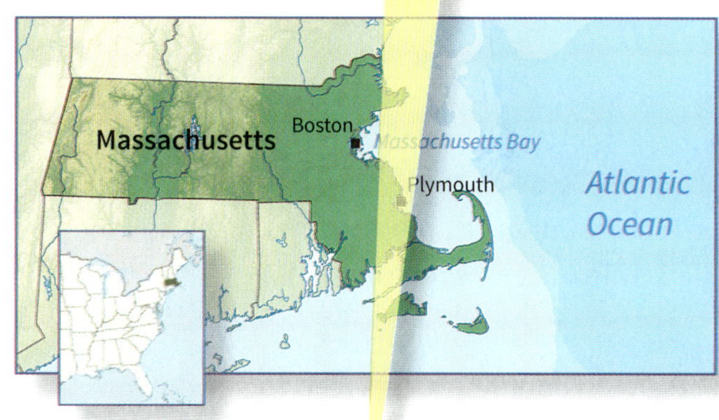

Before leaving their ship, all of the colonists signed a document in which they pledged to form their own community and to obey its laws. This agreement is known as the **Mayflower Compact**.

Signing the Mayflower Compact

The Historian's Apprentice

The Mayflower Compact

In the name of God.

We who are underwritten, the loyal subjects of King James of Great Britain, France, and Ireland, having undertaken for the glory of God, and advancement of the Christian faith, and honor of our country, a voyage to plant the first colony in Virginia, do [agree] and combine ourselves together into a body politic [a community with its own form of government], for our better order and preservation and . . . to enact . . . just and equal laws . . . from time to time, as shall be thought most convenient for the general good of the colony, unto which we promise all due submission and obedience.

In witness whereof we sign our names at Cape-Cod, 11th of November [1620]

Your teacher will divide your class into small groups. Discuss the answers to the following questions in your group.

1. What did the colonists mean by "advancement of the Christian faith"? How did they think they were doing this?
2. Why did the colonists agree to form a "body politic"?
3. Who could participate in this "body politic"?
4. What did the colonists mean by the "general good"?
5. Would you have signed the Mayflower Compact?
6. What was its significance?

At Plymouth, the Pilgrim colonists faced hardships just as difficult as those at Jamestown. Half of them died from illness in just the first few months. William Bradford was elected as governor and worked closely with Myles Standish, an experienced soldier in charge of the colony's defense.

The Pilgrims were also helped by friendly Indians. According to Bradford's journal, *Of Plymouth Plantation*, local Indians showed them how to plant corn and fertilize the soil with fish.

The Puritans at Massachusetts Bay

Ten years after the Pilgrims landed, a second group of English Protestants arrived. These colonists were known as the **Puritans**. They wanted to "purify" the Church of England. Unlike the Separatists, the Puritans were a very large group—perhaps even a majority of the people in England at the time. But England's new ruler, King Charles I, wanted to take the Church of England in a different direction. He was impressed by the power of Catholic rulers, such as the King of France. Charles disliked the Puritans, who did not respect his authority.

King Charles I

In 1629, Charles dismissed Parliament and tried to rule the country without it. Fearing persecution, some Puritans decided to move overseas. In North America, they could establish a community based on their own beliefs without royal interference.

An expedition of 700 Puritan colonists set sail in 1630. They landed in **Massachusetts Bay**, just north of the Pilgrim settlement at Plymouth. Their main settlement was established in Boston. **John Winthrop**, one of their leaders, gave a famous sermon in which he told the colonists that God was watching over them. Using a phrase from the Bible, Winthrop said their colony would be "as a City upon a Hill." Winthrop meant that the Puritan colony would provide a shining example for the entire world.

Like the Pilgrims, the Puritans were very strict. They required attendance in church. They banned many common pastimes such as dancing and watching plays. Life in Puritan Massachusetts centered on avoiding sin and obeying God's commands.

The new colony was governed by a group of elected officials known as the **General Court**. Only members of a Puritan congregation could vote in elections or serve on the General Court. To become members of a congregation, colonists had to persuade church leaders that they sincerely held Puritan beliefs.

John Winthrop

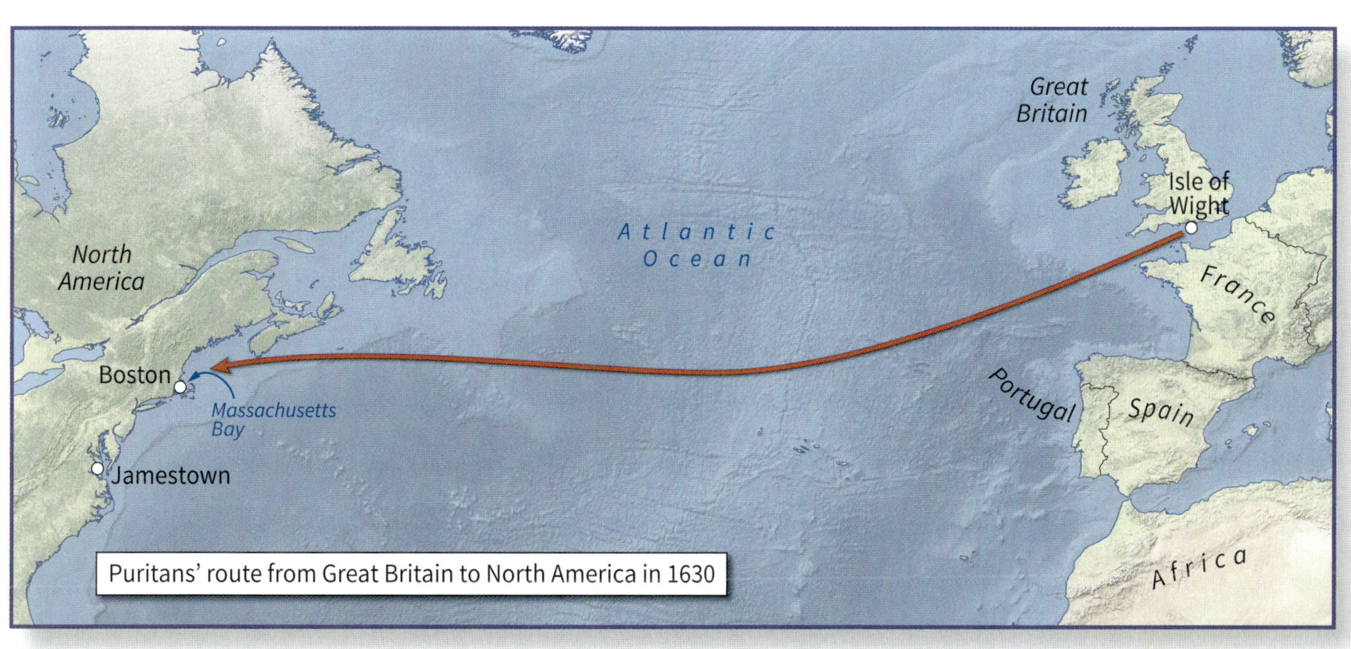

Puritans' route from Great Britain to North America in 1630

The Historian's Apprentice

Write your answers to the following questions in your journal or on a separate sheet of paper and then share your answers with a partner.

1. How did religious disagreements in Europe encourage the English settlement of North America?
2. How did the colonists who went to New England compare to those who went to Jamestown? Complete the Venn diagram below showing their similarities and differences.

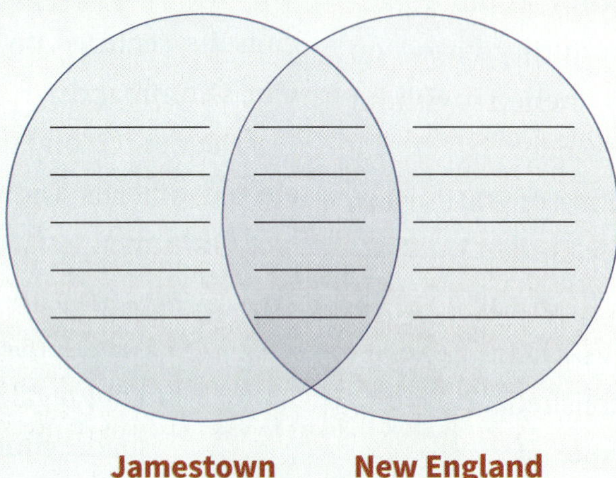

Note:
New England is the area along the northeastern coast of the United States from Maine to Connecticut.

How the Other English Colonies Began

The successful colonies at Jamestown, Plymouth, and Massachusetts Bay encouraged others to start colonies.

Rhode Island

Roger Williams was a Protestant minister in Massachusetts. At first, Williams had believed that neither the Puritans nor the Separatists were "pure" enough in their beliefs. But after visiting the Indians, Williams decided that each person should be allowed to worship God in his or her own way. This challenged the beliefs of the Puritan ministers who governed Massachusetts Bay Colony. Williams was forced to leave Massachusetts. He established a new colony nearby in **Rhode Island**. His colony was the first to declare the principle of **religious toleration**—that people of all faiths should be able to worship freely in their own way without fear of government interference.

Back in Massachusetts, **Anne Hutchinson** was put on trial for expressing the view that ordinary believers, not just Puritan ministers, could understand God's message. She was also banished (*forced to leave*) from Massachusetts. Hutchinson joined Williams in Rhode Island.

Connecticut

Thomas Hooker took settlers from Massachusetts to start a new colony in **Connecticut**. The three towns of the new colony agreed to the **Fundamental Orders of Connecticut** in 1639. This document served as a blueprint for the new colony's government. It established a General Court, like the one in Massachusetts Bay. It also gave all adult male residents the right to vote. Some historians see it as the first modern written constitution.

New Hampshire

A group of investors in England started another colony in New England in **New Hampshire**. Settlers from England started a number of small towns near the coast. The territory was also claimed by Massachusetts, and the settlers in New Hampshire agreed to be governed as part of that larger colony. In 1679, King Charles II gave New Hampshire its own charter. Until the 1740s, the same official served as governor of both colonies.

Pennsylvania

The **Quakers** were a group of Protestants who believed that all people were equal in God's eyes. They were against violence. Quakers had no priests or ministers because they believed that each individual should look to his or her own thoughts to discover God.

William Penn was the son of a wealthy admiral in the British navy. He became a Quaker at the age of twenty-two. Penn was later given land in America by King Charles II to create a home for Quakers. He went to America and established the colony of **Pennsylvania** ("Penn's Woods"). Penn paid the Indians for their land and granted his colonists a written constitution, which he called the **Frame of Government**. Penn's "Frame" included many rights, including freedom of religion and the right to a trial by jury. Penn's colony welcomed not only Quakers but all persecuted minorities, including French Protestants (Hugenots), Jews, Catholics, Mennonites, and Amish.

Maryland

George Calvert, also known as **Lord Baltimore,** was a successful politician. He had served King James I. He obtained a charter to start the colony of **Maryland** as a home for England's Catholics. The new colony was located just across the Chesapeake Bay from Virginia. Lord Baltimore died before the colony could be started, but his two sons went on to establish and govern it.

North and South Carolina

King Charles II gave the right to found a new colony to eight of his nobles, known as **Lords Proprietor**. The proprietors established a colony just south of Virginia and named it **Carolina** after their king. (Carolus was the Latin word for Charles.)

Conditions in the northern and southern parts of Carolina were so different that the colony split into North and South Carolina in 1712. **North Carolina** was a colony of independent farmers with small plots of land. It became known for its forest products (tar and other materials from pine trees used for ships).

South Carolina was dominated by wealthy landowners with large plantations. The plantation owners used the labor of enslaved Africans and African-Americans to grow rice and indigo (*a plant used to make blue dye*) for sale in England.

New York, Delaware, and New Jersey

The Dutch colony of New Netherland was located between the British colonies of New England and the British colonies in the South. It was a long narrow band, stretching from western Long Island up the Hudson River. New Netherland had also taken Delaware (originally a Swedish colony).

In 1664, Britain and the Netherlands were at war. The British sent ships to capture the city of New Amsterdam. The Dutch colonists refused to resist and the colony's governor was forced to surrender. New Netherland was renamed **New York** after the King's younger brother, the Duke of York. New Amsterdam became **New York City** and Fort Orange became **Albany**.

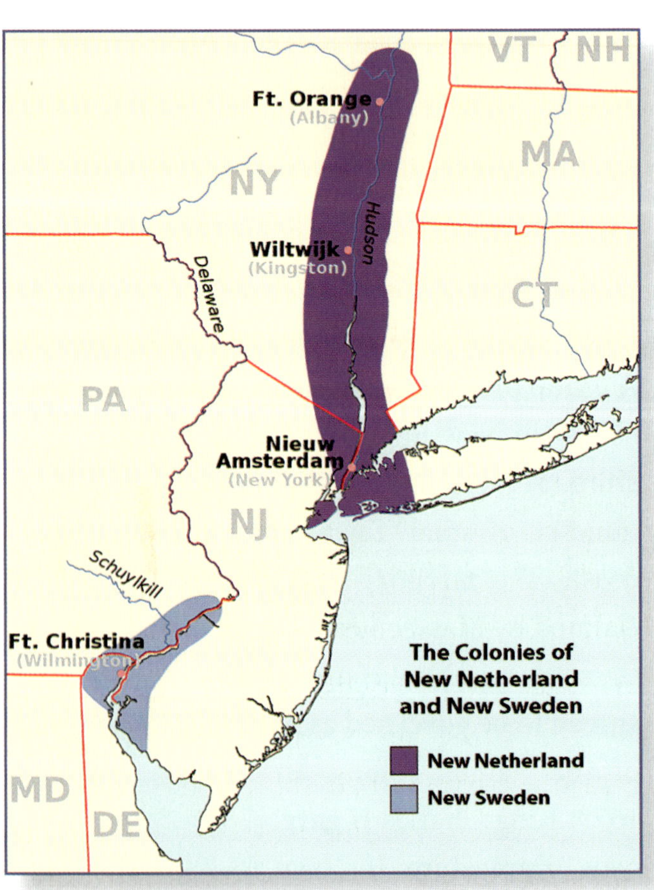

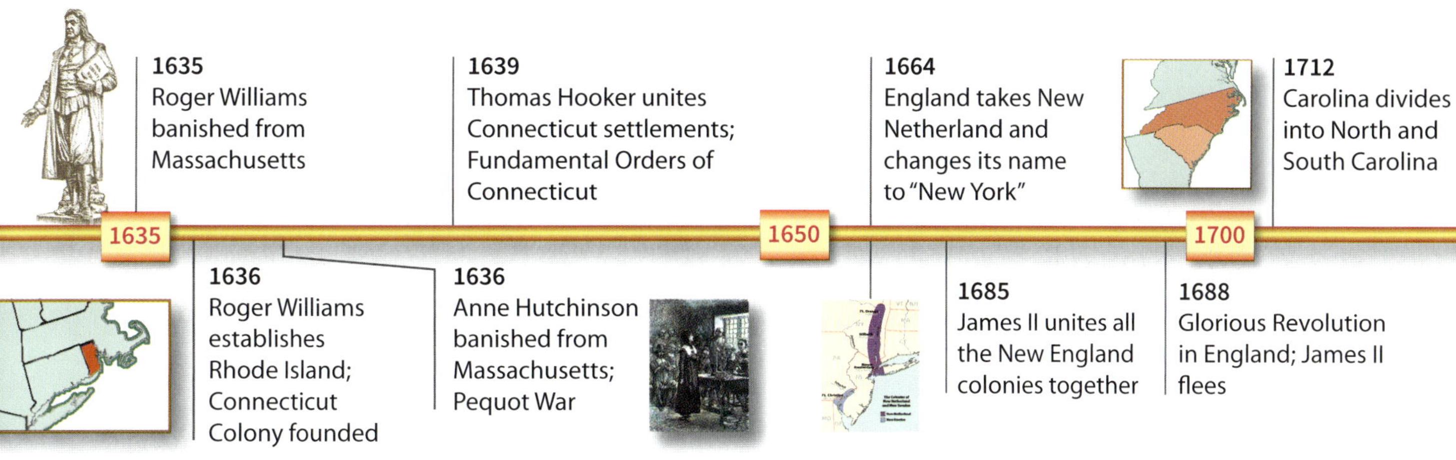

Dutch residents were allowed to stay and to keep all their lands and rights. **Delaware** and **New Jersey**, once part of New Netherland, became separate British colonies. New Jersey, located in an area between Delaware and New York, was given by Charles II to two of his friends.

Georgia

In 1732–1733, **James Oglethorpe** founded **Georgia** as a colony for debtors. **Debtors** are people who owe money and cannot pay it. In England, many debtors were sent to prison. Some debtors were permitted to go to Oglethorpe's colony.

At first, Oglethorpe prohibited slavery. But slavery was permitted in Georgia after 1743.

The Impact of Colonial Settlements on Native Americans

The building of English settlements had very harmful effects on Native American peoples. Native Americans had shared these lands for thousands of years. They used them for hunting, fishing, and growing corn, squash, and beans. The English had very different ideas of land ownership. They believed in **exclusive ownership**: When an Englishman owned a piece of

Complete the Venn diagram below.

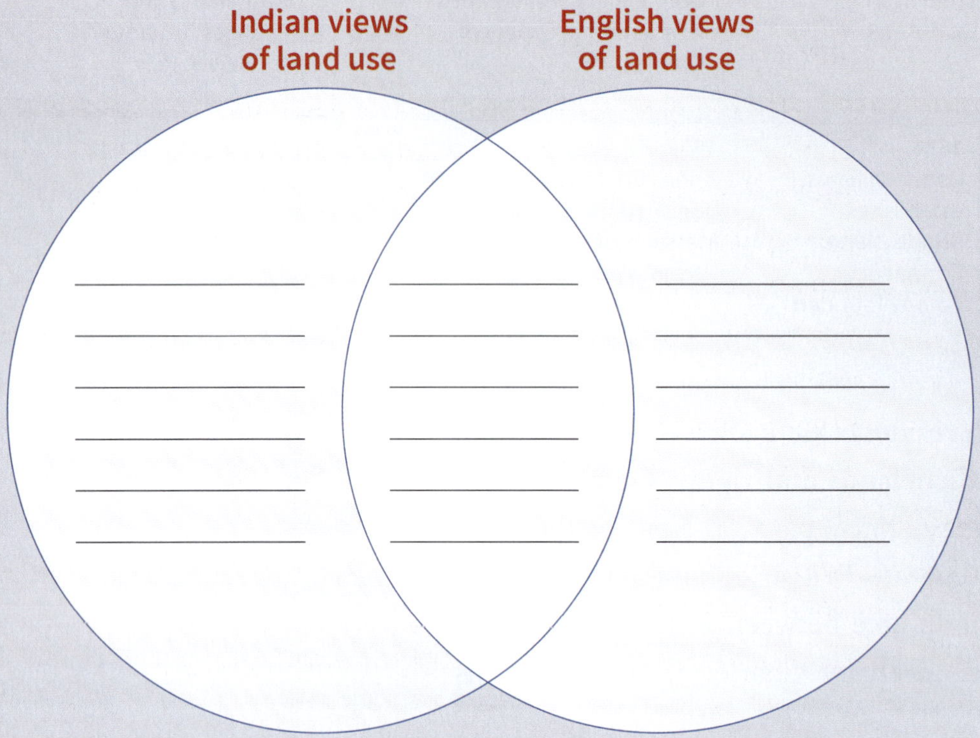

Indian views of land use		English views of land use
____________	____________	____________
____________	____________	____________
____________	____________	____________
____________	____________	____________
____________	____________	____________
____________	____________	____________

land, no one else had the right to use it. English settlers cleared the land by cutting down trees, building wooden houses, plowing the soil, and planting crops.

The spread of English settlements reduced the amount of land that Indian tribes living along the Atlantic coast could use. This led to conflicts between those tribes and other tribes farther west. The introduction of guns and other new weapons made Indian warfare more dangerous. Native Americans became dependent on European goods and neglected their own traditional ways. Native American populations were also reduced by the introduction of European diseases such as smallpox.

The English often took sides with some tribes against others. Relations between colonists and Native Americans sometimes led to open warfare. Metacom, known as King Philip, was the son of the Indian chief who had once welcomed the Pilgrims. Metacom allied with other tribes in New England. They attacked local colonial settlements, taking hundreds of lives in **King Philip's War** (1675–1676). Metacom was finally killed and his allies were defeated. In another example, the Tuscarora Indians started a war against English settlers in North Carolina in 1711. This war lasted several years before the Tuscarora were defeated.

Colonists fighting Indians

The Historian's Apprentice

1. Discuss the following question with a partner:

   Imagine what it would be like if people suddenly landed from outer space and introduced new products and new ideas that replaced those of your own culture. Would the benefits of using these new products and ideas outweigh the loss of traditional ways?

2. Make a chart or graphic organizer identifying some of the effects that the arrival of English colonists had on Native Americans.

3. Pretend that you are at a meeting of Indian leaders. Write a speech about how you think they should respond to the arrival of English colonists.

4. Complete the chart below showing how important leaders influenced the economic, political, and/or social development of the English colonies. Fill in only those sections of the chart you think apply.

   - Economic relations concern how people work and share to meet their material needs, such as for food and shelter.
   - Political relations concern how people are governed.
   - Social relations concern how people relate to one another in society. They can include how people are affected by their religious beliefs.

Leader	Economic Impact	Political Impact	Social Impact
Captain John Smith			
William Bradford			
John Winthrop			
Roger Williams			
Anne Hutchinson			
William Penn			
Lord Calvert			
James Oglethorpe			

Based on the chart, what conclusions can you draw about the impact of early colonial leaders?

Fill in the chart below about England's colonies.

Colony	Date	Reason(s) for Starting	Important Leader(s)	Geography and Other Characteristics
Jamestown	1607		Captain John Smith	
Plymouth	1620		William Bradford	
Massachusetts Bay	1630		John Winthrop	
Rhode Island	1636		Roger Williams	
Connecticut	1636		Thomas Hooker	
New Hampshire	1633			
Pennsylvania	1681		William Penn	
Maryland	1632–1633		Lord Calvert (Baltimore)	
Carolina	1663			
New York	1664			
Delaware	1664			
New Jersey	1664			
Georgia	1732–1733		James Oglethorpe	

Complete the map below by identifying each colony on the blank line.

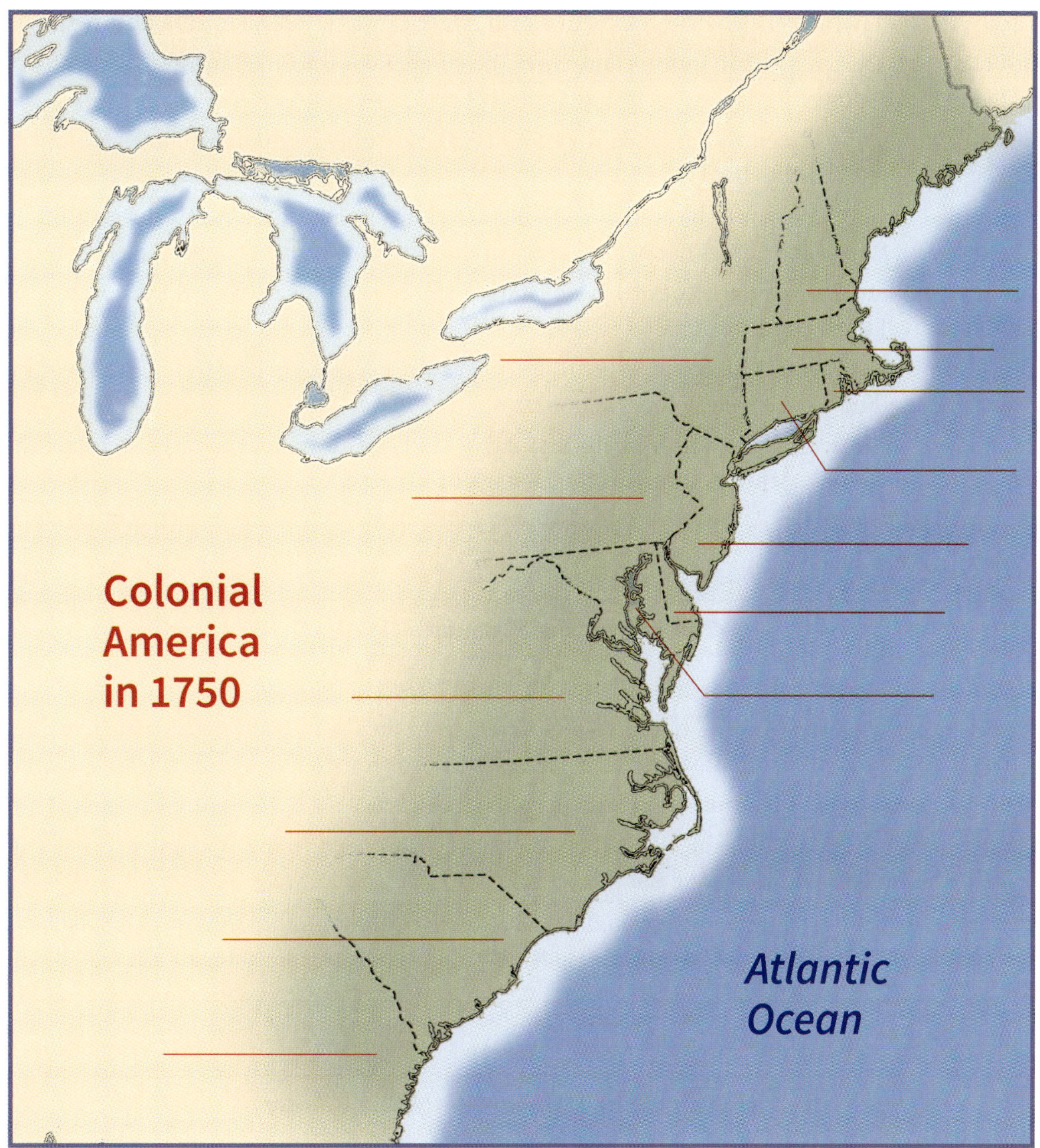

Chapter Review Cards

Roanoke – England's Lost Colony

- In 1585, **Sir Walter Raleigh** established the first English colony on **Roanoke**, a small island off the shore of present-day North Carolina. Settlers in the colony stayed one year and returned to England.
- A second group of settlers went there in 1587, but disappeared.

Jamestown – England's First Permanent Colony

- In 1607, the first permanent English colony in North America was established at **Jamestown**.
- The colony was started by the **London Company**. The company was formed by investors who wanted to make money.
- The first colonists were men who thought they could make fortunes by finding gold. Half of them were gentlemen not used to hard work.
- They started the colony in a marshy area on the James River in Virginia. They built a stockade of sharpened tree trunks and houses out of logs. Many of the settlers died from hunger.
- **Captain John Smith** saved the colony by establishing friendly relations with local Indians and insisting that all the colonists work.
- **John Rolfe** began growing tobacco in 1612. Tobacco was already in great demand in Europe. By growing and selling tobacco, the colonists soon prospered.
- In 1619, women from England and Africans first arrived in Jamestown. The colony also established its own representative assembly, known as the **House of Burgesses**.

The Pilgrims at Plymouth (1620)

- Pilgrims and Puritans came to North America to worship God in their own way.
- The **Pilgrims** were Separatists who wanted to separate from the Church of England. In 1620, they sailed for America on the **Mayflower**. The colonists included women and children as well as men.
- The Pilgrims landed in **Plymouth** in present-day Massachusetts.
- Before they left their ship, the men signed the **Mayflower Compact**. In this document, they pledged to create their own community and obey its laws.
- At Plymouth, half the Pilgrims died from illnesses in the first few months. They were helped by friendly Indians who showed them how to plant corn and to fertilize the soil with fish.

The Puritans at Massachusetts Bay Colony

- The **Puritans** wanted to "purify" the **Church of England**.
- King Charles I of England rejected Puritan ideas for reforming the church. Some Puritans decided to move to America to establish a community based on their own religious beliefs.
- In 1630, about 700 Puritans landed in **Massachusetts Bay**.
- Puritans placed great emphasis on religion. Puritan leader **John Winthrop** told the colonists that their settlement would be "as a City upon a Hill"—a shining example to others.
- Massachusetts Bay Colony was governed by a group of elected officials known as the **General Court**. Only members of Puritan congregations could vote.

Rhode Island

- **Roger Williams** lived in Massachusetts. After spending time with a group of Indians, he came to believe each person should be allowed to worship God in his or her own way.
- Williams challenged the Puritan ministers who controlled Massachusetts Bay Colony. They forced him to leave.
- Williams began a new colony in Rhode Island. It was the first colony to declare the principle of **religious toleration** – the belief that people of all faiths should be able to worship freely and without interference.
- Williams was joined by **Anne Hutchinson**. She was forced to leave Massachusetts for expressing her view that ordinary believers, not just Puritan ministers, could understand God's message.

Connecticut

- **Thomas Hooker** took settlers from Massachusetts to start this colony.
- Three of its towns agreed to the **Fundamental Orders of Connecticut** in 1639. This gave all adult men the right to vote. The Fundamental Orders served as a plan for the new colony's government. Some see it as the first modern written constitution.

New Hampshire

- A group of investors in England started this colony. Settlers in New Hampshire agreed to be governed as part of Massachusetts.
- In 1679, New Hampshire received its own royal charter, making it a separate colony.

Pennsylvania

- **Quakers** were another group of English Protestants. Quakers believed that all people were equal in God's eyes. They supported non-violence.
- **William Penn** was a Quaker. Penn was given land in America by King Charles II to create a land for Quakers.
- Penn began the colony of **Pennsylvania**, which welcomed people of many faiths. He granted the colonists a constitution, known as the **Frame of Government**.

Maryland

- **George Calvert**, also known as **Lord Baltimore**, obtained a charter to start the colony of **Maryland** as a home for England's Catholics.

North and South Carolina

- King Charles II gave eight of his nobles the right to found a new colony. They were known as **Lords Proprietor**. They established the colony of **Carolina**.
- Conditions in the northern and southern parts of the colony were so different that it split into **North** and **South Carolina** in 1712.
- North Carolina had many farmers with small areas of land while South Carolina had wealthy landowners, large plantations, and slaves.

New York, Delaware, and New Jersey

- In 1664, the Dutch and the English were at war. England sent ships to capture the city of New Amsterdam, and the Dutch colony surrendered.
- New Netherland became **New York** and **New Amsterdam** became **New York City**.
- **Delaware** and **New Jersey**, once part of the Dutch colony of New Netherland, became separate colonies. New Jersey was given by King Charles II to two of his friends.

Georgia

- **James Oglethorpe** founded Georgia as a colony for debtors in English prisons in 1732–1733. Rather than stay in prison, debtors could go to Georgia. Oglethorpe prohibited slavery in Georgia but his ban did not last.

Impact of the English Colonies on Native Americans

- English settlements had a harmful effect on Native American peoples.
- Native Americans believed in sharing land. The English believed in exclusive ownership.
- English settlements reduced the land available to Indian tribes. This led to conflicts between tribes. The introduction of guns made tribal warfare more dangerous.
- Many Native Americans died from European diseases, such as smallpox and measles.
- Many Native American tribes became dependent on European goods and trade.

How the English Colonies Began

Background Events

- New World colonies enrich Catholic Spain
- Protestant England feels threatened
- English rulers want their own colonies

Impact of Colonists on Native Americans

- General impact was harmful
- English colonists took over land – exclusive ownership
- Introduced guns
- Brought European diseases like smallpox
- Defeated Indians in wars

The First English Colonies

Roanoke: The Lost Colony

Jamestown, Virginia

- Founded in 1607
- Sponsored by London Company
- First colonists hoped to find gold
- Harsh Conditions: "Starving Time"
- Captain John Smith saved the colony
- Growing tobacco brought profit
- 1619—Women, enslaved persons, House of Burgesses

Plymouth

- Founded by Pilgrims in 1620
- Colonists came to worship God in their own way
- Settled in New England
- Mayflower Compact (1620)—Self-government

Massachusetts Bay

- Founded by Puritans in 1630
- Puritans wanted to "purify" the Church
- 700 colonists settled north of Plymouth
- Governed by a General Court

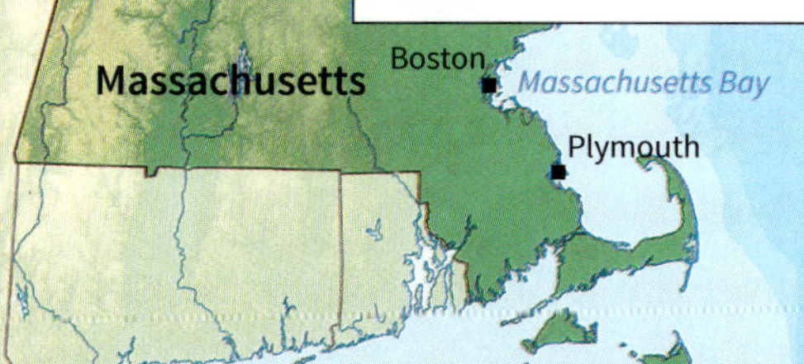

Later English Colonies

Rhode Island

- Roger Williams
- Religious toleration

Connecticut

- Thomas Hooker
- Fundamental Orders of Connecticut (1639)

New Hampshire

- Governed by Massachusetts

Pennsylvania

- William Penn
- Home to Quakers
- Frame of Government (1682)

Maryland

- Lord Calvert (Baltimore)
- Home to Catholics

New York, Delaware and New Jersey

- Taken from Dutch in 1664
- Greater diversity than elsewhere

North and South Carolina

- Lords Proprietor
- Divided in 1712
- South Carolina grew rice and indigo

Georgia

- James Oglethorpe
- Home for debtors

What do you know?

SS.6.A.2.2

1. How did geography influence settlement patterns in the first English colonies?

   A. Because New England had the shortest growing season, most colonists settled in this region.

   B. Because forested land was difficult to clear, colonists first settled along the coastline and rivers.

   C. Because the growing season in the Southern colonies was the longest, few people settled there.

   D. Although the climates of the colonies were different, their populations were all about the same.

SS.6.A.2.1

2. The passage below was written by William Bradford in his history, *Of Plymouth Plantation* (1651).

   > *Their condition was not ordinary; their ends were good & honorable; their calling lawful, & urgent; and therefore they might expect the blessing of God in their proceeding.*

   Which conclusion can be drawn from this passage?

   A. Settlers came to Plymouth to find gold and silver.

   B. Settlers came to Plymouth for their moral and religious ideals.

   C. Settlers came to Plymouth to be released from debtor's prison.

   D. Settlers came to Plymouth to defend England from Spain and France.

SS.6.A.2.4

3. The box below lists four key individuals.

John White	John Smith
William Bradford	John Winthrop

   What did these individuals have in common?

   A. They refused to give food and shelter to all the colonists.

   B. They came to the New World in search of fame and riches.

   C. They led some of the first English colonies in the New World.

   D. They believed they were setting an example of righteousness for the entire world to follow.

SS.6.A.2.2

4. The passage below was written by Captain John Smith.

> *Here are mountains, hills, planes [plains], valleys, rivers, and brooks, all running most pleasantly into a faire Bay . . . with fruitful and delightsome land.*

Based on Smith's description, why did the colonists choose to settle at Jamestown in 1607?

A. The Native Americans had agreed to let the colonists have this area.

B. The area had all the resources the colonists needed for mining gold.

C. Rivers and brooks created the possibility of developing maritime industries.

D. Fresh water, fertile land, and good harbors offered the possibility of successful farming.

SS.6.C.1.4

5. What was the importance of the Mayflower Compact?

A. It was the first example of a written constitution.

B. It established religious toleration in the colonies.

C. It established the practice of self-government in the colonies.

D. It established rules for electing representatives to a colonial assembly.

SS.6.A.2.2

6. The passage below describes the geography of New England.

> *The excellent coastline provided natural harbors and forests provided timber. Whale and fishing beds in nearby waters made whaling and fishing profitable. New England's thin, rocky soil prevented the growth of cash crops.*

Which conclusion about the economy of colonial New England can be drawn from this passage?

A. New Englanders preferred farming to fishing and whaling.

B. Thick forests and rich, fertile soil encouraged manufacturing.

C. Good coastlines and rocky soil encouraged the farming of cash crops.

D. Excellent harbors and forests encouraged the development of shipbuilding.

SS.6.A.2.1

7. Which statement summarizes the reasons for the founding of Jamestown and Plymouth?

A. Both colonies were established as safe places for imprisoned debtors.

B. Both colonies were founded to provide religious freedom to all settlers.

C. The colonists at Jamestown expected riches, while the Pilgrims wanted to practice their religion.

D. The colonists at Jamestown came to convert the Native Americans, while the Pilgrims came to establish trade.

SS.6.A.2.3

8. In colonial times, how were indentured servants different from enslaved individuals?

A. They did not have to work in the fields.

B. They could not be punished for disobedience.

C. They would be freed after four to seven years.

D. They were taken to the colonies against their will.

SS.6.A.2.7

9. How did Native Americans affect the first English settlements in North America?

A. Friendly Indians helped the colonists adapt to their new land.

B. Most colonists married Native Americans and adopted their lifestyles.

C. Colonists were attacked by angry Native Americans before they even landed.

D. English colonists obtained most of their food and clothes from Native Americans.

SS.6.A.2.2

10. The map below shows colonial America in 1740.

Which pair of colonies allowed greater religious freedom?

A. Colonies 2 and 12

B. Colonies 3 and 7

C. Colonies 2 and 11

D. Colonies 3 and 10

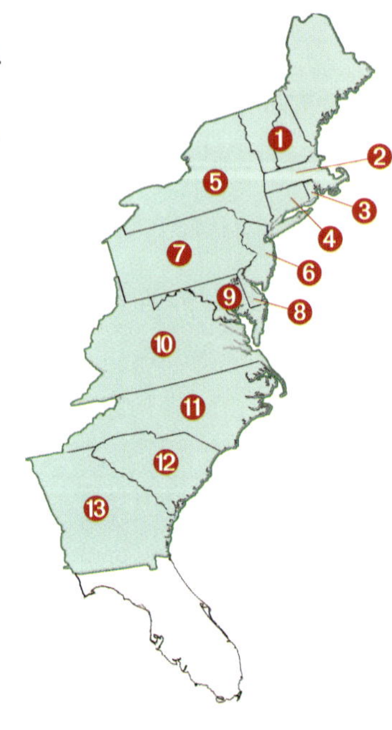

SS.6.A.2.4

11. The passage below was written by Captain John Smith in his 1624 book, *A General History of Virginia.*

> *From May until September, those that escaped sickness lived upon sturgeon [a fish] and sea crabs. Fifty in this time we buried. Captain John Smith, by his own example and strong leadership, set some men to mow, others to bind and thatch, some to build houses, so that in a short time we had lodgings to protect us from the cold. His motto became known as, "If you do not work, you will not eat." This made even the laziest of men get up and do their share of the work!*

Based on this passage, why was Captain John Smith so strict with the Jamestown settlers?

A. He wanted to persuade the colonists to return to England.

B. He wanted to make sure that the London Company made a profit.

C. He wanted to make sure the settlers survived in their new environment.

D. He wanted to test whether everyone in the colony would obey his orders.

SS.6.A.2.3

12. Which is an example of subsistence farming in colonial times?

A. growing tobacco in Virginia

B. growing rice in South Carolina

C. dairy farming outside Philadelphia

D. growing food for one's family in North Carolina

SS.6.A.2.4

13. Which contribution did Lord Calvert make to the social development of the colonies?

A. He helped the colonists survive their first year at Jamestown.

B. He welcomed debtors who had been put in prison in England.

C. He helped finance the Puritan expeditions to Massachusetts Bay.

D. He made Maryland a home for Catholics facing persecution in England.

SS.6.A.2.2

14. In the 1600s, why were colonists in New England generally better educated than elsewhere?

A. New Englanders had more free time than other colonists.

B. Puritans believed each person should be able to read the Bible.

C. Colonists in New England depended more on the labor of slaves.

D. The most wealthy people from England preferred to settle in New England.

SS.8.C.1.4

15. The passage below is from the Mayflower Compact, signed by the colonists at Plymouth in 1620.

> *We .. do [agree] and combine ourselves together into a body politic, for our better order and preservation and . . . to enact . . . just and equal laws . . . from time to time, as shall be thought most convenient for the general good of the colony, unto which we promise all due submission and obedience.*

Which action by a colonist would break this promise?

A. sharing English farming methods with local Indian leaders

B. searching for gold when it was unlikely any would be found

C. sailing back to England after receiving news of a sick relative

D. refusing to help with military duties when asked by colony leaders

SS.6.A.2.2

16. The diagram below describes a colony in New England.

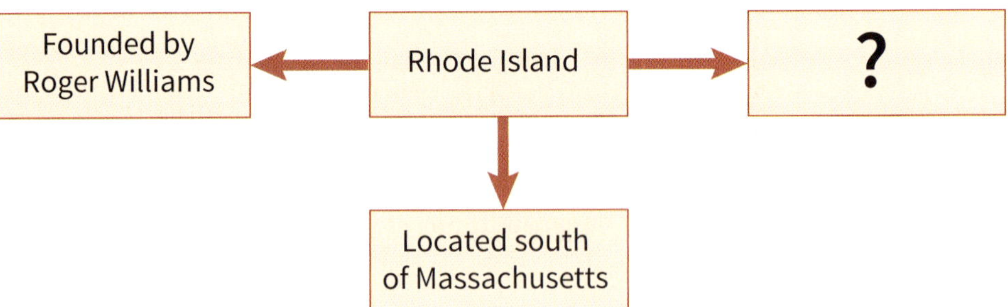

Which phrase belongs in the blank box in the diagram?

A. introduced slavery to the English colonies

B. put eleven men and women to death as witches

C. was the first colony to practice religious toleration

D. founded by English investors seeking to make a profit

SS.6.A.2.4

17. Which individual started a colony for Quakers and provided its colonists with a Frame of Government?

A. Captain John Smith

B. William Bradford

C. Roger Williams

D. William Penn

CHAPTER 3 Life in the Thirteen British Colonies

SS.6.A.2.2 Compare the characteristics of the New England, Middle, and Southern colonies.

SS.6.A.2.3 Differentiate economic systems of New England, Middle, and Southern colonies including indentured servants and slaves as labor sources.

SS.6.A.2.4 Identify the impact of key colonial figures on the economic, political, and social development of the colonies.

SS.6.A.2.5 Discuss the impact of colonial settlement on Native American populations.

SS.6.A.2.7 Describe the contributions of key groups (Africans, Native Americans, women, and children) to the society and culture of colonial America.

Alignment to Grade 7 Civics Standards

SS.7.C.1.1 Recognize how Enlightenment ideas including Montesquieu's view of separation of powers and John Locke's theories related to natural law, and how Locke's social contract influenced the Founding Fathers.

SS.7.C.1.2 Trace the impact that the Magna Carta, English Bill of Rights, Mayflower Compact, and Thomas Paine's *Common Sense* had on colonists' views of government.

Names and Terms You Should Know

New England	Magna Carta
Middle colonies	Common law
Southern colonies	House of Burgesses
Maritime industries	Mayflower Compact
Growing season	Town meetings
Triangular trades	Fundamental Orders of Connecticut
Indentured servant	Frame of Government
Diversity	Glorious Revolution
Religious toleration	English Bill of Rights
Plantations	Enlightenment
Cash crops	John Locke
Slave trade	Social contract
Subsistence farming	Great Awakening

Florida "Keys" to Learning

1. The British colonies formed three regions: New England, the Middle colonies, and the Southern colonies.

2. New England was rocky and cold with a short growing season. New Englanders grew crops, raised animals, worked as blacksmiths, wove cloth, gathered lumber, fished and engaged in maritime industries.

3. New Englanders were active in triangular trades. Their ships carried sugar from the West Indies (Caribbean) to New England, where it was made into rum. The rum was taken to Africa and traded for enslaved Africans. The slaves were taken to the West Indies.

4. New Englanders lived in towns. They were religious because of Pilgrim and Puritan influences. Education was important and most people could read and write.

5. The Middle colonies had a milder climate than New England. Their farmers grew wheat, oats and other grains. People engaged in trade and made goods. Many settlers first arrived in these colonies as indentured servants. They agreed to work 4-7 years for their passage to America. Enslaved Africans were also used for labor. This region had the greatest diversity in colonial America. Its residents were Dutch, German, French, Scottish and English.

6. The Southern colonies were the warmest and had the longest growing season. Most of the region's settlers lived spread out on farms rather than in villages.

7. A few Southern landowners owned large plantations that grew cash crops—tobacco, cotton, rice, indigo. They used enslaved African Americans for labor.

8. Most Southerners owned no slaves at all. Many were former indentured servants and their descendants. They engaged in subsistence farming—growing just enough food for their families.

9. English settlement had a harmful effect on Native Americans. Colonists took away their land while new diseases reduced their population.

10. Colonists inherited English traditions, including rights under Magna Carta (1215) and the common law. The Magna Carta guaranteed trial by jury. It said that the King would not raise taxes without his subjects' consent.

11. The colonists also established their own forms of self-government: the House of Burgesses, the Mayflower Compact, the Fundamental Orders of Connecticut, and William Penn's Frame of Government. Colonial governments dealt with problems that needed to be solved locally.

12. The English Parliament overthrew King James II during the "Glorious Revolution" (1688). Parliament passed the English Bill of Rights—a list of rights guaranteed to all English subjects. John Locke justified the revolution by explaining that the king's authority was part of a "social contract." People gave the king his power to protect their rights. People had the right to overthrow a king who broke the terms of this contract.

13. Several colonies promoted religious toleration, including Rhode Island, Pennsylvania, New York and Maryland.

14. During the Great Awakening, popular preachers like George Whitefield addressed large numbers of colonists in mass meetings and encouraged them to think for themselves.

The Three Regions of British North America

By 1750, British colonies lined the Atlantic coast. They formed three separate regions: New England, the Middle colonies, and the Southern colonies.

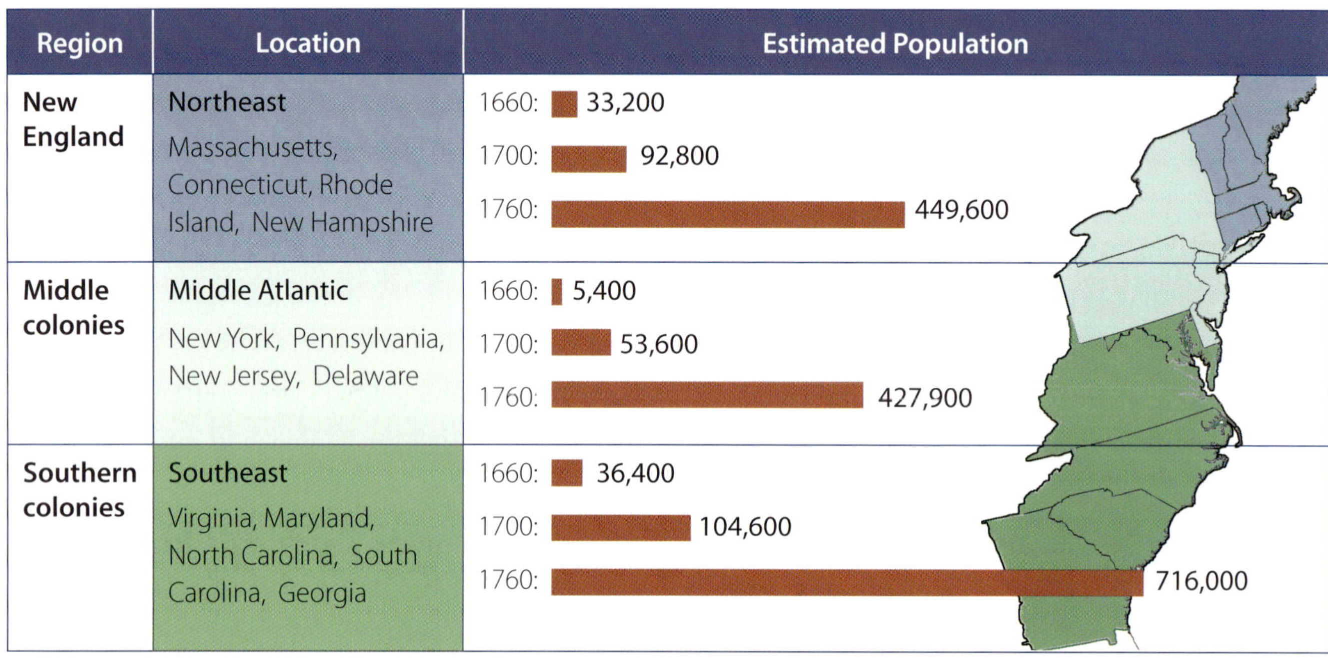

Region	Location	Estimated Population
New England	Northeast Massachusetts, Connecticut, Rhode Island, New Hampshire	1660: 33,200 1700: 92,800 1760: 449,600
Middle colonies	Middle Atlantic New York, Pennsylvania, New Jersey, Delaware	1660: 5,400 1700: 53,600 1760: 427,900
Southern colonies	Southeast Virginia, Maryland, North Carolina, South Carolina, Georgia	1660: 36,400 1700: 104,600 1760: 716,000

Source: US Census Bureau

The colonies in each region had common characteristics.

New England

New England had rocky soil, cooler temperatures, and a short growing season. People often lived longer in New England than in the Southern colonies because its cold winters killed mosquitoes that could carry disease.

Earning a Living

Many colonists in New England grew crops and raised animals for their own use. Others worked in skilled crafts as blacksmiths, weavers, and printers. A large number of New Englanders worked by cutting trees for lumber, as fishermen, or in **maritime industries** such as building ships and carrying cargo over the ocean. Fishing was successful in New England because large numbers of cod, mackerel, and halibut swam in the ocean waters nearby.

New Englanders were active in the **triangular trades**. A triangular trade takes place when three places trade together. New England ships carried sugar from the islands of the Caribbean (known as the **West Indies**) to New England. There it was made into rum. The rum was shipped to Africa where it was traded for enslaved people. New England merchants also sold fish and lumber to plantation owners in the West Indies. Their ships carried sugar from the West Indies to England, where they bought manufactured goods.

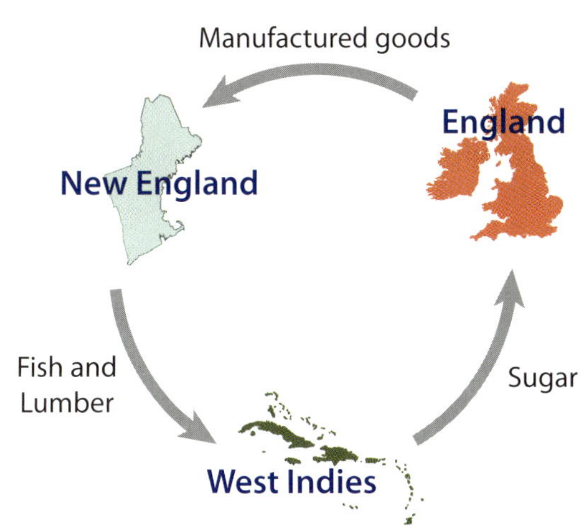

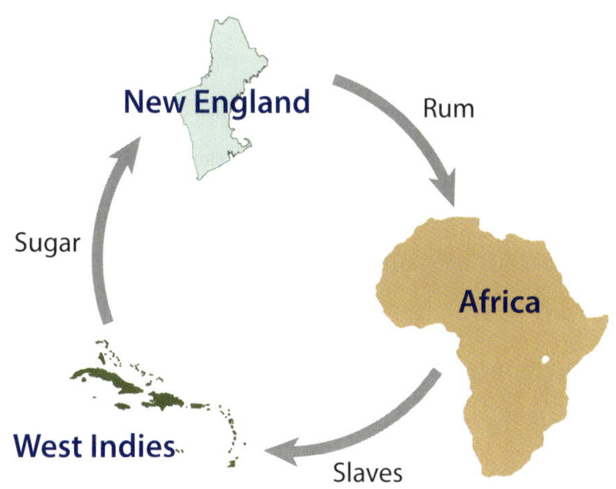

Triangular Trade Routes

Settlement Patterns

New Englanders usually lived in towns, where they could worship together. Each town had a village green for public celebrations. Farms were located in fields just outside the town. Lands were divided among the children, so no great landed properties developed as in England. By the early eighteenth century, some of New England's original settlements, such as Boston and Providence, had become bustling port cities.

Religion

New England was influenced by the fact that many of its original colonists had come there to worship God in their own way. Church ministers continued to hold great authority. In Massachusetts Bay Colony, only members of Puritan congregations could vote for government officials.

People were so religious that Massachusetts was shaken by a "witch craze" at the end of the seventeenth century. Several women in the town of Salem were put on trial for witchcraft. The trials lasted from 1692 to 1693. Neighbors swore they saw the women cast spells. Nineteen women and men were hanged for witchcraft before the trials ended.

Education

New England was an early center of education. Puritans believed that both men and women should be able to read the Bible. Two-thirds of the men and nearly half of the women in New England could read. In 1647, Massachusetts Bay Colony decided that every town with fifty or more families should have its own public school. The first American universities also opened in New England. Harvard, the oldest college in the United States, was founded in 1636. Yale, in nearby Connecticut, is our nation's third oldest college. It started in 1701.

Photo courtesy of Daderot

Massachusetts Hall—Harvard's oldest building

The Middle Colonies

Winters in the Middle colonies were not as harsh as in New England. The growing season was longer and the land was less rocky and more fertile. Much of the region was still forest that had to be cleared to make farms and towns.

Earning a Living

The Middle colonies produced much of the food that was eaten in all 13 colonies. Its farmers grew wheat, oats, and other grains. They raised cattle, pigs, and other animals. Wheat from the Middle colonies was even sent to the West Indies and Great Britain.

People in the Middle colonies engaged in trade and making goods, as well as farming. **Philadelphia**, the capital of Pennsylvania, became the largest city of colonial America by 1760. Another important city in this region was **New York City**.

There was greater **diversity** (*variety*) in the Middle colonies than elsewhere in British America. In addition to the English, many of its residents were Dutch, German, French, or Scottish. Because of the diversity of its religions, **religious toleration** was practiced. Dutch Reformed Protestants, Anglicans (*members of the Church of England*), Catholics, Quakers, Lutherans, and Jews all lived peacefully side-by-side.

Indentured Servants

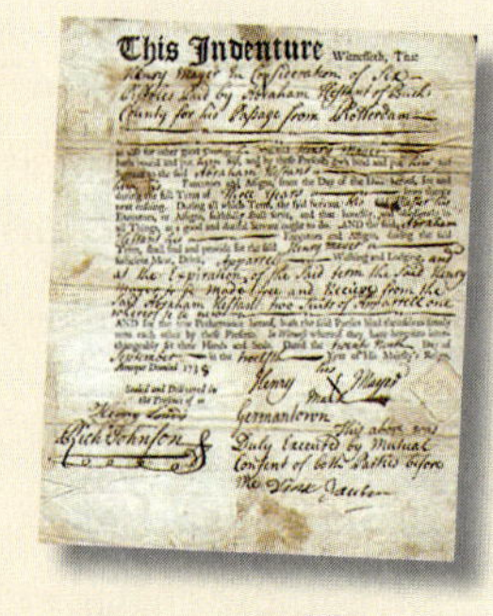

Many later settlers in the Middle colonies came as **indentured servants**. An indentured servant was a person who signed a contract (*written agreement*) in England with a sponsor. The sponsor paid the expenses for the person to come to America. The indentured servant agreed, in return, to work for the sponsor for four to seven years. After that, the indentured servant was free to do whatever he or she wished. Enslaved Africans were also used in the Middle colonies as farm workers and skilled craftsmen.

The Historian's Apprentice

What reasons led to the greater diversity of the Middle colonies? Discuss the answer to this question with a partner. Consider how the policies of the Dutch before 1664 and the later policies of William Penn contributed to diversity in this region.

Southern Colonies

The Southern colonies had warmer weather and a longer growing season than either of the other regions. Virginia was the oldest colony and had the largest population.

Most of the Southern colonists could trace their roots to England, Scotland, or Ireland. A majority were Anglicans. People usually came to these colonies for economic reasons, especially to obtain their own land. In New England, people lived together in towns. In the Southern colonies, people were spread out on farms.

Earning a Living: Plantations and Slavery

A few wealthy landowners owned plantations (*very large farms that grew just a few crops*). Plantations were found along the major water routes (*rivers and streams*) of the coastal plain. Plantation owners enjoyed privileged lifestyles. They bought English clothes, furniture, glass, and other luxury products. They used slaves as their house servants. Their children had private tutors. Some even sent their children back to England to study at the universities of Oxford and Cambridge. Others sent their children to study at the College of William and Mary in Virginia, the second oldest college in the United States.

Southern plantations grew **cash crops** for sale to England—tobacco, cotton, rice, and indigo (*a plant producing a blue dye*). They used enslaved people to work the land and harvest their crops. The slaves were Africans brought to the colonies by force, as well as their **descendants** (*children and later generations*). Several colonies passed **slave codes** (*laws that limited the movement of enslaved people*).

Slavery in the British Colonies

Year	1650	1700	1750	1780
Enslaved Population	1,600	27,817	236,420	575,420
Total Population	50,368	250,888	1,170,760	2,780,369

* Source: U.S. Census Bureau

The Atlantic Slave Trade

New slaves were people first captured in Africa by members of a different tribe. Then they were marched to stone fortresses along the coast of West Africa where they were sold to European slave traders. The slave traders bound them together in chains and crammed them into ships, which carried them across the Atlantic. Often the captives could barely move throughout the long passage. One fifth of them died during the voyage. Those who survived arrived in the West Indies, Brazil, or the British colonies where they were sold to landowners at slave auctions. Most of them were used as field workers where they were subjected to brutal conditions.

A slave auction in 1655

Earning a Living: Other Southern Farmers

Not all white Southerners were slave owners. Many white people first came to the South as indentured servants. In the foothills of the Appalachian Mountains, these people became farmers working their own land, often growing only enough food for their own families. This was called **subsistence farming**. They made their own clothes and furniture, and taught their children at home.

The Historian's Apprentice

The following colonial occupations are listed on the website of Colonial Williamsburg. This city became the capital of Virginia in 1699.

Apothecary: acted as pharmacist, doctor, dentist, and general storekeeper

Barber: cut hair, also was a surgeon

Blacksmith-Armorer: made things from iron and repaired weapons

Bookbinder: made books

Breechesmaker: made breeches (*pants*)

Brickmaker: made bricks

Cabinetmaker: made and repaired furniture

Carpenter-joiner: built interiors of ships and houses

Chandler: made candles

Coachmaker: made coaches and wagons

Cooper: made containers of wood, such as barrels

Cutler: made, sold, and repaired knives and scissors

Farrier: put shoes on horses and acted as a veterinarian (*animal doctor*)

Goldsmith: made hollow ware (such as bowls, cups, and vases) and jewelry

Gunsmith: made and repaired guns

Hatter: made hats

Leather dresser: finished leather by coloring and polishing

Mantuamaker: dressmaker

Milliner: made dresses and hats

Music Teacher: taught music

Printer: published the newspaper, sold books and other printed materials, and often served as postmaster

Roper: made rope and nets

Saddler: made saddles, harnesses, and other leather items

Shoemaker: made shoes

Silversmith: made products out of silver

Tavern Keeper: provided meals, drinks, entertainment, and lodging (*shelter*)

Weaver: wove cloth

Wheelwright: made wheels and carts

Wigmaker: made wigs

Whitesmith: made things of iron and steel, then polished them to make them look like silver

Select a partner and share your answers to the following questions.

1. Which of these occupations most surprised you? Why?
2. Which of these occupations are still important today?
3. Which of these occupations would you have wanted if you had lived in colonial times? Why?

The Contributions of Key Groups

Many different groups made contributions to the development of colonial America.

Native Americans 	Friendly Native Americans showed the first colonists how to grow crops in local conditions. They traded furs and foods with the colonists in exchange for guns and other European goods. However, the colonists kept taking more and more land. This led to conflicts with the Native Americans.
Africans 	Africans were brought to the colonies by force. The earliest Africans may have been brought as indentured servants. Later, they were brought as enslaved persons. Slaves did most of the work on Southern plantations. They also worked as craftsmen in all the colonies. Some brought special expertise from Africa to the Americas. For example, traditional African ways of growing rice were successfully adopted in South Carolina. Over time, some enslaved Africans were freed, creating a community of free blacks.
Women 	In colonial times, women worked in the home, on farms, and in businesses. They helped plant and harvest crops, cooked food, and sewed clothes. They acted as nurses to other family members. Women had the primary responsibility for raising and teaching their children. At the same time, they did not enjoy the same rights as men. For example, women could not vote or hold public office.
Children 	In New England and Pennsylvania, young children usually attended school. Elsewhere in the colonies, children might be "home schooled." In wealthy families, children were often taught by a private tutor. On farms, children helped with important chores such as taking care of livestock (*farm animals*). In villages and towns, children helped with family businesses. They could be sent as apprentices to learn a trade.

How the British Colonies Were Governed

English Political and Legal Traditions

English colonists benefited from centuries-old traditions they brought from England. Four hundred years earlier, English subjects had won very important rights. In 1215, King John had granted his subjects a "Great Charter." This charter is known by its Latin name, **Magna Carta**.

In Magna Carta, John agreed not to collect new taxes without the approval of a council of nobles. He also promised not to put individuals in prison or take away their property without following the laws of the land and giving them a trial by jury.

Magna Carta gave the English people rights that were unknown in the rest of Europe. The charter also led to the later creation of **Parliament**—an assembly that the king called together whenever he wanted to get the support of his subjects or collect new taxes. **Parliament** consisted of all the nobles, who made up the House of Lords, and representatives elected by the common people, who sat in the House of Commons.

Another important tradition that the colonists inherited from England was the **common law**. The English believed that the same rules should apply to everyone. When English judges made important decisions, their judgments were written down and kept. The same reasoning was then applied to similar cases. Even the king was subject to the common law.

A copy of the Magna Carta

Magna Carta affected the colonists' views of government.

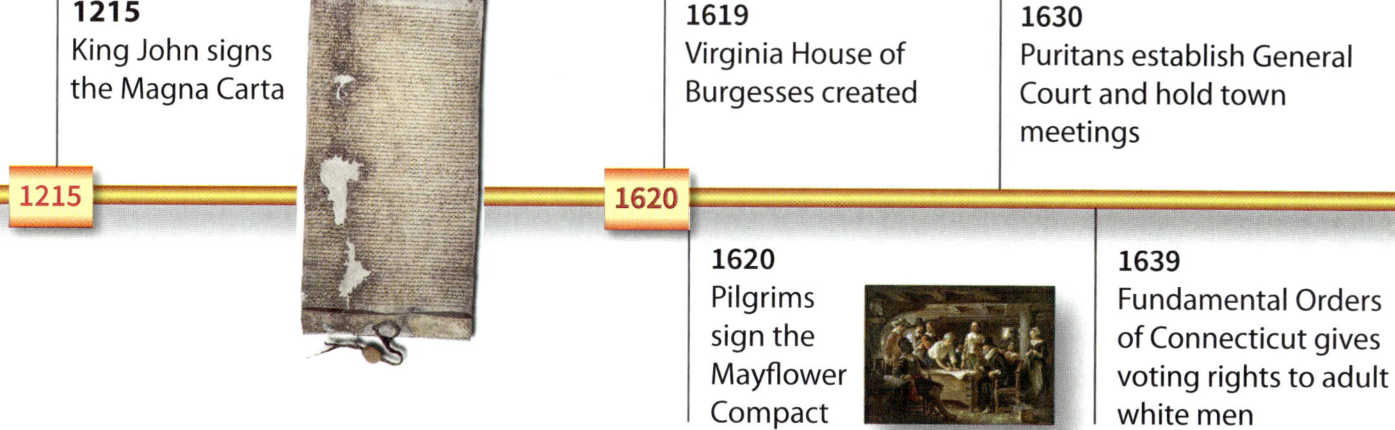

Colonial Government

The colonies were thousands of miles from England. In those days, a ship could take more than a month to sail across the Atlantic. From the beginning, the colonists therefore needed some form of local government to deal with immediate problems as they arose.

- The Virginia Company created the **House of Burgesses**—a representative assembly—in 1619. Each district elected two representatives.
- The Pilgrims pledged to create their own form of government and to obey it in the **Mayflower Compact** of 1620.
- In Massachusetts Bay Colony, Puritan communities held **town meetings**. Members of Puritan congregations voted to elect members of the **General Court**, which acted as an assembly for the entire colony.
- When Thomas Hooker took colonists from Massachusetts to Connecticut, he gave them the **Fundamental Orders of Connecticut**. This document gave all adult men in the colony the right to vote. Hooker's "Fundamental Orders" was an early type of **constitution** (*a plan of government*).
- In 1682, William Penn gave the colonists of Pennsylvania a **"Frame of Government."**

Like the Fundamental Orders of Connecticut, Penn's Frame was an early type of constitution. Penn established a government with three parts: the Governor, the Provincial Council, and the General Assembly. All free adult men in the colony elected members of the General Assembly and the Provincial Council. Voters included those who had once been indentured servants but were now free.

Both the General Assembly and the Provincial Council played a role in passing new laws for the colony. Two-thirds of the Provincial Council had to approve important laws, but only half its members were needed to pass normal laws. The Governor and Provincial Council were put in charge of carrying out, or **executing**, the laws.

Finally, the structure of government could itself be changed. However, it was harder to change the Frame itself than it was to pass an ordinary law. Six-sevenths (6/7) of both the Provincial Council and General Assembly were needed to **amend** (*add to or change*) it.

The Historian's Apprentice

The following excerpts are from William Penn's "Frame of Government." After reading these excerpts, write a paragraph explaining how the colonists of Pennsylvania benefited from these arrangements.

Frame of Government of Pennsylvania, May 5, 1682

That the government of this province shall . . . consist of the Governor and freemen of the said province, in form of a Provincial Council and General Assembly, by whom all laws shall be made, officers chosen, and public affairs transacted . . .

II. That the freemen of the said province shall . . . ch[oo]se out of themselves 72 persons of most note for their wisdom, virtue and ability, who shall meet, on the tenth day of the first month next . . . and act as the Provincial Council . . . .

VII. That the Governor and Provincial Council shall prepare and propose to the General Assembly . . . all bills, which they shall, at any time, think fit to be passed into laws . . .

IX. That the Governor and Provincial Council shall, at all times, have the care of the peace and safety of the province . . .

X. That the Governor and Provincial Council shall, at all times, settle and order the situation of all cities, ports, and market towns in every county, modeling therein all public buildings, streets, and market places, and shall appoint all necessary roads, and highways in the province. . . .

XII. That the Governor and Provincial Council shall [establish] all public schools, and encourage and reward the authors of useful sciences and . . . inventions in the said province. . . .

By 1700, a similar pattern of government could be found in all the British colonies. Each colony had a governor, a governor's council, and a colonial assembly. The colonial government managed local issues, such as relations with the Indians. The royal government in England handled overseas trade and relations with foreign governments.

Town Meetings

People in New England often made group decisions in town meetings. These were meetings in which all the adult men in the town met to vote on important issues. They were usually held once a year.

Bacon's Rebellion

In the Southern colonies, tensions between wealthy planters, poor farmers, and indentured servants finally exploded during **Bacon's**

Colonial Governments in 1700

	The **governor** acted as an **executive**—an official who enforced the laws.
	The **governor's council** was appointed to advise the governor. The council also acted as the "supreme court" for the colony. It looked at appeals from the decisions of judges.
	The **colonial assembly** was made up of elected representatives. It acted as a **legislature**—a law-making body. By 1700, all free white men in most colonies could vote.

The main difference between the colonies was in how their governors were chosen.

	In **royal colonies**, the king chose the governor. This meant the British government in London appointed the governor.
	In **proprietary colonies**, the king gave a charter to one or more proprietors. For example, Charles II granted his brother, the Duke of York, a charter for New York. He also granted charters to William Penn, Lord Baltimore, the Lords Proprietor for the Carolinas, and two Lords Proprietor for New Jersey. In these colonies, the proprietors chose the governor.
	In **self-governing colonies**, such as Connecticut and Rhode Island, the colonial assembly chose the governor.

Over time, a colony's form of government could change. Many proprietary colonies became royal colonies.

Nathaniel Bacon (1647–1676)

Nathaniel Bacon was a wealthy plantation owner who sided with western farmers against the Indians. Bacon was a member of the **governor's council**. He led several attacks on peaceful Indian tribes. Bacon and his followers wanted to seize Indian lands. The Governor of Virginia opposed Bacon's harsh treatment of the Indians and removed Bacon from his council.

The burning of Jamestown

Rebellion in the 1670s. Nathaniel Bacon's supporters felt the Governor of Virginia was not doing enough to defend them against Indian attacks. They also wanted to have more representation in the House of Burgesses.

Bacon had created a small army to fight the Indians. He turned this force against the governor himself. Bacon issued a declaration accusing the governor of corruption. Bacon's followers were so angry they burned down Jamestown. A few months later, Nathaniel Bacon died of a fever and the governor's full powers were restored.

The Dominion of New England and the "Glorious Revolution"

In the north, New England was made up of five separate colonies. In 1685, however, King James II decided to join them all together into a single colony. The new colony was named the "Dominion of New England." It had only one royal governor. The King was trying to tighten royal control over the colonies.

James II also tried to increase his power in England. He converted to Catholicism and became very unpopular. The English Parliament finally overthrew James during the "**Glorious Revolution**" of 1688. The King was replaced by his daughter Mary and her husband William, who also ruled the Netherlands.

The following year, Parliament passed the **English Bill of Rights**—a list of rights that were guaranteed to all English subjects. These included freedom of religion, a ban on cruel and unusual punishment, and freedom of speech in Parliament.

The English Bill of Rights, like the Magna Carta, had an important influence on colonial views of government. Some of these same rights are found in our first ten amendments, known as the Bill of Rights.

English or British?

Just as the United States is made up of different states, the United Kingdom is made up of different kingdoms. At one time, England (red), Wales (brown), Scotland (blue), and Ireland (green) were all separate countries. Together they make up the British Isles. Great Britain is the main island, consisting of England in the southwest, Wales in the southeast and Scotland to the north. In the Middle Ages, Prince Edward conquered Wales and joined it to England. In 1603, the King of Scotland became the King of England. At first, the two countries remained separate. They were finally joined together by the Act of Union in 1707. Historians thus refer to the original American colonies as "English." After the Act of Union in 1707, the colonies became "British."

John Locke's views on natural law and his theory of the "social contract" influenced the Founding Fathers.

Writers like **John Locke** justified the Glorious Revolution. Locke argued that the king's power did not come from God but was the result of a "**social contract.**" The people had given the king his power in order to protect their individual rights. The people had the right to overthrow their king when he violated the terms of this contract.

In New England, the colonists rebelled against the single colony created by James II. They locked up its governor. After James II was overthrown, New England was again divided into the same separate colonies as before. There was one exception: Massachusetts Bay Colony and Plymouth Colony were united into a single colony known as Massachusetts.

The English Common Law and Freedom of the Press

The English common law provided additional protection to the colonists. Colonial courts enforced the laws of England, giving the colonists certain basic rights. This became clear in the trial of John Peter Zenger, which increased freedom of the press.

Freedom of the Press

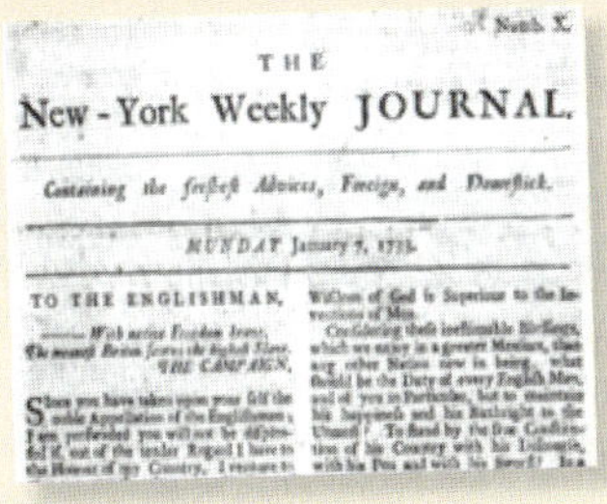

Numb. X.

THE

New-York Weekly JOURNAL.

TO THE ENGLISHMAN,

John Peter Zenger (1697–1746) was a German immigrant. He published the *New York Weekly Journal*, a newspaper in New York City. In 1734, Zenger wrote an article making fun of the Governor of New York. Zenger accused the governor of corruption.

The governor was furious. He accused Zenger of **criminal libel** and had him arrested. To commit **libel** is to print a false statement in public that hurts a person's reputation.

Zenger's attorney was a famous lawyer, Andrew Hamilton. Hamilton argued that if the statement that Zenger made was true, he had not committed libel. The jury agreed with Zenger that the governor was corrupt. It ruled in Zenger's favor.

The case was an important landmark for the freedom of the press. It meant that if a reporter published a statement that criticized government officials, it was not a libel if it was true.

1650

1675 Bacon's Rebellion in Virginia demands greater representation for western farmers

1682 William Penn grants the "Frame of Government" to colonists in Pennsylvania

1685 King James II joins all the New England colonies together

1688 "Glorious Revolution" in England

1689 English Bill of Rights

1700

1734 Zenger trial in New York

The Historian's Apprentice

1. Do you think the Zenger case was decided correctly? Why or why not?
2. Why is freedom of the press so important?

Religion in the Thirteen Colonies

We have seen that several colonies were established so that the colonists might worship God in their own way.

This did not mean, however, that these colonies supported freedom of religion for all. Pilgrims and Puritans favored freedom of religion for themselves but not for others. They felt their religious beliefs were correct and that others should follow their example.

Roger Williams was the first colonial leader to establish freedom of religion and "separation of church and state." Williams believed that government should treat the members of all religions equally. He believed that the government

Colonies Established as Religious Havens

Colony	Group	Leader
Plymouth	Pilgrims (Separatists)	William Bradford
Massachusetts Bay	Puritans	John Winthrop
Rhode Island	All religions (religious toleration)	Roger Williams/Anne Hutchinson
Pennsylvania	Quakers	William Penn
Maryland	Catholics	George Calvert, Lord Baltimore

should not take the side of one religion over another.

In Maryland, Lord Baltimore proposed the **Toleration Act of 1649**. This was passed by Maryland's colonial assembly. The law prohibited any attempt to limit the religious rights of Christians. New York also provided religious toleration. It had already been practiced when the colony was under Dutch rule. Finally, William Penn promoted religious toleration in Pennsylvania.

The Great Awakening

By the 1730s, many Protestants in England and America believed that in order to go to Heaven it was not enough to attend church and participate in religious ceremonies. They believed a good Christian must have strong religious feelings.

In England, some preachers tried to stir up those religious feelings with emotional sermons. Earlier ministers had used their sermons to discuss Bible passages in a dry and scholarly way. Now some preachers became much more emotional. They warned their listeners to look into their very souls to see if they were sinners. Then they told them to put all their faith in Jesus Christ to find salvation; if not, they would face the fires of damnation. This movement became known as the "Great Awakening."

George Whitefield preaching

During the Great Awakening, George Whitefield, an English preacher, visited the colonies. He held large open-air meetings, which thousands of people would attend. In Boston, **Jonathan Edwards** also spread the message of the Great Awakening in his sermons.

During the Great Awakening, people participated actively in religious services instead of just listening to their minister. **Salvation** (*going to Heaven*) became an individual act. This created a new equality among all believers. Puritans had believed that only a chosen few would go to Heaven. Now, preachers taught that all those who put their faith in God and repented for their sins could go there.

The Great Awakening led people to think more for themselves. It questioned the authority of ministers and church officials. It inspired African slaves to accept Christianity, while urging

Phillis Wheatley

Phillis Wheatley was the first published African-American female poet. She remained a slave although she became famous for her poetry. She converted to Christianity after hearing George Whitefield preach. She was only seventeen when she wrote a poem that she dedicated to Whitefield on his death.

better treatment from their masters. The Great Awakening appealed to women and encouraged them to be more independent. It brought large numbers of colonists together in mass meetings. It prepared the colonists to speak more openly. These qualities would be important in the future when colonists had disagreements with the British government.

Imagine you are living in one of the British colonies in the 1730s.

Which colony are you living in? ____________________

Are you an adult white male settler or do you belong to one of the other key groups that made contributions to colonial life, such as Native Americans, African Americans, women or children? Which group do you belong to? ____________________

What is your occupation? ________________

Now suppose that you are writing a short autobiography for later generations. Describe your daily life, religious beliefs and your participation in the political life of your colony.

____

____

____

____

____

____

____

____

Make a question relating to each box of words and phrases. Then exchange questions with a classrooom partner and answer them.

Name ______________________________

New England Short growing season Maritime industries Town meetings

Middle colonies Grains and Livestock Diversity Philadelphia and New York

Southern colonies Plantations Enslaved people Cash crops

Magna Carta Mayflower Compact House of Burgesses Frame of Government

Religious Toleration Roger Williams Great Awakening George Whitefield

Chapter Review Cards

Regions of North America: New England Colonies

- **New England** had rocky soil, cool weather, and a short growing season. Colonists grew crops, raised animals, and worked at skilled crafts as blacksmiths, weavers, and printers. They built ships, gathered lumber, fished and engaged in **maritime industries**.
- Its merchants engaged in **triangular trades** by buying sugar from the Caribbean islands, making rum from the sugar in New England, and trading the rum in Africa for slaves. Or they sold their fish and lumber in the West Indies, carried sugar to England, and bought manufactured goods there for sale at home.
- People lived together in towns and had town meetings.
- The region was still religious from Pilgrim and Puritan influences. Education was important. Puritans believed men and women should be able to read the Bible. Public schools were opened as early as 1647. Harvard College was founded in 1636; Yale College in 1701.

Regions of North America: Middle Colonies

- **Middle colonies** had mild winters, longer growing seasons, and fertile land. The Middle colonies produced much of the food for the colonies. They grew wheat, oats, and other grains. They raised cattle and pigs.
- People in the Middle colonies also engaged in trade and in making goods.
- There was a great diversity of peoples and religious toleration.

Regions of North America: Southern Colonies

- **Southern colonies** had warm weather and a longer growing season than the other regions.
- Southern colonists were spread out on farms. A few wealthy landowners owned plantations. Slaves provided labor on the plantations. They grew **cash crops** for sale in England such as tobacco, rice, cotton and indigo.
- Not all Southerners were slave owners. Many engaged in **subsistence farming** – growing just enough food for their families.

Contributions of Key Groups

- Native Americans showed the first colonists how to grow crops and later traded with the colonists.
- Africans did most of the work on plantations. They also worked as craftsmen.
- Women worked in the home, on the farms, and in businesses. They helped plant and harvest crops, cooked, sewed, raised children and nursed sick family members.
- Children attended schools or learned at home. They helped with important chores or served as apprentices.

English Traditions Inherited by the Colonists

- In 1215, King John granted his subjects a "Great Charter," the **Magna Carta**, which gave Englishmen the right to a trial by jury and the right not to be taxed without the consent of nobles advising the King. These rights led to the creation of **Parliament**—an assembly of nobles and elected commoners.
- Colonial courts enforced English **common law**, based on past court judgments, to which everyone was subject.

Colonial Governments

- England was far away. Colonists needed local governments to deal with their problems.
- In 1619, **Virginia** created the **House of Burgesses**, a representative assembly.
- The Pilgrims pledged to create their own form of government and obey it in the **Mayflower Compact** of 1620.
- In Massachusetts Bay, Puritan communities held **town meetings** and elected members of the **General Court**.
- Thomas Hooker granted the **Fundamental Orders of Connecticut**, an early constitution, which gave all adult males in Connecticut the right to vote.
- In 1682, William Penn gave Pennsylvania a "**framework of government**." It established a government of three parts: Governor, Provincial Council and General Assembly. The members of the Provincial Council and the General Assembly were elected by all free adult males and had the duty of passing laws.
- By 1700, all the colonies had a similar pattern of government made up of a governor, a governor's council, and a colonial assembly.

Bacon's Rebellion

- Bacon's Rebellion resulted from tensions between wealthy planters, poor farmers, and indentured servants.
- **Nathaniel Bacon** led the rebellion. His supporters wanted the Governor of Virginia to do more in defending them from Indian attacks. The rebellion failed when Bacon died of a fever.

The Dominion of New England and the "Glorious Revolution"

- In 1685, James II combined Plymouth, Massachusetts Bay, Rhode Island, Connecticut, and New Hampshire into a single colony called the "**Dominion of New England.**" The colonists rebelled and imprisoned their governor.
- In 1688, the English Parliament overthrew James II in the "**Glorious Revolution**." In 1689, Parliament passed the **English Bill of Right**s—rights guaranteed to all English subjects. These included freedom of religion, a ban on cruel and unusual punishment, and freedom of speech in Parliament.
- New England was divided again into separate colonies.
- **John Locke** justified the Glorious Revolution by explaining that the King's authority was part of a "**social contract**" between the King and his subjects. The King was required to protect the individual rights of his subjects. When he failed in this duty, his subjects had the right to rebel.

The English Common Law and the Freedom of the Press

- The English common law protected the rights of colonists as English subjects. This was shown in the case of **John Peter Zenger**, which involved freedom of the press.
- Zenger wrote an article making fun of the Governor of New York and accusing him of corruption. The Governor arrested Zenger for the crime of **libel** (*making a false public statement about someone that hurts the person's reputation*). At trial, the jury agreed that the governor was corrupt and that the statement made by Zenger was true. Therefore Zenger was not guilty of libel.
- The case meant that even if a reporter published a damaging statement, it was not a libel if it were true.

Religion

- Pilgrims and Puritans favored freedom of religion for themselves but not for others.
- **Roger Williams** was the first colonial leader to establish **freedom of religion** for all and "**separation of church and state**." He believed the government should treat all religions equally.
- **Lord Baltimore** supported religious toleration in Maryland; **William Penn** supported it in Pennsylvania.

The Great Awakening

- In the 1730s, a group of preachers became much more emotional in a "**Great Awakening**." They told listeners to put their faith in Jesus Christ to find salvation or face the fires of damnation.
- The English preacher, George Whitefield, held large open-air meetings, which were attended by thousands. In Boston, **Jonathan Edwards** spread the Great Awakening's message. People participated actively in the service.
- Salvation became an individual act, creating new equality among all believers. The Great Awakening questioned the authority of ministers and church officials. It led people to think more for themselves.
- The Great Awakening inspired African slaves to accept Christianity, while urging better treatment from their owners. It appealed to women and encouraged them to become more independent.
- After hearing Whitefield, **Phillis Wheatley**, a 17 year-old, converted to Christianity. She became the first published African-American poet.

New England
- Rocky soil, short growing season, cold winters
- Farming, fishing, lumber, skilled crafts or maritime industries (sailing, shipbuilding)
- Merchants active in triangular trades: sugar-rum-slaves
- People lived in towns; participated in town meetings; most were literate; oldest university

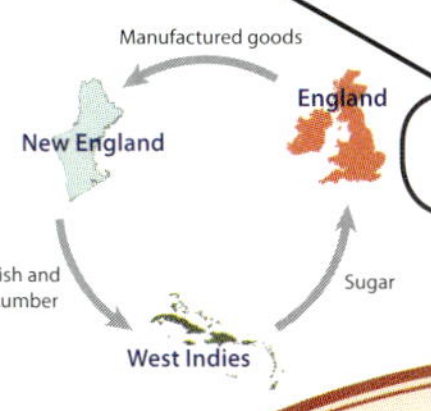

Middle Colonies
- Good soil, climate less harsh than New England
- Great diversity of people
- Farmers grew grain and raised cattle and pigs
- People made or traded goods
- Indentured servants worked 4–7 years and then were freed

Southern Colonies
- Warmest weather and longest growing season
- People lived on their own farms
- Wealthy landowners had plantations with slaves and grew cash crops
- Most Southern colonists owned no slaves
- Farmers in West often engaged in subsistence farming

Three Regions

Life in the Thirteen British Colonies

Government

English Traditions
- Magna Carta
- Parliament
- Common Law

Colonial Government
- Virginia: House of Burgesses
- Plymouth: Mayflower Compact
- Connecticut: Fundamental Orders
- Pennsylvania: Frame of Government
- New England: town meetings

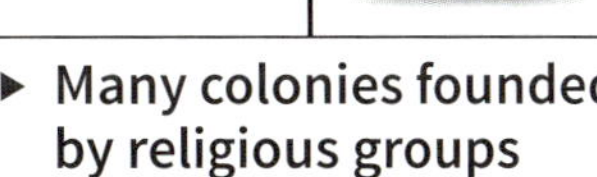

Religion

- Many colonies founded by religious groups
- Growth of religious toleration

- Rhode Island—Roger Williams
- Pennsylvania—Frame of Government
- Maryland—Toleration Act

The Great Awakening (1730s–1740s)
- Emotional sermons
- Everyone has chance to be saved
- Challenged authority of ministers
- George Whitefield and Jonathan Edwards

Contributions of Key Groups
- **Native Americans:** helped first settlers adapt to the new land
- **Africans:** brought to the colonies by force; did much of the work; brought skills in farming
- **Women:** worked in homes, farms and businesses; not treated equally
- **Children:** might or might not go to school; helped family; apprentices

What do you know?

SS.6.A.2.2

1. The map below shows where economic activities took place in colonial America.

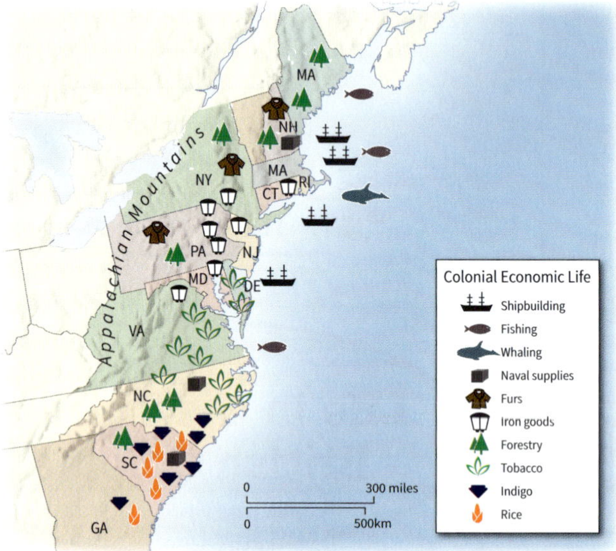

Based on the map, where would a whaler or shipbuilder be most likely to live in colonial times?

A. South Carolina

B. New England

C. Middle colonies

D. Southern colonies

SS.6.A.2.2

2. Based on the map, which two regions of colonial America had good natural harbors and a thriving fur trade?

A. Western and Middle colonies

B. Middle and Southern colonies

C. New England and Middle colonies

D. Southern colonies and New England

SS.6.A.2.4

3. How were Nathaniel Bacon and John Peter Zenger similar?

A. They started popular uprisings.

B. They lived in Southern colonies.

C. They challenged the actions of colonial governors.

D. They published articles critical of the government in the newspaper.

SS.8.C.1.4

4. The list below identifies three features of colonial America.

- Mayflower Compact
- Virginia House of Burgesses
- New England town meetings

Which title best describes the list?

A. Colonial Trade Organizations
B. Self-Government in the Colonies
C. First Attempts to Declare Independence
D. Colonists' Relations with Native Americans

SS.6.A.2.7

5. The passage below describes enslaved people during the colonial period.

The first Africans in North America were probably brought as indentured servants. Later, Africans were brought by force as enslaved persons. Slaves performed most of the work on Southern plantations. Some brought special expertise from Africa to the Americas such as traditional African ways of growing rice. These were successfully adopted in South Carolina.

Which conclusion can be drawn from this passage?

A. Enslaved Africans made their greatest contribution to colonial manufacturing.
B. Southern plantations relied on the labor and skills of enslaved African Americans.
C. Enslaved persons made up the same proportion of the population in every colony.
D. The first Africans in America preferred working on Southern plantations to living in the cold climate of New England.

SS.6.A.2.5

6. What would be the best title for the list below?

- Loss of land
- Increased warfare
- Westward movement
- Epidemics leading to reduced populations

A. Reasons for Settlement of North America
B. Impact of Colonial Settlement on Native Americans
C. Reasons for Different Colonial Regions
D. Effects of Exploration of North America on Europe

SS.6.A.2.3

7. The passage below was published by Alexander Falconbridge, a ship's doctor, in 1788.

> *[The captives] are generally brought upon deck... [A] long chain, which is locked to a ringbolt fixed in the deck, is run through the rings of the shackles of the men and then locked to another ringbolt, fixed also in the deck. By this means, fifty or sixty and sometimes more are fastened to one chain in order to prevent them from rising or endeavoring to escape.*

Which conclusion can be drawn from his description?

A. The ship's doctor treated the enslaved Africans to make them comfortable.

B. Enslaved men were free to roam the deck of the ship, but not to walk below deck.

C. A large number of captive Africans escaped during the voyage across the Atlantic.

D. Enslaved Africans suffered many hardships during Middle Passage across the Atlantic.

SS.6.A.2.3

8. The chart below gives statistics about slavery at two different times.

In 1650, the number of enslaved people in Northern and Southern colonies was almost equal.	In 1770, there were ten times as many enslaved people in the South as in the North.

Which conclusion can be drawn from these statistics?

A. All Northern colonies had abolished slavery by 1770.

B. The South grew faster in population than the North did.

C. The route from Africa to the South was shorter than to the North.

D. Southerners relied more on the work of enslaved laborers than Northerners did.

SS.6.A.2.4

9. How did preachers like Jonathan Edwards and George Whitefield encourage the growth of democracy during the Great Awakening (1720–1750)?

A. They advised colonists to obey royal authority.

B. They threatened their opponents with damnation.

C. They asked colonists to think more for themselves.

D. They accused several colonial women of witchcraft.

CHAPTER 4 The Road to Revolution

SS.6.A.2.1 Compare the relationships among the British, French, Spanish, and Dutch in their struggle for colonization of North America.

SS.6.A.2.6 Examine the causes, course, and consequences of the French and Indian War.

SS.6.A.3.1 Explain the consequences of the French and Indian War in British policies for the American colonies from 1763 to 1774.

SS.6.A.3.2 Explain American colonial reaction to British policy from 1763 to 1774.

SS.6.A.3.3 Recognize the contributions of the Founding Fathers (John Adams, Sam Adams, Benjamin Franklin, John Hancock, Alexander Hamilton, Thomas Jefferson, James Madison, George Mason, George Washington) during American Revolutionary efforts.

SS.6.A.3.6 Examine the causes, course, and consequences of the American Revolution.

SS.6.A.3.8 Examine individuals and groups that affected political and social motivations during the American Revolution.

S.6.A.3.16 Examine key events in Florida history as each impacts this era of American history.

Alignment to Grade 7 Civics Standards

SS.7.C.1.2 Trace the impact that the Magna Carta, English Bill of Rights, Mayflower Compact, and Thomas Paine's *Common Sense* had on colonists' views of government.

SS.7.C.1.3 Describe how English policies and responses to colonial concerns led to the writing of the Declaration of Independence.

Terms and Names You Should Know

- George Washington
- French and Indian War
- Albany Congress
- Benjamin Franklin
- Albany Plan of Union
- Prime Minister
- William Pitt
- Treaty of Paris (1763)
- King George III
- Proclamation Line of 1763
- Mercantilism
- Smuggle
- Stamp Act
- Taxation consent
- Petition
- Boycott
- Patrick Henry
- Stamp Act Congress
- Samuel Adams
- Sons of Liberty
- Daughters of Liberty
- Repeal
- Declaratory Act
- Townshend duties
- Quartering Act of 1765
- Boston Massacre
- Consult
- Massacre
- John Adams
- Tea Act
- Boston Tea Party
- Coercive Acts
- Enlightenment
- Revolution

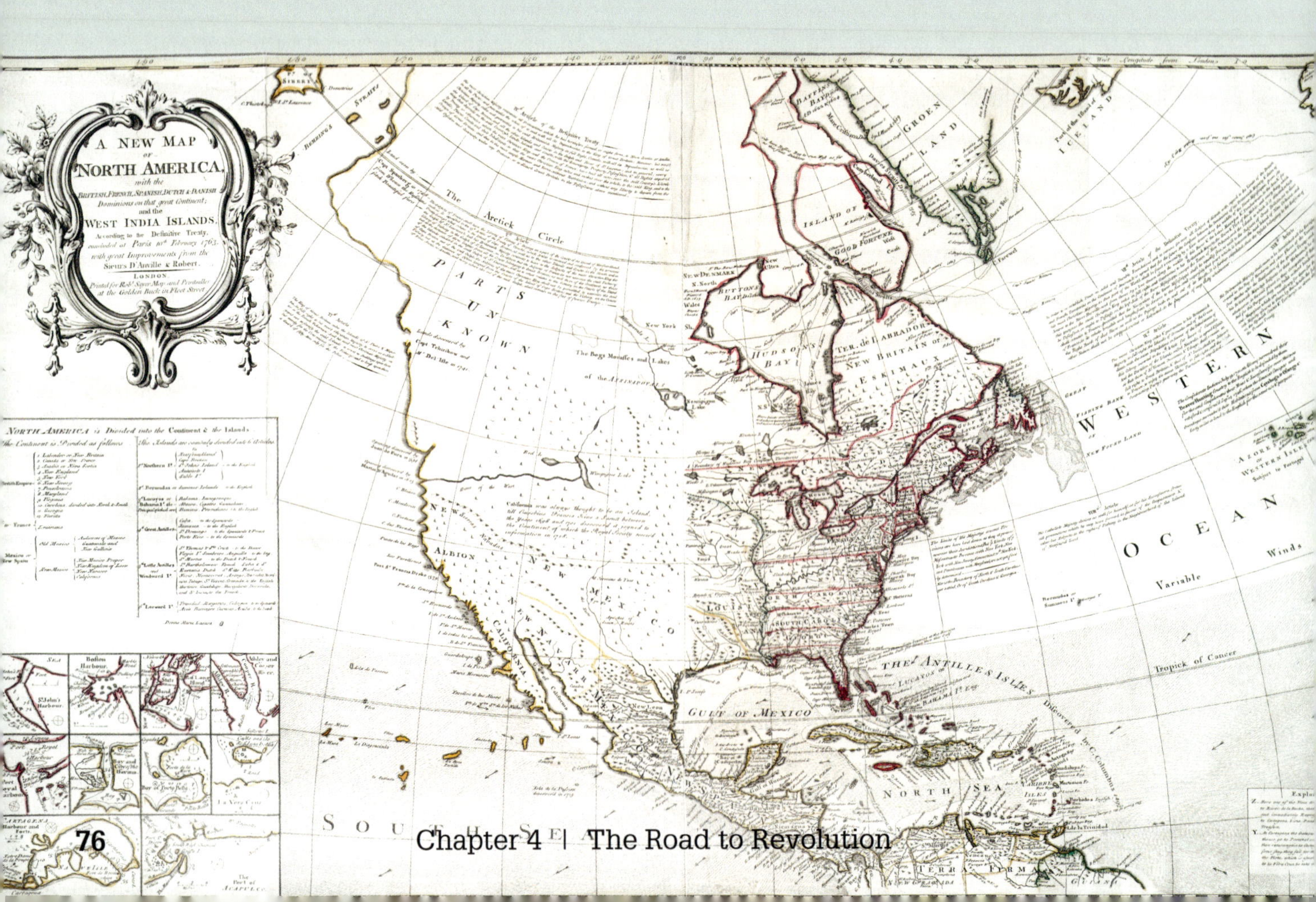

Florida "Keys" to Learning

1. The expansion of New France and the British colonies led to a war for the control of North America. Both powers had interests in the Ohio River Valley.

2. The French and Indian War began when George Washington led an ambush of French soldiers near Fort Duquesne in 1754. The next year, British troops marching towards Fort Duquesne were defeated.

3. After the Seven Years' War broke out in Europe in 1756, France could not devote as many resources to North America. The British took Quebec in 1759. In the Peace of Paris, ending the war in 1763, France gave Canada to Britain.

4. King George III announced the Proclamation Line of 1763, prohibiting settlement west of the Appalachian Mountains to protect the Indians. This angered many colonists.

5. Because of the high cost of the French and Indian War, Britain placed new taxes on the colonists after the war. In 1765, Parliament passed the Stamp Act without the prior consent of the colonists. This act required revenue stamps on newspapers, pamphlets, and legal documents.

6. Colonial assemblies sent petitions to Parliament against the new tax. Colonists boycotted British goods. Patrick Henry declared that only the House of Burgesses had the right to place new taxes on Virginians. James Otis declared that, "taxation without representation is tyranny." Sam Adams formed the "Sons of Liberty." "Committees of Correspondence" informed each other of anti-British activities.

7. Parliament repealed the Stamp Act. At the same time, it passed the Declaratory Act (1766), stating its right to pass laws for the colonies, including new taxes.

8. In 1767, Parliament passed the Townshend duties—taxing household goods like lead and glass. Parliament again passed this law without the consent of the colonists.

9. In 1768, more British soldiers arrived in Boston. In 1770, some of them fired on a crowd and killed five colonists in the "Boston Massacre."

10. Parliament finally repealed the unpopular Townshend duties. In 1773, it passed a new Tea Act. This lowered the cost of tea in the colonies but still collected a tax. Colonists again protested. A group of colonists disguised as American Indians threw chests of British tea into Boston Harbor in the "Boston Tea Party."

11. Outraged by this destruction of property, Parliament passed the Coercive Acts (1774). These acts closed Boston Harbor and suspended the colony's legislature until the tea was paid for. Parliament also passed the Quebec Act, allowing Catholics in Quebec to hold public office and making the Ohio River Valley a part of Quebec.

12. Colonial views were greatly influenced by the Enlightenment. Enlightenment thinkers did not believe that kings and queens received their powers from God. Instead, they accepted John Locke's view that each government was created as part of a "social contract" between a people and their ruler. If the ruler did not respect the rights of the people, then the social contract was broken and the people had the right to overthrow their ruler.

It is a crisp afternoon in May 1754. A young officer from Virginia named **George Washington** is leading a small band of soldiers and Indians through the woods of the Ohio River Valley. Washington has learned from his scouts that French soldiers are nearby and decides to ambush them. Several of the Frenchmen are killed by musket fire. Other Frenchmen are killed by the Indian warriors traveling with Washington.

The French and Indian War

Two Empires Clash in the Ohio River Valley

By the late 1740s, the British colonies and New France were on a collision course. The French had built scattered settlements along the St. Lawrence River, Great Lakes, and the Mississippi River. Their claims reached from Canada southward through the center of the North American continent. The British, on the other hand, had built settlements along the Atlantic coast from Georgia to New Hampshire.

The French mainly used their territory for the profitable fur trade. There were still fewer than 100,000 French colonists on the mainland of North America. In contrast, there were as many as one and a half million British colonists.

As the French moved southward, they built forts and increased their trade with Indian tribes. Meanwhile, British settlers were pressing westward. As the territories of these nations spread across the North American continent, they were bound to clash.

The British finally found themselves face to face with French settlers in the Ohio River Valley. In 1749, the French sent a body of soldiers to enforce French claims and warn local Indian tribes not to trade with the British. In the same year, the British government handed control of these richly forested lands to the Ohio Company of Virginia.

Two years later, the French sent another military force into the valley to build more forts and to punish those Indian tribes trading with the British. Meanwhile the Governor of Virginia, who had invested in the Ohio Company, sent George Washington to warn the French to withdraw.

Fort Duquesne Changes Hands

After Washington's warning, a small force of British soldiers began building a fort where two rivers joined to form the Ohio River. From this position, they could control much of the Ohio

Indians with European goods

Fort Duquesne

River Valley. However, a larger French force arrived and sent the British soldiers home. The French soldiers continued building the fort, which they named "**Fort Duquesne**."

Washington had been sent back to help with the new fort. On the way, he learned that the fort had been taken by the French. As we have seen, Washington's small force then ambushed a group of French soldiers in May 1754. Their exchange of gunfire was actually the start of the **French and Indian War** (1754–1763). In this conflict, Britain and France fought for control of North America.

After the ambush, Washington moved south and began building a new fort of his own. But early in July 1754, his fort was captured. The French let Washington and his men peaceably withdraw and return to Virginia.

The Conflict Spreads

News of these events soon reached Britain and France. Both countries sent more troops across the Atlantic. Although there were more British colonists, the French counted heavily on their Indian allies. Most Indians preferred French to British rule since British settlers took their land to make farms. The French also gave frequent gifts to tribal leaders, which the British failed to do. The powerful Iroquois tribes, on the other hand, sided with the British.

The British had ambitious war plans in 1755. They planned to send forces from Virginia, Pennsylvania, and New York to capture several French forts at once. **General Edward Braddock** took command of the British forces in Virginia. Braddock marched with 1,500 troops towards Fort Duquesne. Washington was one of his officers. However, Braddock was not used to fighting on the frontier. He insisted that his forces march on the open road as they would in Europe. French soldiers and their Indian allies hid behind trees and shot at the British soldiers. Braddock was killed and two-thirds of his men were wounded or killed.

General Braddock's death near Fort Duquesne

Washington helped rally the remaining troops and assisted in their retreat.

Elsewhere, the British also met with defeat. In far away India, the British and French were also competing for influence. British troops surrendered at Calcutta. The local ruler imprisoned them overnight in a crowded room with little air, where most died of suffocation. The situation did not look good for the future of the British Empire.

> The Virginia troops showed a great deal of bravery, and were near all killed. . . . I luckily escaped without a wound, though I had four bullets through my coat and two horses shot from under me.
>
> —George Washington to his mother, July 18, 1754

The Historian's Apprentice

1. Imagine you are one of the soldiers under the command of George Washington. Write a letter describing your experiences between 1754 and 1755.
2. Suppose you are the chief of a tribe of Native Americans in western Pennsylvania. Write a speech to the other members of your tribe explaining why you should ally with either the British or the French in this new war.
3. Make an illustrated map showing the Ohio River Valley, Fort Duquesne, and other nearby forts and cities. Be sure to show boundaries between colonies. Add boxes around the margins of the map for illustrations or comments.

The Albany Congress

Seven colonies sent representatives to the frontier town of Albany, New York, in July 1754, just as the French and Indian War was beginning. The purpose of their meeting was to come up with a common policy for dealing with Native American tribes. **Benjamin Franklin** and Thomas Hutchinson proposed that the colonies create a common government with a President-General, chosen by the King, and a Grand Council, chosen by the colonial assemblies. The delegates to the Albany Congress approved the plan. The plan was sent to the colonial assemblies and the British government in London for approval. These groups, however, rejected the Albany plan.

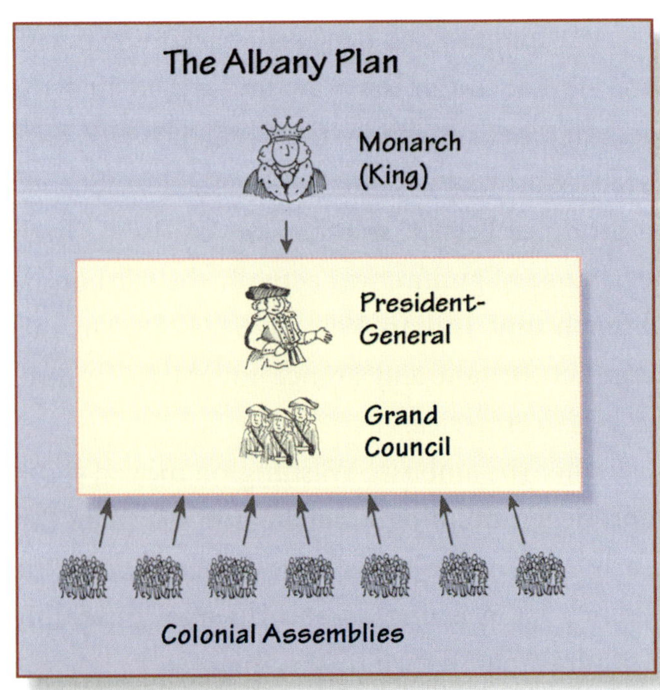

This cartoon was published by Benjamin Franklin to encourage the colonies to participate in his plan for a form of cooperative government.

The Historian's Apprentice

The following excerpts are from the Albany Plan of Union, proposed by Benjamin Franklin and Thomas Hutchinson. It was approved by the delegates to the Albany Congress:

"It is proposed that . . . one general government may be formed in America, including all the said colonies, within and under which government each colony may retain its present constitution . . .

1. That the said general government be administered by a President-General, to be appointed and supported by the crown; and a Grand Council, to be chosen by the representatives of the people of the several Colonies met in their respective assemblies. . . .

10. That the President-General, with the advice of the Grand Council, hold or direct all Indian treaties, in which the general interest of the Colonies may be concerned; and make peace or declare war with Indian nations.

11. That they make such laws as they judge necessary for regulating all Indian trade.

15. That they raise and pay soldiers and build forts for the defense of any of the Colonies. . . .

16. That for these purposes they have power to make laws, and lay and levy such general duties, imposts, or taxes, as to them shall appear most equal and just . . ."

Select a partner and discuss the answers to the following questions:

- Why did Franklin and Hutchinson propose two parts to this new government?
- What were the powers and responsibilities of this new government?
- What did the Albany Plan propose for the existing colonial assemblies?
- Would you have supported the Albany Plan? Why or why not?

Outbreak of War in Europe

By the spring of 1756, the war had spread to Europe. Europe's three largest countries—Russia, Austria, and France—joined together to attack Prussia, a small but rising state in Germany. Britain took Prussia's side in this contest. Because the war in Europe lasted seven years—from 1756 to 1763—it became known in Europe as the **Seven Years' War**.

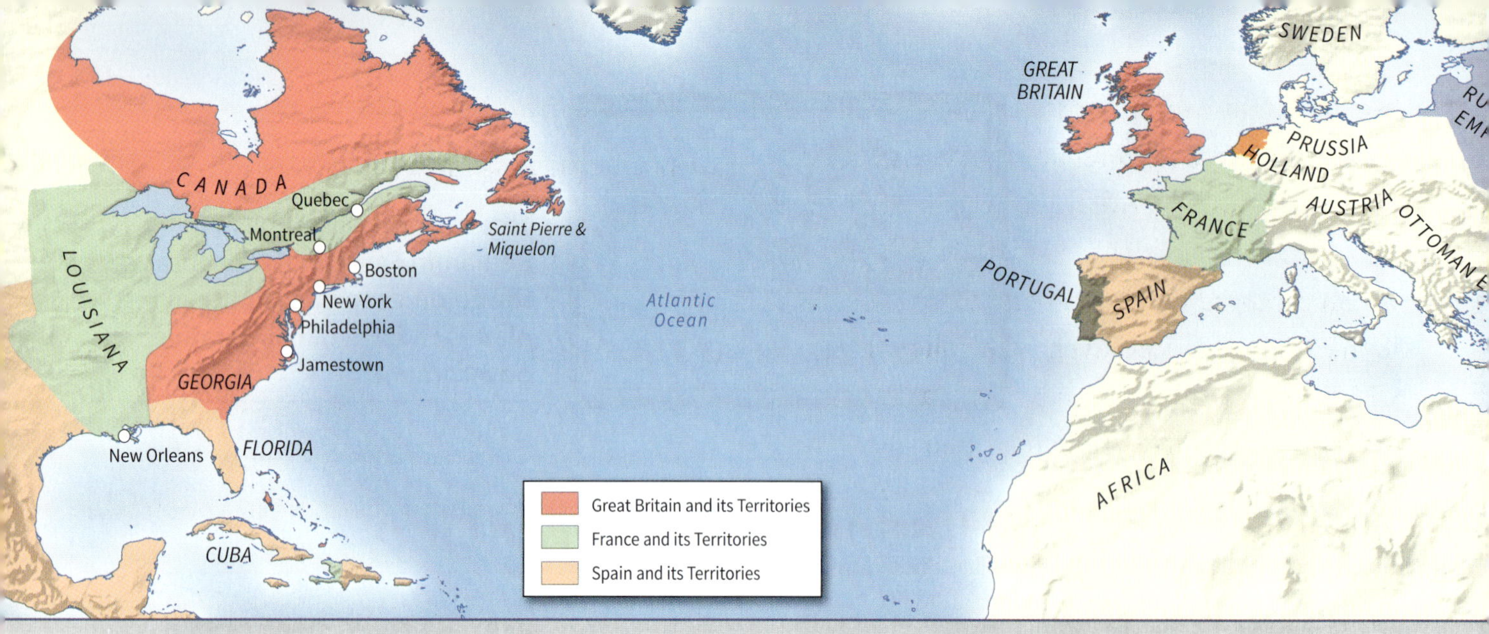

Europe and North America in 1756

After 1756, the French had to concentrate their resources on the fighting in Europe. This meant they could no longer send more troops to North America. In 1757, William Pitt became the **Prime Minister** of Great Britain (*the leader of the British government*). Pitt understood the importance of the war in North America. He was determined to send Britain's best resources to help the colonists.

In October 1758, a new British army marched on Fort Duquesne. This time, the British soldiers were more experienced at fighting in frontier conditions. At the same time, the Indian forces allied to the French were weakened by a new smallpox epidemic. The British captured Fort Duquesne and permitted the French to withdraw. The British renamed the outpost **"Fort Pitt"** after their popular Prime Minister. Fort Pitt later became the city of Pittsburgh.

To the north, the British also captured Fort Louisbourg in Nova Scotia (in northeastern Canada), at the entrance to the St. Lawrence River. Other fighting between Britain and France continued in India and in the ocean off the coast of West Africa. The Seven Years' War was the world's first truly global conflict.

In 1759, the British decided to invade Canada. **General James Wolfe** sailed up the St. Lawrence River in July to attack **Quebec,** a fortress city on the heights above the St. Lawrence River. Wolfe cut the city off from its supplies but was unable to launch a successful attack. In September, he came up with a new plan. At night, he secretly moved his troops upstream and had them scale the tall cliffs on the western side of the city. The French

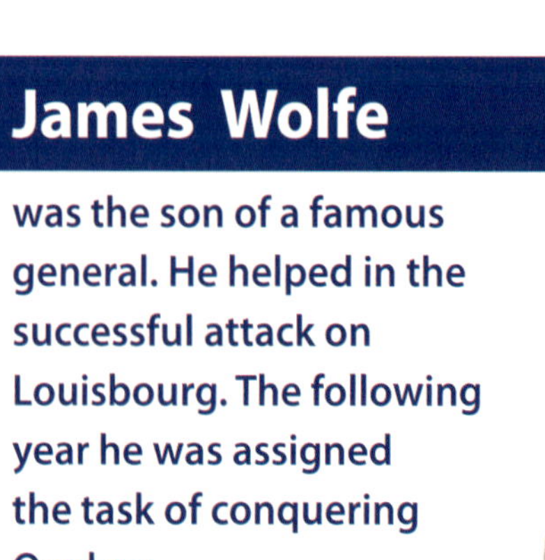

James Wolfe

was the son of a famous general. He helped in the successful attack on Louisbourg. The following year he was assigned the task of conquering Quebec.

thought these were impossible for any army to climb. They were not prepared to defend the city from this direction. After a fifteen-minute battle the next day, the French were defeated and the British captured Quebec, giving them command of the St. Lawrence River. The following year, British forces took Montreal. The war in Europe and the Caribbean continued for two more years, but the fighting on the North American mainland had ended.

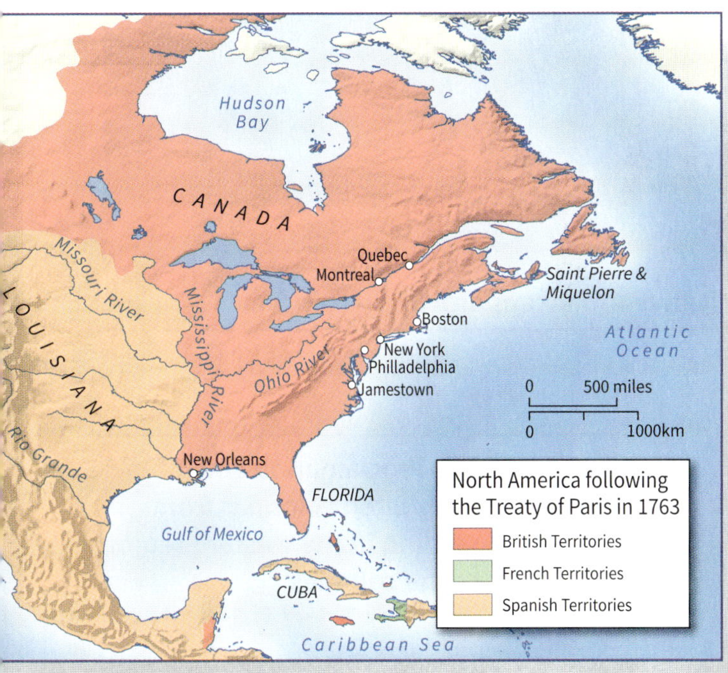

North America following the Treaty of Paris in 1763

The Treaty of Paris (1763)

France lost the war and was forced to surrender its colonies on the mainland of North America. Under the **Treaty of Paris,** Canada and the Ohio River Valley came under British rule. In fact, all French territory east of the Mississippi was given to Britain. French territory west of the Mississippi was handed over to Spain. The British returned several Caribbean islands known for making sugar to France.

The British colonists were pleased with this outcome. They no longer had to worry about defending themselves against the French and their Indian allies. On the other hand, the British government found itself deeply in debt. It had borrowed large sums of money to pay for the war. The British government further had to decide how to govern Canada and its French-speaking, Catholic residents. The government also had to handle relations with the Indians. It faced many challenges ahead.

The Treaty of Paris also affected Florida. At the time, Florida was in Spanish hands. Spain now gave Florida to Britain in exchange for the return of Cuba, which the British had captured during the war.

The Historian's Apprentice

1. Discuss the following two questions with a partner. Then write down your answers in your journals or on a separate piece of paper.
   - What were the main causes of the French and Indian War?
   - Why were the British able to win this war?
2. Pretend you are a soldier during the French and Indian War. Write a letter to relatives back home describing what you have seen.
3. Make your own graphic organizer or concept map showing the causes, course, and consequences of the war.

British Polices after the War Lead to Colonial Discontent

Although the British won the war, the next decade saw increasing tensions between the British government and the colonists in North America.

The Proclamation Line of 1763

Native American tribes were anxious about the defeat of the French. Just as the war was ending, Chief Pontiac of the Ottawa tribe sent messages to other tribes asking them to unite against the British colonists. This was the first time that so many different tribes had acted together, and they were able to capture eight forts along the frontier before they were defeated.

Native Americans and British officers

The Proclamation Line of 1763 prohibited colonists from settling in the western regions of the colonies.

The British government was already considering steps to avoid future conflicts with the Indians. In October 1763, **King George III** issued a royal proclamation. It prohibited colonists from settling west of the Appalachian Mountains. This created a line of settlement to protect the Indians. It was shocking, however, to those colonists who were looking forward to taking new lands in the Ohio River Valley.

The Navigation Acts

The British government followed a policy of **mercantilism**. Under this policy, colonies existed to enrich the "mother country" (Great Britain). Mercantilists believed that the colonies should send inexpensive crops and raw materials to Britain, and that the colonists should purchase more expensive manufactured goods from the British. This relationship would guarantee a steady flow of money to the mother country.

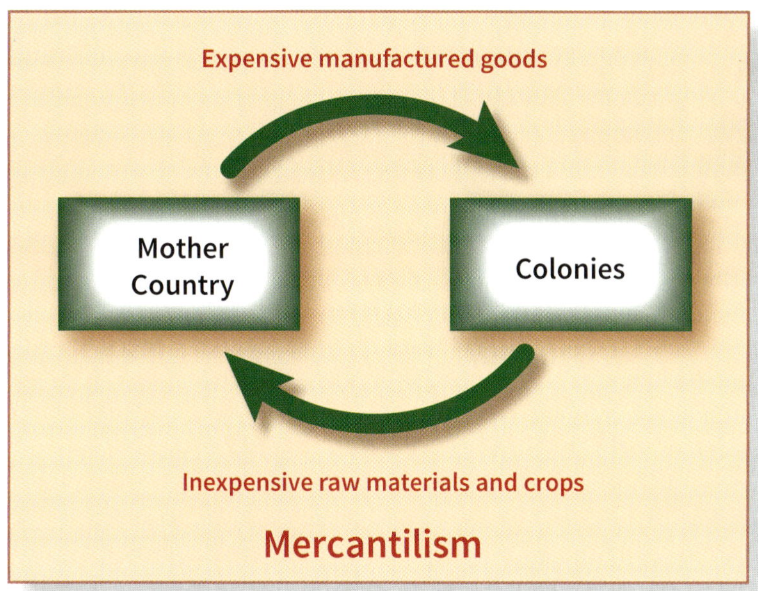

Even before the French and Indian War, the British government had passed many laws, known as the **Navigation Acts**, to help British merchants:

- For example, the government required that all goods from the colonies be shipped to Great Britain before being sold in other European countries.
- The government also placed special taxes on foreign sugar and molasses entering the colonies. The goal of this law was to ensure that the colonists bought their sugar from British merchants. Instead, an active trade in smuggling foreign sugar into the colonies had grown. (To "smuggle" is to bring goods into a country illegally.)
- The **Sugar Act of 1764** actually lowered the **duties** (*taxes*) on foreign sugar, but the government planned to enforce the law more strictly.

The British failure to consult with the colonists and obtain their consent would later influence the colonists' decision to declare independence from Great Britain.

New Revenue Policies: Taxation and Protest

After the French and Indian War, the most important issue dividing the colonists and the British government was taxation.

People living in Britain were already paying more in taxes than the colonists in North America. The British government therefore decided that the colonists should pay more towards their own defense. Parliament passed a series of laws to tax the colonists. Since the colonies were so far from London, no attempt was made to obtain their prior **consent** (*agreement*) to these new taxes.

The Stamp Act

The first of these laws was the **Stamp Act**, passed in 1765. This act required every official document, newspaper, or pamphlet in the colonies to have an expensive government stamp.

The colonists were greatly angered by the Stamp Act. Colonists held marches and rallies against it. Colonial assemblies sent **petitions** (*formal requests*) to Parliament to change the law. Colonists **boycotted** (*refused to buy*) British goods.

May 28, 1754
George Washington fires on French soldiers

July 4, 1754
Washington surrenders Fort Necessity

1750

1755

July 13, 1755
General Braddock killed in Ohio River Valley

May 17, 1756
Start of Seven Years' War in Europe

September 13, 1759
General Wolfe takes Quebec

1760

October 25, 1760
George III becomes King

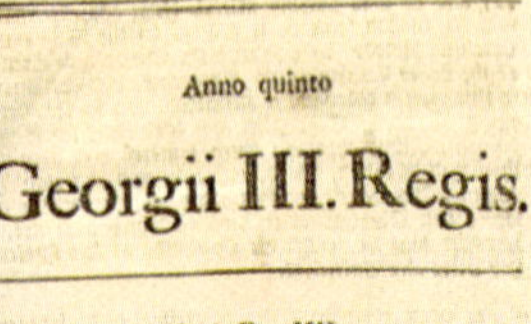

Anno quinto

Georgii III. Regis.

CAP. XII.

An Act for granting and applying certain Stamp Duties, and other Duties, in the British Colonies and Plantations in America, towards further defraying the Expences of defending, protecting, and securing the same; and for amending such Parts of the several Acts of Parliament relating to the Trade and Revenues of the said Colonies and Plantations, as direct the Manner of determining and recovering the Penalties and Forfeitures therein mentioned.

The Stamp Act, 1765

In the Virginia House of Burgesses, **Patrick Henry**, a young lawyer, introduced a series of **resolutions** against the Stamp Act. One of the resolutions declared that only the Virginia House of Burgesses could place new taxes on Virginians. In Massachusetts, another lawyer, **James Otis**, declared that "taxation without representation is tyranny." (A **tyranny** is a government that is cruel and unreasonable.)

"[T]here shall be raised, levied, collected and paid unto His Majesty . . . [f]or every skin or piece of . . . parchment, or sheet or piece of paper, on which shall be . . . written or printed any declaration, plea . . . or other pleading, or any copy thereof, in any court of law, within the British colonies and plantations in America, a stamp duty of 3 pence."

—An excerpt from the Stamp Act, March 22, 1765

The colonial assembly of Massachusetts proposed that each of the colonies send representatives to a special "congress." Nine colonies sent representatives to a "**Stamp Act Congress**," which was held in New York City in October. The Stamp Act Congress sent a strongly worded protest against the Stamp Act to the British Parliament in London.

In Boston, **Sam Adams** and others formed a secret society called the "**Sons of Liberty**." The Sons of Liberty set the building of the local Stamp Tax distributor in Boston on fire and attacked the house of the colony's Lieutenant Governor. Members of the Sons of Liberty seized tax collectors and put hot tar and feathers on them.

Colonists against the Stamp Act also organized "**committees of correspondence**." These committees sent information to one another about their anti-British activities.

Repeal of the Stamp Act

The British government was taken by surprise by the many protests against the Stamp Act. British merchants complained that the law was

February 10, 1763
End of the French and Indian War

October 9, 1763
Proclamation Line

April 5, 1764
Sugar Act

1765

March 25, 1765
Stamp Act

May 15, 1765
King George III approves Quartering Act of 1765

October 7, 1765
Stamp Act Congress meets

March 18, 1766
Parliament repeals Stamp Act

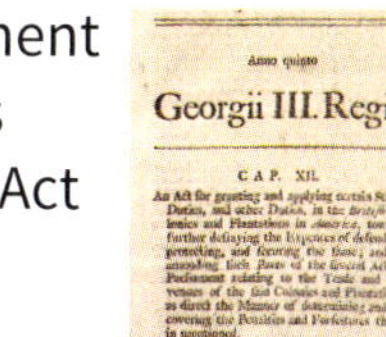
Anno quinto
Georgii III. Regis.
CAP. XII.

June 29, 1767
King George III approves Townshend duties

1. His Majesty's subjects in these colonies owe the same allegiance (loyalty) to the Crown of Great Britain that is owing from his subjects born within the Realm. . . .
2. His Majesty's . . . subjects in these colonies are entitled to all of the . . . rights and liberties of his . . . subjects within the Kingdom of Great Britain.
3. It is . . . essential to the freedom of a people, and the undoubted right of Englishmen, that no taxes be imposed on them but by their own consent. . . .
4. The people of these colonies cannot . . . be represented in the House of Commons in Great Britain.

Resolutions of the Stamp Act Congress, October 19, 1765

actually hurting their businesses. Parliament acted quickly to **repeal** (*cancel; withdraw*) the law. It also further reduced the duties under the Sugar Act.

At the same time, Parliament passed the **Declaratory Act** (1766). This act declared that Parliament had the right to pass laws that were binding on the colonies "in all cases."

The Townshend Duties

The British government still needed to collect money from the colonists. Parliament therefore passed a series of new taxes, known as the **Townshend duties**. These placed taxes on paper, paint, glass, lead, and tea. These were common household goods that were usually shipped to the colonies from Britain.

Once again, Parliament passed these new duties without first obtaining the consent of the colonists. Members of Parliament still felt that the colonists were too far away to consult with them.

The **Daughters of Liberty** had been established in 1765, just after the Sons of Liberty. After the passage of the Townshend duties, these women helped the colonists boycott British goods

Could the colonists have had their own representatives in Parliament?

At a time when crossing the Atlantic was slow, any colonial representatives in London would soon have been out of touch with the colonists they represented. Colonial leaders did not really want to be represented in Parliament. What they wanted was to make their own laws, including those on taxation, in their own colonial assemblies.

by making their own cloth and other products that could be used in their place.

More British Troops Arrive

To enforce the Townshend Acts and to prevent further unrest, the British government sent more troops to North America. Four thousand new soldiers landed in Boston in October 1768. The government quartered some of these troops in colonists' homes. To "**quarter**" means to send soldiers to live in public and private buildings. Under the **Quartering Act of 1765**, the homeowner could be asked to provide food and shelter to these soldiers. British officials were also permitted to search colonists' homes and businesses to prevent smuggling and other violations of the law.

Paul Revere's illustration of British warships landing in Boston Harbor

The Boston Massacre

Tensions reached their peak in Boston in early March 1770. An argument between a colonist and a soldier led a crowd of dockworkers and others to gather in the square in front of the Customs House. A British officer came with several men to the soldier's assistance. Snow covered the ground and some of the crowd threw snowballs, stones, and other objects at the troops. The British officer warned his troops not to fire. With all the noise and excitement, one of the soldiers actually thought he heard the word "fire." The soldiers began firing and soon three of the colonists were dead. **Crispus Attucks**, who was half African and half Native American, was one of those killed. Two others died soon afterwards from their wounds.

The soldiers were put on trial for murder. They were defended by **John Adams**, a young lawyer from Boston who was also a cousin to Sam Adams. Adams argued that the troops had acted in self-defense and won the case.

His cousin, Sam Adams, saw the event differently. He saw it as another opportunity for attacking British rule. In **broadsides** (*one-sided sheets*) and other printed materials, he described the shooting as a deliberate "massacre" (*the murder of many innocent people*). Paul Revere, a silversmith and artist, drew a famous cartoon that was shown throughout the colonies.

The Historian's Apprentice

1. Do you think the soldiers should have been convicted for murder? Write a paragraph explaining your point of view.
2. Do you think Revere's drawing was an accurate representation of the Boston Massacre? Use visual evidence from the drawing to explain your answer.

Paul Revere's illustration of the Boston Massacre

October 1, 1768
British troops land in Boston

1770

March 5, 1770
Boston Massacre

May 10, 1773
Parliament passes the Tea Act

March-May 1774
Coercive Acts

December 16, 1773
Boston Tea Party

Committees of Correspondence

In Massachusetts, Sam Adams set up a more permanent "Committee of Correspondence" in 1772. Virginia and other colonies soon followed this example. These committees communicated with one another. They also spread news from the towns to the countryside, where most colonists lived. By 1774, these committees had thousands of members.

The Tea Act

By 1773, Parliament had finally repealed the hated Townshend duties. However, it passed a new tax on tea in place of the duties. Parliament gave the East India Company, which was in financial difficulties, the right to sell its tea directly to the colonists in North America. This brought down the price of tea, which no longer had to be sold in England. Parliamentary leaders felt that by lowering the cost of tea, they could collect the tea duty without protest. Tea from the East India Company could actually be bought with the tea duty for less than the cost of illegal tea offered by smugglers. Even so, the colonists were still dissatisfied.

The Boston Tea Party

British ships carrying tea from the East India Company arrived in Boston Harbor in December 1773. A group of colonists disguised as American Indians boarded the ship at night and threw 342 chests of tea into the harbor in protest. This event became known as the "**Boston Tea Party**."

The Coercive Acts (1774)

The British government was outraged when it received news of this destruction of property. Parliament passed a series of laws in March and June 1774 known as the **Coercive Acts**. The colonists called these the "**Intolerable Acts**."

These British policies eventually led to the writing of the Declaration of Independence.

- Boston Harbor was closed until the tea was paid for. Warships blockaded the harbor. Even ferryboats were not permitted to carry food across the harbor.
- The Massachusetts legislature was suspended (*temporarily closed*).
- The British government was given the power to appoint all officials in Massachusetts until the tea was paid for.
- Royal officials would no longer be tried for crimes in the colonies, but in Great Britain.
- A harsher Quartering Act was passed.

The Quebec Act (1774)

Just after passing the Coercive Acts, Parliament also passed the **Quebec Act**. This act allowed Catholics in Quebec to hold public office and made the Ohio River Valley part of the province of Quebec. It also established royal rule over the province. Colonists feared the Quebec Act might set the pattern for the future government of the thirteen colonies.

The Historian's Apprentice

1. Design your own poster seeking recruits for the Sons of Liberty.
2. Imagine that your class is the British Parliament in London. Each member of your class is a member of Parliament. Your class should debate how to treat the colonists after the "Boston Tea Party" and whether to approve the Coercive Acts.

The Enlightenment and Colonial Ideas about Government

The views of the colonists were greatly influenced by new ways of thinking in Europe. These views were known as the **Enlightenment**.

Europeans had discovered that science could explain many of the things they observed in nature. Sir Isaac Newton, a British scientist and mathematician, had published his laws of motion and gravity. Newton's laws explained how objects moved both on Earth and in space. The same laws accurately predicted the path of a cannon ball fired on Earth and the movements of the moon and planets thousands of miles away.

Scientists began to think that they could eventually explain everything by using scientific methods, careful observation, and mathematics to discover nature's universal laws.

Many writers also believed that they could apply human reason to better understand people and society—and to make things better. Because they thought reason brought light to the world, their movement became known as the Enlightenment.

Enlightenment thinkers challenged religious prejudice and intolerance. They questioned the inherited privileges of nobles (*Europe's highest social classes*).

Enlightenment thinkers did not believe that kings and queens received their powers directly from God. Instead, they accepted the view of **John Locke** that each government was created as part of a **social contract** between people and their rulers. If rulers did not respect the rights of their subjects, then the social contract was broken and the people had the right to overthrow them.

These ideas, popular in Europe in the late eighteenth century, inspired many of those living in the thirteen British colonies.

Pre-Conditions for Revolution

By 1775, the colonies were seething with discontent. Conditions were ripe for "**revolution**" (*a rapid and complete change in society and government*).

- The colonists no longer feared an invasion by France.
- They were less fearful of Indian attacks.
- They wanted to occupy lands west of the Appalachian Mountains, but had been stopped by the British government.
- They disliked paying taxes required by the British government without their consent.
- They had traditions of self-government.
- They had local colonial assemblies already in operation.
- They resented British restrictions on their trade.
- They claimed the traditional rights and liberties of Englishmen, first established by the Magna Carta.
- They accepted the Enlightenment idea that government actions should be reasonable, and followed John Locke's view that government held its authority through a "social contract."
- They saw British troops as an enemy occupation force.
- Many joined secret organizations, like the Sons of Liberty, that opposed British policies.
- The British government refused to give up its authority over the colonists and actually sent more troops to the colonies to enforce its claims.

In the next chapter, you will learn how war finally broke out between the colonists and Great Britain, and how the colonists obtained their freedom by declaring independence and winning the Revolutionary War.

The Historian's Apprentice

1. After Parliament passed the Coercive Acts in 1774, do you think the American Revolution was "inevitable" (*unable to be avoided*)? Why or why not?
2. What actions would you have taken if you had been the British Prime Minister at this time? Do you think you would have been able to satisfy both the demands of people in Britain and the colonists?
3. What areas of the world do you think might be ripe for revolution today?

1. Complete the following chart by explaining the significance of each of the following to the French and Indian War (1754-1763).

	Significance
Ohio River Valley	
Fort Duquesne	
Albany Plan of Union	
Outbreak of the Seven Years' War in Europe	
Conquest of Quebec (1754)	
Treaty of Paris (1763)	

2. Complete the paragraph frame below on relations between Britain and the colonies from 1763 to early 1775.

The Road to Revolution

After the French and Indian War, the British government was concerned because ____.

The British government passed a series of new taxes on the colonists to help solve this problem.

In 1765, it passed the Stamp Act. This law ____

The colonists were angry about the law because they felt ____

To protest against the new tax, they ____

The British Parliament finally repealed the Stamp Act. The British still needed money. In 1767, Parliament passed the ______________________ . This law ____.

The colonists again felt the law was unfair because ____.

To enforce the law, the British sent more troops to Boston in 1768. In 1770, this led to the ____.

The British government finally repealed these duties. In 1773, the Tea Act lowered the price of tea but collected a tax on it. In December 1773, a group of colonists in Boston protested against the tax on tea by ____.

This action outraged Parliament. Parliament passed the ______________________ Acts. These ____.

Colonists in Massachusetts and elsewhere thought these terms were too harsh. By 1775, the colonists and the British government seemed to be on the road to war.

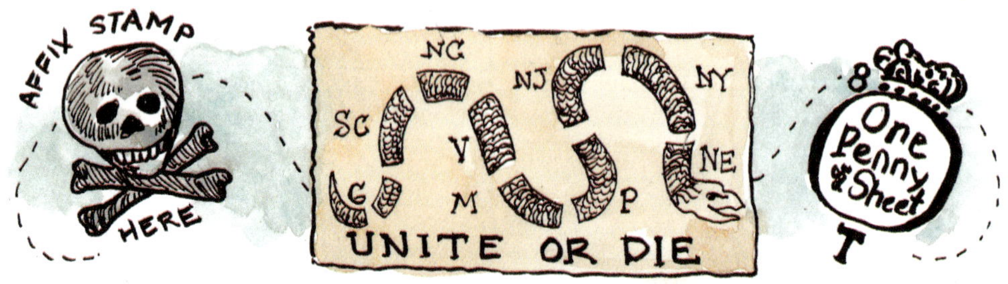

Chapter Review Cards

The French and Indian War: The War Begins (1754-1755)

- The expansion of New France and the British colonies led to a war for control of North America. The French were expanding to the south and the British to the west.
- The **French and Indian War** began when **George Washington** and a small British force ambushed a group of French soldiers near **Fort Duquesne** in the Ohio River Valley in May 1754.
- Britain and France sent troops across the Atlantic. Britain had more colonists in North America, but the French counted on their Indian allies.
- At the **Albany Congress** in 1754, **Benjamin Franklin** and Thomas Hutchinson proposed a cooperative government for all the colonies, with a President and General Council. This government would handle matters affecting all the colonies, such as relations with the Indians. The delegates accepted the "**Albany Plan of Union**." Franklin's "Join or Die" cartoon was published to encourage the colonies to participate in his plan. However, the plan was rejected by both the various colonial assemblies and the British government.

The French and Indian War: The War Spreads (1756-1760)

- By the spring of 1756, the war had spread to Europe. Russia, Austria and France joined together to attack Prussia. Britain took Prussia's side. The war in Europe became known as the **Seven Years' War** (1756-1763). After 1756, the French had to concentrate their resources on the fighting in Europe. The war was fought in Europe, North America, and India and at sea.
- William Pitt, the **Prime Minister** of Great Britain, continued to send resources to the colonists. In October 1758, the British captured Fort Duquesne, which later became **Pittsburgh**.
- The British next captured Louisbourg in Nova Scotia (in northeastern Canada). In 1759, the British invaded Canada. **General James Wolfe** successfully captured **Quebec** by scaling the heights on one side of the city. This gave them command of the **St. Lawrence River**. The following year, British forces took **Montreal**.

The French and Indian War: The Treaty of Paris (1763)

- France lost the war. The **Treaty of Paris** was signed in 1763. France gave all its territory in North America east of the Mississippi River to Britain. French territory west of the Mississippi was handed over to Spain. Spain gave Florida to Britain in exchange for the return of Cuba, which the British captured during the war. The British returned several Caribbean "sugar islands" to France.

The Proclamation Line of 1763

- The colonists were looking forward to having new lands, especially in the Ohio River Valley. The British government was concerned about new conflicts with the Indians.
- King George III issued a royal proclamation in 1763, prohibiting colonists from settling west of the Appalachian Mountains. This line became known as the **Proclamation Line of 1763**. Its goal was to keep peace with the Indians. The colonists resented this restriction (limit).

Mercantilism and the Navigation Acts

- The British government followed a policy of **mercantilism**. Colonies existed to enrich the "mother country." Colonies were meant to send inexpensive crops and raw materials to Britain. The colonists were expected to purchase more expensive finished goods from the British. This would guarantee a flow of income to Britain (the mother country) from the colonies.
- British navigation acts required that colonial goods be shipped to Britain before being sold in other countries.
- The **Sugar Act of 1764** lowered **duties** (import taxes) on sugar. The government planned to enforce it, unlike previous acts, to ensure that the colonists bought their sugar from British merchants.

New Revenue Policies: Taxation

- The British government had a large debt from the French and Indian War. People living in Britain were already paying more in taxes than the colonists. Parliament passed a series of laws to tax the colonists to pay for their own defense. No attempt was made to obtain the colonists' prior **consent** (agreement) to these new taxes.

The Stamp Act

- The first new tax was the **Stamp Act** (1765). This required every official document, newspaper or pamphlet in the colonies to have an expensive government stamp.
- Colonial assemblies sent **petitions** to Parliament, arguing that the Stamp Act had been imposed without colonial **consent**. Colonists **boycotted** British goods. **Patrick Henry** stated that only the Virginia House of Burgesses could place new taxes on Virginians. **James Otis** declared that "taxation without representation is tyranny." **Samuel Adams** formed the "**Sons of Liberty**." They set some buildings on fire and tarred and feathered tax collectors. New "**Committees of Correspondence**" informed each other of anti-British activities. In New York City, a "**Stamp Act Congress**" was held. It petitioned Parliament to repeal the Stamp Act.
- The Stamp Act ended up hurting British businesses. Parliament repealed the law.

The Declaratory Act (1766)

- Parliament passed the **Declaratory Act** (1766). This act declared that Parliament had the right to pass laws, including taxes, that were binding on the colonies.

The Townshend Duties (1767)

- The British government still needed to collect money from the colonists. Parliament passed the **Townshend duties**, which taxed common household goods usually shipped to the colonies from Britain. These included glass, lead, paint, paper and tea. Once again, Parliament did not obtain the consent of the colonists before passing this new tax. These duties led to new colonial protests.

The Boston Massacre (1770)

- In 1768, the British government sent 4,000 more troops to Boston, the center of colonial unrest.
- In 1770, an argument between a colonist and a soldier led to a crowd throwing snowballs at British troops. The soldiers fired on the crowd and killed several colonists. The event became known as the **Boston Massacre**. **John Adams** defended the troops in court. His cousin Samuel Adams and Paul Revere used the event to stir up anti-British feeling. Revere made a famous engraving of the event.

The Tea Act and the Boston Tea Party (1773)

- Parliament repealed the Townshend duties. In 1773, it passed the Tea Act. The new act gave the East India Company the right to sell its tea directly to the colonists. This lowered the price of tea, even though the tea was still taxed.
- British ships carrying tea from the East India Company arrived in Boston Harbor in December 1773. A group of colonists, disguised as American Indians, boarded the ship at night and threw 342 chests of tea into the harbor in protest. This event became known as the "**Boston Tea Party**."
- Outraged by this destruction of property, Parliament passed the **Coercive Acts** (1774), also known to the colonists as the "**Intolerable Acts**." Boston Harbor was closed, the Massachusetts colonial assembly was suspended, and the British government was given the power to appoint all officials until the tea was paid for. Royal officials were to be tried in Britain rather than in colonial courts and a harsher Quartering Act was passed.
- **The Quebec Act** (1774) allowed Catholics in Quebec to hold public office and made the Ohio River Valley part of Quebec. It also established royal rule over the province.

The Impact of the Enlightenment

- The **Enlightenment** influenced the colonists. Enlightenment thinkers believed they could discover nature's universal laws by using scientific methods, careful observation, and mathematics. They thought to apply the same methods to improve society.
- Enlightenment thinkers did not believe that kings and queens received their powers from God. Instead, they accepted **John Locke**'s view that each government was created as part of a "**social contract**" between a people and their rulers. If rulers did not respect the rights of their subjects, then the social contract was broken and the people had the right to overthrow their government.

The Road to Revolution

Enlightenment and Colonial Views on Government

- Enlightenment applies reason to improve society
- John Locke's "Social Contract"

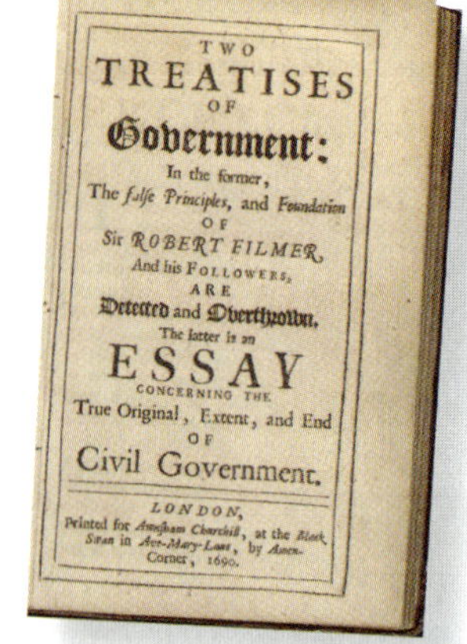

TWO
TREATISES
OF
Government:
In the former,
The false Principles, and Foundation
OF
Sir ROBERT FILMER,
And his FOLLOWERS,
ARE
Detected and Overthrown.
The latter is an
ESSAY
CONCERNING THE
True Original, Extent, and End
OF
Civil Government.
LONDON,
Printed for Awnsham Churchill, at the Black Swan in Ave-Mary-Lane, by Amen-Corner, 1690.

French and Indian War

Clash in Ohio River Valley

- French expanding to the south
- British expanding to the west

Albany Congress

- Held in Albany, 1754
- Franklin and Hutchinson propose common government with President-General and Grand Council

Fort Duquesne

- Key location on Ohio River
- First British, then French fort
- Washington's ambush starts war
- Braddock's march fails, 1755
- British retake fort in 1758

- Seven Years' War in Europe
- Wolfe captures Quebec, 1759
- Treaty of Paris, 1763: France gives Canada to Britain

British Policies Create Discontent

Proclamation Line of 1763

- Prohibits western settlement

Navigation Acts

- Mercantilism
- Sugar Act of 1764

Stamp Act (1765)

- Colonial protests
- Stamp Act Congress
- Sons of Liberty
- Parliament repeals Stamp Act

Declaratory Act (1766)

Townshend Duties (1767)

- Taxes on glass, lead, tea, and other items
- Colonial protests
- Parliament repeals duties except on tea

Arrival of more British troops (1768)

- Boston Massacre (1770)
- Samuel Adams sets up Committees of Correspondence (1772)

Tea Act (1773)

- Boston Tea Party (December 1773)

Quebec Act (1774)

Coercive Acts (1774)

What do you know?

SS.6.A.3.1

1. Why did the British government decide to start taxing the colonists in the 1760s?

   A. to build new roads and make other improvements in the colonies

   B. to raise money after the costs of the French and Indian War

   C. to increase the powers of royal governors in the colonies

   D. to encourage more colonists to return to Great Britain

SS.6.A.3.2

2. Why did the Proclamation Line of 1763 anger many American colonists?

   A. It prohibited colonists from settling in the Ohio River Valley.

   B. It promoted peaceful relations with Indian tribes in the west.

   C. It increased the taxes that the colonists paid to Britain.

   D. It gave too much land away to Canada.

SS.6.A.3.1

3. The timeline below lists laws from the colonial period, 1764–1774.

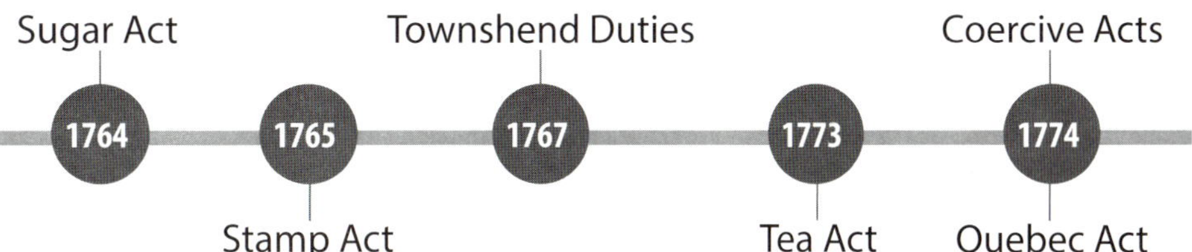

   Which would be the best title for this timeline?

   A. Colonial Reactions to British Taxes

   B. Examples of British Navigation Laws

   C. Abuses of Power by Colonial Legislatures

   D. British Policies Leading to Colonial Protests

SS.6.A.3.3

4. Which phrase best describes Samuel Adams?

   A. Commander of the Continental Army

   B. Founder of the Sons of Liberty

   C. Governor of Massachusetts

   D. Ambassador to France

SS.6.A.3.2

5. The passage below is an entry from Samuel Adams' diary in March 1770.

> *I awoke to the news that some of the cursed Redcoats had fired their muskets upon a crowd of colonists near the Customs' House. Innocent colonists murdered by the vicious British soldiers on our own American soil. Not only do they tax us without a vote, now they are murdering us in the streets of Boston.*

Based on the passage, which right would Samuel Adams have supported?

A. the right of the British government to tax the colonists

B. the right of Patriots to protest British policies and actions

C. the right of colonists to elect their own members of Parliament

D. the right of soldiers in the colonies to be tried for any crimes back in Britain

SS. 6.A.3.6

6. How did the Boston Massacre make the American Revolution more likely?

A. It showed the colonists that the British would use violence against them.

B. It was used by the British as an excuse to punish the colonists with more taxes.

C. It made Patriots more willing to reach a compromise with the British government.

D. It showed that the British did not plan to let the colonists elect members to Parliament.

SS.6.A.3.8

7. How were the Committees of Correspondence, Sons of Liberty and Daughters of Liberty similar?

A. They were all Loyalist organizations.

B. They were limited to the New England colonies.

C. They all invited the participation of both men and women.

D. They were organizations formed in opposition to British policies.

SS.6.A.3.2

8. Paul Revere completed an engraving of five coffins with the initials of the colonists who were killed by the British soldiers during the Boston Massacre on March 5, 1770.

What was the main purpose of this engraving?

A. to blame the Loyalists for the massacre

B. to persuade the colonists to act together against British policies

C. to encourage witnesses to the event to testify before Parliament

D. to illustrate the events of the Boston Massacre as impartially as possible

CHAPTER 5 "The Times that Try Men's Souls": The Story of the American Revolution

SS.6.A.3.3 Recognize the contributions of the Founding Fathers (John Adams, Sam Adams, Benjamin Franklin, John Hancock, Alexander Hamilton, Thomas Jefferson, James Madison, George Mason, George Washington) during American Revolutionary efforts.

SS.6.A.3.4 Examine the contributions of influential groups to both the American and British war efforts during the American Revolutionary War and their effects on the outcome of the war.

SS.6.A.3.5 Describe the influence of individuals on social and political developments during the Revolutionary era.

SS.6.A.3.6 Examine the causes, course, and consequences of the American Revolution.

SS.6.A.3.7 Examine the structure, content, and consequences of the Declaration of Independence.

SS.6.A.3.8 Examine individuals and groups that affected political and social motivations during the American Revolution.

SS.6.C.1.2 Compare views of self-government and the rights and responsibilities of citizens held by Patriots, Loyalists, and other colonists.

Alignment to Grade 7 Civics Standards

SS.7.C.1.2 Trace the impact that the Magna Carta, English Bill of Rights, Mayflower Compact, and Thomas Paine's *Common Sense* had on colonists' views of government.

SS.7.C.1.3 Describe how English policies and responses to colonial concerns led to the writing of the Declaration of Independence.

SS.7.C.1.4 Analyze the ideas (natural rights, role of the government) and complaints set forth in the Declaration of Independence.

SS.7.C.3.1 Compare different forms of government (direct democracy, representative democracy, socialism, communism, oligarchy, autocracy).

Terms and Names You Should Know

Militia
Patriots
Loyalists
First Continental Congress
Petition
John Hancock
Second Continental Congress
George Washington
Thomas Paine
Common Sense
George Mason
Richard Henry Lee
Thomas Jefferson
Declaration of Independence
Unalienable rights
Grievances
Abolish
Despotism
Monarchy
Democracy
Ally
Battle of Saratoga
Battle of Yorktown
Peace of Paris

Florida "Keys" to Learning

1. The First Continental Congress sent a petition to George III, who never answered.

2. In April 1775, the royal governor sent troops to Lexington and Concord to arrest Sam Adams and John Hancock and to seize arms. Patriot "minutemen" and British troops fired on each other, starting the war. In June 1775, Patriot minutemen seized Breed's Hill in Boston. The British charged the hill several times before taking it in the Battle of Bunker Hill.

3. The Second Continental Congress met in May 1775. It sent the Olive Branch Petition, which was refused. The Congress created the Continental Army and made George Washington its commander.

4. Americans seized Fort Ticonderoga but failed to invade Canada. Guns were taken from Ticonderoga to Boston. Washington placed them on a hill, forcing the British to leave Boston.

5. Washington moved his army to New York City. The British landed there and defeated Washington at the Battle of Long Island. Washington had to retreat into New Jersey. The colonists' morale was low when Washington took his army across the Delaware River to defeat the Hessians at Trenton.

6. Colonists identified as Patriots favored independence; Loyalists did not want to leave the British Empire; still others were undecided.

7. In January 1776, Thomas Paine published *Common Sense*. He encouraged the colonists to declare independence and establish a democracy.

8. In June 1776, Richard Henry Lee of Virginia proposed a resolution in favor of independence to the Continental Congress.

9. The Congress appointed a committee to draft a declaration of independence. Thomas Jefferson was its main author. Lee's resolution for independence was passed on July 2, 1776. The Declaration of Independence was signed on July 4, 1776.

10. The Declaration announced that (1) men have certain "unalienable rights"—the "right to life, liberty and the pursuit of happiness"—that cannot be taken away; (2) governments are created to protect these rights; and (3) when a government tries to destroy these rights, the people have the right to change their government, by force if necessary.

11. Two months after the Declaration, the British army captured Philadelphia. Washington spent the winter at Valley Forge (1776–1777).

12. British plans to divide the colonies in two through New York failed when General Burgoyne surrendered at Saratoga. The French concluded an alliance with the Americans.

13. The British took the war to the Southern colonies, where they thought they had more support. They captured Savannah and Charleston. But British troops were trapped at Yorktown by American and French forces. The British surrendered and sought to end the war. In 1783, the Peace of Paris recognized American independence and gave the United States all land east of the Mississippi River.

14. Many Loyalists, Native Americans and former slaves granted freedom by the British left for the West Indies, Canada, and Great Britain.

In the spring of 1775, Boston Harbor was closed and the city was filled with British "redcoats" (*soldiers in bright red uniforms*). The Massachusetts colonial assembly had been shut down. People were tense. Would the situation end in violence? Or would wise leaders be able to work out a skillful compromise?

In this chapter, you will learn how the colonists finally took up arms against British rule and declared their independence, giving birth to the United States.

The Fighting Begins

The First Continental Congress

Because of all the troubles with Britain, the colonies decided to send representatives to Philadelphia for a "**Continental Congress**." Each colony sent delegates except Georgia. Samuel Adams, John Adams, Patrick Henry, George Washington, John Dickinson, and John Jay were among its members.

The First Continental Congress met in September 1774. Its members were still loyal to King George III, but they wanted to resolve their **grievances** (*complaints*). They sent a **petition** (*a written plea asking for change*) to the King. It demanded that the Coercive Acts be repealed. The delegates also made plans for a future boycott of British goods. Finally, they decided that another Continental Congress should be held in May if the King rejected their petition. Then they went home.

King George III never answered the colonists' petition. Instead, he gave a speech to the British Parliament condemning the colonists for their actions.

The Battles of Lexington and Concord—the "Shot Heard Round the World"

Meanwhile, colonists opposed to British policies were organizing in Boston. They called themselves "**Patriots**." The Patriots formed groups of **militia** (*citizens in temporary military service*). Because they claimed to be ready on a minute's notice, these volunteers were also called "**minutemen**." The Patriots secretly collected guns and ammunition for the day when they might have to defend their liberties.

John Hancock was one of the wealthiest merchants in Boston. He was also an important Patriot leader. In April 1775, the royal governor of Massachusetts learned that Hancock and Samuel Adams were in Lexington, a small town just outside Boston. The governor sent a force of 700 soldiers to arrest them and to capture the arms that the Patriots were storing in the nearby town of Concord.

When Patriot leaders in Boston learned that British soldiers were about to march, they sent Paul Revere and other riders on horseback to warn the countryside. The first British troops

Fighting at Lexington

arrived in Lexington early the next day, April 19th. They were surprised to find 70 Patriots with muskets standing on the village green. After some hesitation, the colonists and British redcoats both fired. Several Patriots lay dead. The first blood of the American Revolution had been spilled. Then the British charged and the colonial volunteers fled.

The British soldiers next marched to Concord. Patriot militia attacked them on a local bridge. News of the fighting spread to neighboring towns and villages. Soon hundreds of militia joined the minutemen along the road. They fired at the British soldiers as they marched back to Boston. More than 70 British soldiers and almost 50 colonists lost their lives that day.

The Historian's Apprentice

1. Would you have been willing to risk your life in the Patriot militia?
2. Why did poet Ralph Waldo Emerson call this "the shot heard round the world"?

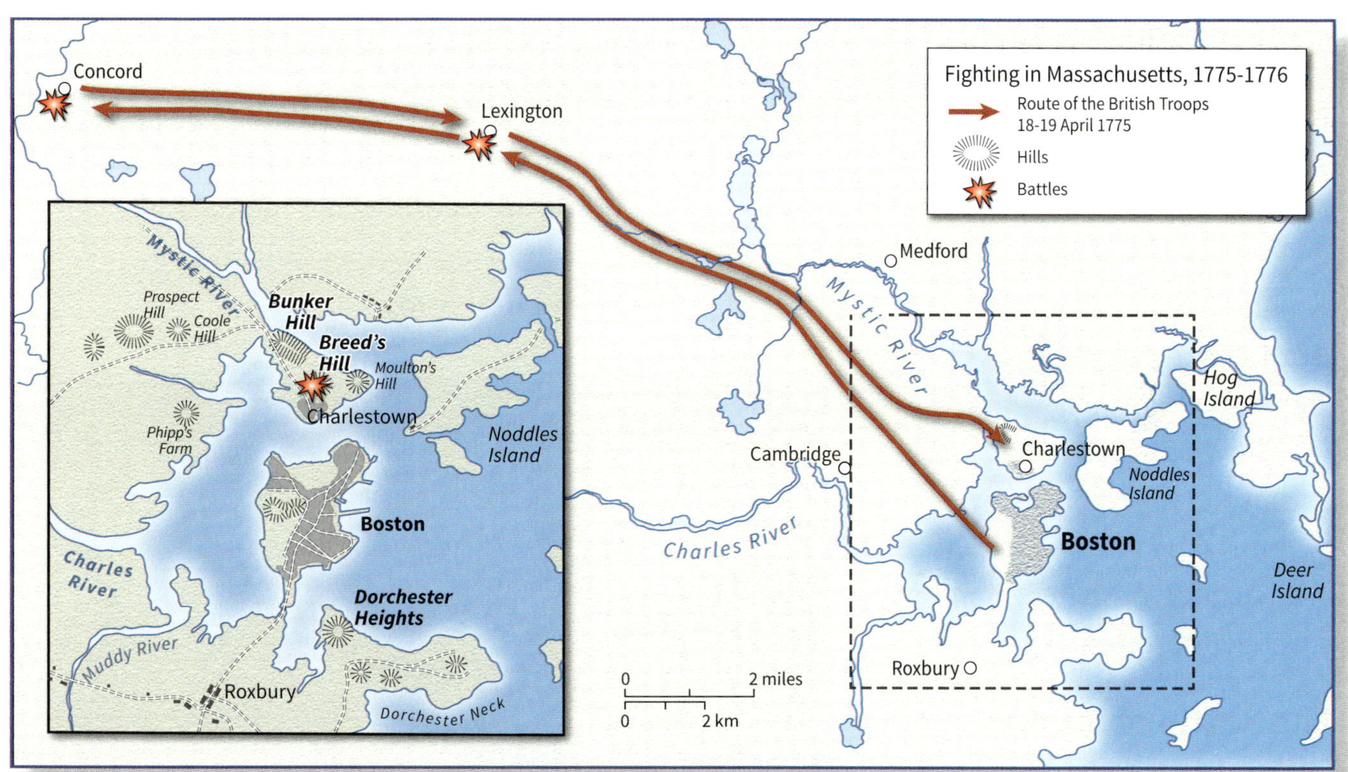

Fighting in Massachusetts in 1775–1776

The Conflict Spreads

The Second Continental Congress

George III refused to consider the colonists' petition, so the colonists held a **Second Continental Congress**. Many of its delegates were on their way to Philadelphia when they received news of the shots fired at Lexington and Concord.

The new Congress began its meetings early in May 1775. John Hancock was elected as its

President. Other important members included John Adams, Samuel Adams, Benjamin Franklin, Thomas Jefferson, and John Dickinson.

The delegates agreed to support the colonists in Massachusetts. If the British government could take away the rights of Massachusetts, it could take away the rights of any colony. The defense of Massachusetts had become the cause of all the colonies.

The Olive Branch Petition

While colonists in New England and the South were ready to join in the fight, many people in the Middle colonies still hoped for peace. To reassure them, the Continental Congress sent a new petition to King George III. This was known as the **Olive Branch Petition**. John Dickinson of Pennsylvania wrote most of it. The petition stated that the colonists were still loyal subjects of the King but wanted a fair resolution of the disputes over taxation and trade. The Congress sent a separate explanation of why the colonists had taken up arms.

King George III again failed to consider the colonists' petition. He proclaimed the colonies to be in a state of open rebellion and outside his protection.

The Battle of Bunker Hill (June 17, 1775)

After the Battles of Lexington and Concord, colonial militia from all over New England gathered around Boston. On a quiet night in June, they took Breed's Hill, one of the hills overlooking the city. Overnight, the Patriots built walls of earth to protect themselves from enemy gunfire. The next day, the British were surprised to see that Patriot forces had occupied this high ground. British soldiers charged up the hill three times before they were able to retake it. The Patriot volunteers retreated to Bunker Hill and across a narrow neck of land to escape. The British were victorious in what became known as the **Battle of Bunker Hill**, but at a heavy cost—almost half the attackers were injured or killed. The colonists had shown that they could withstand attacks by regular British troops.

Washington Appointed as Commander in Chief

In Philadelphia, the Continental Congress adopted the New England militia as the core of its own new army. They called their force the "**Continental Army**."

The Battle of Bunker Hill

Colonial and British Forces

By August 1776, Washington had about 20,000 troops under his command. The members of the Continental Army were all volunteers who had enlisted (*signed up for military service*). Most enlisted for only six months. Washington often complained about the shrinking of his forces, as men returned to their families and farms at the end of their enlistment period. At the beginning of the war, soldiers in the Continental Army had little or no experience in fighting. Washington grumbled that they needed more discipline. A few key units were made up of men with longer service. These soldiers formed the backbone of the Continental Army.

In the same month of August 1776, the British landed 32,000 troops in New York Harbor. Their troops consisted of both British soldiers and Hessian **mercenaries** (*troops for hire*). British soldiers usually came from the lowest classes and were "pressed" (*forced*) into service, often for life. Despite their backgrounds, they were trained to become highly disciplined, professional soldiers. British officers came from the upper classes of British society. Officers were often chosen for their social connections rather than their actual talents. "**Hessians**" were paid troops from the German state of Hesse-Cassel. About half the German troops who fought in the Revolutionary War came from this part of Germany.

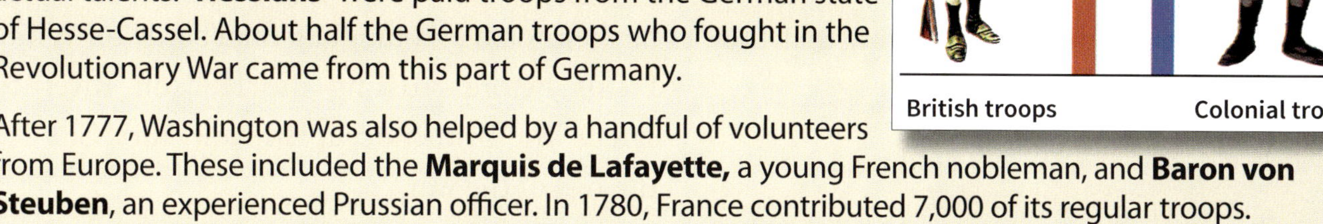

After 1777, Washington was also helped by a handful of volunteers from Europe. These included the **Marquis de Lafayette,** a young French nobleman, and **Baron von Steuben**, an experienced Prussian officer. In 1780, France contributed 7,000 of its regular troops.

At the time of the American Revolution, soldiers used a type of gun known as a musket. Soldiers had to insert a bullet, push it with a ramrod, add gunpowder from a cartridge, and fire the musket with a spark that came from a flintlock. Muskets were not accurate except at close range. In Europe, soldiers were taught to load, fire, and reload their muskets while standing in a line, creating a deadly wall of gunfire. Highly disciplined troops could load and fire several rounds a minute.

George Washington, now 43 years old, was appointed to command it. Washington had valuable military experience from the French and Indian War. It was hoped his appointment would encourage Virginia to support the Patriot cause. Appointed the day before the Battle of Bunker Hill, Washington left immediately for Boston.

The Guns of Ticonderoga

Less than a month after the Battles of Lexington and Concord, Ethan Allen and the Green Mountain Boys from New Hampshire, joined by Benedict Arnold from Massachusetts, led an attack on **Fort Ticonderoga**—a British fort on the southern end of Lake Champlain. They took the fort by surprise at night.

A few months later, 59 heavy cannons from Ticonderoga were pulled on sleds through the winter snow all the way to Boston. On the night of March 4, 1776, Washington had the guns carried up Dorchester Heights, another hill overlooking Boston. The next day, the British commander woke up to see the cannons overlooking the harbor. Two weeks later, he marched his troops onto ships and sailed away. Boston was freed from British occupation and remained so for the rest of the war.

The Invasion of Canada

American Patriots hoped that Canadians would support their cause. There was a clear invasion route using a chain of lakes and rivers—the Hudson River, Lake George, Lake Champlain, and the Richelieu River—leading all the way from New York to Canada. An American army took this route and captured Montreal. Some of its men went farther north towards Quebec. A second army, commanded by Benedict Arnold, marched through the wilderness from Maine to Quebec. Both forces were reduced by winter conditions when they finally met outside the city of Quebec. They attempted to attack the city on December 31, 1775, but their forces were so weakened by cold weather and snow that they were easily crushed.

The American Invasion of Canada

The Battle for New York City

Washington thought that the British might move their main army to New York City, so he marched his army southward. His instincts proved right. The British landed their troops on Long Island, just south of Washington's own forces. The Continental Army was outnumbered, and the British moved some of their troops behind Washington's army so that they could attack from two sides. Washington lost the **Battle of Long Island**. However, he skillfully retreated across the East River to Manhattan at night. He fought a second battle against the British from the heights of Harlem. Again, his forces were defeated. Washington retreated farther north and fought a final battle on White Plains before crossing the Hudson River to safety. The British occupied New York City for the rest of the war.

The Battles of Trenton and Princeton

Soldiers in the Continental Army were greatly discouraged by these defeats. Washington decided on a daring attack to boost morale. On Christmas Day of 1775, he crossed the Delaware River to surprise Hessian mercenaries camped at Trenton. The Hessians did not expect to be attacked at Christmas time in such cold weather. They were defeated and captured at the **Battle of Trenton**. Washington followed this with a second victory against several units of British troops in the **Battle of Princeton**.

Patriots versus Loyalists

People in the colonies were greatly divided during the Revolutionary War. Many colonists actually sided with the British. They had British

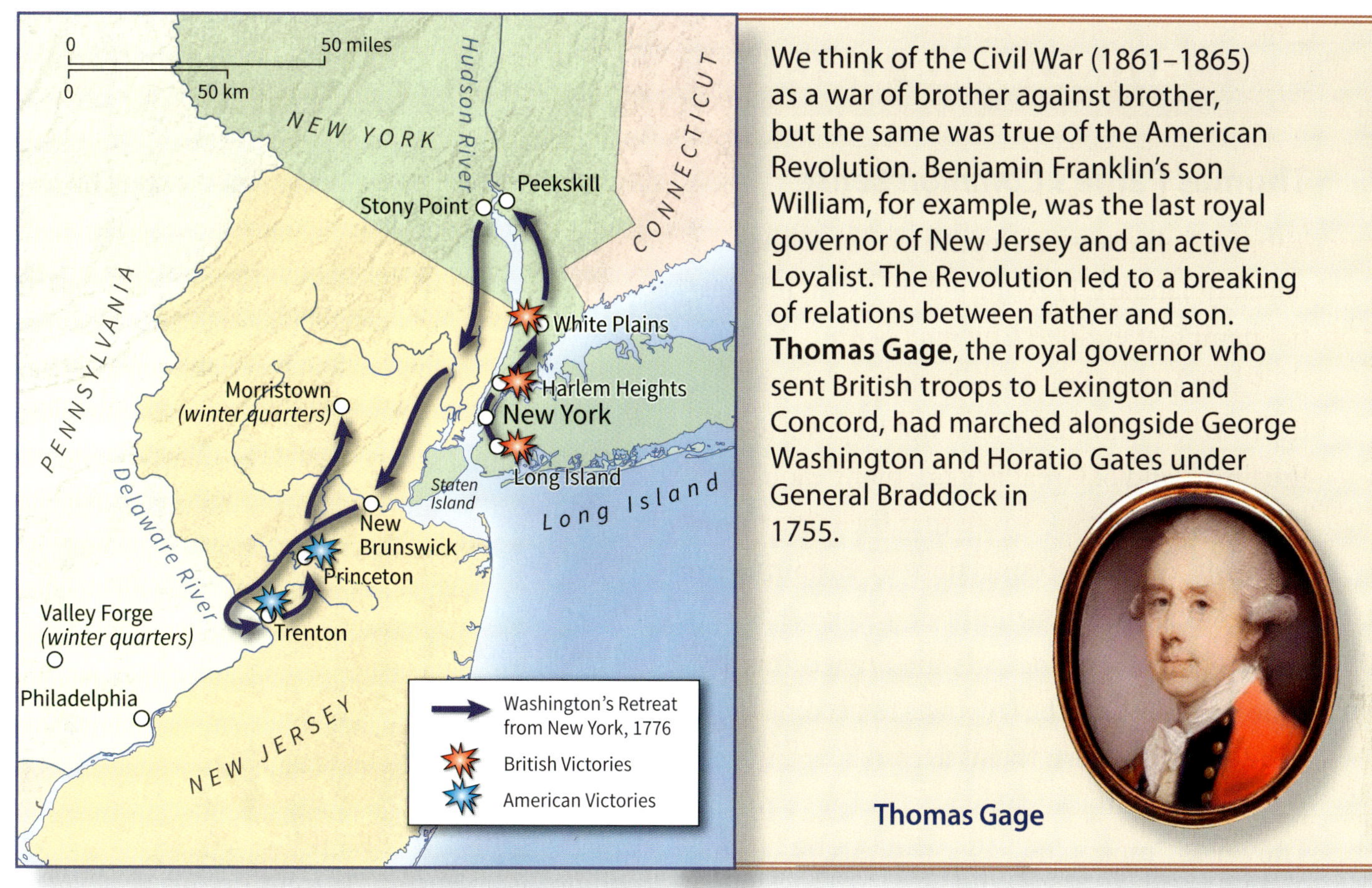

Battles in New York and New Jersey, 1776

We think of the Civil War (1861–1865) as a war of brother against brother, but the same was true of the American Revolution. Benjamin Franklin's son William, for example, was the last royal governor of New Jersey and an active Loyalist. The Revolution led to a breaking of relations between father and son. **Thomas Gage**, the royal governor who sent British troops to Lexington and Concord, had marched alongside George Washington and Horatio Gates under General Braddock in 1755.

relatives, admired British culture, and valued the trade they enjoyed as members of the British Empire. They did not want to leave the empire but hoped that King George III might be persuaded to change his policies. These British sympathizers were known as **Loyalists**. They were also called **Tories**, after a political party in Britain that was very loyal to the King.

Patriots thought that the colonists should govern themselves. At the beginning of the war, many Patriots thought this could still be done without leaving the British Empire. As the war dragged on, this became less and less likely. Most Patriots began to look forward to the day when the colonies would be free and independent.

Besides Loyalists and Patriots, there were also a great many colonists who remained **undecided** during the war.

The Historian's Apprentice

- At the end of 1775, would you have been a Loyalist, a Patriot, or an undecided? Pretend you were living at the time and write a letter to a friend explaining your point of view.
- In a small group, create your own political cartoons in favor of either the Patriots or Loyalists.

Americans Declare Their Independence

Thomas Paine's *Common Sense*

Thomas Paine was an English visitor to the colonies. In January 1776, he published an influential pamphlet entitled *Common Sense*.

Paine argued that it was "common sense" that the thirteen colonies should not be governed by the tiny island of Great Britain, many thousands of miles away. Paine wrote that the costs to the colonists of their connection to Britain were greater than the benefits they received. Based on Enlightenment ideas, Paine argued that the time had come for the colonists to become independent and govern themselves.

Paine also attacked the system of government known as "monarchy." In a **monarchy**, a king or queen inherits power from a parent or other family member. Paine thought this was wrong. He called on the colonists to create a **democracy**—a system in which the people are the source of all political power. In a democracy, people either make decisions themselves (a direct democracy), or they elect representatives to do so (a representative democracy).

> I have heard it stated by some that America has prospered from her connection with Great Britain, and that this connection is necessary for her future happiness. We may as well say that because a child has had milk, that it is never to have meat. I challenge the warmest supporter of Britain to show a single advantage that this Continent can gain by being connected with Great Britain. . . .
>
> —Thomas Paine, *Common Sense*

The Desire for Independence Grows

More and more colonists agreed with Paine that the colonies should end their connection with Great Britain. Patriot leaders also knew that they could not have **allies** (*countries that agree to act together*) in the war as long as they remained the King's subjects. Only by becoming independent could they conclude alliances with foreign powers such as France and Spain. They needed the support of these foreign powers to win the war.

The Second Continental Congress therefore began debating the question of American independence early in 1776. John Adams was one of the loudest voices in its favor. Back in Virginia, Patrick Henry, James Madison and George Mason also urged the Continental Congress to declare independence.

Richard Henry Lee Proposes Independence

Richard Henry Lee, one of Virginia's delegates to the Congress, finally introduced a **resolution** (*formal proposal*) for independence in early June.

The Declaration of Independence

The Continental Congress appointed a special committee to draft a declaration explaining the colonists' reasons for declaring independence. John Adams, Benjamin Franklin, and Thomas Jefferson were among its members. Jefferson was given the tough job of writing the first draft. The other members of the committee were so

Richard Henry Lee Proposes Independence

Resolved, That these United Colonies are, and of right ought to be, free and independent States, that they are absolved from all allegiance to the British Crown, and that all political connection between them and the State of Great Britain is, and ought to be, totally dissolved.

Word Helper

absolve = to release or set free

allegiance = loyalty to a superior

British Crown = the King

connection = a link or formal association

dissolved = ended or eliminated

pleased with Jefferson's text that they made almost no changes to it.

After much debate, the Continental Congress approved Lee's resolution for independence on July 2nd. The Declaration of Independence was signed by the members of the Congress two days later. That date, July 4th, is now our national holiday.

The Main Ideas of the Declaration of Independence

The Declaration of Independence begins by announcing that it sometimes becomes necessary for a people to end the ties that once joined them to another people. When they do, they should explain their reasons for doing so to the rest of the world.

The next section may be the most famous part of the Declaration. It sets forth the American theory of government. This theory is based on a belief in natural rights and John Locke's social contract. It begins by stating that all people are created equal. They enjoy certain **unalienable rights** under natural law. These are God-given rights that cannot be taken away. Among these rights are **life, liberty, and the pursuit of happiness**.

The Declaration next explains that people have created governments to protect these rights. When a government acts to destroy these rights, its citizens have the right to end that government and create a new one.

The Declaration recognizes that people should not change their government lightly. Disagreement with a few government decisions does not justify changing an entire system of government. But when there has been a long pattern of abuses showing that the government has become **despotic** (*oppressive* and *dictatorial*), then the people clearly have the right to change their government. Such has been the case, the Declaration argues, for the American colonists.

The British King and his government had committed repeated injuries against them. The Declaration lists many of these abuses. This list of grievances is the longest part of the Declaration. These abuses include:

- refusing to approve necessary laws
- imposing taxes without the colonists' consent
- quartering troops in colonists' homes

- making judges dependent on the King's will
- trying royal officials and colonists in Britain instead of in the colonies
- suspending or dissolving colonial legislatures

The Declaration works up to the most serious grievances at the very end of the list. The King:

- has cut off their trade
- has made war on the colonists
- has hired foreign mercenaries against them
- has ordered the burning down of towns
- has even stirred up neighboring Indians to attack them

The final paragraphs of the Declaration explain that the colonists have tried to settle their disagreements with Britain peacefully, but all their attempts have failed. The time has therefore come for the colonies to declare their independence. The very last paragraph contains the wording of Richard Henry Lee's famous resolution: the former colonies "are, and of right ought to be, free and independent states."

Reading from the Declaration of Independence

Now try reading two paragraphs from the Declaration of Independence for yourself. Some of their more difficult words are defined in the second column. After you have read each paragraph, rewrite it in your own words in the space on the next page.

In CONGRESS, July 4, 1776.

The unanimous Declaration of the thirteen United States of America . . .

We hold these truths to be self-evident, that all men are created equal, that they are endowed by their Creator with certain unalienable Rights, that among these are Life, Liberty, and the pursuit of Happiness.

Word Helper

self-evident = obvious, clear

endowed = given

Creator = God

unalienable = not capable of being taken away

- What is meant by the phrase "unalienable rights"?
- What examples are given of "unalienable rights"?

That to secure these rights, Governments are instituted among Men, deriving their just powers from the consent of the governed. That whenever any Form of Government becomes destructive of these ends, it is the Right of the People to alter or to abolish it, and to institute new Government . . . organizing its powers in such form, as to them shall seem most likely to effect their Safety and Happiness. Prudence, indeed, will dictate that Governments long established should not be changed for light and transient causes . . . But when a long train of abuses and usurpations, pursuing invariably the same object evinces a design to reduce them under absolute Despotism, it is their right, it is their duty, to throw off such Government, and to provide new Guards for their future security.

Word Helper

secure = to obtain
instituted = created
derive = to obtain from; to come from
consent = agreement
alter = to change
abolish = to end; to get rid of
organize = arrange in order
institute = to start; to create
effect = to bring about
prudence = cautious and careful judgment
dictate =to demand; to determine
transient = temporary; not permanent
long train = long chain or series of events
usurpation = a wrongful taking of someone else's rights
pursue = to chase after something in order to obtain it
object = goal
invariably = always, without change
evince = to provide evidence of
despotism = an oppressive and arbitrary power

Write what this means in your own words.

....

....

....

....

....

....

....

....

The Declaration of Independence actually did several things at once:

1. It declared American independence. It boldly stated that the colonies were no longer part of the British Empire and the former colonists were no longer subjects of King George III.

2. It announced a new theory of government. Governments, it said, are created to protect individual rights. These rights are not just the rights of British subjects, but the natural rights of all human beings. Governments that fail to protect these rights should be changed.

3. It listed the grievances (*complaints*) that the colonists had against King George III and the British government.

> Do you recollect the pensive and awful silence which [filled] the house when we were called up, one after another, to the table of the President of Congress, to subscribe [to] what was believed by many at that time to be our own death warrants?
>
> —Dr. Benjamin Rush to John Adams, July 20, 1811

4. It justified the conduct of the colonists, both to their fellow countrymen and to the rest of the world.

5. It announced the arrival of the United States as an independent member of the international community. This cleared the way for the former colonies to conclude military alliances with France and Spain.

The Historian's Apprentice

1. Pretend that your class is the Second Continental Congress in early 1776. Debate whether the colonies should declare their independence from Great Britain and George III.
2. Look at a copy of the complete Declaration of Independence from a printed source or online. See how much of the language of the Declaration you can understand.
3. Discuss with a partner why the Declaration of Independence has been so influential. Then share your ideas with the rest of the class.
4. Make a poster or chart summarizing the Declaration of Independence.

The War Continues

The British Capture Philadelphia

While the Continental Congress was debating independence, the fighting continued. The commander of the British forces, General William Howe, thought he might end the war quickly if he could defeat Washington in one great battle. He sailed with most of his troops from New York to Chesapeake Bay in order to attack Philadelphia from the southwest. Howe defeated Washington's army at the **Battle of Brandywine** (September 1777) and marched into Philadelphia. The Continental Congress had to flee to western Pennsylvania.

Howe's victory and the flight of the Continental Congress did not end the war as Howe had hoped. And Howe paid a great price for his victory. He did not leave enough troops behind in New York to help in a new British plan for dividing the rebellious colonies in two.

The Battle of Saratoga: The Turning Point of the War

Earlier in 1777, the British government had come up with a new strategy for winning the war. Three British armies would march from different places to the middle of New York, separating the colonies into two parts.

- The first army would use the same route that the Americans had used to invade Canada, but in the opposite direction—moving south from Quebec to Lake Champlain, Lake George, and finally the Hudson River.
- A second army would march from New York City north along the Hudson River.
- A third army from western New York would travel east along the Mohawk River Valley. It would consist largely of Britain's Indian allies, especially the Iroquois.

The three British armies planned to meet in Albany. Their movement would cut New England off from the rest of the colonies.

From the beginning, things went wrong. General Howe went to attack the Continental Congress in Philadelphia. He did not leave enough soldiers behind in New York to allow some to march north to Albany. A few soldiers were finally sent, but only after it was too late.

Secondly, **General John Burgoyne**, who took command of the British force from Canada, marched too slowly and missed short cuts that might have reduced his march. His men marched through wilderness and faced attacks

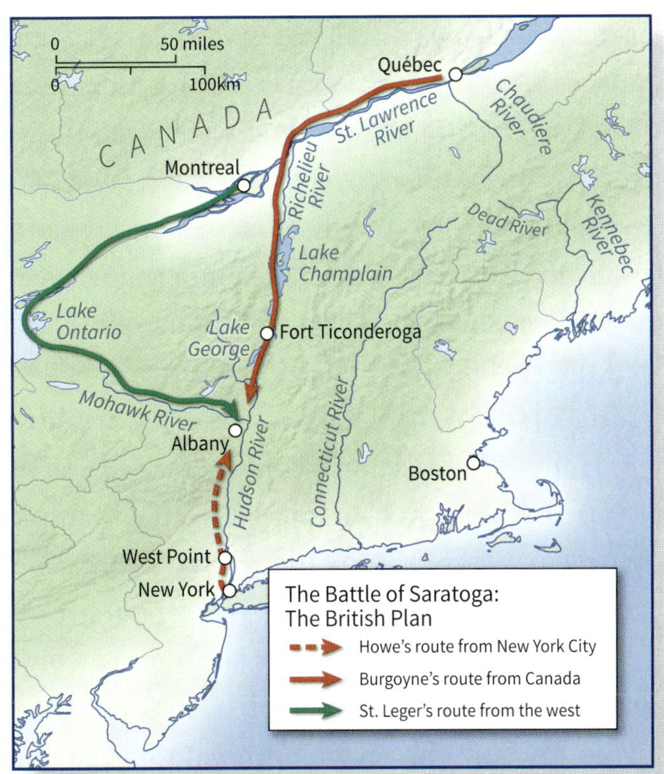

from hostile colonists and Indian tribes. His heavy baggage train, with tents, wine and food, was difficult to carry. The Continental Army had pulled down trees to block his path.

Finally, the army from the west never appeared. The American general, Benedict Arnold, sent messages to the Indians in the British camp misleading them into believing that the Americans had many more troops than they did. The Indians deserted the British, so the army from the west never reached Albany.

General Burgoyne was left on his own. Militia from nearby New England and New York kept joining the Continental Army, whose numbers swelled. Burgoyne found himself facing forces much larger than those he commanded. His troops fought two short battles in September and October, but they failed to break through. Surrounded and without any hope of reinforcement, Burgoyne finally surrendered 6,000 men and supplies to General Horatio Gates on October 17, 1777. It was a great victory for the Americans.

The French Alliance

The French were still angry at the loss of their North American colonies in 1763. The Continental Congress sent Benjamin Franklin to France to negotiate an alliance with France. News of the victory at Saratoga helped persuade King Louis XVI and his ministers to step in. In February 1778, the French signed a treaty of alliance with the new United States.

The British had feared just such an alliance between the Americans and the French. In the same month that the alliance was signed, the British Parliament repealed all its taxes on the colonists and gave up its right to tax them. A special commission was sent to negotiate with the Continental Congress. But it was all too late.

Above all, the British feared that the French might attack their "sugar islands" in the Caribbean. They withdrew 5,000 soldiers from the thirteen colonies and moved them to the West Indies. For the rest of the war, British commanders in North America could no longer count on fresh troops from Britain. General Howe was even ordered to leave Philadelphia.

The Winter at Valley Forge (1777–1778)

Conditions were terrible when Washington and the 12,000 men of the Continental Army reached their winter headquarters at **Valley Forge** for the winter of 1777–1778. Washington chose this grim, windy location because it was 20 miles northwest of Philadelphia, which the British still occupied at the time.

Only a third of Washington's men still had shoes. The rest wrapped their feet in rags. Their shoes had been destroyed by their long marches. Their clothes were also torn and blankets were scarce. Food was just as scarce. The men ate a tasteless mixture of flour and water, and occasional broth. At first they had no shelter and had to build their own rough cabins out of logs and mud. Even their horses were undernourished, and 700 of them died. Many farmers refused to sell their crops to the Continental Army, which paid in paper money that was almost worthless.

Hunger, disease, and cold took the lives of 2,500 of Washington's men that winter. Many of his men deserted. **Alexander Hamilton**, who served as Washington's assistant, sent a stream of complaints to the Continental Congress. Five members of the Continental Congress finally came to view the shocking conditions of the

Washington and Lafayette at Valley Forge

"Unless some great . . . change suddenly takes place, . . . this army must . . . starve, dissolve or disperse, in order to obtain subsistence [*food*] in the best manner that they can."

—General George Washington

army in late January. Afterwards, the Continental Congress increased its payments.

Despite the terrible conditions, Washington made use of the time in Valley Forge to train his troops. **Baron von Steuben**, a volunteer from the German kingdom of Prussia, drilled the soldiers, taught them how to use their firearms and bayonets, and created a more disciplined army. News of the French alliance also lifted the men's spirits.

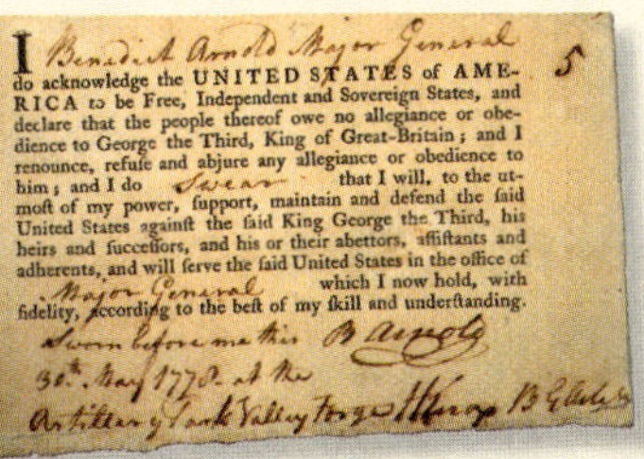

I Benedict Arnold Major General 5
do acknowledge the UNITED STATES of AMERICA to be Free, Independent and Sovereign States, and declare that the people thereof owe no allegiance or obedience to George the Third, King of Great-Britain; and I renounce, refuse and abjure any allegiance or obedience to him; and I do Swear that I will, to the utmost of my power, support, maintain and defend the said United States against the said King George the Third, his heirs and successors, and his or their abettors, assistants and adherents, and will serve the said United States in the office of Major General which I now hold, with fidelity, according to the best of my skill and understanding.

Sworn before me this 30th. May 1778. at the Artillery Park Valley Forge B Arnold

At Valley Forge, troops were required for the first time to take an oath of allegiance to the new United States.

The Battle of Monmouth

The Continental Army stayed at Valley Forge until spring. In June 1778, British forces left Philadelphia to return to New York City. Washington decided to attack them. At Monmouth, a force of 6,000 Americans attacked the rear of the retreating British army. However, the British troops turned around and almost defeated their attackers. Only Washington's arrival on the scene helped to turn the situation around. By nightfall, the battle was inconclusive. There was no clear victor. The British continued their march to New York. It was the last time the two main armies in the war faced one another.

The Final Phase of the War

Naval and Frontier Warfare

The Revolutionary War spread to the oceans and the western frontier. Several states established their own navies, while the Continental Congress voted to build thirteen ships. Later, both France and Spain brought their larger fleets into the war. The colonists were especially thrilled by the adventures of **John Paul Jones**. Jones went to France to get a larger ship

John Paul Jones and the capture of the British warship *Serapis*

and captured the British warship *Serapis* off the English coast. On the western frontier, General George Rogers Clark marched his men through the wilderness in winter to surprise the British on the Wabash River.

The Treason of Benedict Arnold

Benedict Arnold, a former Connecticut merchant, was one of the bravest officers in the Continental Army. He had attacked Ticonderoga in 1775, led men through the wilderness to attack Quebec in 1776, and played a key role in the fighting at Saratoga in 1777.

After the recapture of Philadelphia, Washington appointed Arnold to command the forces in the city, but Arnold still felt resentful. He had been passed over several times by men who had not fought as hard or as well as he had. Arnold was also having money troubles. While in Philadelphia, he married a pretty young Loyalist who was half his age. She had important family connections with British officers, and Arnold used her letters to make a secret offer to the British commander. For a large sum of money, he offered to turn over West Point, a key fort on the Hudson River.

Benedict Arnold

Arnold managed to get appointed as the Governor of West Point and might have succeeded in his plan, except that his British contact, Major André, was caught with papers proving Arnold's treason. Arnold escaped but Major André was hanged as a spy. Afterwards, Arnold commanded British troops against Americans in Virginia before retiring to England.

The War in the South

After the failure at Saratoga, the British government came up with a new plan for winning the war. This time it was the "Southern strategy." The British believed there were more Loyalists in the South than in the North. Therefore, they would send a large army to the South, where they could count on Loyalist volunteers.

The plan began well. The British fleet sailed to Savannah, an important port in Georgia. British troops took the city in December 1778. Later attempts by American Patriots to recapture the city failed. In May 1780, the British also took **Charleston**, the largest city in South Carolina. The British captured 5,000 American soldiers as prisoners—almost as many men as Burgoyne had surrendered at Saratoga. The loss of Charleston was the worst defeat for the Americans in the course of the war.

From Charleston, Lord Cornwallis, the British general in charge of the Southern campaign, marched inland. He defeated Horatio Gates, the hero of the Battle of Saratoga, at the Battle of Camden (August 1780). But Patriot resistance to the British remained strong in the hills of South Carolina. Continental forces defeated a group of British troops at the **Battle of Cowpens** (January 1781). Shortly afterwards, Cornwallis marched north to Virginia.

The Surrender at Yorktown

Cornwallis took his soldiers to a peninsula alongside Chesapeake Bay, only a few miles from where the first English colonists had once settled in Jamestown. Learning this, Washington and his French allies decided to lay a trap.

At first, Cornwallis' forces were just opposed by a smaller force commanded by Lafayette. However, the French navy under Admiral de Grasse sailed into Chesapeake Bay, blocking Cornwallis' escape. At the same time, Washington marched his army from New York southward. Another army was brought to Yorktown by the French general, Count Rochambeau.

Cornwallis did not know that the troops against him were being reinforced. Once he realized he faced an overwhelming force and had no escape route, Cornwallis surrendered with 9,000 men and arms. It was another major victory for the Americans.

There was an immediate reaction to the surrender at Yorktown in the British Parliament. The war was already unpopular. Taxes were high. Spain and Holland had recently joined France in opposing Britain. British leaders were afraid of losing their profitable islands in the West Indies. There was no longer any chance of reaching a compromise that kept the American colonists in the British Empire. For all these reasons, Parliament refused to send any more troops to North America. There were no more major actions in the war after Cornwallis' surrender. The British had decided to end the war.

The Peace of Paris (1783)

Benjamin Franklin, John Adams, and John Jay were sent to Europe to negotiate a peace treaty with the British. The negotiations were delayed by France and Spain, who were still fighting. The peace treaty was finally concluded in 1783. The British recognized the independence of the former British colonies. The treaty also gave the United States all the land up to the Mississippi River. Britain returned Florida to Spain. The colonists had surprisingly defeated the greatest military power of the age.

This painting of the delegations at the Treaty of Paris shows John Jay, John Adams, Benjamin Franklin, Henry Laurens, and William Temple Franklin. The British delegation refused to pose, and the painting was never completed.

Why the British Lost

In 1775, Britain's population was more than five times that of the colonies. The British also had one of the world's best fighting forces. Why did the British lose the war?

Lord Cornwallis surrenders at Yorktown

1. **The American colonists were fighting on home soil.** The British army had to be supplied from overseas. The Continental Army had the support of local militia, who appeared when most needed. Volunteers played a role at Lexington and Concord, Saratoga, and other battles.
2. **The Americans were more determined.** The Declaration of Independence meant they could not go back to British rule. Washington showed his determination in holding the army together. The Americans didn't have to win every battle. They lost the battles of Long Island, Brandywine, and Camden. At different times, they lost control of the cities of New York, Philadelphia, Savannah, and Charleston. Yet the war continued. When the British lost at Saratoga and Yorktown, these defeats were enough to cause them to give up.
3. **British generals did not always pursue their opportunities.** This may have been poor leadership. Some, like General Howe, may have been looking to the future when the colonies would be brought back into the empire. In Britain, Howe had personally opposed both the Stamp Act and the Coercive Acts.
4. **The French alliance played a crucial role.** It made the British pull 5,000 troops out of the war to protect the West Indies. It kept the British from sending further reinforcements. The French provided the colonists with money and supplies. Finally, the French army and navy played a key role at Yorktown. Yorktown was as much a French as an American victory.
5. **British public opinion was divided.** Many in Britain sympathized with the colonists. As the war dragged on, public opposition to it grew.

This important fact led to the first ten amendments, known as the Bill of Rights, and to later amendments that extended rights to more groups.

The Impact of the War

The Loyalists

One of the most important effects of the Revolution was that 100,000 Loyalists left the United States for Canada, the West Indies, and Great Britain.

> *"If there be an object truly ridiculous in nature, it is an American patriot, signing resolutions of independency with the one hand, and with the other brandishing a whip over his [frightened] slaves."*
>
> —A London pamphlet, 1776

African Americans, Native Americans, and Women

The Declaration of Independence loudly proclaimed that "all men are created equal." Three important groups were obviously left out: African Americans, Native Americans, and women. Perhaps it is not surprising that white men at that time did not consider members of these groups as equals, and we should not judge people in the past by our own standards. Yet even in the 1770s, there were already some voices demanding rights for all: "Liberty is equally as precious," wrote African-American minister Lemuel Haynes, "to a black man as to a white one."

Lemuel Haynes was an African-American minister who served in the Massachusetts militia after the fighting at Lexington and Concord. He served at Fort Ticonderoga in 1776. After the Revolution, Haynes became a popular preacher in Vermont.

African Americans. British critics made fun of American slaveholders who claimed to be fighting for freedom. Thomas Jefferson, for example, owned more than 100 slaves.

At the beginning of the Revolutionary War, the British promised freedom to all enslaved people who enlisted in the British army. Some slaves did so and left the United States at the end of the war with other Loyalists.

During the Revolutionary period, many states in the North began to think about **abolishing** (*ending*) slavery. A society for abolishing slavery was founded in Pennsylvania in 1775. Vermont became the first state to abolish slavery in 1777. Pennsylvania abolished slavery for the children of slaves in 1780. Massachusetts ended slavery in 1783. Three other New England states began the gradual abolition of slavery in 1783–1784. Even Southerners like George Washington could see the contradiction in having slaves. Washington's private letters show his conscience bothered him about slavery, which he thought was very wrong. He finally freed his slaves on his death.

Benjamin Banneker was a free black who lived in Baltimore. He helped survey the land that became Washington, D.C. He also published a series of almanacs. Banneker wrote to Thomas Jefferson. He complained that Jefferson had written the Declaration of Independence but kept his own slaves. Banneker also sent Jefferson copies of his almanac. Jefferson was impressed and saw this as proof that African Americans could equal other Americans in their talents and accomplishments.

I thank you sincerely for your letter . . . and for the almanac it contained. [N]o body wishes more than I do to see such proofs as you exhibit, that nature has given to our black brethren, talents equal to those of the other colors of men, & that the appearance of a want of them is owing merely to the degraded [inferior] condition of their existence both in Africa & America. . . . I considered [your almanac] as a document to which your whole color had a right for their justification against the doubts which have been entertained of them.

—Thomas Jefferson to Benjamin Banneker, August 30, 1791

If they appeared to have fewer accomplishments, it was only because of the inferior conditions in which they were kept in slavery.

Unlike Washington, however, Jefferson never freed his slaves, even on his death.

Native Americans. The rights of Indian tribes were also ignored by the signers of the Declaration. In general, the American Revolution was a disaster for them. The American victory meant that pioneers would soon be seizing their lands.

Most Indian tribes sided with the British during the Revolutionary War. They knew that American Patriots would take their lands to make new farms. The British had promised the Indians they could keep their hunting grounds behind the Proclamation Line of 1763. Unfortunately for the Native Americans, the British lost the war. After the Revolution, a few tribes moved north to Canada along with other Loyalists. Those that remained were gradually pushed westward.

Women. Women played an important role in the American victory in the Revolution. They made homespun cloth for the coats and shirts needed by the soldiers of the Continental Army. They took care of family farms when their men left to fight. Benjamin Franklin's daughter Sarah Franklin Bache helped raise $300,000 to buy clothes for soldiers. Despite their contributions to the war effort, women had few rights. The property of a married woman, for example, belonged to her husband. Women had no right to vote or to hold public office. No woman had the opportunity to sign the Declaration of Independence. Abigail Adams, the wife of John Adams, begged her husband to consider the rights of women.

Many Indians allied with the British

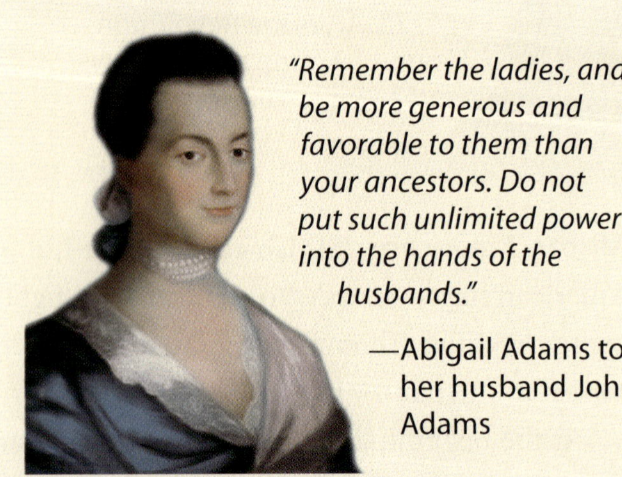

"Remember the ladies, and be more generous and favorable to them than your ancestors. Do not put such unlimited power into the hands of the husbands."

—Abigail Adams to her husband John Adams

The Historian's Apprentice

1. A "revolution" is a major turning point in history. The term often refers to the violent overthrow of a government by force. Do you think it is correct to describe the events of 1775–1783 as "revolutionary"?
2. Who belongs in the American Revolution Hall of Fame?

In this chapter, you read about the main events of the American Revolution. You also learned about the most important leaders in these events. Imagine you are creating a Hall of Fame for the American Revolution. Each year, this Hall of Fame can enroll five new members. Which five individuals from the list below would you bring into the Hall of Fame for the first year? Consider the accomplishments of your candidates, what they contributed to the American Revolution, and what problems they had to overcome.

Abigail Adams	John Hancock	James Madison
John Adams	Alexander Hamilton	George Mason
Samuel Adams	Lemuel Haynes	Thomas Paine
Benjamin Banneker	Thomas Jefferson	Baron von Steuben
John Dickinson	Marquis de Lafayette	George Washington
Benjamin Franklin	Richard Henry Lee	Horatio Gates

3. Become an "armchair general."

Your teacher should divide your class into small groups. Each group should select one of the battles described in this chapter. Your group should also choose one side in that battle—either American or British. The members of your group should then use the Internet or school library to find out more about the battle. You should complete a chart that includes: the name of the battle, the location of the battle with any special geographic characteristics, the military leaders in the battle, the number of soldiers on each side, the number of cannons or other weapons, and any other important information. Then your group should plan a strategy for your side to win that battle. Finally, each group should present its battle strategy to the class. Your classmates should then decide which side would have won the battle if your strategy had been used.

Chapter Review Cards

Causes of the War

- The Revolutionary War arose from the conflicting views of the British government and the American colonists on British attempts to tax the colonists.

The First Continental Congress

- Delegates from the colonies met in September 1774 for the **First Continental Congress**. They wrote a petition asking King George III to repeal the **Coercive Acts**. They also decided to boycott British goods and to hold another Continental Congress if the King denied their petition—which he did.

Shots Fired at Lexington and Concord

- In April 1775, the royal governor of Massachusetts sent troops to arrest Patriot leaders **John Hancock** and **Samuel Adams**, and to seize arms the Patriots were storing in Concord. Patriots learned of these plans and gave warnings.
- British soldiers arrived first at Lexington, where they were met with armed opposition from Patriot militia. The first shots of the Revolution were fired.
- British troops next went to Concord and were attacked on a bridge. On their march back to Boston, colonists along the road shot at British troops.

The Second Continental Congress

- The **Second Continental Congress** assembled in May 1775. The Congress sent the **Olive Branch Petition** to the King asking for a peaceful resolution of their disagreements. The King again denied the petition and declared the colonies to be in a state of rebellion.
- The Congress appointed **George Washington** as commander of the new **Continental Army**.

Fighting Continues

- **Battle of Bunker Hill**: In June 1775, Patriots took Breed's Hill, which overlooked Boston. The British took back the hill, but lost many men in the attack, known as the **Battle of Bunker Hill**. It showed colonists could resist British troops.
- **Guns of Ticonderoga**: The colonists had taken Ticonderoga on Lake Champlain. They dragged the guns from the fort to Boston where Washington placed them on a hill overlooking Boston. This caused the British to leave Boston, which remained free of British troops for the rest of the war.
- **Invasion of Canada**: In December 1775, American Patriots failed in their attempt to attack Quebec.

Divided Opinions among the Colonists

- **Loyalists** were American colonists who did not want to leave the British Empire. They hoped King George III would change his policies.
- **Patriots** opposed British policies. As the fighting continued, most came to believe that the American colonies should declare independence from British rule.

The Declaration of Independence

- In January 1776, Thomas Paine published ***Common Sense***, which argues for colonial independence from Great Britain. Paine called for the colonists to create a **direct democracy** or **representative democracy**.
- In 1776, the **Second Continental Congress** began discussing American independence.
- **Richard Henry Lee** of Virginia made a resolution for independence in the Continental Congress.
- A committee was appointed to write a public declaration explaining the reasons for independence. Thomas Jefferson wrote most of the Declaration. It explained that all people enjoy "**unalienable rights**"—**life, liberty and the pursuit of happiness**. Governments are established to protect these rights. Citizens therefore have a right to overthrow governments that destroy these rights. The Declaration listed the colonists' many grievances against the King and announced that the colonies had become free and independent states.
- On July 2, 1776, the Continental Congress approved Lee's resolution for independence. On July 4, 1776, the **Declaration of Independence** was signed.

Fighting in the Middle Colonies: New York, New Jersey, Pennsylvania

- Washington took his men to **New York City**, thinking the British would land there. He proved right: the British landed close to his own army.
- **Battle of Long Island**: Washington and his troops were outnumbered by the British. They fought three battles as they retreated from New York to New Jersey. The British occupied New York City for the rest of the war.
- **Battle of Trenton**: On Christmas 1776, Washington's troops surprised and defeated Hessian mercenaries (hired troops) camped at Trenton.
- Washington followed this success with a victory at the **Battle of Princeton** against several units of British troops.
- In September 1777, British commander General Howe defeated Washington's army at the **Battle of Brandywine**. Howe occupied Philadelphia.

The Turning Point: Saratoga and the French Alliance

- The British developed a plan to bring three armies together at Albany, New York. They hoped to weaken the colonies by splitting them in two. Lack of troops, difficult terrain, and miscommunication ruined the plan. General Howe went to Philadelphia instead of north. Colonel Barry St. Leger and his Iroquois allies went only a short distance from Lake Erie and then turned back.
- **General John Burgoyne** marched south but took longer than expected and became surrounded by colonial militia. In October 1777, **General Burgoyne** surrendered at Saratoga to **Horatio Gates**.
- This was seen as a turning point. News of his surrender led the French to sign a treaty of alliance with the colonists in February 1778. France now entered the war. Spain soon followed.

Valley Forge (1777–1778)

- **Winter at Valley Forge**: During the winter of 1777–1778, many of Washington's troops died from cold and hunger. Others deserted.
- At Valley Forge, **Baron von Steuben** taught the men how to better use their weapons and helped create a more disciplined army.
- With France entering the war, Howe was ordered to leave Philadelphia and return to New York.

The War in the South

- The British decided to take the war to the South, where there were a large number of Loyalists.
- In December 1778, the British captured Savannah, Georgia. In May 1780, the British took Charleston, South Carolina—the worst defeat for the colonists of the Revolutionary War. In August 1780, Lord Cornwallis defeated Horatio Gates at the **Battle of Camden**.
- In January 1781, Continental troops defeated a group of British troops at the **Battle of Cowpens**.
- Cornwallis took a large number of troops to Yorktown in Virginia.
- **The Battle of Yorktown**: Washington, French General Count Rochambeau, and Lafayette led troops to trap Cornwallis at Yorktown, Virginia. French Admiral De Grasse cut off his retreat at sea. Cornwallis surrendered with 9,000 troops at **Yorktown**.

Peace of Paris, 1783

- The war became unpopular in Britain. After the surrender at Yorktown, the British gave up all hope of keeping the colonies. They also feared losing their profitable islands of the West Indies. The British now sought to end the war.
- The **Peace of Paris of 1783** ended the war. Britain recognized the independence of the United States. It gave all land east of the Mississippi River to the United States. Land west of the river went to Spain. Britain also returned Florida to Spain.

Consequences (Effects) of the Revolutionary War

- The United States became an independent nation.
- **Loyalists** left the United States for Canada, the West Indies, or Great Britain. Enslaved individuals who had enlisted in the British army left the United States.
- Most Indians had sided with the British. Some of these moved to Canada. Those who remained in the United States would later be pushed westward.
- African Americans, Native Americans, and women were not given the rights mentioned in the Declaration of Independence. In 1777, Vermont became the first state to abolish slavery. Its example was followed by other Northern states.
- **Benjamin Banneker,** a free African American, helped survey the land that became Washington, D.C. He published a series of almanacs and gave one to Jefferson. Jefferson saw this as proof that African Americans could be the equals of whites.
- **Women** did not have any opportunity to sign the Declaration of Independence. They still did not have the right to vote or hold public office.

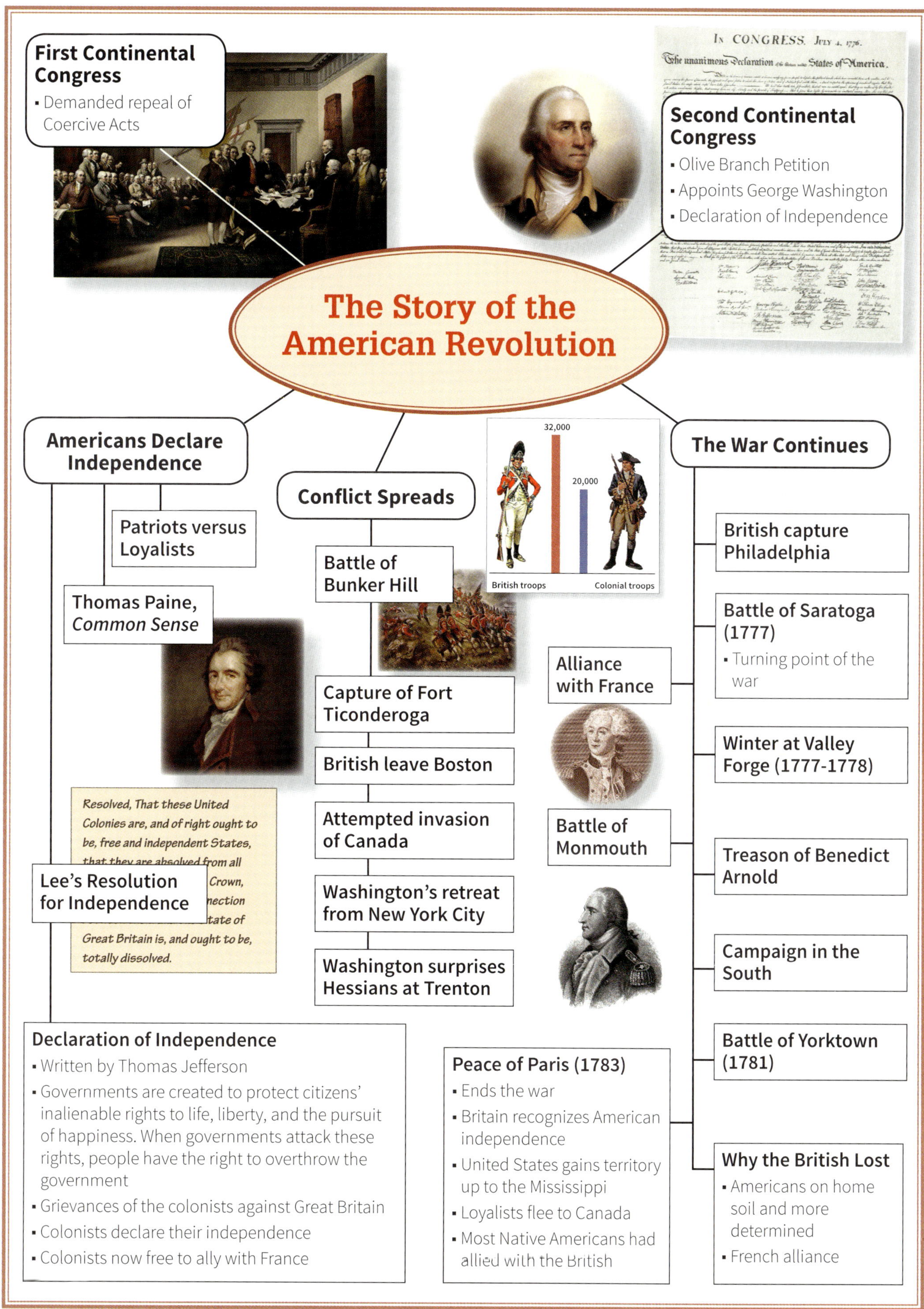

First Continental Congress
▪ Demanded repeal of Coercive Acts
In CONGRESS. July 4, 1776.
The unanimous Declaration of the thirteen united States of America.
Second Continental Congress
▪ Olive Branch Petition
▪ Appoints George Washington
▪ Declaration of Independence
The Story of the American Revolution
Americans Declare Independence
Patriots versus Loyalists
Thomas Paine, *Common Sense*
Resolved, That these United Colonies are, and of right ought to be, free and independent States, that they are absolved from all ... Crown, ... nection ... tate of Great Britain is, and ought to be, totally dissolved.
Lee's Resolution for Independence
Declaration of Independence
▪ Written by Thomas Jefferson
▪ Governments are created to protect citizens' inalienable rights to life, liberty, and the pursuit of happiness. When governments attack these rights, people have the right to overthrow the government
▪ Grievances of the colonists against Great Britain
▪ Colonists declare their independence
▪ Colonists now free to ally with France
Conflict Spreads
Battle of Bunker Hill
Capture of Fort Ticonderoga
British leave Boston
Attempted invasion of Canada
Washington's retreat from New York City
Washington surprises Hessians at Trenton
32,000
20,000
British troops
Colonial troops
Alliance with France
Battle of Monmouth
Peace of Paris (1783)
▪ Ends the war
▪ Britain recognizes American independence
▪ United States gains territory up to the Mississippi
▪ Loyalists flee to Canada
▪ Most Native Americans had allied with the British
The War Continues
British capture Philadelphia
Battle of Saratoga (1777)
▪ Turning point of the war
Winter at Valley Forge (1777-1778)
Treason of Benedict Arnold
Campaign in the South
Battle of Yorktown (1781)
Why the British Lost
▪ Americans on home soil and more determined
▪ French alliance

What do you know?

SS.6.A.3.6

1. What was the significance of the fighting at Lexington and Concord in 1775?
   A. The British plan to divide the colonies in two at Lexington and Concord failed.
   B. General Washington and his troops endured great hardships from hunger.
   C. The fighting at Lexington and Concord marked the outbreak of the American Revolution.
   D. Right after these battles, British leaders recognized the independence of the United States.

SS.6.A.3.7

2. The passage below is from the Declaration of Independence, signed on July 4, 1776.

   That to secure these rights, Governments are instituted [created] among Men, deriving [obtaining] their just powers from the consent of the governed, that whenever any Form of Government becomes destructive of these ends, it is the Right of the People to alter or to abolish it, and to institute new Government, laying its foundations on such principles and organizing its powers in such form, as to them shall seem most likely to affect their Safety and Happiness.

   Which theory of government led directly to the views expressed in this passage?
   A. the Mayflower Compact
   B. the Divine Right of Kings
   C. John Locke's social contract
   D. Baron Montesquieu's separation of powers

SS.6.A.3.7

3. What was the main purpose for writing the Declaration of Independence?
   A. to create a framework for a new democratic government in America
   B. to explain the colonists' reasons for separating from Great Britain
   C. to offer King George III a compromise that would end the conflict
   D. to persuade the Loyalists to move to Canada

SS.6.A.3.7

4. Which argument is found in the Declaration of Independence?

   A. The British government has failed to respect the rights of the Native Americans.

   B. The colonists have a right to change their government because it has violated the very rights it is supposed to protect.

   C. The colonists have the right to declare independence because the British government is too far away to govern effectively.

   D. The colonists should be able to elect their own representatives to Parliament before the British government imposes any more taxes.

SS.6.A.3.8

5. The passage below is from *The Crisis*, written by Thomas Paine in 1776.

   These are the times that try men's souls. The summer soldier and the sunshine patriot will, in this crisis, shrink from the service of his country; but he that stands it now deserves the love and thanks of man and woman.

   What effect did Thomas Paine intend this passage to have on his readers?

   A. persuade Loyalists to desert the British cause

   B. explain to colonists why they were fighting against the British

   C. encourage soldiers of the Continental Army to keep on fighting

   D. help colonists understand the reasons for recent British victories

SS.6.A.3.5

5A. The cartoon below was published in Great Britain in August 1779. Below the picture, it states: "The horse America, throwing his Master."

   In this picture, who does the person on the horse most likely represent?

   A. Thomas Paine

   B. King George III

   C. George Washington

   D. Members of the Continental Congress

SS.6.A.3.6

6. The two maps below provide details about the Battle of Saratoga.

Based on a comparison of these maps, why did the British plan to divide the colonies in two fail?

A. The British plan was impossible to carry out.

B. Not all the British generals followed their plan.

C. Too many American Indians had sided with the colonists.

D. The Continental Army had many more regular troops than the British had.

SS.6.A.3.6

7. What was the significance of the Battle of Saratoga in 1777?

A. The Continental Army ended the British threat in the South.

B. The British decided to grant the colonists their independence.

C. The British were able to divide the colonies into two separate parts.

D. The French were persuaded to enter the war as an ally of the colonists.

SS.6.A.3.3

8. Which pair of individuals made significant military contributions to the outcome of the American Revolution?

A. John Adams and Patrick Henry

B. Samuel Adams and John Hancock

C. Benjamin Franklin and Thomas Jefferson

D. George Washington and the Marquis de Lafayette

SS.6.A.3.3

9. How did Thomas Jefferson contribute to the outcome of the American Revolution?

   A. by serving as a U.S. Senator from Virginia

   B. by writing the Declaration of Independence

   C. by being elected as President of the United States

   D. by serving as a general in the Continental Army

SS.6.A.3.3

10. The passage below is from a diary entry by a leader in the American Revolution.

    > *I served my country as the Commander of the Continental Army during the American Revolution. I retired to Virginia but was called back to serve my country as its chief executive under the new United States Constitution.*

    Which leader was the author of this passage?

    A. John Adams

    B. James Madison

    C. Thomas Jefferson

    D. George Washington

SS.6.A.3.6

11. Which factor most contributed to the American victory in the Battle of Yorktown (1781)?

    A. the support of the French navy and of French troops

    B. George Washington's victory at the Battle of Trenton

    C. the orders of King George III, which confused General Cornwallis

    D. support from the German mercenaries who surrendered at Trenton

SS.6.A.3.4

12. Why did so many American Indian tribes support the British during the American Revolution?

    A. They felt a sense of loyalty to King George III.

    B. They feared the colonists would take away their lands.

    C. They felt regret for supporting the French in the French and Indian War.

    D. They did not believe in the equality promised by the Declaration of Independence.

SS.6.A.3.6

13. The information below provides details about the American Revolution.

- American Patriots fought on their own land.
- The British had to ship supplies across the ocean.
- American Patriots knew the local land and could lay ambushes.
- France and Spain provided the American Patriots with assistance.
- The British could capture coastal cities, but could not control the interior.

What do these details have in common?

A. They tell the ways in which the Americans Loyalists influenced the war's outcome.

B. They describe the effects of geographic factors on the American Revolutionary War.

C. They identify the reasons why the British army was defeated in the American Revolution.

D. They explain why the French and the Spanish decided to support the American Revolution.

SS.6.A.3.6

14. How was the signing of the Peace of Paris in 1783 a victory for the United States?

A. Great Britain was forced to form an alliance with France.

B. Great Britain recognized the United States as an independent nation.

C. The French and Indian War was over and colonists could move west.

D. American Patriots signed an alliance with France to help them win the American Revolution.

SS.6.A.3.8

15. Two individuals are described in the chart below.

Person A	Person B
I supported the American Revolution and was sent to Paris to obtain help from France.	I signed the Declaration of Independence as a representative from Massachusetts and as President of the Continental Congress.

Which pair of individuals is described in the chart?

A. John Burgoyne and Earl Cornwallis

B. Patrick Henry and Thomas Jefferson

C. Benjamin Franklin and John Hancock

D. Alexander Hamilton and John Dickinson

Part 2
When Americans Established a New Republic

Some Events that Took Place between 1781 and 1828

Americans established the Articles of Confederation as their first national government.

Daniel Shays' rebellion made many think the government was too weak.

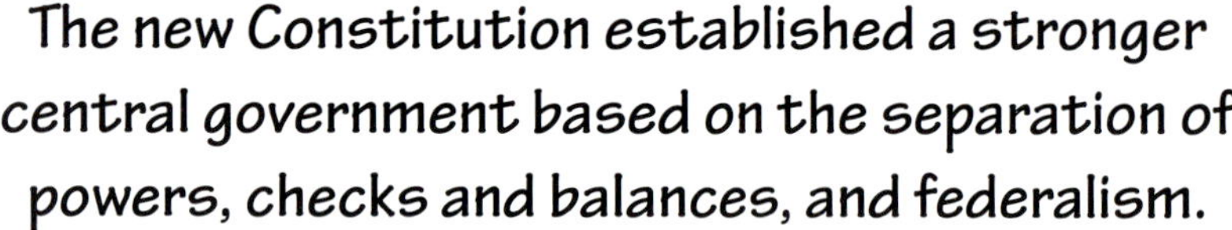
The new Constitution established a stronger central government based on the separation of powers, checks and balances, and federalism.

President Washington appointed Alexander Hamilton to set the nation's finances in order.

The nation's first political parties emerged.

The King of France was executed in Paris during the French Revolution.

The Louisiana Purchase doubled the size of the United States.

Americans fought against the British a second time in the War of 1812.

After the war, Americans strengthened the federal union during the "Era of Good Feelings."

North America after the Treaty of Paris in 1783
United States
Spanish
British
Russian
French
Unclaimed
Disputed Territory
Quebec
Montreal
Great Lakes
Saint Pierre & Miquelon
Boston
New York
Philadelphia
Jamestown
Missouri River
Mississippi River
Ohio River
Rio Grande
Atlantic Ocean
New Orleans
Gulf of Mexico
Bahamas
Cuba
Jamaica
St. Domingue
Caribbean Sea
Pacific Ocean
0
500 miles
0
1000 km

To all to whom these Presents shall come, we the under signed Delegates of the States affixed to our Names send greeting. Whereas the Delegates of the United States of America in Congress assembled did on the fifteenth day of November in the Year of our Lord One Thousand Seven Hundred and Seventy seven, and in the Second Year of the Independence of America agree to certain articles of Confederation and perpetual Union between the States of Newhampshire, Massachusetts bay, Rhodeisland and Providence Plantations, Connecticut, New York, New Jersey, Pennsylvania, Delaware, Maryland, Virginia, North Carolina, South Carolina and Georgia

CHAPTER 6 The Critical Period: America under the Articles of Confederation

SS.6.A.3.9 Evaluate the structure, strengths, and weaknesses of the Articles of Confederation and its aspects that led to the Constitutional Convention.

Alignment to Grade 7 Civics Standards

SS.7.C.1.5 Identify how the weaknesses of the Articles of Confederation led to the writing of the Constitution.

SS.7.C.3.2 Compare parliamentary, federal, confederal, and unitary systems of government.

Terms and Names You Should Know

- State constitutions
- Unitary state
- Federation
- Confederation
- Articles of Confederation
- Confederation Congress
- Sovereign
- Exclusive
- Northwest Ordinance
- Daniel Shays
- Foreclose
- Shays' Rebellion
- Annapolis Convention

respectively represent, and that the union shall be perpetual. In Witness whereof we have hereunto set our hands in Congress. Done at Philadelphia in the State of Pennsylvania the ninth Day of July in the Year of our Lord one Thousand seven Hundred and Seventy-eight, and in the third year of the independence of America.

John Dickinson May 5th 1779
Nicholas Van Dyke
Josiah Bartlett
John Wentworth Junr August 8th 1778
John Hancock
Samuel Adams
Francis Dana
James Lovell
William Ellery
Henry Marchant
John Collins
Richard Henry Lee
John Banister
Thomas Adams
Jno Harvie
Francis Lightfoot Lee
John Penn July 21st 1778
William Henry Drayton

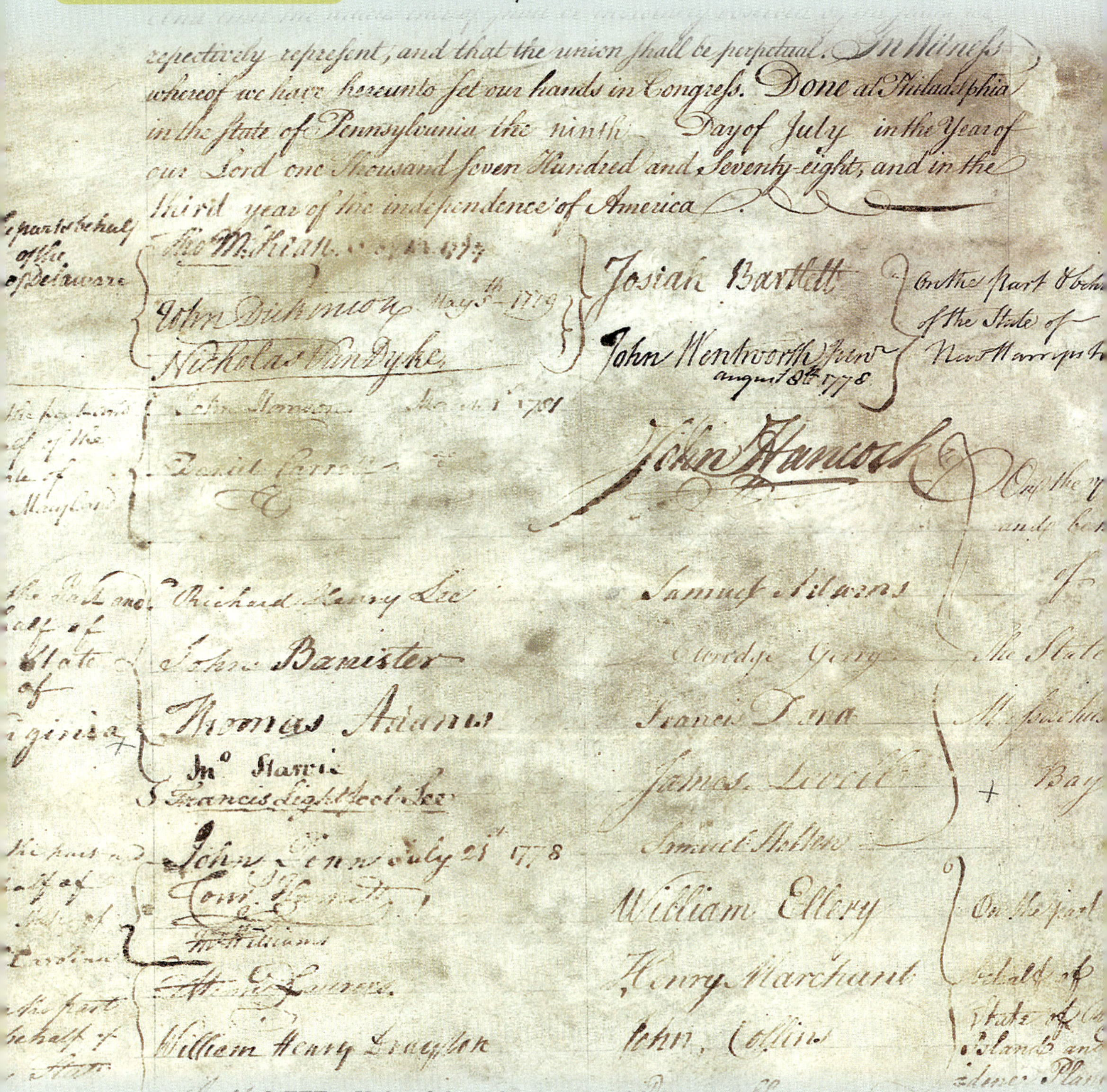

Florida "Keys" to Learning

1. The period after the American Revolution (1781–1787) is sometimes known as the "critical period" of American history.

2. After declaring independence, each colony became a separate state. Each state wrote its own constitution. Each state constitution created a government with three branches and included a bill of rights.

3. The new states could no longer rely on the British to hold them together. They had to establish their own national government. The Second Continental Convention approved the Articles of Confederation, the blueprint for our first national government.

4. Most Americans feared a central government that was too powerful. The Articles created a very weak central government—a simple "league of friendship" between the thirteen states.

5. The Congress of the Confederation was the only branch of national government. Each state had one vote in the Congress. The new Congress had very limited powers. It had the power to declare war, to exchange ambassadors with foreign nations, to enter into treaties and alliances, to resolve disputes between states, to regulate relations with certain Indian tribes, to borrow money, to build a navy, and to "direct" an army.

6. Any new law had to be approved by nine states. All thirteen states had to agree to any changes to the Articles themselves.

7. There was no national executive or judicial branch. The Confederation Congress could not raise its own troops or tax citizens or states. It relied on the states to raise troops and to contribute funds. The states remained sovereign except for those limited powers given to Congress.

8. The Congress could not print money, tax, regulate trade, or enforce laws. Only state governments had such powers. State governments had their own executives and courts, while the national government lacked both of these.

9. The Confederation Congress had some achievements. It signed the peace treaty ending the Revolutionary War. It passed the Northwest Ordinance in 1787. This established rules for the Northwest Territory to be divided up into smaller territories that would be admitted as new states on an equal footing with the original states. It also prohibited slavery throughout the Northwest Territory and guaranteed freedom of religion and the right to a trial by jury.

10. Because the central government was so weak, foreign nations posed a threat. Trade between states became difficult, there was a shortage of money, and some state governments refused to pay their debts.

11. The government of Massachusetts raised taxes and foreclosed on farms. Daniel Shays led a rebellion of poor farmers and veterans. The state militia eventually stopped them. Shays' Rebellion made many Americans desire a stronger central government.

12. In 1786, delegates at a meeting in Annapolis, Maryland, called for another meeting to be held in Philadelphia the following year to revise the Articles of Confederation.

A sick patient is in "critical" condition when facing a life-or-death situation. The years just after the American Revolution were critical for the new republic. No group of colonies had ever declared independence before. No large country had ever governed itself as a representative democracy. In Europe, every large country was a monarchy ruled by a king or queen. The United States was a great experiment. It was unclear whether the former colonies would survive as free and independent states. Many historians therefore refer to the years 1781–1787 as the "critical period" of American history.

> *The establishment of our new government seemed to be the last great experiment for promoting human happiness.*
>
> —George Washington, January 9, 1790

The New State Governments

Once the Declaration of Independence was signed, each colony became a free and independent state. A **state** is an area with its own government. A **government** is an organization that helps people cooperate, resolve disputes, defend themselves, punish criminals, and achieve things they could not do as individuals.

The colonies had once relied on the British government to do all these things. But without British rule, each state needed to establish its own government. Americans already had some experience in self-government with their colonial assemblies. Special conventions were now held in each state to write a **constitution**, or plan of government. These new state constitutions replaced earlier colonial charters.

Each new state constitution decided which form of government that state would have, what powers its government would be given, and what rights its citizens would enjoy.

The Constitution of the Commonwealth of Massachusetts was written by **John Adams** in 1779. It remains one of the oldest written constitutions still in effect today. It includes both a "declaration of rights" and a "frame of government." This constitution established a government with three "branches": legislative, executive, and judicial. The state legislature was made up of a Senate and a House of Representatives. Based on the declaration of rights in its state constitution, Massachusetts' courts ruled that slavery was illegal in 1783.

John Adams

The Articles of Confederation

The thirteen new states no longer had the British government to hold them together. They therefore needed a new form of association. They required some authority to settle disputes. They also needed a way to cooperate for facing foreign nations or defending themselves against Native Americans.

The same day that the Second Continental Congress appointed Jefferson and others to write the Declaration of Independence, it appointed a

Page 1 of the Articles of Confederation

separate committee to decide how the thirteen new states would cooperate. This committee wrote the **Articles of Confederation**. Its main author was John Dickinson—the same delegate from Pennsylvania who wrote the Olive Branch Petition in 1775.

After their struggle with Great Britain, many Americans were afraid of giving too much power to the central government. They did not want a far-away government taxing them or giving them orders, as the British government had done. But they needed some form of national government to protect all Americans and to look after relations between the states. Could they design a national government that was not too weak and not too strong, but just right?

Americans' first attempt at forming a national government was in the Articles of Confederation. The Articles created a simple "league of friendship" to which all thirteen states

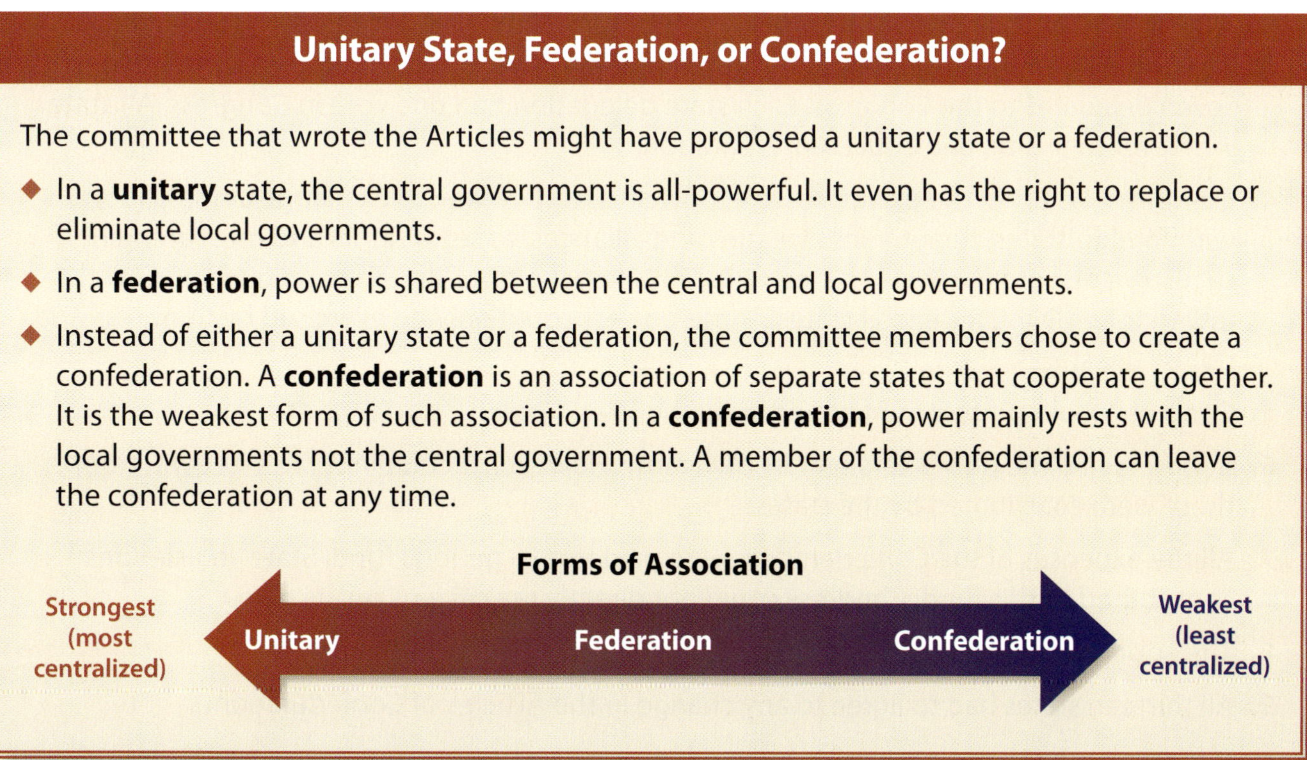

Unitary State, Federation, or Confederation?

The committee that wrote the Articles might have proposed a unitary state or a federation.

- In a **unitary** state, the central government is all-powerful. It even has the right to replace or eliminate local governments.
- In a **federation**, power is shared between the central and local governments.
- Instead of either a unitary state or a federation, the committee members chose to create a confederation. A **confederation** is an association of separate states that cooperate together. It is the weakest form of such association. In a **confederation**, power mainly rests with the local governments not the central government. A member of the confederation can leave the confederation at any time.

The Historian's Apprentice

Your teacher will divide your class into small groups. Each group should consider this question: What kind of national government should the former colonies create? Make a plan for some form of national government. Then have a reporter from your group share your ideas with the rest of your class.

belonged. Most governmental powers were left in the hands of the states.

In this loose association, all thirteen states could cooperate, especially in dealing with **foreign affairs** (*relations with other countries*). This association had a "**Congress**." It was the only branch of the national government. There was no national executive or national court system under the Articles. The Confederation Congress was actually a council made up of the representatives of thirteen powerful, independent states. Each state had **one vote** in Congress.

The Articles were debated for almost a year in the Continental Congress. Then they were sent to the state legislatures. The Articles of Confederation were finally approved by all thirteen states in 1781. The individual states did not hold special elections or even send new representatives to the Confederation Congress. Instead, once the Articles were

Major Provisions of the Articles of Confederation

1. The new Confederation was known as the "United States of America."
2. Each state remained **sovereign** (*had final authority*). The states kept all governing powers except those given exclusively (*only*) to the Confederation Congress.
3. The Congress of the Confederation was to meet every year. Each state could send two to seven delegates to the Congress. Each state delegation had one vote in Congress. All states, whatever their size, had equal representation.
4. Congress was given the exclusive (*sole*) power to declare war, to exchange ambassadors with foreign states, to enter into treaties and alliances, to set weights and measurements, to resolve disputes between states, to establish post offices, and to handle relations with Indian tribes living in several states. These powers could only be exercised by Congress and not by the states.
5. Congress could borrow money, and could build and equip a navy.
6. Congress had the power to direct its own army. However, it could not raise its own troops: these were contributed by the states.
7. All the expenses of the Confederation were paid from a general fund. State legislatures contributed to this fund. Congress could not directly tax citizens on its own.
8. The approval of nine states was needed to pass any new law in Congress.
9. All thirteen states had to agree to any change in the Articles of Confederation.

The balance of power under the Articles of Confederation.

approved, the Second Continental Congress became the Congress of the Confederation. All the members stayed the same.

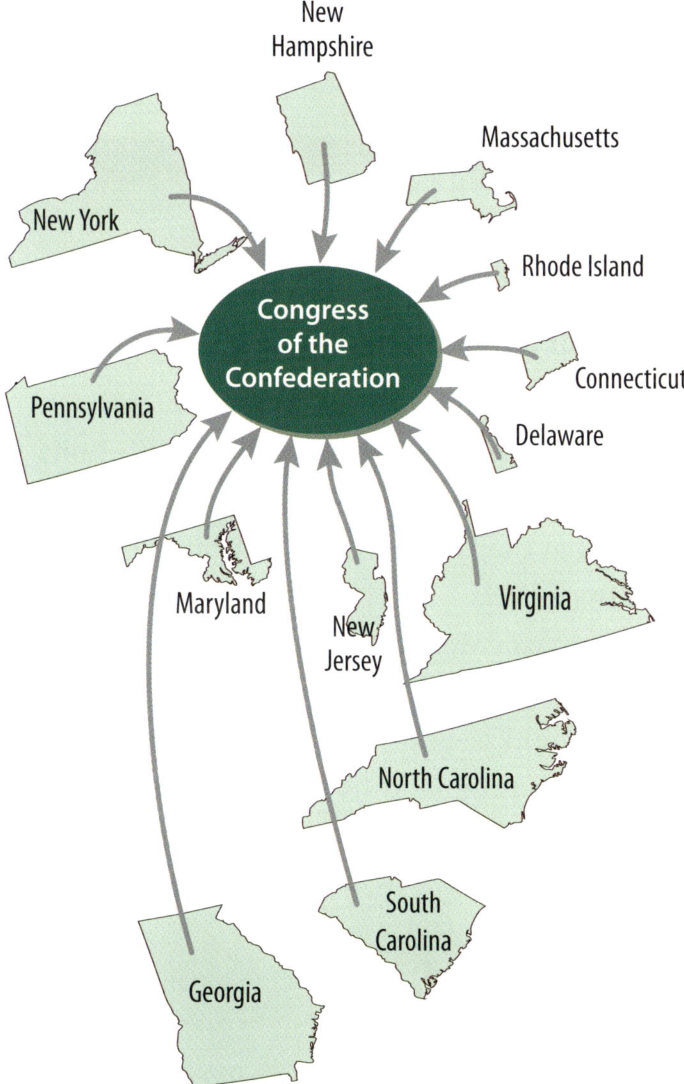

Each state had one vote in the Confederation Congress.

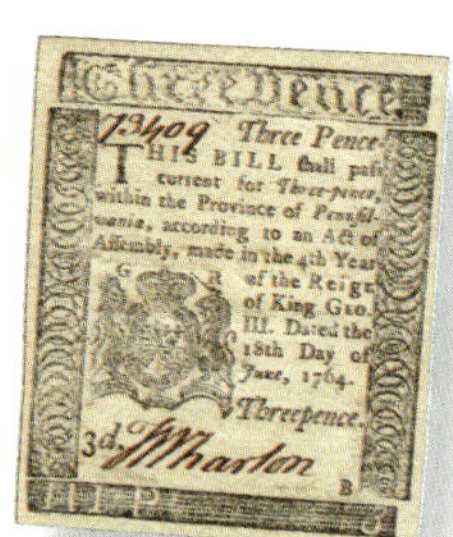

Under the Articles, individual state governments remained more powerful than the central government. For example, states could print their own money. They could tax goods brought in from other states. Only the state governments could collect taxes and raise troops. The Congress of the Confederation relied on contributions from the states to pay its expenses, yet had no power to force states to contribute. Each state government had its own executive and courts, while the Confederation lacked both of these. Could such a government work?

These weaknesses led to the later writing of the U.S. Constitution

1. Congress had no power to tax.
2. Congress had no power to raise its own troops.
3. Congress had no power to regulate trade.
4. Congress had no power to enforce its laws.
5. There was no national court system.
6. There was no national executive to provide leadership.

The Historian's Apprentice

1. Why was it necessary to create the Articles of Confederation? What would have happened if the new states had not created any form of association at all?
2. How did the experience of British rule influence John Dickinson and the other authors of the Articles of Confederation?
3. Imagine that the Continental Congress has hired you to design a poster in favor of the new Articles of Confederation. The purpose of your poster is to sway public opinion. What would it say?
4. You have just read about some of the weaknesses of the Articles of Confederation. What do you think were its major strengths?
5. Do you think the authors of the Articles of Confederation succeeded in creating a national government that was "just right"? Or was the new government too strong or too weak? Pretend you are a citizen in 1781. Write an editorial for a local newspaper giving your opinion on this question. An editorial is a short article in which the writer expresses his or her own opinions.

The "Critical Period": America under the Articles of Confederation

As we have seen, once the Articles of Confederation were approved in 1781, the Continental Congress became the Confederation Congress.

The new Confederation Congress had two major achievements. You read about the first of these in the last chapter: The Congress approved the peace treaty with Great Britain that ended the American Revolution. The second achievement was in the treatment of frontier lands. The Confederation Congress passed the Northwest Ordinance.

The Northwest Ordinance

The thirteen colonies had become thirteen new states with their own state constitutions and governments. But what about the frontier lands that the United States had gained by the Treaty of Paris—all of the lands between the Appalachian Mountains and the Mississippi River? What would happen to these territories? Should they be divided up and handed over to the original thirteen states? Or should something else be done?

The Historian's Apprentice

Select a partner. Imagine you are both members of the Confederation Congress. Discuss how you would treat the frontier territories that belong to the United States. Then share your ideas with the rest of the class.

The Northwest Territory

Settlers moving into the Northwest Territory

To solve this problem, the Confederation Congress passed a series of **ordinances**, or laws. The frontier lands north of the Ohio River became known as the **Northwest Territory**. The first of these ordinances, in 1785, divided the Northwest Territory into townships six miles on each side. Each township was further divided into 36 smaller sections. One square mile in each township was set aside to support a public school. The rest of the sections were to be sold. Some of the land was to be given to veterans who had fought in the Revolutionary War.

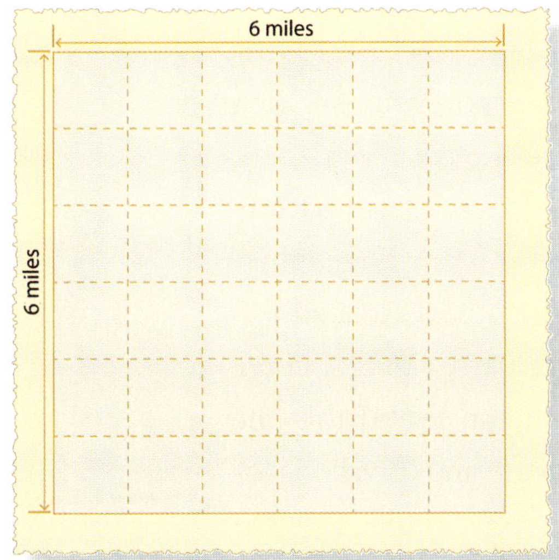

Dimensions of a Township

A second ordinance, known as the **Northwest Ordinance**, was passed in 1787. The Northwest Ordinance divided the Northwest Territory into several smaller territories. It then set up a procedure for each of them to be admitted to the United States as a new state once its population reached a certain size.

1. At first, Congress would appoint a governor and judges to run the territory.
2. When 5,000 free adult males were living in the territory, they could elect their own representatives to govern the territory.
3. When 60,000 "free inhabitants" (people) were living in the territory, they could write a constitution and be admitted to statehood "on an equal footing with the original states."

The Northwest Ordinance also prohibited slavery throughout the Northwest Territory. It guaranteed freedom of religion and the right to a trial by jury in the Northwest Territory. Any male adult who owned fifty acres of land had the right to vote.

The Northwest Ordinance (July 13, 1787)

Article I

No person . . . shall ever be molested on account of his mode of worship or religious sentiments.

Article II

All persons shall be bailable, unless for capital offenses . . . [N]o cruel or unusual punishment shall be inflicted. No man shall be deprived of his liberty or property but by judgment of his peers or by the law of the land . . .

Article V

. . . And whenever any of the said states shall have 60,000 free inhabitants therein, such state shall be admitted by its delegates into the Congress of the United States on an equal footing with the original states in all respects . . .

Article VI

There shall be neither slavery nor involuntary servitude in the said territory. . .

Problems under the Confederation Grow

Despite these achievements, serious problems quickly arose.

First, there were problems with foreign nations. The British refused to hand over several forts in the Northwest even though they had promised to do so. Spain challenged the borders of the new United States to the Southwest. In far away North Africa, pirates attacked American ships that were once protected by the British navy. Without a strong national government, there was no one to watch over American interests.

Second, there were growing economic difficulties at home. Despite winning the Revolution, many Americans faced hard times. To raise revenues, states taxed each other's goods. This hurt trade. So did the fact that the British refused to sign a trade agreement with the United States because trade was supposed to be handled by the individual states.

Third, there was a general shortage of money. Some state governments refused to honor their debts from the Revolution or to repay overseas lenders. The Confederation Congress could not raise its own money, but it owed back pay to veterans who had fought in the American Revolution.

Finally, there was no coordination between the states and very few national rules. For example, American authors like Noah Webster complained that there was no copyright law to protect their writings.

Webster's Dictionary

A growing number of Americans believed that the state governments were becoming tyrannical and corrupt. Some state governments threatened freedom of religion; others violated private property rights. George Washington feared that the jealousies and divisions of the states would prevent the development of a genuine national spirit. James Madison feared the "tyranny of the majority"—that

[Can] thirteen states . . . be said to be united in government when each state reserves to itself the sole powers of legislation? . . . If the states propose to form and preserve a confederacy, there must be a supreme head in which the power of all the states is united. . . . Without such a head, the states cannot be united and all attempts to conduct the measures of the continent will prove governmental farces. So long as any individual state has the power to defeat the measures of the other twelve, our pretended union is but a name and our confederation a cobweb.

—Noah Webster, *Sketches of American Policy* (1785)

Daniel Shays, a Massachusetts farmer, had served as a captain during the American Revolution. Shays led a group of angry farmers and debtors in an attack on one of the state's courthouses. They demanded freedom for debtors, cheap paper money, and lower taxes.

state governments would not respect the rights of minorities, including property owners.

Shays' Rebellion

In Massachusetts, an economic crisis led the state government to raise taxes and to increase its efforts to collect debts. It **foreclosed** (*took back ownership*) on farms and sent some debtors to prison. Many of these farmers had fought as soldiers in the Revolution. Poor farmers protested. They shut down courts trying to collect taxes and debts. They demanded that Massachusetts print cheap paper money as nearby Rhode Island had done. This would have raised prices and made farmers' debts easier to repay.

Shays' Rebellion created a wave of fear among wealthy landowners and merchants across the country. There was no national army to put down the rebellion if Massachusetts was unable to stop its spread to other states.

In the end, the Massachusetts militia (*citizens' military force*) was able to crush Shays' Rebellion. But with all the other problems facing the country under the Articles of Confederation, many Americans began to think that it was time for a change. Merchants feared the loss of trade, army officers feared the loss of their back pay, and lenders feared the loss of their loans to the government.

The Annapolis Convention: A Call for Action

In 1786, a meeting was held in Annapolis, Maryland. The purpose of the meeting was to discuss trade between the states. Five states sent representatives. The members could see that the country was in trouble. They called for a new meeting to be held in Philadelphia the following year. Its purpose would be to revise the Articles of Confederation. All thirteen states were invited to send representatives.

We have probably had too good an opinion of human nature in forming our confederation. Experience has taught us that men will not adopt and carry into execution measures the best calculated for their own good without the intervention of a coercive power [*power based on force*]. I do not conceive [*think*] we can exist long as a nation without having lodged [*put*] somewhere a power which will pervade [*fill*] the whole Union . . .

—George Washington to John Jay, August 1, 1786

Meetings of Representatives of the Colonies or States

Meeting	Date	Location	Purpose/Accomplishments
Albany Congress	1754	Albany	Met to discuss cooperation of the colonies just as the French and Indian War was beginning; approved the Albany Plan of Franklin and Hutchinson, which proposed a President-General and a Grand Council.
Stamp Act Congress	1765	New York City	Sent a petition to King George III to repeal the Stamp Act.
First Continental Congress	1774	Philadelphia	Sent a petition to King George III to repeal the Coercive Acts; planned a colonial boycott of British goods.
Second Continental Congress	1775–1781	Philadelphia (except during the British occupation)	Met to discuss a response to the Coercive Acts and other British policies; sent Olive Branch Petition; created Continental Army; appointed George Washington; signed Declaration of Independence; approved Articles of Confederation.
Confederation Congress	1781–1788	Philadelphia, Princeton, Annapolis, Trenton, and New York City (had no fixed capital and moved from place to place)	Had the same members as the Second Continental Congress but acted as the national government under the Articles of Confederation; approved the Treaty of Paris (1783) and passed the Northwest Ordinance (1787).
Annapolis Convention	1786	Annapolis	Met to discuss trade between the states; called for meeting of delegates to revise the Articles of Confederation.
Constitutional Convention	1787	Philadelphia	Met in Philadelphia to revise the Articles of Confederation, but wrote a whole new constitution instead.

The Historian's Apprentice

1. Which of the representatives' meetings shown in the table was most important? Why?
2. Can you see any patterns in the degree of cooperation between the colonies/states? Explain your answer.

Name: ______________________________

Complete the concept ladder below by adding your own descriptions and explanations.

The Articles of Confederation (1781)

Shays' Rebellion

Trade between States

Achievements of the Confederation

Weaknesses of the Confederation

The Confederation Congress

Powers of the Confederation

Chapter Review Cards

The Great Experiment: America during the "Critical Period"

- The first years after the American Revolution—from 1781 to 1787—are sometimes known as the "**critical period.**"
- No colony had ever declared its own independence before.
- No large country had ever chosen to govern itself as a **representative democracy**.
- America was a great experiment and it was not at all certain that the country would survive.

The State Constitutions

- Each state became independent.
- Each state wrote its own state constitution.
- Each state constitution usually had a bill of rights and established a state government with three branches: a governor, a state legislature, and a state court system.

The Articles of Confederation

- After declaring independence, the states no longer could rely on the British government to hold them together. They had to establish some form of national government for themselves.
- Members of the Second Continental Congress wrote the **Articles of Confederation**—the blueprint for their national government from 1781 to 1787.
- Members of the Continental Congress believed the best form of national government would be a **confederation**—a loose association of separate states. The state governments remained **sovereign**, except for those powers given to Congress.
- Americans were afraid of creating a central government that was too strong or tyrannical.
- That was how they felt the British government had been.
- The Articles of Confederation therefore created a **very weak national government** with just one branch: the "**Congress**" of the Confederation.
- The Confederation Congress was to meet every year. It had very limited powers. These powers included the ability to declare war, to enter into treaties and alliances, to resolve disputes between states, to establish post offices, to handle relations with Indian tribes, to borrow money, to build and equip a navy, and to direct its own army.
- Congress could not raise its own troops. It also could ***not*** tax. Instead, it had to rely on contributions from the states to raise money or to have troops in an emergency.
- Individual state governments remained more powerful than the central government: states could print their own money, tax goods brought in from other states, collect taxes, and raise their own troops. Each state had its own executive and courts, while the Confederation lacked either of these.

Achievements of the Confederation Congress

- Even though the new national government was weak, the Confederation Congress had two major achievements: it negotiated a peace treaty with Britain and established a process for admitting new states into the United States.

The Northwest Ordinance

- The Confederation Congress passed two **ordinances** (laws) to deal with the frontier lands gained in the Peace of Paris. These new lands made up the Northwest Territory—the land between the Ohio River and the Great Lakes.
- In 1785, an ordinance divided the Northwest Territory into "townships." Each township was a square six miles on a side. Each township was further divided into 36 smaller sections. One section in each township was reserved for supporting a public school.
- In 1787, the **Northwest Ordinance** stated that the Northwest Territory would eventually be divided into three to five separate territories, which would become new states. (For example, the Ohio Territory was created in 1800 and the Territory of Illinois was created in 1809.)
- The ordinance set up a procedure for admitting each territory, once it reached a certain size in population (60,000 free inhabitants), to the United States as a new state "on an equal footing" with the original states.
- The Northwest Ordinance **prohibited slavery** throughout the Northwest Territory. It also **guaranteed freedom of religion** and the **right to a trial by jury**. All adult males had the right to vote.

Problems under the Confederation

- The new government had problems with foreign nations. The British held onto several forts in the Northwest. Spain challenged the southwest border of the United States. Pirates in North Africa attacked American ships, which had once been protected by the British navy.
- There were economic problems as well. States taxed each other's goods, hurting trade between them. The British refused to sign a trade agreement with the Confederation government. They claimed that trade was actually handled by individual states and not by the national government. There was a general shortage of money. Some state governments refused to pay their debts from the Revolution and overseas creditors.
- There was little coordination between the states and very few national rules.

Shays' Rebellion

- In Massachusetts, the state government raised taxes. It foreclosed on farms to collect debts. It also refused to print cheap paper money as Rhode Island had done.
- Many poor farmers protested. Some of them had fought as soldiers in the Revolution. They attacked courthouses for trying to collect taxes and debts. They demanded that the state government print cheap paper money to make it easier for them to pay their debts.
- **Daniel Shays**, a Massachusetts farmer and a veteran from the Revolutionary War, led farmers in a protest. The state militia finally ended his protest.
- Events like Shays' Rebellion made many Americans desire a stronger central government.

Annapolis Convention

- In 1786, a meeting was held in Annapolis, Maryland to discuss trade between the states.
- The delegates at Annapolis called for the states to send representatives to meet again in Philadelphia the following year to revise the Articles of Confederation.

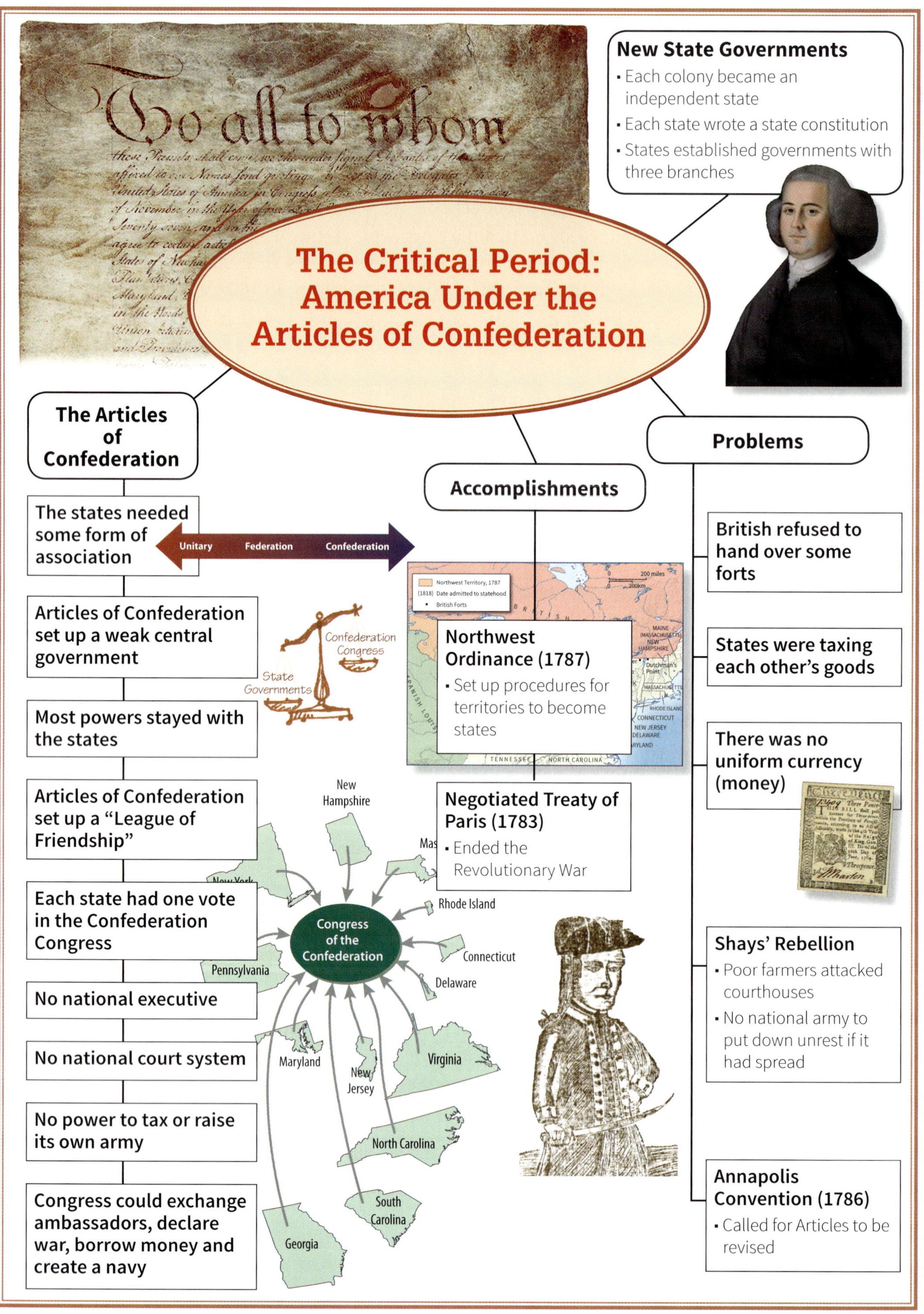

To all to whom
The Critical Period: America Under the Articles of Confederation
New State Governments
Each colony became an independent state
Each state wrote a state constitution
States established governments with three branches
The Articles of Confederation
The states needed some form of association
Unitary
Federation
Confederation
Articles of Confederation set up a weak central government
Confederation Congress
State Governments
Most powers stayed with the states
Articles of Confederation set up a "League of Friendship"
Each state had one vote in the Confederation Congress
No national executive
No national court system
No power to tax or raise its own army
Congress could exchange ambassadors, declare war, borrow money and create a navy
Congress of the Confederation
New Hampshire
Rhode Island
Connecticut
Delaware
Pennsylvania
Maryland
New Jersey
Virginia
North Carolina
South Carolina
Georgia
Accomplishments
Northwest Territory, 1787
(1818) Date admitted to statehood
British Forts
Northwest Ordinance (1787)
Set up procedures for territories to become states
TENNESSEE
NORTH CAROLINA
Negotiated Treaty of Paris (1783)
Ended the Revolutionary War
Problems
British refused to hand over some forts
States were taxing each other's goods
There was no uniform currency (money)
Shays' Rebellion
Poor farmers attacked courthouses
No national army to put down unrest if it had spread
Annapolis Convention (1786)
Called for Articles to be revised

What do you know?

SS.6.A.3.9

1. Which statement identifies a major achievement of the Articles of Confederation?

A. The Articles created a powerful national executive.

B. The Articles established a single national currency.

C. The Articles established a national government during the American Revolution.

D. The Articles announced the reasons why the colonists had separated from England in 1776.

SS.6.A.3.9

2. The information below lists several weaknesses of the Articles of Confederation.

- No power to collect taxes
- No national court system
- No national currency
- No taxing authority

How did these weaknesses affect the delegates to the Annapolis Convention in 1786?

A. They decided to give greater power to state governments.

B. They asked the states to send representatives to revise the Articles.

C. They drafted a bill of rights to protect the liberties of individual citizens.

D. They encouraged groups of states to enter into their own separate arrangements.

SS.6.A.3.9

3. The information below provides details about the Articles of Confederation.

Under the Articles of Confederation, each state set its own taxes on imported goods—goods from other countries brought into the United States for sale. The Confederation Congress had no power to raise or lower these import taxes.

What was an important consequence of this situation?

A. Debtors demanded that state governments print more paper money.

B. Merchants demanded the Articles be revised to promote more trade.

C. State governments demanded the right to tax exports as well as imports.

D. Merchants demanded that the Confederation Congress create a national bank.

SS.6.A.3.9

4. How did Shays' Rebellion contribute to the desire to revise the Articles of Confederation?

   A. Poor farmers felt they were not being treated fairly by the states.

   B. Debtors wanted a stronger national government that would create a stable currency.

   C. Property owners feared the national government was not strong enough to put down a rebellion.

   D. Veterans from the Continental Army wanted a stronger national government that could pay their back pay.

SS.6.A.3.9

5. The conversation below occurred in 1786.

Speaker 1:	Our national government should be strong. State governments should have only limited powers.
Speaker 2:	A bicameral legislature would protect the power of both the large states and the small states.
Speaker 3:	Any further expansion of our national government might give our leaders too much power.
Speaker 4:	The executive branch of our government should have greater power than the other branches.

   Which speaker is most likely to have wanted to keep the Articles of Confederation?

   A. Speaker 1

   B. Speaker 2

   C. Speaker 3

   D. Speaker 4

SS.6.A.3.9

6. Why did many Americans feel a need to revise the Articles of Confederation in 1787?

   A. They wanted to give more power to the upper classes.

   B. They wanted to provide the right to vote to all citizens.

   C. They wanted to provide better safeguards for individual rights of life, liberty, and property.

   D. They wanted to create a stronger national government to protect Americans from invasion or domestic unrest.

SS.6.A.3.9

7. In the passage below, a modern historian describes conditions in the United States in the early 1780s.

> *The states were quick to look to Congress for support when British troops were marching across their farmlands and through their towns and cities, but as soon as the danger left, Congress' pleas for contributions fell on deaf ears. Few Marylanders saw the need to finance a war fought in New York, and few Virginians were willing to pay troops to defend Massachusetts.*

Based on the passage, which conclusion can be drawn about the Articles of Confederation?

A. Each state was willing and eager to act in defense of the other states.

B. The national government lacked the power to sign treaties with foreign countries.

C. The Confederation Congress had the power to collect taxes in an emergency.

D. The Confederation Congress had no way to enforce its requests for contributions.

SS.6.A.3.9

8. Why did the Continental Congress create a weak central government in the Articles of Confederation?

A. Former Loyalists demanded a weak government to protect their property.

B. Wealthy former colonists wanted a weak government that they could control.

C. The Treaty of Paris of 1783 had defined the structures of a new national government.

D. Its members feared that a strong central government would threaten individual rights.

SS.6.A.3.9

9. How did passage of the Northwest Ordinance of 1787 demonstrate a strength of the Articles of Confederation?

A. It showed that the Confederation Congress could sometimes act to meet national needs.

B. It showed that the Confederation Congress had the power to resist British demands.

C. It showed that several of the original states would be able to make claims on western lands.

D. It showed that the Confederation Congress had the power to extend slavery to settlements in the west.

SS.6.A.3.9

10. The excerpt below is from Article 2 of the Articles of Confederation.

> *Each State retains its sovereignty, freedom and independence, and every power and right . . . not expressly granted to the United States, in Congress assembled.*

Which conclusion can be drawn from this excerpt?

A. The Articles of Confederation gave Congress the power to tax the states.

B. The Articles of Confederation kept the states totally independent of Congress.

C. The Articles of Confederation left most governing power with the state governments.

D. The Articles of Confederation gave most governing power to the national government.

SS.6.A.3.9

11. The passage below is from the Supreme Court decision of *Gibbons v. Ogden* in 1824.

> *Reference has been made to the political situation of these states [under the Articles of Confederation]. It has been said that they were sovereign, were completely independent and were connected with each other only by a league. This is true.*
>
> *But when these allied sovereigns converted their congress of ambassadors . . . into a legislature empowered to enact laws . . . the whole character in which the states appear underwent a change.*

According to this passage, what was the relationship of states to the national government under the Articles of Confederation (1781–1787)?

A. The states gave most of their powers to the national government.

B. The national government could make its own laws on any subject.

C. The states were independent and acted together only on a few issues.

D. The national government could eliminate the state governments at any time.

SS. 6.A.3.9

12. Which step took place after the Second Continental Congress declared independence and each state adopted its own state constitution?

A. Americans agreed to abolish slavery.

B. American colonists threw crates of British tea into Boston Harbor

C. A new central government was formed by the Articles of Confederation.

D. The British won the French and Indian War and obtain control of Canada.

CHAPTER 7 The "Miracle at Philadelphia": The Story of Our Constitution

SS.6.A.3.9 Evaluate the structure, strengths, and weaknesses of the Articles of Confederation and its aspects that led to the Constitutional Convention.

SS.6.A.3.10 Examine the course and consequences of the Constitutional Convention (New Jersey Plan, Virginia Plan, Great Compromise, Three-Fifths Compromise, compromises regarding taxation and slave trade, Electoral College, state vs. federal power, empowering a president).

SS.6.A.3.11 Analyze support and opposition (Federalists, Federalist Papers, Anti-Federalists, Bill of Rights) to ratification of the U.S. Constitution.

SS.6.C.1.3 Recognize the role of civic virtue in the lives of citizens and leaders from the colonial period through Reconstruction.

SS.6.C.1.4 Identify the evolving forms of civic and political participation from the colonial period through Reconstruction.

SS.6.C.1.5 Apply the rights and principles contained in the Constitution and Bill of Rights to the lives of citizens today.

Alignment to Grade 7 Civics Standards

SS.7.C.1.5 Identify how the weaknesses of the Articles of Confederation led to the writing of the Constitution.

SS.7.C.1.6 Interpret the intentions of the Preamble of the Constitution.

SS.7.C.1.7 Describe how the Constitution limits the powers of government through separation of powers and checks and balances.

SS.7.C.1.8 Explain the viewpoints of the Federalists and the Anti-Federalists regarding the ratification of the Constitution and inclusion of a bill of rights.

SS.7.C.2.5 Distinguish how the Constitution safeguards and limits individual rights.

SS.7.C.2.4 Evaluate rights contained in the Bill of Rights and other amendments to the Constitution.

Terms and Names You Should Know

- Constitutional Convention
- James Madison
- Virginia Plan
- New Jersey Plan
- Great Compromise
- Three-fifths Compromise
- Commerce Compromise
- Preamble
- "We the People"
- Domestic tranquility
- Congress
- Senate
- House of Representatives
- President
- Electoral College
- Supreme Court
- Separation of Powers
- Legislature
- Executive
- Judiciary
- Checks and Balances
- Federalism
- Ratification
- Federalists
- Anti-Federalists
- *The Federalist Papers*
- Bill of Rights
- First Amendment

Congress of the United States,
begun and held at the City of New-York, on
Wednesday the fourth of March, one thousand seven hundred and eighty nine.

Florida "Keys" to Learning

1. In May 1787, delegates gathered in Philadelphia to revise the Articles of Confederation. Instead, they set about writing a new constitution altogether. The assembly became known as the Constitutional Convention.

2. The delegates agreed to create a national government with three branches: a legislature, executive and judiciary.

3. They could not agree on representation in the legislature. Virginia, a large state, proposed two houses based on proportional representation—larger states would have more members. New Jersey, a small state, proposed each state have equal representation. The delegates adopted the "Great Compromise": each state would have two Senators in the Senate and a number of members in the House of Representatives proportional to its size.

4. Delegates from slave and non-slave states disagreed on how slaves should be counted. They again compromised: slaves would be counted as three-fifths of their actual number for purposes of both representation and taxation.

5. The Convention agreed that the new Congress could not prohibit the slave trade for the next twenty years and could never tax exports.

6. The first three articles of the Constitution establish the basic structure of our federal government. Article I defines Congress and its powers. Congress has the power to declare war, to lay and collect taxes, to raise and support an army and navy, to coin money, to borrow money, to regulate interstate commerce, to establish post offices, and to create lower courts.

7. Article II focuses on the Presidency. The President is chosen by an Electoral College and serves for a four-year term. The President enforces federal laws, serves as Commander-in-Chief of the armed forces, appoints and receives ambassadors, negotiates treaties, gives a "State of the Union" address, and appoints judges and other federal officials. Congress can impeach the President for misconduct.

8. Article III establishes the Supreme Court as the highest court in the land.

9. The delegates struggled with one main issue: they wanted a central government strong enough to protect the country but not so strong that it would oppress them. To prevent this, the delegates introduced three key principles: federalism, separation of powers, and checks and balances.

10. Article VII stated that the new Constitution would go into effect once nine states ratified (*approved*) it. During the ratification debates, Anti-Federalists opposed the Constitution. They complained that there was no bill of rights. Federalists argued a stronger government was needed and that the three key constitutional principles would prevent it from becoming too strong. They also promised to add a bill of rights.

11. The first ten amendments, added in 1791, are known as the Bill of Rights. The First Amendment guarantees freedom of speech, of the press, of religion, and of assembly, and the right to petition the government. Other amendments protect the right to bear arms, protect citizens from unreasonable search and seizure, and guarantee rights to those accused of a crime, such as the right to a public trial by a jury.

There is a famous saying: "If you don't succeed at first, try, try again." This describes perfectly the approach that Americans took in establishing their own national government. In this chapter, you will learn why.

The "Miracle at Philadelphia": The Constitutional Convention

In the last chapter, you learned how many groups of Americans had become frustrated with the Articles of Confederation. A meeting of several states at Annapolis had invited all the states to send representatives to revise the articles.

In response, fifty-five delegates gathered at the state house in Philadelphia in May 1787. It was the same building where eight of them had signed the Declaration of Independence eleven years before.

Back in 1776, the colonists had cut their ties to Britain in the name of liberty. The challenge now was to make a central government that was strong enough to defend the nation and promote its citizens' well-being, but not so strong that it would threaten individual liberties. The Continental Congress had tried to do this with the Articles of Confederation but many Americans felt they had not succeeded. Now it was time to try again.

Every state except Rhode Island sent representatives to this new meeting. All of the delegates were men who owned property. More than half of them were trained lawyers. One third of these men had fought in the Revolution.

The delegates immediately elected George Washington to preside over their proceedings. Just as quickly, they voted to keep their discussions secret from the public to encourage a freer exchange of ideas.

Next, the delegates took a surprising step. They had been asked to revise the Articles of Confederation. Instead, they decided to replace the Articles altogether. The delegates set about writing a new **constitution**—a plan of basic rules for government. Their assembly became known as the **Constitutional Convention**.

The Historian's Apprentice

Imagine that your class is about to create its own government. You must answer a series of questions to do so:

- Who should make the class rules?
- Who should make sure those rules are obeyed?
- Who should settle disputes between class members?
- Who should pay for class expenses?
- Who should be in charge of communicating with other classes?

Make a chart or outline showing your ideas for a plan of government for your class.

What the Delegates Agreed On

The delegates who met in Philadelphia in 1787 were in general agreement on a number of important issues. Most agreed, for example, that the national government was too weak.

The Historian's Apprentice

In his opening address, Governor Edmund Randolph of Virginia pointed to these weaknesses in the present system of government:

Edmund Randolph

"(1) the Confederation produced no security against foreign invasion . . .

(2) the [Confederate] government could not check the quarrels between states nor a rebellion in any . . .

(3) there were many advantages which the United States might acquire [*get*], which were not attainable under the Confederation, such as a productive impost [*a tax on goods coming from other countries*]—counteraction of the commercial regulations of other nations—pushing of commerce . . .

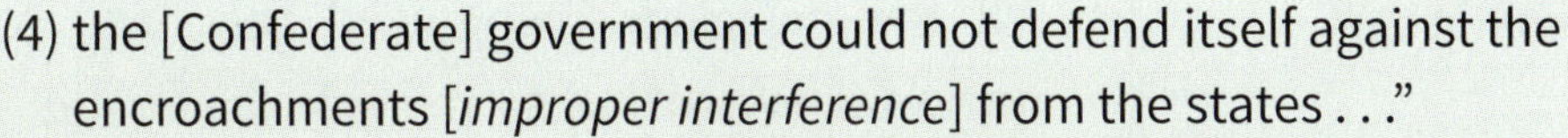

(4) the [Confederate] government could not defend itself against the encroachments [*improper interference*] from the states . . ."

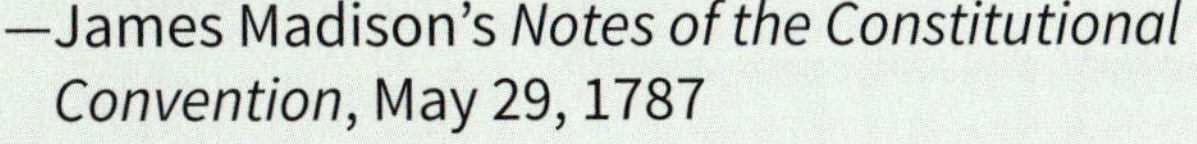

—James Madison's *Notes of the Constitutional Convention*, May 29, 1787

James Madison

- Which of the weaknesses identified by Governor Randolph do you feel were most important? Explain your answer.
- Imagine that you are a delegate at the Constitutional Convention. Write a private letter to a friend explaining how the weaknesses of the Articles of Confederation have led the delegates to decide to write a whole new constitution.

The Signing of the United States Constitution by Louis S. Glanzman, 1987

Only a few days after Governor Randolph's opening speech, the delegates passed this resolution:

> *"That a national government ought to be established consisting of a supreme legislative, executive, and judiciary."*

In other words, they agreed to form a new national government with three separate branches, just as their state governments already had.

In a government, the **legislature** is the body that makes the laws. The **executive** "executes," or carries out, the laws. The **judiciary** (or court system) applies the laws to particular cases.

The legislature makes the law:

The city council passes a law setting the speed limit on Main Street at 30 miles per hour.

The executive enforces the law:

A police officer stops a driver on Main Street who is going 40 miles an hour and gives her a speeding ticket.

The judiciary applies the law:

The driver claims she drove faster to avoid an accident when a truck crossed over onto her lane. A court must decide whether she broke the law and should pay a penalty in this particular situation.

The Legislature

The members of the Constitutional Convention also seemed to agree, at least at first, that the new legislature should have two houses, just like the British Parliament:

- The first house would be known as the **House of Representatives**. It would represent the people. Its members would be elected directly by the people.
- The second house would be the **Senate**. It would represent the wisdom, wealth, and property of America. As one delegate put it, the Senate should have "the most distinguished characters by rank and property." Senators would serve for longer terms than members of the House of Representatives. This way, they would not be as subject to pressures from the public.

The Executive

All the delegates recognized the need for a **national executive** to provide leadership and to carry out the laws. This had been missing from the Articles of Confederation. The delegates were not sure, however, if this new executive should be a single person or a small group.

After some debate, the members of the Constitutional Convention decided that the

The Historian's Apprentice

- Alexander Hamilton greatly admired the British monarchy. He said that the king identified with his people's interests as a whole, rather than with any special group. Hamilton proposed that the delegates create a powerful executive for life: "The English model was the only good one on this subject. . . . [W]e ought to go as far in order to attain stability . . . as republican principles will admit . . . Let one executive be appointed [for life] who dares execute his powers." The other delegates rejected Hamilton's idea. If you had been present, would you have supported or opposed Hamilton? Write your answer in your journal or on a separate sheet of paper.
- Do you think it is better to have a single person or a committee as the head of the executive branch of government? Explain your opinion to a partner and then share your ideas with the class. Be sure to consider the advantages and disadvantages of each.

national executive should be a single individual, known as the **President**. They further decided that the President should be given the power to **veto** (*deny or refuse*) new laws passed by Congress. However, to make sure the President was not too powerful, the delegates also decided that two-thirds of both houses of Congress should be able to override the President's veto.

Disagreement and Compromise

Although the delegates agreed on the need for a stronger national government, they disagreed on a number of other issues.

Large against Small

The most important disagreement was about representation in Congress. Here, the larger states **opposed** (*were against*) the smaller ones.

- The larger states argued they should have more representatives because they had more people. They felt it would be unfair for small states with fewer people to have an equal voice in Congress. This would violate republican principles.
- The smaller states feared that the larger states would abuse their power if they were given more representatives. They wanted each state to have equal representation in Congress as they had under the Articles of Confederation.

The Virginia Plan

Virginia was still the most populous state in the nation. Its delegates proposed that the representation of each state in Congress should be **in proportion** to its population. That is, the number of each state's representatives should be based on the size of its population. The delegates from Virginia wished to apply this principle to *both* houses of Congress. They suggested that the members of the House of Representatives would select the members of the Senate. Since Virginia, Massachusetts, and Pennsylvania had the largest populations, they would be given the most seats in both the House of Representatives and the Senate. This was known as the "**Virginia Plan**."

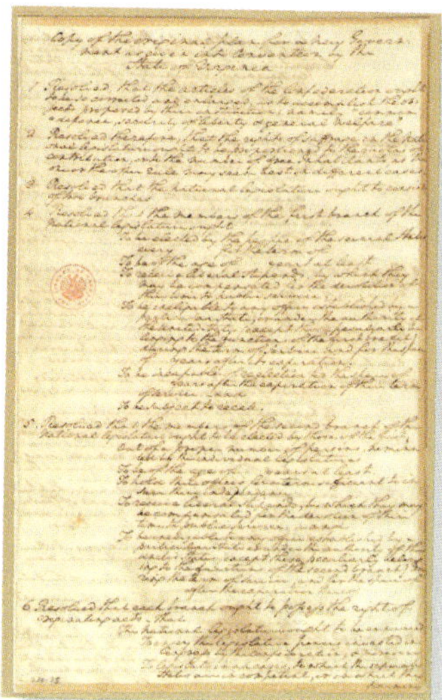

The New Jersey Plan

New Jersey was one of the smallest states. Its delegates opposed (*were against*) the Virginia Plan. By mid-June, they even turned against the idea of a legislature with two houses. Instead, they argued that representation in the legislature should remain as it had been under the Articles of Confederation. They proposed that the legislature have only one house and that each state continue to have **equal** representation in that house. This became known as the "**New Jersey Plan**."

At the heart of this disagreement were conflicting views on the role of the states in the future government. The larger states wanted a national government that represented the people. The smaller states wanted a national government that represented the states.

The Historian's Apprentice

Mr. William Paterson (*New Jersey*): "Give the large states an influence in proportion to their [size], and what will be the consequence? Their ambition will be proportionally increased, and the small states will have everything to fear. New Jersey will never [agree]. She would be swallowed up. He had rather submit to a monarch, to a despot, than submit to such a fate. . . ."

Mr. James Wilson (*Pennsylvania*): "[A]s all authority was derived from the people, equal numbers of people ought to have an equal number of representatives, and different numbers of people different numbers of representatives. This principle had been improperly violated in the Confederation, owing to the urgent circumstances of the time . . . If small states will not [agree] to this plan, Pennsylvania . . . would not [agree] to any other . . ."

—James Madison's *Notes of the Constitutional Convention*, June 9, 1787

Dr. Benjamin Franklin (*Pennsylvania*): The diversity of opinions turns on two points. If a proportional representation takes place, the small states [argue] that their liberties will be in danger. If an equality of votes is to be put in its place, the large states say their money will be in danger . . .

—James Madison's *Notes of the Constitutional Convention*, June 30, 1787

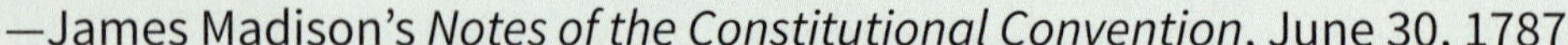

- What was meant by proportional representation?
- Why did larger states want proportional representation?
- Why did smaller states want equal representation?
- Imagine that you are a delegate to the Constitutional Convention in 1787. Would you have agreed with Mr. Paterson or Mr. Wilson? Prepare a short speech to the other delegates at the Constitutional Convention in which you respond to their arguments.

The "Great Compromise"

Have you ever had an argument with someone and settled it with a compromise? A **compromise** occurs when each side to a dispute gives up something in order to reach a solution that both sides can accept.

In 1787, the Virginia Plan proposed proportional representation in both houses of Congress. The New Jersey Plan proposed equal representation. The delegates from Connecticut proposed a compromise to end the dispute:

- States should enjoy **proportional representation** in the **House of**

Representatives. States with larger populations would have more representatives. This benefited the larger states.

- States should enjoy **equal representation** in the **Senate**. Each state should have the same number of Senators. This benefited the smaller states.

After two months of debate, a revised version of the Connecticut plan was finally adopted. The delegates agreed that each state would have **two Senators** in the Senate. Each state would have a number of representatives in the House of Representatives **proportional** to its size. This solution became known as the **Great Compromise.** It explains the organization of Congress that we still have today.

The Electoral College

The delegates also disagreed over how to choose the President. Most of the delegates did not trust the people enough to let them elect the President directly. James Madison of Virginia, for example, thought that Congress should actually select the President. The Virginia and New Jersey Plans both proposed that Congress should choose the President.

The Historian's Apprentice

Mr. Elbridge Gerry (*Massachusetts*): The evils we experience flow from the excess of democracy. The people do not [lack] virtue but are the dupes [*fools*] of pretended patriots. In Massachusetts . . . they are daily misled into the most baleful [*harmful*] measures and opinions by the false reports [spread] by [evil] men . . .

—James Madison's *Notes of the Constitutional Convention*, May 31, 1787

Based on this quotation, why do you think Elbridge Gerry opposed the direct election of the President by the people?

The President is elected by the Electoral College. The magic number a candidate needs today is 270 electoral votes.

The delegates eventually decided that the President should be chosen by a group of special "electors" known together as the **Electoral College**. Each state would have a number of electors equal to the total number of its representatives in both houses of Congress.

To become President, a candidate would need to win the support of a majority of these electors. If no candidate won a majority, then the election would be decided by the House of Representatives, where each state would have one vote.

The "Three-fifths Compromise"

In 1787, Southern states had large slave populations. They wanted to count their slaves as part of their populations when calculating how many seats they had in the House of Representatives. But they didn't want their slaves to count for purposes of taxation.

Citizens in Northern states had few slaves or none at all. Several Northern states had already outlawed slavery or were in the process of doing so. The delegates from these states thought that slave populations should not be counted as part of a state's population for Congressional representation since slaves were not free citizens. However, they thought the slaves should be counted for purposes of taxation.

In the end, the delegates struck a compromise. Slave populations would be counted at three-fifths of their actual number. In other words, every five slaves would be counted as three persons. The same rule would apply for purposes of both representation and taxation.

The Historian's Apprentice

A Southern state has a population of 600,000 free citizens and 500,000 slaves. What is this state's population for purposes of both Congressional representation and taxation under the "Three-fifths Compromise"?

The "Commerce Compromise"

Most members of the Convention condemned the horrors of the slave trade—the shipment of captives by force from West Africa across the Atlantic to the Americas. Some members of the Convention wanted to prohibit it. However, wealthy Southerners relied on the slave trade to supply their plantations with new slaves.

The members of the Convention finally agreed that the new Congress should not be permitted to **abolish** (*end*) the slave trade for the next twenty years. After 1808, Congress would have the power to outlaw the slave trade if it wanted to.

To **export** is to sell goods to people in other countries. Southern farmers relied on exporting their cotton, tobacco, rice, and other cash crops to Britain. They were afraid that the federal government might try to tax their exports. The Convention agreed that Congress should not have the power to do so.

Mr. Oliver Ellsworth (*Connecticut*): There are solid reasons against Congress taxing exports. It will discourage industry . . . The taxing of exports would [create] jealousies.

—James Madison's *Notes of the Constitutional Convention*, August 21, 1787

The Historian's Apprentice

1. Some historians have described the Constitution as a "bundle of compromises." Which compromise do you think was most important? Why?
2. Create a foldable describing the three main compromises at the Constitutional Convention: the "Great Compromise," the "Three-fifths Compromise," and the "Commerce Compromise."

A Summary of the U.S. Constitution

By August 1787, the delegates had completed the first draft of the new constitution. The final document was approved by the Constitutional Convention one month later. It consisted of a preamble and seven articles. The same document still governs us more than two hundred years later.

The Preamble

The first part of the Constitution is the Preamble. A **preamble** is an introductory statement. The Preamble to the U.S. Constitution announces that the new government is the creation of the American people. The rest of the Preamble then explains the goals of the people in establishing this government. You can read the preamble below.

We the People of the United States, in order to form a more perfect Union, establish justice, insure domestic tranquility, provide for the common defense, promote the general welfare, and secure the blessings of liberty to ourselves and our posterity, do ordain and establish this Constitution for the United States of America.

Word Helper

"We the People" = the individual citizens of the United States.

Union = a group of states united together under one government.

Establish justice = to administer laws fairly; to treat fairly and reasonably; to punish crimes and reward good deeds.

Tranquility = peacefulness and calm. (Also often spelled "tranquillity.")

Domestic tranquility = peacefulness and calm inside a country.

Common defense = the defense of the entire community.

General welfare = the well-being (happiness, health, and prosperity) of the entire community.

Posterity = all future generations; those who will live after us.

Ordain = to order or make official.

The Historian's Apprentice

- Why did the Preamble begin with the words "We the People"?
- Explain what the Preamble says in your own words.

How Our National Government Is Organized

The first three articles of the Constitution establish the basic structure of our national government, known as the "**federal government**." These articles define three separate branches of government with different powers and responsibilities.

Article I
Congress

Article II
The President

Article III
The Supreme Court

Article I: The Legislative Branch: Congress

- The first article establishes the legislative branch, known as **Congress.**
- Congress has two houses: the **Senate** and the **House of Representatives**.
- In the Senate, each state is represented by two Senators.
- In the House of Representatives, each state is represented by a number of members in proportion to its population.
- Members of the House of Representatives are elected by the people for two-year terms.
- Senators are appointed for six-year terms by their state legislatures. (This method of selecting Senators was changed in 1913.)
- Article I gives Congress very specific powers. These powers are far greater than those given to the Confederation Congress under the Articles. They include the power to declare war, to lay and collect taxes, to raise and support an army and navy, to coin money, to borrow money, to regulate interstate commerce, to establish post offices, and to create lower courts.
- Congress also has the power to pass any law "necessary and proper" for carrying out the powers listed above.
- A **bill** must pass both houses of Congress and be signed by the President in order to become a law. A two-thirds majority in each house can pass a bill without the President's signature (known as "**overriding a veto**").

The Historian's Apprentice

List two important rules about Congress found in Article I of the Constitution.

Article II: The Executive Branch: the Presidency

- The second article establishes the offices of **President** and **Vice President**.
- The President must be a natural-born citizen who is at least thirty-five years old. The President is chosen by the **Electoral College**. After being elected, the President serves for a four-year term.
- The President enforces federal laws, serves as commander-in-chief of the armed forces, appoints and receives ambassadors, negotiates treaties, gives a "State of the Union" address, and appoints judges and other officials.
- Congress can remove the President from office for misconduct by **impeachment**.

The Historian's Apprentice

List two important rules about the President found in Article II of the Constitution.

Article III: The Judicial Branch: the Supreme Court

- The third article establishes the **Supreme Court** as the highest court in the land.
- The Supreme Court decides all disputes between states or concerning foreign ambassadors. The Supreme Court can also hear appeals of other cases.
- Federal judges hold office for life (unless they commit some crime or other bad behavior).
- The Constitution did not create any lower federal courts, but it gave Congress the power to create lower federal courts in the future.

The Historian's Apprentice

List two important rules about the judicial branch found in Article III of the Constitution.

The Constitution also has a number of other important provisions.

Article IV: The States

- Citizens of every state enjoy the same rights and privileges in all other states.
- Congress can admit new states into the "Union" (*our nation*).
- Every state is guaranteed the **republican** form of government (*a government of representatives elected by the people*).

Article V: The Amending Process

- The Constitution can be **amended** (*added to or changed*).
- An amendment must be proposed by two-thirds (2/3) of each house of Congress and **ratified** (*approved*) by three-fourths (3/4) of the states.

Article VI: The Supreme Law of the Land

- The Constitution and all federal laws are the "supreme law of the land." They are superior to state laws.

Article VII: Ratification

- This last article established a procedure for adopting the Constitution. It stated that the new Constitution would go into effect once nine of the thirteen states **ratified** (*approved*) it.

The Historian's Apprentice

How did the new Constitution remedy the major weaknesses of the Articles of Confederation? Fill in the chart below.

Weaknesses of the Articles of Confederation	How the Constitution Remedied this Weakness
Congress had no power to tax.	
Congress had no power to raise its own troops.	
Congress had no power to regulate trade.	
Congress had no power to enforce its laws.	
There was no national court system.	
There was no national executive to provide central leadership.	

Make a chart or Venn diagram comparing the Articles of Confederation and the Constitution.

Constitutional Principles

The delegates to the Constitutional Convention struggled with one central issue. They wanted to create a central government that would be strong enough to protect the country and promote greater cooperation while not becoming so strong that it would oppress them.

The system of government they introduced to solve this problem rested on several key principles. Three of the most important were federalism, separation of powers, and checks and balances.

Federalism

The Articles of Confederation had created a confederation. The Constitution created a **federation** in which powers and responsibilities were divided between the national government, known as the **federal government**, and the state governments.

The federal government is responsible for affairs affecting the nation as a whole, such as national defense. Only the federal government has the power to appoint ambassadors, negotiate treaties, and declare war. State governments cannot do these things.

Local matters, such as keeping up local roads and running schools, are left to the states. Congress has no power to say what children should learn in school, or what speed people can drive their cars on local roads. This division of power and responsibility between our national and state governments is known as **federalism**.

The authors of the Constitution believed that this division of powers between the federal and state governments would prevent the federal government from becoming too strong. They also believed this division of authority would provide an effective way of governing an area as large as the United States.

Separation of Powers

Within the federal government, power is further divided by the separation of powers. The Constitutional Convention gave our federal government three separate branches: legislative, executive, and judicial. Each branch exercises its own separate power:

- **Legislative Power**—the power to make federal laws—is exercised by Congress.
- **Executive Power**—the power to carry out and enforce federal laws—is exercised by the President.
- **Judicial Power**—the power to hear and decide cases applying federal law to specific situations—is exercised by the Supreme Court.

This separation of powers was based on the ideas of a Frenchman, **Baron de Montesquieu**, who wrote during the Enlightenment. By 1787, each state already had a separation of powers in its own state constitution.

The authors of the Constitution saw the separation of powers as another way of making sure that the federal government did not become too strong. In an absolute monarchy, a king or queen has all of the powers of government. The monarch makes the laws, enforces the laws, and decides if the laws are applied correctly. It is impossible for ordinary citizens to challenge anything that such an all-powerful king or queen has done.

With the separation of powers, it becomes more difficult for the government to commit arbitrary and unfair acts. Each branch acts as a watchdog over the other. "Ambition," James Madison later wrote, "counteracts ambition."

Checks and Balances

Closely related to the separation of powers was the creation of a system of **checks and balances**. Each branch was given specific powers to "**check**"—or *stop*—the other two. This would prevent any single branch of the central government from becoming too powerful. It also created an incentive for the different branches to cooperate.

Checks on Congress

- Each house of Congress checks the other house. The approval of both houses is needed to pass any new law.
- To pass a bill into law, Congress requires the signature of the President. The President can check Congress by **vetoing** its proposed legislation (refusing to sign the bill).
- The Supreme Court can check Congress by ruling that a federal law is **unconstitutional** (*violates some aspect of the Constitution*).

Checks on the President

- The President appoints Justices to the Supreme Court, ambassadors, and other

Examples of Checks and Balances

officials, but these appointments must be approved by the Senate.

- The President negotiates treaties with foreign nations, but these treaties must be approved by two-thirds of the Senate.
- The President controls foreign policy and acts as commander-in-chief of the armed forces, but only Congress can declare war.
- The President establishes programs, but Congress can refuse to provide money for these programs.
- Congress can **impeach** (*remove from office*) the President.
- The Supreme Court can check the President by ruling that an executive order or Presidential action is unconstitutional.

Checks on the Supreme Court

- Congress can override decisions of the Supreme Court on federal law by passing a new law.
- Congress and the states can override the Supreme Court's interpretation of the Constitution by amending the Constitution.
- The President can influence the composition of the Supreme Court through judicial appointments.
- Congress can impeach federal judges for wrongdoing.
- The President can grant a pardon to someone convicted of a crime.

The Historian's Apprentice

- How do the separation of powers and the system of checks and balances limit our federal government and prevent it from growing too strong?
- Make your own poster or chart describing one of these constitutional principles.

The Debate over Ratification

The Constitution began with these words: "We the People." But did the American people truly support the new Constitution?

Article VII of the Constitution set up a procedure for its adoption. The Constitution would come into force only if it was **ratified** (*officially approved*) by nine states. To decide on ratification, states held special ratifying conventions.

Federalists against Anti-Federalists

Debates now sprang up in all thirteen states to decide whether or not the Constitution should be ratified. Those who favored the new constitution called themselves **Federalists**. Opponents of the new constitution became known as **Anti-Federalists**.

Many of the Anti-Federalists, including Samuel Adams, Patrick Henry, and Richard Henry Lee, had been leading Patriots during the American Revolution. They feared that the proposed Constitution would establish a central government that was just as oppressive as the British government had been. The Anti-Federalists were convinced that the new government would threaten personal liberties.

The Federalists warned that if a stronger central government were not soon adopted, the country might split apart or be invaded by foreign powers. They also argued that the proposed new government would never become despotic or oppressive. This was because of several safeguards found in the Constitution itself:

1. **The division of power between the federal government and the states**
2. **The separation of powers within the federal government**
3. **The system of checks and balances**

The most important Federalist arguments were published by Alexander Hamilton, James Madison, and John Jay in a series of articles known as *The Federalist Papers*. The purpose of *The Federalist Papers* was to persuade the ratifying convention of New York to approve the Constitution. *The Federalist Papers* argued that a stronger government was badly needed, while the principles of federalism, the separation of powers, and checks and balances would protect the liberty of every citizen.

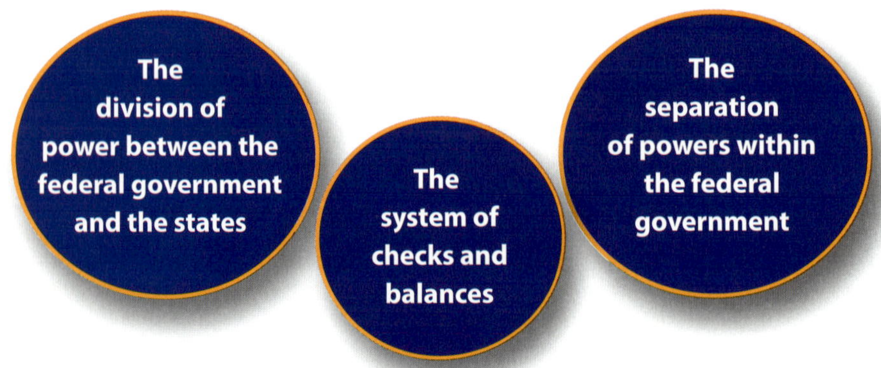

The Historian's Apprentice

"[How can we maintain] in practice the necessary [separation] of power among the several departments, as laid down in the Constitution? The only answer that can be given is . . by so contriving [designing] the interior structure of the government as that its several . . . parts may, by their mutual relations, be the means of keeping each other in their proper places . . . [T]he great security against a gradual concentration of the several powers in [one] department consists in giving to those who administer [conduct; manage] each department the necessary constitutional means and personal motives to resist encroachments of the others. . . . In the . . . republic of America, . . . power . . . is first divided between two distinct governments [federal and state]. Hence a double security arises to the rights of the people. The different governments will control each other, at the same time that each will be controlled by itself."

—*James Madison, Federalist No. 51, February 6, 1788*

- In what two ways, according to Madison, does the Constitution prevent potential abuses of power?
- Imagine that the students in your class are the members of a state convention in 1788, deciding whether or not to ratify the new Constitution. Some members of the class should pretend to be Federalists. Others should pretend to be Anti-Federalists. The "convention" should debate the question of ratification. Be sure to consider the absence of a bill of rights. After the debate is over, the class should take a vote on whether the Constitution should be ratified.
- Imagine it is 1788. Write your own newspaper article, make your own political flyer, or make your own political cartoon either for or against ratification of the Constitution.
- Federalists and Anti-Federalists held beliefs in common even though they disagreed on whether to adopt the new Constitution. Make your own Venn diagram comparing the views of Federalists and Anti-Federalists, showing their similarities as well as their differences.

The Bill of Rights

Clashing Views on a Bill of Rights

During the ratification debates, the Anti-Federalists complained that there was no bill of rights in the Constitution. They said this showed that the authors of the Constitution secretly planned to rob the people of their liberties.

A **bill of rights** is a list of rights guaranteed to individuals, such as freedom of religion or freedom of speech. Parliament had issued the English Bill of Rights in 1689. Most states included a bill of rights in their state constitutions. However, the idea of a bill of rights was hardly discussed at all at the Constitutional Convention and quickly dismissed.

In *The Federalist Papers*, Alexander Hamilton argued that a bill of rights was needed in a monarchy to protect the people from their ruler. It was not needed in a republic where the people governed themselves. However, to win popular support for the new Constitution, the Federalists promised they would add a bill of rights in the future.

The Bill of Rights: The First Ten Amendments

The Federalists kept their word. After the Constitution was adopted, the first Congress proposed a bill of rights in the form of the first ten amendments in 1789. These amendments were quickly ratified by the states and became part of the Constitution in 1791. The first ten amendments are thus known as the "**Bill of Rights**." They establish individual rights that Congress has no power to take away. The First Amendment may be the most famous of them all. It guarantees freedom of speech, freedom of the press, the right to assemble, the right to petition the government, and freedom of religion.

A SUMMARY OF THE BILL OF RIGHTS

First Amendment

The right to freedom of speech, freedom of the press, freedom of religion, freedom of assembly, and freedom to petition the government.

Second Amendment

The right to bear arms.

Third Amendment

The right not to have troops quartered without permission in one's home in peacetime.

Fourth Amendment

No unreasonable search or seizure (*arrest*); these normally require a warrant (*an order signed by a judge*).

Fifth Amendment

No accusation for a "capital" offense without indictment by a grand jury; no double jeopardy (*being tried twice for the same crime*); no self-incrimination (*being forced to testify against ourself*); no taking away of "life, liberty, or property" without "due process of law" (*fair and impartial procedures*); and no taking of property by eminent domain (*taking for a necessary public use)* without just compensation.

Sixth Amendment

The right to a speedy and public trial by an impartial jury for a criminal offense; the right to be informed of all criminal charges; the right to face and question witnesses; and the right to have legal counsel (*a lawyer*).

Seventh Amendment

The right to a trial by jury in some civil matters.

Eighth Amendment

No excessive **bail** (*money paid as security for release of an accused person awaiting trial*); no excessive fines; and no "cruel and unusual punishments."

Ninth Amendment

People may have other rights that are not mentioned in the Constitution or the Bill of Rights. Just because individuals are given several specific rights does not mean that they do not also enjoy other unlisted rights.

Tenth Amendment

Powers not given to the federal government by the Constitution are reserved for the states and the people.

How the Constitution and Bill of Rights Apply Today

Although created more than two hundred years ago, the rights and principles found in the Constitution and Bill of Rights continue to influence our lives today:

- Because of the Constitution, we elect our members of Congress and the President of the United States.
- Because of the Constitution, we have federal courts to enforce our national laws.
- Because of the Constitution, Congress is able to regulate (*make laws for*) trade between states and with other countries.
- Because of the Constitution, we have armed forces ready to defend our country.
- Because of the Bill of Rights, we enjoy freedom of religion, freedom of speech, and freedom of the press. We are not afraid to criticize (*make comments that point out faults*) our public officials. We are not afraid to say what we think.
- Because of the Bill of Rights, we are not afraid of being arrested at any time without a good reason. We feel safe in our homes.

The Historian's Apprentice

- Select one of the amendments in the Bill of Rights and create a poster about it.
- Eileen has written an article about the government. It points out that her representative in Congress has taken a bribe. She includes persuasive evidence. Police go to her home and seize her computer and arrest her. They cannot explain what they are looking for but keep her locked up in the police department for five days. She is not allowed to speak to anyone and is not given a chance to see a lawyer. Next she is brought before a judge, who tells her she is guilty of a serious crime for writing the story and sentences her to three years' imprisonment. Select a partner and discuss which of Eileen's rights in the Bill of Rights have been denied. Make a list of those rights and share your results with the rest of the class.

Civic Virtue and Civic Participation

The Constitution of 1787 relied on a secret ingredient: civic virtue. **Civic virtue** is the willingness of citizens to set aside their personal interests for the good of the community. Without civic virtue, the new system of democratic government could not work.

Civic virtue was especially shown in people's loyalty to democratic values and through their military service. During the Revolution, American Patriots had volunteered for militia service or enlisted in the Continental Army for little pay. They risked their lives for independence and freedom. In the new republic, ordinary citizens continued to volunteer in state militia. The new Constitution also depended on citizens giving some of their time to public service to make the government work.

Civic virtue requires **civic participation**. This is the participation of ordinary citizens in the process of government. In a democracy, ordinary citizens participate in government by voting in elections and by serving in public office.

There are also many informal ways in which citizens can participate. They can join political clubs or parties. They can participate in public demonstrations that celebrate achievements or that protest policies. They can write and publish articles and letters. They can have parades and listen to speeches. They can petition government leaders for change.

In the Revolutionary period, citizens made use of all these methods of civic participation. Critics of British policies wrote articles in newspapers and published pamphlets. The Sons of Liberty organized boycotts, demonstrations, and even violent actions like attacks on British tax collectors and the Boston Tea Party. After the Revolution, some citizens continued using these same methods. The followers of Daniel Shays in Massachusetts attacked courthouses to express their anger. Other citizens wrote articles and pamphlets, gave speeches, or ran for public office. By 1787, America was a society in which citizens expected to be able to express their views and to participate in government.

The Historian's Apprentice

1. With a partner, discuss recent examples of civic virtue or civic participation that you have read about or know about.
2. Think of a person you know who has shown civic virtue. Write a paragraph explaining how that person shows civic virtue.
3. Why is civic virtue more important in a democracy than in a monarchy?

Chapter Review Cards

The Constitutional Convention

- In May 1787, fifty-five delegates gathered in Philadelphia to revise the Articles of Confederation. Instead, they decided to write a whole new **constitution**. Their assembly became known as the **Constitutional Convention**.
- The delegates agreed that the new national government should have three separate **branches**: a **legislature**, **executive**, and **judiciary**.
- At first, they also agreed that the legislature—**Congress**—should have two houses: a **House of Representatives**, directly elected by the people; and the **Senate**, whose members would serve for longer terms and be protected from public pressures.
- The delegates also quickly decided that the executive should be a single individual—the **President**—with the power to **veto** new laws passed by Congress. Two-thirds of both houses of Congress would be able to override the President's veto.

The "Great Compromise": Large vs. Small States

- The delegates did not agree on everything. The biggest disagreement was between large and small states. Larger states wanted more representatives in Congress.
- The **Virginia Plan** proposed that each state should be represented **in proportion** to its population in both houses of Congress. This is known as **proportional representation**.
- The **New Jersey Plan** proposed a one-house legislature with **equal** representation for each state.
- Connecticut delegates proposed a compromise in which states would enjoy proportional representation in the **House of Representatives** and **equal representation** in the **Senate**.
- In the end, delegates agreed that each state should have **two Senators** in the Senate and **proportional** representation in the House of Representatives. This solution became known as the "**Great Compromise**."

Electoral College

- The delegates feared having the people elect the President directly. Instead, they decided that the President should be chosen by an **Electoral College**.
- Each state's electors would equal the sum of its representatives in both houses (Members in the House + 2 for its two Senators).
- If no candidate won a majority of the Electoral College, the House of Representatives would select the President.

"Three-Fifths Compromise": South vs. North

- Southerners wanted enslaved people to count as part of the population of each state in determining the number of representatives in Congress. Northerners believed slaves should not be counted because they did not vote.
- Northern delegates thought slaves should be counted, however, for purposes of taxation.
- The delegates reached the "**Three-fifths Compromise**." They agreed that slaves would count as three-fifths of their actual number for purposes of both representation and taxation.
- The delegates agreed on the "**Commerce Compromise**." The Constitution prevented Congress from passing any laws prohibiting the slave trade for the next twenty years (before 1808).
- The delegates also agreed that Congress should not have the power to tax **exports**. Southern states depended on exporting their cash crops to Britain.

Structure of the U.S. Constitution

- The **Preamble** (introduction): "We the People"
- Article I. The legislative branch: Congress
- Article II. The executive branch: the Presidency
- Article III. The judicial branch: the Supreme Court
- Article IV. The states
- Article V. The constitutional amendment process
- Article VI. Federal law is the supreme law of the land
- Article VII. Process for the ratification (*approval*) of the Constitution

Constitutional Principles

- These constitutional principles prevented the federal government from becoming too strong.
- **Federalism**: The division of power between the federal government and the state governments. The federal government deals with issues affecting the nation; state governments deal with matters affecting the individual states.
- **Separation of powers**: The separation of power between the legislative, executive and judicial branches.
- **Checks and balances**: Each branch has specific powers allowing it to "**check**"—or stop—the other two branches. This prevents any one branch from becoming too powerful. It also encourages cooperation between branches.

The Ratification Debate: Federalists vs. Anti-Federalists

- **Federalists** favored the new Constitution. They argued that a stronger government was needed to protect Americans and to hold the nation together. The constitutional principles of federalism, the separation of powers, and checks and balances would protect individual liberties and prevent the new federal government from becoming too strong.
- Federalist arguments were best expressed by James Madison, Alexander Hamilton and John Jay in a series of essays known as *The Federalist Papers*. These essays were written to persuade New Yorkers to ratify the Constitution.
- **Anti-Federalists** opposed the new Constitution. They feared the new central government was just as oppressive as the British government had been.
- Anti-Federalists complained that there was no **bill of rights** (a list of rights guaranteed to individuals) in the Constitution.
- To win popular support for the new Constitution, the Federalists promised a bill of rights.
- The first Congress proposed ten amendments in 1789, which were ratified by the states in 1791. These amendments are known as the "**Bill of Rights**."

The Bill of Rights: The First Ten Amendments

- **First Amendment**: The right to **freedom of speech**, **freedom of the press**, **freedom of religion**, **freedom of assembly**, and **freedom to petition the government**.
- **Second Amendment**: The **right to bear arms**.
- **Third Amendment**: The right not to have troops quartered without permission in one's home in peacetime.
- **Fourth Amendment**: **No unreasonable search or seizure**; these normally require a warrant.
- **Fifth Amendment**: No accusation for a "capital" offense without indictment by a grand jury; **no double jeopardy**; **no self-incrimination**; no taking away of "life, liberty, or property" without "due process of law"; and no taking of property by eminent domain without just compensation.
- **Sixth Amendment**: The **right to a speedy and public trial by an impartial jury** for a criminal offense; the right to be informed of all criminal charges; the right to face and question witnesses; and the right to have legal counsel.
- **Seventh Amendment**: The right to a trial by jury in some civil matters.
- **Eighth Amendment**: No excessive **bail**; no excessive fines; and **no cruel and unusual punishments**.
- **Ninth Amendment**: People may have other rights that are not mentioned in the Constitution or the Bill of Rights.
- **Tenth Amendment**: Powers not given to the federal government by the Constitution are reserved for the states and the people.

Civic Virtue and Civic Participation

- **Civic virtue** is the willingness of citizens to set aside their personal interests for the good of the community.
- **Civic participation** is the participation of ordinary citizens in the process of government. Citizens participate by voting, attending public meetings, joining political parties, and running for public office.

"Miracle at Philadelphia": The Story of Our Constitution

The Constitutional Convention Meets (1787)
- Delegates decide to write a new constitution
- Delegates agree to create a national legislature, executive and judiciary

Disagreement and Compromise

Summary of the U.S. Constitution
- Preamble-We the People
- Article I- Congress: Senate and House of Representatives - Powers include the power to tax, raise an army, borrow money, regulate interstate commerce
- Article II- The President
- Article III- The Supreme Court
- Article IV- The States
- Article V- Amending Process
- Article VI- Supremacy of Federal Law
- Article VII- Ratification Process

Large vs. Small States
- Virginia Plan-Proportional Representation
- New Jersey Plan- Equal Representation
- "Great Compromise"- House based on proportional representation; Senate based on equal representation

Electoral College—Electors choose the President

"Three-fifths Compromise"—Only 3/5 of slaves are counted

Commerce Compromise
- No taxes on exports
- Congress can only prohibit slave trade in 20 years

Constitutional Principles
- Federalism
- Separation of Powers
- Checks and Balances

The division of power between the federal government and the states

The system of checks and balances

The separation of powers within the federal government

Ratification Debate
- Federalists vs. Anti-Federalists
- *The Federalist Papers*
- Demand for a bill of rights

Bill of Rights

1st Amendment
- Freedom of religion, speech and the press, and right to assemble and petition

Other Rights:
- Right to bear arms
- Freedom from unreasonable search or seizure
- Right to a fair and public trial by jury
- No cruel and unusual punishment
- No excessive bail, double jeopardy or self-incrimination

What do you know?

SS.6.A.3.11

1. The passage below is from *The Federalist*, No. 51, written by James Madison in 1788.

> *But what is government itself, but the greatest of all reflections on human nature? . . . In framing a government which is to be administered by men over men, the great difficulty lies in this: you must first enable the government to control the governed; and in the next place oblige it to control itself.*

How did the proposed Constitution address the problem identified by Madison in the passage?

A. It included a bill of rights to protect individual liberties.

B. It allowed the slave trade to continue for twenty more years.

C. It included checks and balances to prevent abuses of power by government.

D. It prevented the federal government from waging war without the support of the states.

SS.6.A.3.10

2. The headlines below appeared in American newspapers in 1787.

National Gazette

Proposed Congress to Have Two Houses

Philadelphia The first house would be known as
the House of Representatives. It would represent the
members would be elected directly by the people.
The second house would be the Senate. It would
represent the wisdom, wealth, and property of
America. As one delegate put it, the Senate should
have "the most distinguished characters by rank and
property." Senators would serve for longer terms than
members of the House of Representatives. This way,
they would not be as subject to pressures from the

National Gazette

Each Slave to Count as Three-Fifths of a Person

Delegates strike a compromise.

Philadelphia Slave populations will be counted at
three-fifths of their actual number. In other words,
every five slaves would be counted as three persons.
The same rule would apply for purposes of both
representation and taxation.

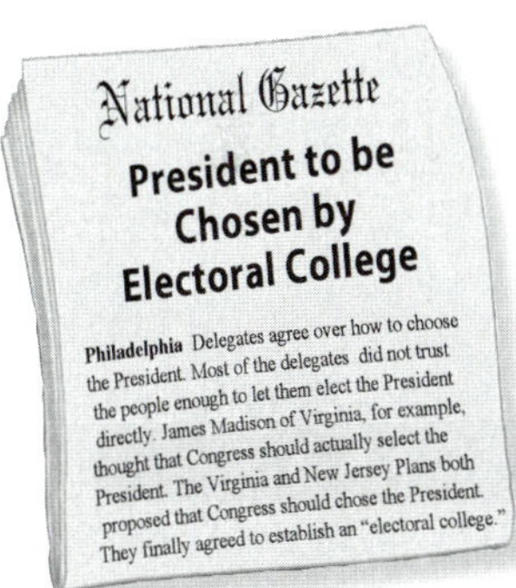
National Gazette

President to be Chosen by Electoral College

Philadelphia Delegates agree over how to choose
the President. Most of the delegates did not trust
the people enough to let them elect the President
directly. James Madison of Virginia, for example,
thought that Congress should actually select the
President. The Virginia and New Jersey Plans both
proposed that Congress should chose the President.
They finally agreed to establish an "electoral college."

Which conclusion about the Constitutional Convention is supported by these headlines?

A. It was controlled by states with large enslaved populations.

B. Its members were able to compromise on important issues.

C. Most of its members wanted the President to be chosen directly by the people.

D. It gave states that were small in population the most power in the new Constitution.

SS.6.C.2.1

3. The excerpts below are from the Constitution of the United States.

> ***Article I Section 1***
>
> *All legislative powers . . . shall be vested in a Congress of the United States, which shall consist of a Senate and House of Representatives.*
>
> ***Article II Section 1***
>
> *The executive power shall be vested in a President of the United States of America . . . together with the Vice President, chosen for the same term . . .*
>
> ***Article III Section 1***
>
> *The judicial power of the United States, shall be vested in one Supreme Court, and in [other lower] courts as the Congress may from time to time ordain and establish . . .*

Which important constitutional principle is illustrated by these excerpts?

A. federalism

B. individual rights

C. popular sovereignty

D. separation of powers

SS.6.A.3.11

4. Which statement describes the debate between the Federalists and Anti-Federalists over ratification of the Constitution?

A. They argued over the question of establishing a national bank.

B. They disagreed over whether slavery should continue in the new nation.

C. They disagreed over whether the national executive should be a single person or a group.

D. They disagreed over the distribution of power between the federal and state governments.

SS.6.A.3.9

4A. The information below lists several weaknesses of the Articles of Confederation.

- No power to collect taxes
- No national court system
- No national currency

How did the delegates to the Constitutional Convention attempt to correct these weaknesses?

A. They gave greater power to state governments.

B. They drafted a plan for a stronger national government.

C. They drafted a bill of rights to protect individual liberties.

D. They encouraged state to enter into their own agreements.

SS.6.A.3.11

5. The excerpt below is from the Sixth Amendment.

> *A person accused of a crime in the United States "shall enjoy the right to a speedy and public trial by an impartial jury."*

Why was this amendment included in the Bill of Rights?

A. to override a decision of the Supreme Court

B. to remedy a weakness of the Articles of Confederation

C. to approve an amendment recently added to most state constitutions

D. to satisfy the demands of Anti-Federalists for greater protection of individual liberties

SS.6.A.3.10

6. At the Constitutional Convention, how did the New Jersey Plan differ from the Virginia Plan?

A. The New Jersey Plan favored the direct election of the President by the people.

B. The New Jersey Plan favored equal representation for each state in a Congress.

C. The New Jersey Plan favored proportional representation in two houses of Congress.

D. The New Jersey Plan proposed the selection of the President by the Electoral College.

SS.6.C.1.5

7. Citizens attend a public demonstration against government policies. Speakers at the demonstration criticize the government and print flyers to distribute to listeners and the general public.

Which rights in the Bill of Rights are exercised in this scenario?

A. Freedom of speech, the press and assembly.

B. Freedom of speech, religion, and the right to bear arms.

C. Freedom from unreasonable search, and the right to a trial by jury.

D. Freedom of assembly, religion, and the right to petition.

SS.6.A.3.10

8. The discussion below took place between four delegates to the Constitutional Convention.

Delegate 1:	Our national government should be strong. State governments should have only limited powers.
Delegate 2:	A bicameral legislature will allow Congress to represent the interests of both large states and small states.
Delegate 3:	Any further expansion of our national government may lead to tyranny.
Delegate 4:	The executive branch should have more power than the other branches because it can act the most quickly in emergencies.

Which delegate expresses ideas included in the "Great Compromise"?

A. Delegate 1

B. Delegate 2

C. Delegate 3

D. Delegate 4

SS.6.A.3.10

9. Which disagreement led to the "Three-fifths" Compromise?

A. Delegates at the Constitutional Convention argued over whether to tax trade. Southern delegates feared this would hurt landowners who exported cash crops to England.

B. Delegates at the Constitutional Convention discussed whether to include women in determining a state's representation in Congress. Some feared this would end in giving women the right to vote.

C. Delegates at the Constitutional Convention debated whether to count enslaved people in calculating a state's representation in Congress or the taxes it should pay to the federal government.

D. Delegates at the Constitutional Convention discussed how each state should be represented in Congress. Smaller states proposed equal representation for states, while larger states proposed proportional representation.

SS.6.A.3.11

10. The passage below was written by Brutus, an Anti-Federalist, in 1788.

> *Let us inquire whether the thirteen states should be reduced to one republic or not? The territory is vast and has nearly three million [people] . . . Is it realistic for a country so numerous to elect representatives to speak [for them] . . . A free republic cannot exist in such a large territory . . . citizens will have little [familiarity] with those chosen to represent them . . . it will consist of men whose names they have never heard . . .*

In this passage, which argument does Brutus make against ratification of the proposed Constitution?

A. Citizens do not need to have a direct contact with their representatives in government.

B. Having people elect representatives to govern the whole nation is impractical in a country with such a large size and population.

C. The geographic size and population of the country should not be considered when debating the benefits of a representative government.

D. The proposed Constitution will place the thirteen states under the direction of a single government that is incapable of carrying out the business of the country.

SS.6.C.2.1

11. The grievance below was listed in the Declaration of Independence.

> *He [King George] has made Judges dependent on his will alone for the tenure [length] of their offices, [service] and the amount and payment of their salaries.*

Which feature of the Constitution addressed this concern and still affects us today?

A. Congress can veto Supreme Court decisions.

B. State legislatures elect Supreme Court Justices.

C. Supreme Court Justices are appointed for life terms.

D. The President can impeach Supreme Court Justices.

SS.6.C.2.1

12. The diagram below describes how laws are handled in the United States.

Laws in the United States

The legislative branch passes laws	The executive branch enforces laws	The judicial branch interprets laws

Which important Constitutional principle is reflected in the diagram above?

A. federalism

B. individual rights

C. popular sovereignty

D. separation of powers

SS.6.C.1.5

13. Which newspaper headline illustrates the operation of the system of checks and balances?

A.

Miami Herald

Senate Rejects the President's Choice of Supreme Court Justice

Washington D.C. — Senate Republicans overwhelmingly rejected Obama's nomination of Merrick Garland amd have refused to hold confirmation hearings ahead of the November election. The Senate has almost a full year to consider and confirm a nominee. In fact, since 1975, the average time from nomination to confirmation is 67 days. It will be harmful and create unsustainable uncertainty if Congress fails

B.

Orlando Observer

Florida Gains Two Seats in the United States House of Representatives

Tallahassee — Florida now has 27 seats in the U.S. House of Representatives. Congressional representation is based on population. Apportionment is the process of dividing the 435 memberships, or seats, in the U.S. House of Representatives among the 50 states. The average size of a congressional district based on the 2010 Census apportionment population will be 710,767, more than triple the average district size of 210,328 based on the 1910 Census.

C.

Tampa Morning Post

Broward County Receives $4 Million from Congress for Transportation Development

Fort Lauderdale— Based on transportation data, Florida's Turnpike is considered one of the busiest highways in the country (according to the IBBTA), the highway is the nation's 3rd most heavily traveled toll road. Congress voted on Thursday to fund needed maintenance on the two busiest sections in Broward County. Funds have also been earmarked for new buses that run on natural gas as part of an modernization

D.

JACKSONVILLE COURIER

Florida Challenges Federal Regulations on Drug Testing for State Employees

Tallahassee— State officials including the Attorney General are calling for more rigorous standards for insuring that state employees remain drug free while on the job. The new measures requires employees to submit to a drug test if the test is conducted as part of a routinely scheduled employee fitness-for-duty medical examination that is part of the employer's established policy or that is scheduled routinely for all members of

CHAPTER 8 Launching the Ship of State: The Presidency of George Washington

SS.6.A.3.12 Examine the influences of George Washington's presidency in the formation of the new nation.

SS.6.C.1.3 Recognize the role of civic virtue in the lives of citizens and leaders from the colonial period through Reconstruction.

SS.6.C.2.1 Evaluate and compare the essential ideals and principles of American constitutional government expressed in primary sources from the colonial period to Reconstruction.

SS.6.E.2.2 Explain the economic impact of government policies.

Alignment to Grade 7 Civics Standards

SS.7.C.3.3 Illustrate the structure and function (three branches of government established in Articles I, II, and III with corresponding powers) of government in the United States as established in the Constitution.

SS.7.C.3.8 Analyze the structure, functions, and processes of the legislative, executive, and judicial branches.

SS.7.C.4.1 Differentiate concepts related to U.S. domestic and foreign policy.

Terms and Names You Should Know

- George Washington
- Inauguration
- Civic Virtue
- Precedent
- Cabinet
- Secretary of State
- Secretary of the Treasury
- Judiciary Act of 1789
- Bill of Rights
- Debts
- Credit
- Government Bond
- Interest
- Washington, D.C.
- Bank of the United States
- "Strict" constructionist
- "Loose" constructionist
- "Necessary and Proper" Clause
- Protective tariff
- Whiskey tax
- Political party
- Federalists
- Democratic-Republicans
- Domestic Policy
- Foreign Policy
- French Revolution
- Proclamation of Neutrality
- Whiskey Rebellion
- Washington's Farewell Address

THE ADDRESS OF GEN. WASHINGTO

To the People of America,

ON HIS DECLINING THE PRESIDENCY

OF THE

UNITED STATES.

Friends and Fellow-Citizens,

THE period for the new election of a citizen to administer the Executive Government of the United States being not far distant, and the time actually arrived when your thoughts must be employed in designating the person who is to be clothed with that important trust, it appears to me proper, especially as it may conduce to a more distinct expression of the public voice, that I should now apprize you of the resolution I have formed, to decline being considered among the number of those out of whom a choice is to be made.

I beg you, at the same time, to do me the justice to be assured, that this resolution has not been taken without a strict regard to all the considerations appertaining to the relation which binds a dutiful citizen to his country; and that, in withdrawing the tender of service which silence in my situation might imply, I am influenced by no diminution of zeal for your future interest; no deficiency of grateful respect for your past kindness; but am supported by a full conviction that the step is compatible with both.

The acceptance of, and continuance hitherto in the office to which your suffrages have twice called me, have been a uniform sacrifice of inclination to the opinion of duty, and to a deference for what appeared to be your desire. I constantly hoped that it would have been much earlier in my power, consistently with motives which I was not at liberty to disregard, to return to that retirement from which I had been reluctantly drawn. The strength of my inclination to do this, previous to the last election, had even led to the preparation of an address to declare it to you; but mature reflection on the then perplexed and critical posture of our affairs with foreign nations, and the unanimous advice of persons entitled to my confidence, impelled me to abandon the idea.

I rejoice that the state of your concerns, external as well as internal, no longer renders the pursuit of inclination incompatible with the sentiment of duty or propriety; and am persuaded, whatever partiality may be retained for my services, that, in the present circumstances of our country, you will not disapprove my determination to retire.

The impressions with which I first undertook the arduous trust were explained on the proper occasion. In the discharge of this trust I will only say, that I have, with good intentions, contributed towards the organization and administration of the government the best exertions of which a very fallible judgment was capable. Not unconscious, in the outset, of the inferiority of my qualifications, experience in my own eyes, perhaps still more in the eyes of others, has strengthened the motives to diffidence of myself; and every day the increasing weight of years admonishes me more and more that the shade of retirement is as necessary to me as it will be welcome. Satisfied, that if any circumstances have given peculiar value to my services, they were temporary, I have the consolation to believe, that while choice and prudence invite me to quit the political scene, patriotism does not forbid it.

In looking forward to the moment which is intended to terminate the career of my public life, my feelings do not permit me to suspend the deep acknowledgment of that debt of gratitude which I owe to my beloved country for the many honours it has conferred on me; still more for the stedfast confidence with which it has supported me; and for the opportunities I have thence enjoyed of manifesting my inviolable attachment by services faithful and persevering, though in usefulness unequal to my zeal.

fortunate than his competitors, turns this disposition to the purposes of his own elevation, on the ruins o Liberty.

Without looking forward to an extremity of this kind (which nevertheless ought not to be entirely out o the common and continual mischiefs of the spirit of party are sufficient to make it the interest and duty o people to discourage and restrain it.

It serves always to distract the public councils, and enfeeble the public administration. It agitates the co with ill-founded jealousies and false alarms; kindles the animosity of one party against another; foments occ riot and insurrection. It opens the door to foreign influence and corruption, which find a facilitated a government itself through the channels of party passions. Thus the policy and the will of one country are s to the policy and the will of another.

There is an opinion that parties in free countries are useful checks upon the administration of the governm serve to keep alive the spirit of liberty. This, within certain limits, is probably true; and in governme monarchical cast patriotism may look with indulgence, if not with favour, upon the spirit of party: but, in the popular character, in governments purely elective, it is a spirit not to be encouraged. From their natural it is certain there will always be enough of that spirit for every salutary purpose. And there being consta of excess, the effort ought to be, by force of public opinion, to mitigate and assuage it. A fire not to be q it demands a uniform vigilance to prevent its bursting into a flame, lest, instead of warming, it should cons

It is important, likewise, that the habits of thinking in a free country should inspire caution in those entru its administration to confine themselves within their respective constitutional spheres, avoiding in the exerci powers of one department to encroach upon another. The spirit of encroachment tends to consolidate the all the departments in one, and thus to create, whatever the form of government, a real despotism. A just of that love of power, and proneness to abuse it, which predominates in the human heart, is sufficient to sat the truth of this position. The necessity of reciprocal checks in the exercise of political power, by divi distributing it into different depositories, and constituting each the guardian of the public weal against inv the others, has been evinced by experiments ancient and modern; some of them in our own country, and own eyes. To preserve them must be as necessary as to institute them. If, in the opinion of the people, t bution or modification of the constitutional powers be in any particular wrong, let it be corrected by an a in the way which the constitution designates. But let there be no change by usurpation; for though thi instance, may be the instrument of good, it is the customary weapon by which free governments are destroy precedent must always greatly overbalance, in permanent evil, any partial or transient benefit which the u any time yield.

Of all the dispositions and habits which lead to political prosperity, Religion and Morality are indispens ports. In vain would that man claim the tribute of patriotism who should labour to subvert these great

Florida "Keys" to Learning

1. In 1788, George Washington was elected by the Electoral College as the first President of the United States.

2. Washington faced many challenges. Many of his actions would establish precedents—ways of doing things that would be copied in the future.

3. Washington held regular meetings of his Cabinet, made up of the appointed heads of government departments. The Cabinet discussed issues and gave him advice.

4. John Jay became the first Chief Justice of the Supreme Court. Congress passed the Judiciary Act of 1789, creating a system of federal courts below the Supreme Court. Congress also proposed the Bill of Rights as the first ten amendments.

5. Alexander Hamilton, Secretary of the Treasury, had a plan to deal with the nation's finances. He proposed the federal government issue interest-paying bonds to pay off its debts from the Revolutionary War. It would also pay off the debts of the states. The plan seemed to favor the North. Jefferson and Madison accepted Hamilton's proposal on the basis of a compromise: they agreed that the nation's new capital city would be located in the South at Washington, D.C.

6. Hamilton next proposed that Congress create the Bank of the United States.

7. Hamilton's plan further called for tariffs. A tariff is a tax on goods coming from other countries (imports). Hamilton wanted to protect infant Northern industries from British competition. The tariff raised prices on British goods and was unpopular in the South.

8. To get more revenue, Hamilton also proposed a tax on whiskey made by western farmers (the "whiskey tax").

9. A political party is a group of people who share similar views and who try to get their candidates elected to office. The disagreement over Hamilton's plan led to the rise of two political parties. Federalists supported Hamilton's plan. Jefferson and Madison led the Democratic-Republicans, who opposed it.

10. The Northwest Territory opened to settlers when General Anthony Wayne defeated Chief Blue Jacket at the Battle of Fallen Timbers in 1794.

11. To avoid involvement in the war between Britain and France during the French Revolution, President Washington issued a Proclamation of Neutrality. It declared that the United States would remain neutral.

12. The Jay Treaty with Britain dealt with British seizures of American ships. The Pinckney Treaty with Spain gave Americans the use of the port of New Orleans.

13. Farmers in western Pennsylvania rebelled against the whiskey tax. Washington led 13,000 men against the rebels. The rebels avoided a fight and returned home.

14. President Washington refused to run for a third term. In his Farewell Address, he reminded Americans that their unity was "the main prop" of their liberty. He advised against political parties and warned about the dangers of entering into entangling alliances in Europe.

In the spring of 1789, George Washington and his wife Martha packed up their belongings and slowly made the journey from their home in Virginia to New York City. All along the way, they were met by cheering crowds. On April 30, Washington stood on the balcony of Federal Hall. He placed his hand on the Bible and took the oath of office as the first President of the United States. It was a stirring moment.

And yet Washington—the hero who had won the Revolution—felt afraid. He worried that he would not be able to meet the demands of his new office.

The Challenges of the First Presidency

The members of the Constitutional Convention already had Washington in mind when they created the office of President. To most Americans, Washington represented the very ideal of **civic virtue**—a willingness to act selflessly for the good of one's community and country. It was therefore no surprise when, in 1788, all the members of the Electoral College cast their votes for him. No one else could better unite the country.

As the nation's first President, Washington faced a number of serious challenges. First, he had to set up procedures for the new government. Second, he had to decide how to pay the debts left from the Revolutionary War. Third, he had to stop Indian attacks on settlers in the Northwest. Finally, he had to deal with foreign powers. It is no wonder Washington was unsure how well he would succeed.

Setting Up the New Government

Washington knew that everything he did in office would create a **precedent**—something that was being done for the first time and would be copied by others in the future. Even whether he should be called "Mr. President" became a subject for debate.

The Cabinet. The first thing Washington did was to appoint the heads of government departments. These officials met together regularly as his Cabinet. The **Cabinet** is the group of top officials who advise the President. The Cabinet is not mentioned in the Constitution. However, Cabinet meetings were held by Washington and have continued under every other President ever since.

The Judiciary. The next task was to set up the country's judicial branch. Washington appointed **John Jay** as the first Chief Justice of the Supreme Court.

The First Cabinet

Office	Responsibility	Individual	Background
Secretary of State	Foreign relations	Thomas Jefferson	Author of the Declaration of Independence, former Governor of Virginia, and former Ambassador to France
Secretary of the Treasury	Finances	Alexander Hamilton	Assistant to Washington during the Revolution, successful lawyer, and delegate to the Constitutional Convention
Secretary of War	Military affairs	Henry Knox	Brought guns from Fort Ticonderoga to Boston in 1775 and was placed in charge of artillery (large guns such as cannons) during the Revolution
Attorney General	Legal affairs	Edmund Randolph	Former Governor of Virginia who spoke at the opening meeting of the Constitutional Convention

The Constitution had established the Supreme Court, but did not create any courts below it. This important job was left to Congress. The first Congress passed the **Judiciary Act of 1789**. This law created a system of federal courts below the U.S. Supreme Court. These included both district courts and courts of appeal.

The Bill of Rights. Federalists had promised a bill of rights to get the Constitution ratified. The first Congress proposed the **Bill of Rights**. This became the first ten amendments to the Constitution, which you read about in the last chapter. These were ratified by the states and added to the Constitution in 1791.

The Historian's Apprentice

1. Why did Washington believe his actions would serve as precedents for later Presidents?
2. Why did Washington bring the heads of departments together for regular meetings?

Paying the Nation's Debts

The next challenge Washington faced was how to pay the debts left by the Revolutionary War. During the war, the Continental Congress and states had printed paper money. They had also sold **war bonds** (called "bills of credit"). Each bond was like a government IOU ("I owe you"). The government promised to repay the holder of the bond at a later date. The government had also borrowed money from French and Dutch bankers. **Alexander Hamilton**, the Secretary of the Treasury, drew up a plan to deal with the nation's financial problems. Hamilton presented his financial plan to Congress in three reports.

Hamilton's "Report on the Public Credit" (January 1790)

Hamilton's first report dealt with the nation's credit.

Hamilton told Congress that in an emergency, such as a war, every country must be able to borrow money. It can only do so if it has good "credit."

Credit is like reputation. People trust a person with good credit. They believe this person will repay his or her debts. The same is true for a country. If a country repays its debts, it will have good credit and find it easier to borrow money in future. Hamilton told Congress: "To be able to borrow upon good terms, it is essential that the credit of a nation should be well established."

To establish its good credit, Hamilton said the United States had to pay its debts. Hamilton said that the federal government should also pay the war debts of the individual states. Altogether, the total was about $75 million. This was a huge amount for this time.

Hamilton proposed that the federal government replace all the bonds and other notes made out at the time of the Revolution with its own new bonds. These new bonds would pay interest (*money based on a percentage*). The federal government would pay this interest to bondholders each year. This step would attach the holders of the new bonds to the nation.

Just as important, the new government bonds would serve as a form of money. Once people knew that the government would repay its debts, they would start using these bonds to pay one another. This would increase how much money was available and promote prosperity.

Jefferson and Madison were against Hamilton's plan. They had two main reasons for opposing it:

First, wealthy investors had already bought up most of the war bonds issued during the Revolution. They had paid very low prices for them. Under Hamilton's plan, the government would now pay the full value for each bond. This would just make the rich much richer. It seemed very unfair to those poor farmers and shopkeepers who had sold the bonds at low prices.

Second, Hamilton wanted the federal government to pay the debts of the states. Virginia and other Southern states had already paid most of their war debts. Their citizens did not want to pay a share of other states' debts when they had just paid all of their own.

Locating the Nation's Capital

Both parts of Hamilton's plan seemed to favor the North over the South. However, a skillful compromise was worked out. Americans had already agreed to build a new capital city for their new nation. Its location had yet to be decided. Jefferson and Madison agreed to let the federal government take on the remaining state debts. In return, Hamilton agreed that the new capital of the United States should be located in the South along the Potomac River. Because of this compromise, our national capital of Washington, D.C., is located in the South, next to Virginia and Maryland. It also meant that Southerners could bring slaves to the capital as household servants.

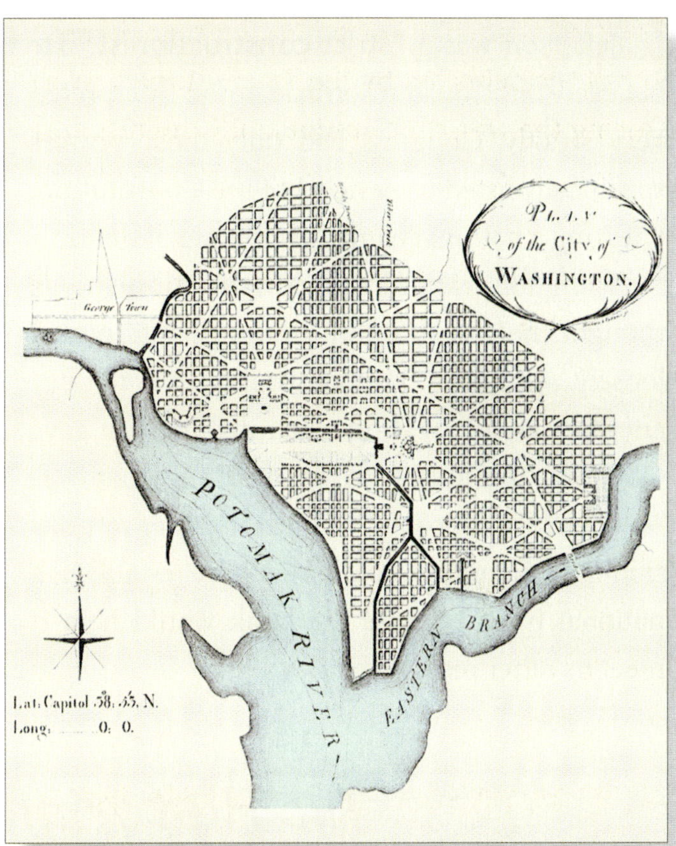

An early plan for Washington, D.C., in March 1791

The Historian's Apprentice

1. How did Hamilton's plan favor the North over the South?
2. If you had been a member of Congress in 1790, would you have supported Hamilton's plan for dealing with debts from the Revolution?
3. Like countries, individuals have credit. Before a bank lends money to a person to buy a house, it checks that person's "credit score." When a person buys something with a "credit card," a bank actually pays the store and the cardholder pays back the bank. Why is having good credit just as important today as it was in Hamilton's time?

The Rest of Hamilton's Financial Plan

Hamilton's "Report on a National Bank" (December 1790)

Hamilton's second report to Congress came almost a year later. Hamilton proposed that the federal government should create a **national bank**. The government could take the money it collected from taxes and deposit it in this bank. It could also pay its expenses and make loans from the bank.

Jefferson especially disliked this part of Hamilton's plan. He felt that starting a bank was not one of the powers of Congress.

Jefferson was a "**strict constructionist**." He believed the Constitution had to be interpreted very strictly. Congress had only those powers specifically listed in Article I of the Constitution. Creating a national bank was not one of them.

Hamilton was a "**loose constructionist**." He thought the Constitution should be interpreted loosely. Although the Constitution did not say anything about creating a national bank, it gave Congress the ability to do anything that was "necessary and proper" to meet its other responsibilities. Congress could therefore establish a national bank because the bank would help it meet its other responsibilities.

In the end, President Washington and Congress agreed with Hamilton. The first Bank of the United States was established in Philadelphia in February 1791.

The First Bank of the United States

The Historian's Apprentice

1. Do you favor a "strict" or "loose" construction of the Constitution? Discuss your opinion with a partner. Then share your views with the class.
2. Did Hamilton, Jefferson, and Madison work out a good compromise by agreeing to locate the nation's capital in the South?

Hamilton's "Report on Manufactures" (December 1791)

Hamilton gave his last report to Congress a year later. This time he argued that America's new workshops and factories needed protection from the government to compete with British manufacturers.

Hamilton proposed a protective tariff. A **tariff** is a special tax placed on goods coming from another country. The purpose of a **protective tariff** is to help American businesses compete by making foreign goods more expensive.

Imagine that cotton cloth from Britain costs $10 a yard. The same cloth from American manufacturers costs $12 a yard. The British cloth is less expensive. But if a tariff of $5 a yard is added, it will cost $15 a yard. The American cloth is now cheaper.

Southern farmers did not want to pay tariffs on goods coming from Britain. They also did not want to buy higher priced American goods. All this just raised their own expenses. In addition, they worried that the British might react by placing tariffs on crops coming from America.

The Whiskey Tax. At this time, western farmers grew corn, rye and other grains. Their crops were too heavy to carry over the Appalachian Mountains. Instead, they turned their grain into whiskey, a strong alcoholic drink. Whiskey was becoming popular in the cities of the east. Many western farmers depended on the extra income they earned by selling whiskey.

Western farmer making whiskey

When Hamilton discovered that the government did not receive enough money from the tariff to meet its needs, he proposed an excise tax on whiskey. (An excise tax is a tax on goods sold within a country.) The **whiskey tax** was approved by Congress and went into effect in March 1791. It was the country's first domestic tax. Once again, Hamilton's proposal hurt farmers, not merchants or manufacturers.

A SUMMARY OF HAMILTON'S FINANCIAL PLAN, 1790–1791

- The nation must establish "**good credit.**"
- The government should issue **new bonds** to cover its debts from the war.
- The federal government should take on the **war debts** of the states.
- The federal government should create a **national bank**.
- The government should have a **protective tariff** to help American manufacturers.
- The government should collect an **excise tax on whiskey**.

The Historian's Apprentice

1. Make a poster or advertisement either for or against Hamilton's financial plan.
2. Would you have supported Hamilton's financial plan? Why or why not?

The Rise of Political Parties

A **political party** is a group of people who share similar views. Members of a political party cooperate to elect their candidates to public office.

Political parties had existed for a long time in England. President Washington greatly disliked them. He believed that party members put the interests of their party above those of the country. Washington preferred to think of himself as an American, not as a party member.

The disagreement over Hamilton's plan led to the rise of the first American political parties. Those who supported Hamilton became known as **Federalists**. They took their name from the earlier supporters of the Constitution. Supporters of Jefferson and Madison, who opposed Hamilton's plan, became known as **Democratic-Republicans**.

Today, we have different political parties. The two major ones are the Democrats and Republicans.

Federalists	Democratic-Republicans
★ Wanted a strong national government.	★ Favored strong state governments and a weak national government.
★ Favored a "loose construction" of the Constitution.	★ Favored a "strict construction" of the Constitution.
★ Wanted to promote manufacturing and trade. They favored merchants and bankers.	★ Favored independent farmers.
★ Thought that the wealthy and best-educated Americans should control the government.	★ Were friendly to France.
★ Were friendly to Great Britain.	★ Were strongest in the South and West.
★ Were strongest in the Northeast.	

The Northwestern Frontier

As late as 1790, Indian tribes in the Northwest Territory were still attacking frontier settlements. Some British officers helped them by providing guns. Chiefs Little Turtle and Blue Jacket attacked settlers in Ohio. In November 1791, Chief Blue Jacket defeated a small force led by the Governor of the Northwest Territory. Washington sent General Anthony Wayne to Ohio to fight the Indians there. General Wayne defeated Blue Jacket at the **Fallen Timbers Battle** (1794). In 1795, Blue Jacket and other tribal leaders signed a treaty giving up most of the Ohio Territory to the United States. This finally opened up the Northwest Territory to American settlements.

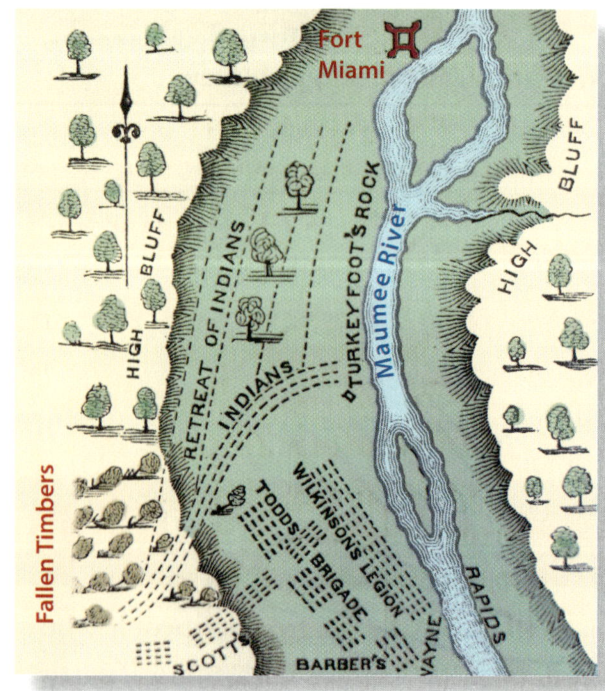

Battle of Fallen Timbers

Domestic and Foreign Policy

Domestic policy consists of all government decisions and policies that concern activities *within* the nation. These include taxes, law enforcement, personal rights, and rules on business conducted within the country. **Foreign policy** consists of a nation's actions towards *other countries.* In this chapter so far, you have learned about Washington's domestic policy. In the next section, you will learn about his foreign policy.

The Challenge of the French Revolution

Federalists and Democratic-Republicans moved farther apart because of events in France. The American Revolution had placed **King Louis XVI** of France in debt. In 1788, the King called on his nobles for help. They insisted that he summon an **Estates General**. This was an assembly representing all the social classes of France. Influenced by Enlightenment ideas and the example of America, middle-class members of the Estates General demanded sweeping reforms. Poorer citizens in Paris also became involved. In July 1789, they attacked the **Bastille**—an old fortress in the center of Paris that served as a prison. Jefferson was living in Paris when the revolution first began. He looked with pride on these early events, which he believed were inspired by the American Revolution.

By 1793, the French Revolution had turned violent. Many French citizens were arrested and killed. Louis XVI was executed in front of a crowd of thousands. A few months later, France and Britain went to war.

Despite the violence, Jefferson remained sympathetic to the French Republic. John Adams and Alexander Hamilton took a different view. They were shocked at French mob violence. They preferred the calm stability of England.

The Proclamation of Neutrality

Once France and Britain were at war, many Americans felt the United States should help France. After all, just a few years earlier the French had helped Americans against Britain.

However, President Washington wanted to stay out of European wars. He declared that the United States would remain **neutral** (*not take either side*) in his **Proclamation of Neutrality**:

> *"The duty and interest of the United States require that they should with sincerity and good faith adopt and pursue a conduct friendly and impartial [not partial or biased] towards the belligerent powers [the countries at war]."*

Citizen Genêt

The French Ambassador to the United States was Edmond-Charles Genêt. During the French Revolution, Frenchmen referred to each other as "citizen," so Genêt became known as **Citizen Genêt**. Citizen Genêt believed that the American public was friendly to the French Republic. He went to Charlestown to hire American captains to attack British ships. His actions caused a scandal. President Washington finally asked Citizen Genêt to leave the country.

Two Treaties

The Jay Treaty. With war in Europe raging, the British navy began seizing (*taking*) American ships carrying sugar from the West Indies to France. Americans were angry, but Washington did not want a war with Britain any more than with France. He sent **John Jay** to London for discussions with the British. The British agreed to pay American merchants for their losses. They also agreed to give up the forts they still held in the Northwest Territory. Jay agreed that Americans should pay any debts owed to the British. A new treaty was signed with these terms. The British would not agree, however, to stop searching American ships. Jefferson opposed the Jay Treaty, but it was approved in the Senate.

Pinckney's Treaty. Spain also became involved in the war in Europe. After receiving news of the Jay Treaty, the Spanish government made an offer to Thomas Pinckney, an American official in Spain. They offered to allow Americans to use the port of New Orleans. They also reached an agreement with Pinckney on where the northern boundary of Florida should be. These terms were put into another treaty, which was also approved by the Senate.

The Historian's Apprentice

Discuss the following questions with a partner. Then share your conclusions with the class.

1. If you had lived in America at this time, would you have been a Federalist or a Democratic-Republican? Explain why.
2. Do you think Washington's domestic or foreign policy was more important?
3. If you had been a member of the Senate in the 1790s, would you have approved the Jay and Pinckney Treaties? Explain your position.

The "Whiskey Rebellion"

Farmers in western Pennsylvania were especially hard hit by Hamilton's new whiskey tax. They held several conventions outside Pittsburgh in protest. They attacked tax collectors and refused to pay the tax. In August 1794, a large number of armed farmers gathered in protest. They threatened resistance and carried banners with the famous slogan of the French Revolution: "Liberty, Equality and Fraternity (*brotherhood*)." Washington and Hamilton decided to use armed force to put down the rebellion. They hoped this would strengthen the authority of the federal

Washington leading troops in 1794

government. Washington collected a force of 13,000 made up of various state militia. His army was as large as any he had commanded during the Revolution. Rather than fight, the rebel army simply dissolved. The farmers returned to their homes. The power and authority of the federal government had been successfully upheld.

The Historian's Apprentice

Make your own Venn diagram comparing Shays' Rebellion and the Whiskey Rebellion. Show both similarities and differences.

Washington's Farewell Address

By 1796, Washington had served two terms as President. Many wanted him to serve for a third term, but Washington refused. Before leaving office, he put a message in the newspapers with parting advice for the new nation. It is known as his "Farewell Address." Washington's address attacked the rising party spirit and geographic differences that were dividing Americans. "The name of American," Washington wrote, should bring greater pride than membership in any particular region or group. "Your union," he reminded Americans, should be the "main prop [*support*] of your liberty."

Washington also spoke about the dangers to America from foreign powers. He urged his countrymen to avoid alliances in Europe and to focus on their own hemisphere. Europeans had entered a long war, and Washington was sure it would be better for Americans to stay out of it. He advised:

"The great rule of conduct for us in regard to foreign nations is in extending [stretching] our commercial relations, to have with them as little political connection as possible. . . . Europe has a set of primary [main] interests which to us have none; or a very remote relation. Hence she must be engaged in frequent controversies, the causes of which are essentially foreign to our concerns . . . It is our true policy to steer clear of permanent alliances with any portion [part] of the foreign world . . .

The Historian's Apprentice

1. Why was Washington so suspicious of political parties?
2. Why did Washington advise his countrymen to "steer clear of permanent alliances" with other countries?
3. What advice would you have given to Americans in 1796? Imagine that you are George Washington. Write a paragraph that you think he should have included in his "Farewell Address."

Imagine that you have been invited to give a speech at George Washington's funeral in 1799. Write a short speech describing some of his accomplishments. Focus your speech on his time as President. Include the obstacles he faced and how he overcame them. Consider why many people saw him as a model of civic virtue.

Chapter Review Cards

Challenges of the First Presidency

- In 1789, George Washington became the first President of the United States.
- He faced many challenges: to set up the new government, to repay debts from the Revolutionary War, to stop the Indian attacks on settlers in the Northwest Territory, and to deal with foreign powers.

Precedent

- Washington knew many of his actions would establish **precedents**—the first time something was done, which would be copied by others in the future.

The Cabinet

- Washington appointed the heads of government departments. Thomas Jefferson was the first **Secretary of State**, handling foreign affairs. Alexander Hamilton was the first **Secretary of the Treasury**, handling the nation's finances.
- These heads of departments met together in regular meetings as Washington's **Cabinet**. The Cabinet advises the President.

Supreme Court

- Washington appointed John Jay to be the first **Chief Justice** of the Supreme Court.
- Congress passed the **Judiciary Act of 1789** creating a system of federal courts below the Supreme Court. Congress also proposed the **Bill of Rights**, which became the first ten amendments to the Constitution in 1791.

Hamilton's Financial Plan: Establishing Credit and Paying the Debt

- **Alexander Hamilton** explained that it was essential for the new nation to have good credit.
- Hamilton proposed that the federal government should pay the nation's debts from the Revolutionary War. It should give out new government bonds to replace the older war bonds. The government would then pay interest on these new bonds.
- Hamilton also proposed that the federal government pay the states' war debts.
- Jefferson and Madison objected that wealthy investors had bought the war bonds from poor farmers and shopkeepers at very low prices. If the government now paid the debt in full, the rich would simply become richer.
- They also complained that Virginia and other Southern states had already paid off their war debts. Now Hamilton was asking them to contribute to the national government to repay the debts of other states.
- The plan seemed to favor the North over the South.
- A compromise was reached. Hamilton won on his debt proposals, but the new U.S. capital would be located in the South at Washington, D.C., along the Potomac River.

Hamilton's Financial Plan: The National Bank

- Hamilton's plan also called for the creation of a national bank.
- Thomas Jefferson objected that the Constitution did not give Congress the power to do this. He was a "**strict constructionist.**" This meant he interpreted the Constitution strictly.
- Hamilton was a "**loose constructionist**." This meant he thought that the Constitution should be interpreted loosely.
- Since the Constitution gave Congress the power to do anything "**necessary and proper**" for fulfilling its duties, Hamilton argued that it gave Congress the power to create a national bank.
- President Washington and the Congress agreed with Hamilton. The first **Bank of the United States** was founded in Philadelphia in 1791.

Hamilton's Financial Plan: Tariffs and the Whiskey Tax

- Hamilton's plan called for tariffs on imports. This meant special taxes on goods coming into the United States from other countries.
- Hamilton's tariff would protect Northern industries, which were just getting started, by making British manufactured goods more expensive.
- Southern farmers did not like taxing imports because this raised the prices of goods they needed to buy.
- To raise more money for the federal government, Hamilton also proposed a tax on whiskey made by western farmers. The **whiskey tax** was passed by Congress in 1791. Hamilton's proposals helped merchants and manufacturers but hurt farmers.

The Rise of Political Parties

- A **political party** is a group of people who share similar views and support candidates to public office.
- The disagreement over Hamilton's plan led to the rise of political parties.
- Those who supported Hamilton were known as **Federalists**. (They took their name from the original supporters of the Constitution during the debates over ratification.) Federalists wanted a strong federal government. They favored the interests of merchants, manufacturers and bankers.
- Those who opposed his plan, like Jefferson and Madison, became **Democratic-Republicans**. They wanted a weaker federal government. They favored the interests of farmers.

Stopping Indian Attacks in the Northwest

- The Northwest Territory opened to settlers when General Anthony Wayne defeated Chief Blue Jacket and his warriors at the Battle of Fallen Timbers in 1794.

Washington's Foreign Policy

- While Washington was President, a revolution broke out in France. The French Revolutionaries executed the King and became involved in a war with Britain and the other powers of Europe.
- Jefferson and the Democratic-Republicans remained friendly towards France. Hamilton and the Federalists favored Britain.
- In conducting **foreign policy** (which consists of the actions taken towards other countries), Washington declared in his **Proclamation of Neutrality** that the United States would remain **neutral**. It would be "friendly and impartial" to countries at war.
- The United States concluded two treaties: the **Jay Treaty** dealt with the British seizing American ships headed to France carrying sugar and other foods. Britain agreed to pay Americans for their losses and to give up forts in the Northwest. Americans agreed to pay any debts owed to the British.
- In the **Pinckney Treaty**, Spain offered Americans the use of the port of New Orleans. They also agreed on the northern boundary of Florida.

Upholding Federal Authority

- Farmers in western Pennsylvania, who opposed the whiskey tax, rebelled.
- Washington marched against the rebels with a force of 13,000 troops.
- Rather than fight, the western farmers simply returned home.
- Federal power and authority were upheld.

Washington's Farewell Address

- When Washington finished his two terms in office, he refused a third term.
- In his "**Farewell Address**," he opposed the rise of parties. He reminded Americans that "Your union" should be "the main prop" of your liberty.
- He also warned about the dangers from foreign powers, and urged Americans to avoid alliances with Europe.

Precedent:
The first time something is done

The Presidency of George Washington

Northwest Territory
- Americans defeat Indians at Battle of Fallen Timbers, opening Ohio to settlement

Bill of Rights

Setting up a New Government

Cabinet
- Secretary of State: Jefferson

- Secretary of the Treasury: Hamilton

Judiciary Act of 1789
- Set up lower courts

Hamilton's Financial Plan
- The federal government will pay its war debts to have good credit
- The federal government will pay the states' war debts
- A protective tariff to protect American manufacturers
- A national bank to help the government conduct its functions
- A tax on whiskey to raise revenue

Whiskey Rebellion (1794)
- Washington and Hamilton threaten to use force to put down unrest

First Political Parties: Groups of people who share ideas and support candidates to political office
- Jefferson and Madison oppose Hamilton's financial plan
- Jefferson was a "strict" constructionist; Hamilton was a "loose" constructionist
- Hamilton's supporters known as the Federalists
- Jefferson's supporters known as the Democratic-Republicans

Federalists	Democratic-Republica
★ Wanted a strong national government.	★ Favored strong state government weak national government.
★ Favored a "loose construction" of the Constitution.	★ Favored a "strict construction" of t Constitution.
★ Wanted to promote manufacturing and trade. They favored merchants and bankers.	★ Favored independent farmers.
★ Thought that the wealthy and best-educated Americans should control the government.	★ Were friendly to France.
★ Were friendly to Great Britain.	★ Were strongest in the South and W
★ Were strongest in the Northeast.	

Impact of the French Revolution
- French people overthrow their rulers
- French Revolution grows violent
- France and Britain go to war in 1793
- Washington's Proclamation of Neutrality
- Jay Treaty-avoids war with Britain
- Pinckney Treaty-allows Americans to use port of New Orleans

Washington's Farewell Address (1796)
- Attacks political parties
- Advises Americans to avoid entangling alliances with Europe

What do you know?

SS.6.A.3.12

1. Which action of President George Washington had the most lasting influence in creating a precedent for the federal government?

   A. signing treaties with Britain and Spain

   B. using the army to enforce the Whiskey Tax

   C. creating the First National Bank of the United States

   D. establishing a Cabinet of department heads to advise the President

SS.6.A.3.12

2. The passage below is from President George Washington's Farewell Address in 1796.

   > *The great rule of conduct for us in regard to foreign nations is, in extending our commercial [business] relations, to have with them as little political connection as possible. So far as we have already formed engagements let them be fulfilled with perfect good faith. Here let us stop . . . . It is our true policy to steer clear of permanent alliances with any portion of the foreign world.*

   Based on the passage, with which statement would President Washington have most likely agreed?

   A. There are no threats to the security of the United States.

   B. Permanent alliances with foreign nations should be avoided.

   C. Foreign nations profit too much by importing American goods.

   D. Permanent alliances should be a part of every nation's foreign policy.

SS.6.A.3.12

3. The list below summarizes part of Alexander Hamilton's financial plan for the United States.

   1. The United States should pay its debts from the war.

   2. The federal government should pay the war debts of the states.

   3. The federal government should issue new government bonds to cover the debt. These bonds should pay interest. People will be able to rely on these bonds as a form of money.

   How did these recommendations influence the development of the new nation?

   A. They helped the new nation establish good public credit.

   B. They made it difficult for Americans to trade with other countries.

   C. They benefited farmers who had borrowed money during the war.

   D. They helped shopkeepers and farmers who had supplied the Continental Army.

SS.6.A.3.12

4. The Venn diagram below shows features of the Federalists and Democratic-Republicans.

Federalists	Both	Democratic-Republicans
Favored Hamilton's financial plan. Friendly to Britain.	?	Opposed Hamilton's financial plan. Friendly to France.

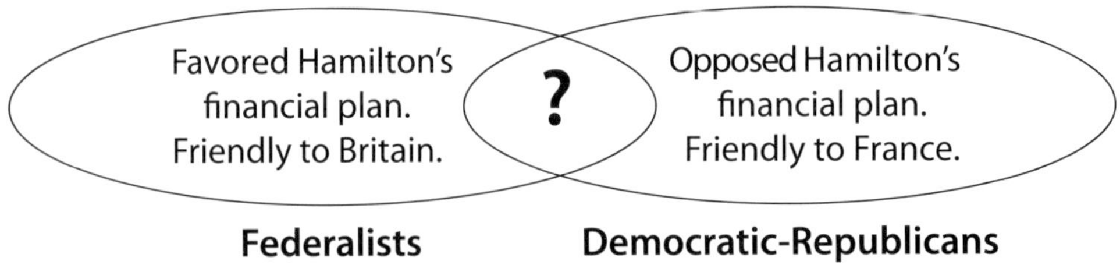

Which best completes the Venn diagram?

A. Became the first political parties
B. Believed in a strong central government
C. Opposed ratification of the U.S. Constitution
D. Believed that manufacturing was more important than farming

SS.6.A.3.12

5. The chart below summarizes characteristics of the Federalists and Democratic-Republicans.

Federalists were in favor of:	Democratic-Republicans were in favor of:
Rule by an educated, wealthy class	Rule by common people
A strong federal government	Strong state governments
Emphasis on manufacturing	Emphasis on agriculture
A "loose" interpretation of the Constitution	A "strict" interpretation of the Constitution
A British alliance	A French alliance
National bank	State banks
Protective tariffs	Free trade

What was an important consequence of these differences?

A. The Democratic-Republicans decided to re-write the Constitution.
B. Increasing differences arose between the North and South.
C. The Democratic-Republicans created a stronger central government.
D. The Federalists refused to hand over power to the Democratic-Republicans in 1800.

SS.8.C.1.3

6. How did George Washington demonstrate qualities of civic virtue?

A. He freed his slaves after his death.
B. He helped to write the Declaration of Independence.
C. He tried to ambush French soldiers in the French and Indian War.
D. He was willing to serve his country as commander of the Continental Army and as President.

SS.6.A.3.12

7. The beliefs below were expressed in the 1790s, during George Washington's first term as President.

1. The federal government should not pay the debts of states because this would be unfair to those states that had already paid their debts.
2. The federal government should not place a protective tariff on imported manufactured goods because this hurts American farmers.
3. The Constitution should be interpreted strictly.

Which pair of leaders would have agreed with these views?

A. John Marshall and John Adams
B. Thomas Jefferson and James Madison
C. Benjamin Franklin and Thomas Jefferson
D. Alexander Hamilton and George Washington

SS.8.E.2.2

8. The chart below summarizes Alexander Hamilton's financial plan for the new nation, 1790–1792.

Hamilton's Plan			
Repay the Debt	**National Bank**	**Whiskey Tax**	**Protective Tariff**
The national government should pay off the debts of both the states and the national government to establish the nation's credit.	The creation of a national bank would provide a place to deposit taxes, provide a sound currency, and make loans to the national government.	A tax on whiskey would raise money from western farmers.	A tariff would protect American industries from foreign competition.

Based on the chart, what was Alexander Hamilton's chief goal as Secretary of the Treasury?

A. to build a strong national economy
B. to replace the Articles of Confederation
C. to encourage cheap British imports into the United States
D. to increase the powers of Congress over interstate commerce

SS.6.A.3.12

9. How was the outcome of the Whiskey Rebellion important to the development of the new nation?

A. It proved to foreign nations that the U.S. government was still weak.
B. It reduced Alexander Hamilton's influence over the national economy.
C. It increased the power of the individual state governments over new taxes.
D. It demonstrated the power of the new federal government to enforce its policies.

SS.6.A.3.12

10. The excerpt below is from President George Washington's Proclamation of Neutrality in 1793.

> *The duty and interest of the United States require that they should adopt a conduct friendly and impartial toward the [warring] powers. I have thought fit to declare the position of the United States to observe a conduct towards those powers respectfully; and warn our citizens to avoid all acts which may in any manner tend to [go against] this position.*

Why did President Washington issue this document?

A. He believed the United States should try to avoid any involvement in European wars.

B. He thought the United States was required by treaty to come to the defense of France.

C. He wanted to respond to those demanding revenge for the death of King Louis XVI of France.

D. He knew the British Royal Navy was stopping American merchant ships in its search for deserters.

SS.6.A.3.12

11. The drawing below shows the execution of Louis XVI during the French Revolution.

How did this event affect Americans?

A. Americans decided that they should make George Washington their King.

B. Federalists were shocked while Democratic-Republicans remained friendly to France.

C. Americans rejected Hamilton's financial plan because they feared instability in troubled times.

D. Americans wanted to ally with the French, who had helped them during the American Revolution.

CHAPTER 9 The Young Republic: America under Presidents Adams and Jefferson

SS.6.A.3.13 Explain major domestic and international economic, military, political, and socio-cultural events of John Adams' presidency.

SS.6.A.3.14 Explain major domestic and international economic, military, political, and socio-cultural events of Thomas Jefferson's presidency.

SS.6.A.4.12 Examine the effects of the 1804 Haitian Revolution on the United States acquisition of the Louisiana Territory.

SS.6.A.3.16 Examine key events in Florida history as each impacts this era of American history.

SS.6.A.4.8 Describe the influence of individuals on social and political developments of this era in American history.

SS.6.E.3.1 Evaluate domestic and international interdependence.

Alignment to Grade 7 Civics Standards

SS.7.C.3.3 Illustrate the structure and function (three branches of government established in Articles I, II, and III with corresponding powers) of government in the United States as established in the Constitution.

SS.7.C.3.8 Analyze the structure, functions, and processes of the legislative, executive, and judicial branches.

SS.7.C.3.12 Analyze the significance and outcomes of landmark Supreme Court cases including, but not limited to, *Marbury v. Madison* . . .

SS.7.C.4.1 Differentiate concepts related to U.S. domestic and foreign policy.

Terms and Names You Should Know

Bribery

Alien

Sedition

Alien and Sedition Acts

Resolution

Kentucky and Virginia Resolutions

Inaugural Address

Violate

Majority

Napoleon Bonaparte

Louisiana Purchase

Chief Justice John Marshall

Marbury v. Madison

Judicial Review

Blockade

Embargo

Boycott

Raising the American flag in New Orleans for the first time in March 1804.

Florida "Keys" to Learning

1. John Adams was elected the second President of the United States in 1796. Adams was a Federalist who favored a strong and stable central government.

2. The French were angry at the United States for signing the Jay Treaty with Britain and began attacking American ships. Adams sent negotiators to Paris to see the French foreign minister Prince Talleyrand. Talleyrand insisted the American officials pay bribes to three French officials before he talk to them. This became known as the "XYZ" affair and outraged the Congress, leading to an undeclared "quasi-war" between the United States and France. Relations did not improve until 1800.

3. Adams worried about potential spies. Congress passed the Alien and Sedition Acts, which gave the President the power to send any foreigner out of the country, to imprison any foreigner whose country was at war with the United States, and to fine or imprison anyone who spoke or wrote against the government. Madison and Jefferson believed these acts violated the Bill of Rights. They wrote the Kentucky and Virginia Resolutions, claiming that individual states could reject the federal laws they believed to be unconstitutional.

4. In 1800, Jefferson was elected President of the United States. He considered his election the "Revolution of 1800" because power peacefully passed to an opposing party.

5. Jefferson opposed a strong central government. He cut spending on the army and navy, and ended the whiskey tax. However, he went to war with the Barbary States for attacking American ships.

6. Jefferson also purchased the Louisiana Territory from France in 1803. This purchase almost doubled the size of the United States. Napoleon sold Louisiana to the United States when he could not restore Haiti to French control. Jefferson sent Meriwether Lewis and William Clark to explore the Louisiana Territory.

7. In the decision of *Marbury v. Madison* (1803), John Marshall established the Supreme Court's power of judicial review—its power to determine whether laws are constitutional. Marbury sued Madison for not giving him his commission. Under the Judiciary Act of 1789, the Supreme Court had the power to order a government official to perform his duties. However, Chief Justice Marshall concluded that this part of the Judiciary Act of 1798 was unconstitutional.

8. In 1804, Alexander Hamilton was killed in a duel by Vice President Aaron Burr.

9. Jefferson was re-elected in 1804. He spent most of his second term dealing with foreign affairs. Economic warfare between France and Britain placed American merchants in a difficult situation. The British Royal Navy started seizing American ships to inspect them for British deserters. If any were found, they were taken back into service. This practice is known as impressment. The British also took many innocent American sailors.

10. In 1807, a British warship attacked the *Chesapeake*, a U.S. warship that refused to be searched. This led to a public outcry for war. Jefferson did not want to enter into a conflict and instead pushed the Embargo Act of 1807 through Congress. This law prohibited Americans from exporting goods to foreign countries until Britain and France lifted their restrictions on neutral shipping.

Despite the warning in George Washington's "Farewell Address," Americans remained divided along party lines. For the next twenty years, the rivalry between Federalists and Democratic-Republicans continued to affect the nation.

The Presidency of John Adams

The second President of the United States, John Adams, was well known to most Americans. He had pushed for American independence. He had helped negotiate the treaty ending the Revolutionary War. He had served as ambassador to Britain and as the first Vice President of the United States.

Like Hamilton, Adams was a Federalist who favored a strong and stable government. He looked with horror at the events of the French Revolution, which had led to mob violence and war.

In the election of 1796, Adams narrowly defeated Thomas Jefferson. The biggest challenge Adams faced as he began his term was the continuing war between Britain and France. Although friendly to Britain, Adams preferred Washington's policy of avoiding any direct involvement in the conflict.

The "XYZ" Affair

The French were angry at the United States for signing the Jay Treaty with Britain. They began attacking American ships. Adams sent negotiators to Paris to see the French foreign minister, Prince Talleyrand. Talleyrand insisted that the Americans pay bribes to three French officials before he would even talk with them.

The American negotiators refused and left. News leaked to the American press. The newspapers referred to the bribery request as the **"XYZ" affair** because the unnamed French officials were called X, Y, and Z. Congress was outraged. It increased the size of both the army and the navy. American ships began attacking French ships in an undeclared "**quasi-war**," which lasted from 1798 to 1800 (*quasi* means "almost"). The government created the **Department of the Navy** and started building new ships. Relations between France and the United States did not improve until 1800, when there was a change of government in France.

A cartoon criticizing the French request for bribes

The Alien and Sedition Acts

Many immigrants were coming to America from Britain, Ireland, and France. Some of the newcomers became active in American politics. Adams feared that some of them might actually be spies. Congress passed the **Alien and Sedition Acts**, which Adams signed into law early in 1798.

> An **alien** is a foreigner living in the United States. **Sedition** is any speech, writing, or act that encourages people to rebel against their government.

FIFTH CONGRESS OF THE UNITED STATES:

At the Second Sesion.

Begun and held at the city of *Philadelphia*, in the ftate of PENNSYLVANIA, on *Monday*, the thirteenth of *November*, one thoufand feven hundred and ninety-feven.

An ACT *in addition to the act, entitled "An Act for the punishment of certain crimes against the United States."*

BE it enacted by the Senate and Houfe of Reprefentatives of the United States of America, in Congrefs affembled. *That if any persons shall unlawfully combine or conspire together, with intent to oppose any measure or measures of the government of the United States, ...*

One of the Alien and Sedition Acts

Each branch of government has different powers. This law briefly increased the executive power exercised by the President.

The Alien Acts increased the length of time that a foreigner had to live in the United States before becoming a citizen. They gave the President the power to send any foreigner out of the country. They also gave the President the power to put in jail or send out of the country any foreigner whose country was at war with the United States. The Sedition Act permitted the President to fine or send to jail anyone who spoke or wrote against the government. Several writers were actually thrown into jail based on the new law.

The Historian's Apprentice

[I]t shall be lawful for the President of the United States . . . to order all such aliens as he shall judge dangerous to the peace and safety of the United States, or shall have reasonable grounds to suspect are concerned in any treasonable or secret machinations against the government thereof, to depart out of the territory of the United States . . .

—An Act Concerning Aliens, Section 1 (November 13, 1797)

[I]f any person shall write, print, utter or publish . . . any false, scandalous and malicious writing or writings against the government of the United States, or either house of the Congress of the United States, or the President of the United States. ... then such person, being thereof convicted before any court of the United States having [authority] thereof, shall be punished by a fine not exceeding two thousand dollars, and by imprisonment not exceeding two years.

—The Sedition Act, Section 2 (November 13, 1797)

Read the excerpts above from the Alien and Sedition Acts and discuss the following questions with a partner. Then share your responses with your class.

1. Did Section 1 of the Alien Act give too much power to the President?
2. Did Section 2 of the Sedition Act violate (*go against*) the rights of free speech and free press in the First Amendment?

The Kentucky and Virginia Resolutions

Madison and Jefferson believed the Alien and Sedition Acts **violated** (*went against*) the Bill of Rights. They wrote resolutions that were passed by the state legislatures of Kentucky and Virginia in 1798 and 1799.

These resolutions argued that the federal union was a "compact"—an association by agreement—of states. If the federal government exercised powers that did not belong to it, the states had the right to reject those actions.

Based on this reasoning, the Kentucky and Virginia legislatures declared that the Alien and Sedition Acts would not be enforced in their states because Congress had no power to limit free speech.

The Historian's Apprentice

1. Discuss the following questions with a partner:
   - Were the Alien and Sedition Acts constitutional?
   - Should individual states have the power to declare federal laws invalid (*not enforceable*) within their own borders? What is your view?
2. Imagine you are living in Virginia in 1798. Write a letter to the editor of your local newspaper either for or against the Kentucky and Virginia Resolutions.

The Presidency of Thomas Jefferson

The "Revolution of 1800"

The election of 1800 was a bitterly fought contest between John Adams and Thomas Jefferson. Adams had served only one term so far. The quasi-war with France and the Alien and Sedition Acts had made him very unpopular.

Jefferson and the Democratic-Republicans won a great victory. Jefferson became the next President. His political party won a **majority** (*more than half the members*) in each house of Congress. It was the first time that power peacefully changed hands from one party to an opposing one. Jefferson considered this transfer of power to be a "revolution."

Jefferson hoped that the United States would become a democracy of self-reliant citizens. (A self-reliant person doesn't rely on others.) His ideal was the independent farmer who worked his own land. Jefferson wanted a smaller government, not a larger one. He disliked the bankers and merchants whom Hamilton had favored.

In his Inaugural Address, Jefferson made an appeal to all Americans. He

> Let us, then, fellow-citizens, unite with one heart and one mind. . . . We are all Republicans, we are all Federalists. . . . Let us, then, with courage and confidence pursue our own Federal and Republican principles, our attachment to union and representative government.
>
> —Thomas Jefferson,
> First Inaugural Address, March 4, 1801

The Barbary States of North Africa

reminded them that, despite party differences, they all shared common principles.

Jefferson called for "a wise and frugal government" that left citizens free to follow their own pursuits. "This," he concluded, "is the sum of good government." He wanted to maintain peace, avoid "permanent alliances" with foreign countries, encourage agriculture and commerce, and promote freedom of religion, speech, and the press.

Cutting Down the Size of Government

A dictator is someone who uses force to have total power over a nation.

Jefferson was lucky when his first term began. The worst crisis in France appeared to be over. A successful general named **Napoleon Bonaparte** had seized power and brought stability. Bonaparte made himself dictator and signed a peace treaty with Britain. With peace in Europe, Jefferson was able to cut spending on the army and navy. He ended the hated whiskey tax and reduced the national debt.

The First Barbary War

Jefferson was willing to protect national interests when necessary. He refused to pay **tribute** (*money*) to the Barbary States along the coasts of North Africa. When this was not paid, the ruler of the state of Tripoli attacked American merchant ships. Jefferson sent the U.S. Navy across the Atlantic. It conducted a blockade of Tripoli. U.S. Marines captured the city of Derna in Tripoli early in 1805. This allowed the United States to bargain for the freedom of American hostages and a promise from the ruler of Tripoli to stop his attacks on American ships.

Attack on Derna

The Louisiana Purchase

The **Louisiana Territory** had belonged to Spain since the end of the French and Indian War. In 1800, Napoleon forced Spain to give the Louisiana Territory back to France. Napoleon had

The Haitian Revolution and Napoleon's Dreams of Empire

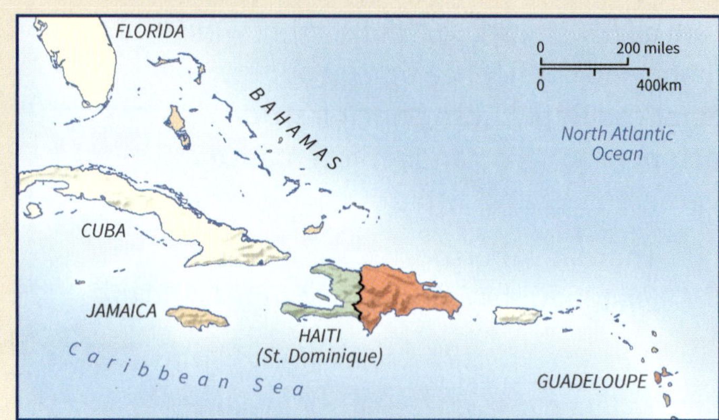

Haiti is the western part of Hispaniola, an island in the Caribbean. When the French Revolution declared the equality of man, slaves in Haiti rebelled against their masters. After some delay, the French legislature outlawed slavery in the colonies in 1794. General **Toussaint L'Ouverture** defended Haiti against British and Spanish troops that tried to conquer Haiti and restore slavery. He wrote a constitution for the island. L'Ouverture prohibited slavery but also made himself dictator, like Napoleon Bonaparte in France. Napoleon sent an army to Haiti with the goal of restoring slavery. He tricked L'Ouverture, who surrendered and died in a cold prison cell in the French Alps.

Napoleon successfully restored slavery on the nearby island of Guadeloupe in 1802. This led Haitians to rebel again. They declared their independence from France in 1803. Haiti became the first country of former slaves to declare its independence. Once Napoleon realized he could not reconquer Haiti, his dreams for a new French Empire in North America collapsed. He suddenly became willing to sell the Louisiana Territory to the United States.

plans to create a new French empire in North America. France would control Haiti and other islands in the Caribbean Sea, the port of New Orleans on the Gulf of Mexico, and all lands west of the Mississippi.

In those days, western farmers sent their crops in flatboats down the Mississippi River. The crops were loaded onto ships in New Orleans, where the Mississippi River empties into the Gulf of Mexico. The rights of Americans to use the port had been guaranteed by Spain in the Pinckney Treaty. The return of Louisiana to France threatened those rights.

Jefferson sent negotiators to Paris to see if the United States could purchase the city of New Orleans from France. Instead, Napoleon surprisingly offered to sell the whole Louisiana Territory to the United States for the bargain price of $15 million.

Jefferson snapped up the offer. Nothing in the Constitution gave him the power to make such

Map of Lewis and Clark's route

a purchase. Yet Jefferson put all his doubts aside. The Louisiana Purchase was just too good to turn down. The Louisiana Purchase doubled the size of the United States. It ended French claims to North America. Finally, it put the United States on the road to further westward expansion.

Meriwether Lewis and William Clark

The Lewis and Clark Expedition (1804–1806)

Jefferson was a scientist as well as a government official. He wanted to learn as much as he could about America's new territories. Most of this land was still unknown to Americans. Jefferson sent **Meriwether Lewis** and **William Clark** (a younger brother of General George Rogers Clark) to explore the new territory. He asked them to collect information about its geography, Indian tribes, and plant and wildlife. Lewis, Clark, and their "Corps of Discovery" (about 50 men) set out from St. Louis in May 1804. They crossed the Mississippi River, went up the Missouri River, crossed the Rocky Mountains, and traveled through the Oregon Territory to reach the Pacific Ocean in November 1805. Then they turned around to make the trip back. It took more than two years to make the entire journey of 7,000 miles. They

were greatly helped by **Sacajawea**, an Indian woman who went with them from North Dakota to the Pacific Ocean. She acted as an interpreter and guide. She also helped make trades with tribes along the way.

Sacajawea helped guide Lewis and Clark

The Supreme Court: *Marbury v. Madison* (1803)

One of the most important events during Jefferson's Presidency was a decision by the U.S. Supreme Court. The head of the Court, known as the Chief Justice, was **John Marshall**. Marshall was a Federalist who believed in strengthening the power of the national government. In the case of ***Marbury v. Madison***, Marshall established the Court's power of **judicial review**—its power to judge whether laws are constitutional. This power still affects us today.

Factual Background

During the last months of the Adams Presidency, Federalists in Congress strengthened the federal judiciary by passing the **Judiciary Act of 1801**. This act created several new federal judgeships. President Adams acted quickly to fill these and other posts with Federalists. The Senate only confirmed these nominations on his last day in office. Because Adams was supposedly still filling these posts at midnight, they became known as the "**Midnight Judges**."

As Secretary of State, John Marshall had helped Adams to select these nominations. At the same time, Marshall had just recently been appointed as Chief Justice of the Supreme Court. In the last month of Adams' Presidency, Marshall actually filled both roles.

William Marbury was one of Adams' last-minute appointments. Marbury did not receive his commission (*the official letter with his appointment*) before Adams left office. Jefferson's Secretary of State, **James Madison**, then refused to deliver it to him.

Marbury's Lawsuit

Marbury sued Madison for failing to deliver his commission. The Judiciary Act of 1789 gave the U.S. Supreme Court the power to order a government official to perform his duties. Marbury sued in the Supreme Court, seeking a court order to Madison to deliver his commission.

The case put Chief Justice Marshall in an awkward situation. Could he be impartial under these circumstances?

The Decision

Chief Justice Marshall came to a surprising conclusion. He decided that part of the Judiciary Act of 1789 was unconstitutional.

The Constitution of the United States had listed the cases that the Supreme Court could hear directly. These were cases in which states or foreign countries were parties to the lawsuit. All other cases could only be brought before the Supreme Court on appeal—after a lower court had heard the case and reached a decision.

In the Judiciary Act of 1789, Congress expanded the Supreme Court's "original jurisdiction"—the cases it could decide directly. Marshall said this expansion of the Court's powers violated (*went against*) the Constitution. Because the Constitution already listed the cases that the Supreme Court could hear directly, only an amendment to the Constitution could change this list. That part of the Judiciary Act that added to the types of cases the Court could hear was therefore invalid. Because of this, the Court did not have the power to hear Marbury's complaint or to issue an order to Madison to deliver Marbury's commission.

Significance

The case was important because it established the Supreme Court's power to determine the constitutionality of laws passed by Congress.

The Historian's Apprentice

In *Marbury v. Madison*, Chief Justice Marshall reasoned as follows:

1. The Constitution is the "fundamental," or most basic, law of the United States.
2. When the Constitution and an ordinary law are in conflict, the Constitution must be upheld.
3. It is the job of the Supreme Court to interpret and apply the law. "It is emphatically the province and duty of the Judicial Department to say what the law is."
4. It is the job of the Supreme Court to interpret both the Constitution and laws passed by Congress.
5. The Supreme Court can declare laws unconstitutional if it finds they conflict with the Constitution.
6. Unconstitutional laws are invalid and cannot be enforced.

Do you agree with Marshall's reasoning? Why or why not? Discuss this question with a partner and share your opinions with your class.

The Hamilton-Burr Duel (1804)

Alexander Hamilton

Aaron Burr

Americans were shocked when Jefferson's long-time political opponent **Alexander Hamilton** was killed in a duel in the summer of 1804.

The reasons for the duel went back to Jefferson's election. When the Constitution was first written, it gave each member of the Electoral College two votes. In the election of 1800, Thomas Jefferson and **Aaron Burr** ran together as Democratic-Republicans on the same "ticket." Jefferson was supposed to become President. All the Democratic-Republican electors voted for Jefferson and Burr, giving both men the same number of votes. This created a tie in the Electoral College.

The election went over to the House of Representatives. The House voted 36 times before a winner was declared. Although Jefferson and Hamilton had opposing views, Hamilton had a great dislike for Burr. He finally threw his support behind Jefferson, who became President. Burr held Hamilton responsible for his defeat.

Four years later, Burr blamed Hamilton again when Burr also lost the election for Governor of New York. Shortly after the election, Burr learned that Hamilton had made insulting comments about him at a dinner party. Burr, who was still Vice President, challenged Hamilton to a duel. Hamilton and Burr met in the woods in New Jersey on the morning of July 11, 1804. Hamilton's only son had been killed in a duel on the same spot three years earlier. According to some reports, Hamilton fired his pistol in the air. Burr fired back and hit Hamilton above the hip. Hamilton died the next day, while Burr's political career was finished.

The Duel

Jefferson's Second Term: Economic Warfare in Europe

Jefferson was re-elected in 1804. He spent most of his second term dealing with foreign affairs. In Europe, the peace made by Napoleon did not last long. By 1803, the other European powers were already forming a new alliance against him. Napoleon crowned himself Emperor of the French at the end of 1804. He defeated the other powers in an astounding victory in 1805. This brought much of the continent of Europe under Napoleon's control.

While the French were supreme on land, the British were supreme at sea. The **Royal Navy** (*the British navy*) defeated the French fleet, giving them command of the world's seas and oceans. Napoleon had no way to attack Britain, so he decided to use trade as a weapon. This was a new idea at the time. The French Emperor announced that people in France could no longer trade with Britain. Countries allied to France were also forced to participate in this boycott.

The British reacted by using their powerful navy to set up a blockade of Napoleonic Europe. They sealed off the French-controlled continent.

No one could sail in or out without their permission. Neutral American ships could still go to France, but only if they first stopped in British ports. British officials would inspect them to see if they carried prohibited war goods. Napoleon responded to the new British rules by threatening to seize any neutral ship that stopped at a British port.

American merchants were caught in the middle of this contest. It was impossible for them to obey both countries' requirements. At the same time, both the British and the French were eager for American crops and other goods. There were enormous profits to be made as well as risks.

The Embargo of 1807

Not only were the British attempting to control American trade, but their warships were also stopping American ships at sea. The British were boarding (*going on*) American ships to look for deserters from the Royal Navy. If any were found, they could be forced back into service. This practice was known as **impressment**. Even worse, such sailors might be hanged for desertion.

In fact, many British sailors had deserted to escape the harsh conditions and discipline of the Royal Navy. Some deserters found work on American ships, but the British were also taking innocent American sailors as well as actual deserters.

In 1807, a British warship attacked the *Chesapeake*, a warship in the U.S. Navy. The attack took place just off the coast of Virginia. The captain of the *Chesapeake* refused to be searched. The British fired and forced the *Chesapeake* to surrender. After searching the ship, the British took three sailors. One was hanged.

In the United States, there was a public outcry for war. Jefferson refused to bring Americans into the conflict in Europe. He was determined to keep the peace at almost any price. Instead of war, he pushed the **Embargo of 1807** through Congress. An **embargo** is a ban on trade. American ships were stopped from leaving American ports. The law stated that no goods could be shipped from the United States to any foreign ports at all until Britain and France ended their restrictions. Jefferson thought Britain and France needed American foodstuffs so badly they would change their rules.

Jefferson's embargo was unpopular across the country. American goods lay in warehouses instead of being sold to foreign buyers. Some merchants could not continue their businesses. western and southern farmers could not sell many of their crops. Jefferson's embargo probably hurt Americans far more than it harmed either the British or the French. Frustration with the embargo even helped to revive support for the Federalist Party. Thomas Jefferson's two terms as President, once so full of promise, ended on this unhappy note.

A cartoonist criticizes the Embargo of 1807. The word "embargo" has been rewritten as "o-grab-me."

The Historian's Apprentice

1. Jefferson feared that the United States might be drawn into the war in Europe. He thought it was better to delay joining that war as long as possible. Every twenty years, the United States was doubling its population. Jefferson therefore thought the country would be stronger in the future. Was he right to have acted as he did?
2. One Federalist complained that the Embargo of 1807 was like "cutting one's throat to cure a nosebleed." What did he mean by this?
3. Pretend it is 1807. Write a letter to a friend for or against the embargo.

President Jefferson defends the embargo.

John Adams and Thomas Jefferson were Presidents at a turbulent time in the life of the young republic. Britain and France were at war over the French Revolution. America's first political parties took sides in this contest.

The Federalists supported ______________________________
because ______________________________
______________________________.

The Democratic-Republicans supported ______________________________
because ______________________________
______________________________.

Congress passed the Alien and Sedition Acts when Adams was President. These stated
____
______________________________.

The acts were very unpopular because ______________________________
______________________________.

When Jefferson was President, Britain and France started attacking American merchant ships. Congress passed the Embargo Act of 1807. This law stated that ______________________________
______________________________.

The embargo was very unpopular because ______________________________
______________________________.

John Adams

Chapter Review Cards

The Presidency of John Adams

- John Adams, the second President of the United States, was a Federalist who believed in a strong and stable government.
- His biggest challenge was the continuing war between Britain and France.

The XYZ Affair

- The French were angry at the United States for signing the Jay Treaty with Britain, and they began attacking American ships. The French foreign minister, Prince Talleyrand, refused to even talk to the American negotiators unless they first paid bribes to three French officials. The negotiators refused and left.
- The American press, hearing of this news, referred to this bribery as the **"XYZ" affair**. "X, Y, and Z" stood for the three unnamed French officials. Congress was outraged, and the American Navy began attacking French ships from 1798 to 1800 in a "quasi-war" ("quasi" means almost).
- The government created the **Department of the Navy** and started building new ships. Relations only improved when there was a change of government in France.

The Alien and Sedition Acts

- Adams feared that some immigrants in America might be spies for France or Britain. Congress passed the Alien and Sedition Acts in 1798.
- The Alien Acts gave the President the power to: send a foreigner out of the country; put a foreigner whose country was at war with the U.S. in jail; fine or send to jail anyone who wrote or spoke against the government.
- The Alien Acts also increased the length of time a foreigner had to live in the United States before becoming a citizen.

The Kentucky and Virginia Resolutions

- In 1798 and 1799, Kentucky and Virginia passed laws that declared the Alien and Sedition Acts would not be enforced in their states. They claimed Congress had no right to limit free speech in violation of the Bill of Rights.
- Jefferson and Madison wrote these resolutions.

The Revolution of 1800 and the Presidency of Thomas Jefferson

- The "quasi-war" with France and the Alien and Sedition Acts made Adams very unpopular. When his first term was over, he lost the election of 1800 to Thomas Jefferson.
- Jefferson won the election and became the third President of the United States. His party, the Democratic-Republicans, won a majority of the seats in both the Senate and the House of Representatives. Jefferson considered this peaceful transfer of power between two opposing parties to be a "revolution." His ideal was the independent farmer. He also wanted a smaller government. He disliked bankers and merchants.
- He appealed to all Americans to work together to form "a wise and frugal government" that allowed citizens to be free to follow their own pursuits. He wanted peace and no entangling alliances with foreign countries. Jefferson encouraged agriculture and commerce. He also promoted freedom of speech, religion, and the press.

Cutting Down the Size of Government

- France made peace with Britain under **Napoleon Bonaparte**. With peace in Europe, Jefferson was able to cut spending on the army and navy. He ended the whiskey tax and reduced the national debt.

The First Barbary War

- Jefferson refused to pay **tribute** (money) to the Barbary States along the coast of North Africa to keep them from attacking American merchant ships.
- Jefferson sent the U.S. Navy to deal with the Barbary States. The U.S. Navy blockaded **Tripoli**, and U.S. Marines captured the city of Derna in Tripoli in 1805. This allowed the United States to obtain a promise from the ruler of Tripoli not to attack American ships.

The Louisiana Purchase

- In 1800, Napoleon forced Spain to give the Louisiana Territory back to France. Previously, under the Pinckney Treaty with Spain, Americans were able to use the port of New Orleans. This was important to American farmers who sent their crops through New Orleans. This right was threatened now that France controlled New Orleans.
- Jefferson sent negotiators to Paris to purchase New Orleans.
- Napoleon had been unable to reconquer Haiti. Former slaves had rebelled and established their own independent nation. Without Haiti, Napoleon gave up on his dreams of an American empire.
- Napoleon surprisingly offered the entire Louisiana Territory to the United States for $15 million. Jefferson immediately agreed.
- The Louisiana Purchase doubled the size of the United States, ended French claims to North America and allowed Americans to further pursue westward expansion.

The Lewis and Clark Expedition (1804–1806)

- Jefferson wanted to know more about America's new territories. He sent **Meriwether Lewis** and **William Clark** to explore and collect information about their geography, Indian tribes, plants and wildlife. They went over rivers, valleys, plains, and mountains, reached the Pacific Ocean, and then turned back. Their journey covered 7,000 miles and took two years. **Sacajawea**, an Indian woman who joined Lewis and Clark, was an important help as a guide and interpreter.

Marbury v. Madison (1803)

- This case established the Supreme Court's power of **judicial review**: its right to determine whether laws are constitutional.
- Marbury was a Federalist. He was one of President Adams' midnight appointments in 1800. The new Secretary of State, James Madison, refused to deliver his commission.
- Marbury asked the Supreme Court to require Madison to do so. The power to decide such disputes was given directly to the Supreme Court by the Judiciary Act of 1789.
- Chief Justice John Marshall ruled that this section of the Judiciary Act of 1789 had expanded the Supreme Court's powers beyond what the Constitution had specified. It was therefore in conflict with the Constitution. This part of the law was therefore unconstitutional and could not be enforced.
- The Court had no power to order Madison to deliver the commission to Marbury. With this decision, the Court established its power as the highest authority on the interpretation of the Constitution.

Jefferson's Second Term: Economic Warfare in Europe

- Jefferson was re-elected in 1804.
- His second term dealt mostly with foreign affairs. Much of Europe was under Napoleon's control. The French were supreme on land; the British, supreme on the seas. Britain's Royal Navy blockaded Napoleonic Europe. No one could sail in or out of Europe without the permission of the British Royal Navy. Neutral American ships could still go to France, but they had to first stop at a British port to be inspected for prohibited war goods. Napoleon responded by stating that any neutral ship that stopped at a British port would be seized. American merchants were caught in the middle with no clear path to follow.
- In 1807, a British warship attacked the American warship, the *Chesapeake*. The British ship fired and forced the *Chesapeake* to surrender. The British searched the ship and took 3 sailors, one of whom was hanged.
- In America there was a public outcry for war. Jefferson was determined to keep neutral. He pushed through Congress the **Embargo of 1807**. This law banned all trade with foreign nations until France and Britain ended their measures against American shipping. Jefferson's embargo was very unpopular. It hurt American merchants and farmers. The embargo even helped to revive (*bring back*) support for the Federalist Party.

The Young Republic Under Presidents Adams and Jefferson

Presidency of John Adams

The XYZ Affair
- French requested bribes; Americans refused

"Quasi-War"
- French and Americans attacked each other's ships

FIFTH CONGRESS OF THE UNITED STATES:

Alien and Sedition Acts
- Gave President Adams the power to send foreigners away and to fine or jail those speaking or writing against the government

Kentucky and Virginia Resolutions
- Jefferson and Madison told states they did not have to enforce unconstitutional laws

Presidency of Thomas Jefferson

Reduced spending on army and navy

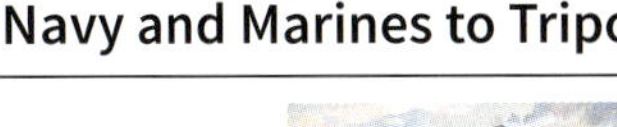

First Barbary War—Sent U.S. Navy and Marines to Tripoli

***Marbury v. Madison* (1803)**
- Chief Justice John Marshall established the Supreme Court's power of judicial review
- Marshall ruled part of the Judiciary Act of 1789 was unconstitutional
- A law is unconstitutional if the Court finds it conflicts with the Constitution

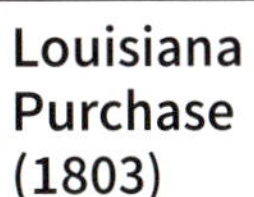

Louisiana Purchase (1803)
- Napoleon decided to sell all of the Louisiana Territory to the United States for $15 million
- Jefferson bought Louisiana although he was unsure if the Constitution gave him the right to do so
- Doubled the size of the United States and opened the way to westward expansion
- Lewis and Clark were sent to explore the Louisiana Territory

Hamilton-Burr Duel (1804)
- Hamilton was killed by Vice President Aaron Burr

Embargo of 1807
- Britain and France blockaded each other
- American merchants were caught in the middle
- Jefferson imposed an embargo: American ships could not take goods to any foreign ports
- The embargo hurt Americans more than others

What do you know?

SS.6.A.3.13

1. The passage below is from Section 2 of the Sedition Act of 1797.

   > *[I]f any person shall write, print . . . or publish . . . any false, scandalous and malicious writing . . . against the government of the United States . . . [then] such person, being thereof convicted . . . shall be punished by a fine . . . and by imprisonment not exceeding two years.*

   Which conclusion can be drawn from this section of the Sedition Act?

   A. The Sedition Act violated the right to a trial by jury.

   B. The Sedition Act denied citizens the right to obtain a writ of habeas corpus.

   C. The Sedition Act violated the First Amendment's guarantee of freedom of the press.

   D. Many people were unjustly deported from the United States because of the Sedition Act.

SS.6.3.14

2. Which statement describes the significance of the "Revolution of 1800"?

   A. John Adams refused to run for another term.

   B. States threatened to secede if John Adams was re-elected.

   C. The Jefferson administration established many new precedents.

   D. There was a peaceful transfer of power to an opposing political party.

SS.6.A.4.12

3. What impact did the Haitian Revolution have on the United States?

   A. Enslaved individuals in the United States rose up in revolt.

   B. The United States warned France not to try to restore its control over Haiti.

   C. American leaders sent assistance to the Haitian people in their struggle for liberty.

   D. Napoleon Bonaparte gave up on his plans for a North American empire and sold Louisiana to the United States.

SS.6.A.3.14

4. How was the judicial branch strengthened during the Presidency of Thomas Jefferson?

   A. Congress created a system of lower federal courts.

   B. *Marbury v. Madison* established the principle of judicial review.

   C. Supreme Court decisions upheld the constitutionality of the national bank.

   D. *Marbury v. Madison* restricted Congress' ability to use the "Necessary and Proper" clause.

SS.6.A.3.14

5. What does the power of judicial review permit the Supreme Court to do?
   A. break tie votes in the Electoral College
   B. repeal amendments to the Constitution
   C. determine the constitutionality of a law
   D. impeach the President and other high-level officials

SS.6.A.3.14

6. The information below lists events during the Presidency of Thomas Jefferson.

- Purchase of Louisiana Territory
- First Barbary War
- Embargo of 1807

Which conclusion can be drawn from this list?

A. President Jefferson conducted an active foreign policy.
B. President Jefferson disagreed with Washington's advice in his "Farewell Address."
C. President Jefferson risked war to help the nations of Latin America gain their independence from Spain.
D. President Jefferson believed most foreign policy matters should be handled by Congress not the President.

SS.6.A.3.13

7. The cartoon below was published in 1798, during the Presidency of John Adams.

Which issue is addressed in the cartoon?

A. the need for greater stability in France
B. the reasons behind the outbreak of the French Revolution
C. the request of French officials for bribes from the United States
D. the attempt to end the continuing war between Britain and France

SS.6.A.3.14

8. The statement below is from the Supreme Court decision of *Marbury v. Madison* (1803).

> *It is emphatically the province and duty of the judicial department to say what the law is.*

Which conclusion did Chief Justice Marshall draw from this statement?

A. The President should have the final say in interpreting the Constitution.

B. The judiciary of each state has the final say in interpreting the U.S. Constitution for that state.

C. It is the role of the Supreme Court to act as the final authority in interpreting the Constitution.

D. Because Congress makes the laws, it should act as the final authority in interpreting the Constitution.

SS.6.A.3.14

9. The painting below illustrates the supremacy of the British Royal Navy on the high seas during the Presidency of Thomas Jefferson.

How were American merchants affected by this supremacy?

A. The British navy stopped American ships to search for deserters.

B. The British protected American ships from attacks by the French navy.

C. The British protected American ships from attacks by the Barbary States.

D. The British attempted to take over the carrying trade between Europe and America.

CHAPTER 10 The War of 1812 and the "Era of Good Feelings"

SS.6.A.4.1 Examine the causes, course, and consequences of United States westward expansion and its growing diplomatic assertiveness (War of 1812, Convention of 1818, Adams-Onís Treaty, Missouri Compromise, Monroe Doctrine . . .).

SS.6.A.4.3 Examine the experiences and perspectives of significant individuals and groups during this era of American history.

SS.6.A.4.8 Describe the influence of individuals on social and political developments of this era in American history.

SS.6.A.4.13 Explain the consequences of landmark Supreme Court decisions (*McCulloch v. Maryland* [1819], . . . significant to this era of American history.

SS.6.A.4.17 Examine key events in Florida history as each impacts this era of American history.

SS.6.E.3.1 Evaluate domestic and international interdependence.

SS.6.G.6.1 Use appropriate maps and other graphic representations to analyze geographic problems and changes over time throughout American history.

(continues next page)

Names and Terms You Should Know

James Madison
Repeal
Recession
Secession
War Hawks
John C. Calhoun
Henry Clay
Impressment
War of 1812
"Star-Spangled Banner"
"Era of Good Feelings"
Tariff
Protective Tariff
Convention
Nationalism
James Monroe
Internal Improvements
Clay's "American System"
Adams-Onís Treaty
McCulloch v. Maryland (1819)
Supremacy
"Necessary and Proper" Clause
Implied Powers
Missouri Compromise (1820)
Monroe Doctrine (1823)
Caucus
Electoral College
Popular Vote
Electoral Votes

Alignment to Grade 7 Civics Standards

SS.7.C.3.3 Illustrate the structure and function (three branches of government established in Articles I, II, and III with corresponding powers) of government in the United States as established in the Constitution.

SS.7.C.3.8 Analyze the structure, functions, and processes of the legislative, executive, and judicial branches.

SS.7.C.3.12 Analyze the significance and outcomes of landmark Supreme Court cases . . .

SS.7.C.4.1 Differentiate concepts related to U.S. domestic and foreign policy.

SS.7.C.4.3 Describe examples of how the United States has dealt with international conflicts.

Florida "Keys" to Learning

1. Chief Tecumseh and his brother, "The Prophet," tried to unite Indian tribes against giving away more lands. The Prophet was defeated at Tippecanoe in 1811. Tecumseh fled to Canada. Americans blamed the British for supplying arms to the Indians.

2. Congress replaced the Embargo of 1807 with the Non-Intercourse Act of 1809. This law permitted trade with all nations other than Britain and France. In 1810, Congress permitted trade with France and Britain. Congress later re-imposed its ban on trade with Britain.

3. The British also continued to stop American ships on the high seas to seize British deserters. This practice was known as impressment.

4. The "war hawks" in Congress pushed for war so that Americans could take Canada from Britain. Congress finally declared war on Britain in 1812.

5. American attempts to invade Canada failed. In the Battle of Lake Erie in 1813, Oliver Perry defeated British ships and gained control of the lake, forcing British troops to leave Fort Detroit.

6. In 1814, the war in Europe ended and Britain sent more troops to America. A British force landed in Chesapeake Bay, occupied Washington, D.C., and burned public buildings, including the White House. The British decided to attack Baltimore next. British ships bombarded Fort McHenry but could not take the fort. Francis Scott Key wrote "The Star-Spangled Banner," our national anthem.

7. Americans also defeated British ships in Lake Champlain. American control of the lake forced British troops to retreat.

8. America and Britain signed the Treaty of Ghent, ending the war in December 1814.

9. News of the treaty had not reached America when British troops attacked New Orleans in 1815. General Andrew Jackson became a hero after defeating the attack.

10. At the Hartford Convention, Federalist delegates from New England criticized the war. A few delegates proposed leaving the union. Soon afterwards, peace was signed and Federalists were branded as unpatriotic.

11. After the war, feelings of patriotism were high during the "Era of Good Feelings." Congress passed the Tariff of 1816 to protect American manufacturers from competition with cheap British goods. Congress also created the Second Bank of the United States. The Supreme Court later upheld the constitutionality of the bank in its decision *McCulloch v. Maryland* (1819).

12. The Federalist Party dissolved, leaving a one-party America. James Monroe was elected President in 1816.

13. Congressman Henry Clay proposed his "American System": high tariffs would support American manufacturers and provide funds for internal improvements in the West, such as roads and canals.

14. Spain gave Florida to the United States in the Adams-Onís Treaty (1819).

15. The Missouri Compromise (1820) admitted Missouri as a slave state and Maine as a free state.

16. Monroe issued the Monroe Doctrine in 1823. It announced that the United States would not allow European powers to start new colonies or to restore rule over former ones that had achieved independence.

17. In the election of 1824, Andrew Jackson received the most votes but not enough electoral votes to win. The House of Representatives chose John Quincy Adams as President.

George Washington had warned Americans to avoid European wars. But this was not so easy to do in the troubled early 1800s. The French Revolution had brought twenty years of war to Europe. France and Britain were locked in a life-and-death struggle. Both sides looked to America for support. American merchants enjoyed making huge profits by trading in Europe, but they did not like the risks. In this chapter, you will learn how Americans finally went to war, and how the war affected them.

James Madison and the War of 1812

Thomas Jefferson followed George Washington's example by serving only two terms as President. His political party, the Democratic-Republicans, remained in power. Jefferson's close friend **James Madison** became the next President in 1809. Madison was a fellow Virginian, the "Father of the Constitution," and one of the authors of *The Federalist Papers*. He had served as Jefferson's Secretary of State.

James Madison

The Non-Intercourse Act (1809)

Only a few days before Jefferson left office, Congress **repealed** (*cancelled*) the unpopular Embargo of 1807. That law had prevented Americans from shipping their goods to any foreign country. It had led to an economic recession in the United States. Congress replaced it with the **Non-Intercourse Act.** This act stopped Americans from trading with Britain or France, but permitted trade with other nations.

The Non-Intercourse Act lasted only one year. In 1810, Congress tried yet another approach. It passed a law allowing Americans to trade with both Britain and France. But the law also stated that if either Britain or France lifted their restrictions on American trade, then the United States would prohibit trade with the other country.

The French Emperor Napoleon acted quickly to accept the American offer. He announced that he would lift all restrictions on American shipping. Based on his promise, Americans placed new restrictions on their trade with Britain. Meanwhile, Napoleon did not keep his word. He continued to seize American ships.

Trouble in the Northwest

In the Northwest Territory, British officers in Canada were still giving guns to Indian tribes. A Shawnee chief named **Tecumseh** and his brother, known as "**the Prophet**," tried to unite all the tribes. The two brothers had grown up at the time of the American Revolution and the wars in the Northwest. Their parents and many of their relatives and friends had been killed in wars with white settlers.

Tecumseh

The Prophet had a powerful religious message. He urged all the tribes to give up their guns, European-style clothes, and alcohol. He wanted them to return to their traditional ways.

Some Indians believed that if they fought alongside the Prophet, they would not be harmed by American bullets.

Tecumseh and the Prophet argued that Indian lands belonged to all the tribes. No single tribe had the right to give any of this land away. Tecumseh and the Prophet persuaded twenty tribes to join their confederacy. Its capital was located at the Indian village of Prophetstown on the Tippecanoe River in present-day Indiana.

While Tecumseh was trying to unite the Indians, William Henry Harrison, the Governor of the Indiana Territory, signed a treaty with other tribal leaders. These leaders gave away millions of acres of Indian land to the United States. Tecumseh spoke loudly against the new treaty. He tried to persuade other tribal leaders to reject it.

Believing that Tecumseh had plans to attack, Governor Harrison approached Prophetstown with a force of a thousand men in 1811. Tecumseh was away visiting other tribal leaders. His brother the Prophet decided to attack Harrison's camp in order to surprise the soldiers. The Indians were defeated and fled. This became known as the Battle of Tippecanoe. After the battle, Harrison burned down Prophetstown. Governor Harrison was especially annoyed when he found that the Indians at Prophetstown had crates of brand new British guns.

The Outbreak of the War of 1812

The troubles in the Northwest Territory led several young Congressmen to conclude that Britain stood in the way of the United States. They blamed Britain for the Indian attacks. These "war hawks" (people who favor war) believed that the United States should invade and take Canada. Only then would the Northwest Territory be safe. The war hawks included **John C. Calhoun** from South Carolina and **Henry Clay** from Kentucky.

Meanwhile, officers of the British navy were continuing to board American ships on the high seas in their search for deserters. The British were also still interfering with American shipping. For all these reasons, President Madison finally asked Congress for a declaration of war against Britain. The conflict became known as the **War of 1812**, although it lasted until 1815.

Congress, the legislative branch, has the power to declare war.

Main Causes of the War of 1812

1. British ships were stopping American ships on the high seas. The British boarded these ships to look for deserters from the British navy. Some American sailors were, in fact, British deserters. But the British also took sailors from American ships who were not deserters at all. This practice was called the *impressment* of sailors because the men were "pressed" into service.
2. After the Battle of Tippecanoe (1811), Chief Tecumseh fled to Canada where he allied with the British. Americans blamed the British for Indian attacks along the Northwest Frontier.
3. Some Americans, especially the "war hawks" in Congress, thought this would be a good time to seize Canada from Great Britain. Since Spain was allied to Britain, they wanted to take Florida as well.

The Course of the War

The War of 1812 was mainly fought along the Canadian border, in the Great Lakes, and at sea. The British were already in a war for survival against Napoleon in Europe. They could not spare many troops for North America. They had fewer then 7,000 regular troops in Canada. The United States did not have many more, but could rely on its militia.

The war was greatly influenced by geography. Americans never attacked Britain itself—it was too far away. Instead, their focus was on Canada. They even thought French Canadians might welcome joining the United States. British strategy during the war was based on the defense of Canada and using British naval power.

Attempted Invasions of Canada

There were three routes for Americans to invade Canada:

1. To the east, there was the Hudson River Valley, Lake Champlain, and the Richelieu River. This route had been used during the American Revolution.
2. Farther west, there was the land bridge between Lake Ontario and Lake Erie, separated by the Niagara River.
3. Even farther west, there was the land bridge between Lake Erie and Lake Huron, separated by the Detroit River.

In the first year of the war, the Americans sent forces across all three routes. The first was a force of about 2,000 American troops. They left Fort Detroit in July and crossed the Detroit River into Canada. They were beaten back, retreated to Fort Detroit, and then surrendered the fort in late August to the British, who were helped by Tecumseh and his Shawnee warriors.

The second American force crossed the Niagara River and advanced into Upper Canada (Ontario) in October. New York militia marching with the American army refused to leave the state. As a result, the British were able to defeat the invaders.

The third American invasion force was sent along the Lake Champlain route to attack Montreal in November. However, the weather was so cold that the Americans turned back after the first signs of resistance.

Naval Warfare

In the first year of the war, Americans did much better at sea than on land. New American ships defeated the British in several small battles in which one ship fought another. The *U.S.S. Constitution* became known as "Old Ironsides" because enemy cannonballs seemed to bounce off its hard oak hull. These early naval victories led the British

to send more of their fleet to North America. In 1813, the British tightened their blockade of the American coast.

The Battle of Lake Erie

Americans and British both began building new warships in the Great Lakes. In September 1813, the American commander **Oliver Perry** fought two large British warships. When his own flagship was almost destroyed in the battle, Perry retreated to another ship. He then led a second attack, which caused the two British warships to crash into one another. Perry's great victory in the **Battle of Lake Erie** forced British troops to leave Fort Detroit.

Perry's ships next carried Harrison and his troops across the lake into Canada, where they defeated the British retreating from Detroit. Chief Tecumseh was killed in this battle.

The Battle of Lake Erie

Wartime Atrocities

In the fall of 1813, another American force crossed the Niagara River into Canada. Once again, they were defeated and forced to withdraw. Before leaving Canada, they burned down the village of Newark. Its homeless residents were left to freeze. Angry British troops took revenge by burning the American town of Buffalo in December 1813.

The Burning of Washington and the Siege of Fort McHenry

In April 1814, Napoleon surrendered and the war in Europe ended. The British sent thousands of their best soldiers to North America to help in the war effort against the United States. In July 1814, some of these troops occupied part of Maine.

In August 1814, a British fleet sailed into Chesapeake Bay. The ships carried an army of 4,500 soldiers. The soldiers landed and marched towards Washington, D.C. An American force was sent to stop their advance, but it was defeated. President Madison and the members of Congress fled the capital city in a panic. President Madison's wife, **Dolley Madison**, took care of the removal of important government documents, paintings, and other valuables from the White House. British troops arrived just in time to finish President Madison's dinner. Then they set the White House, the Capitol, and other public buildings aflame.

Dolley Madison

The British left Washington soon afterwards to prepare for an attack on Baltimore. Their plan was to attack the city by land and sea. Their soldiers decided to retreat once they saw the city's well-prepared defenses. Instead, the British sent their ships to attack Fort McHenry, which guarded the entrance to the harbor. British ships kept out of reach of American guns by firing primitive rockets filled with gunpowder at the fort.

An American lawyer, **Francis Scott Key**, watched these events from a British ship, where he was being held prisoner. The British bombardment failed to force the fort to surrender. Key was so excited to see the American flag still flying over the fort when he woke up the next morning that he wrote the poem that has become our national anthem.

The British burning the Capitol

The Historian's Apprentice

The Star-Spangled Banner

O! say can you see, by the dawn's early light,
What so proudly we hailed at the twilight's last gleaming,
Whose broad stripes and bright stars through the perilous fight,
O'er the ramparts we watched, were so gallantly streaming?
And the rockets' red glare, the bombs bursting in air,
Gave proof through the night that our flag was still there;
O! say does that star-spangled banner yet wave
O'er the land of the free and the home of the brave?

How does Key's poem show a spirit of patriotism? Write your answer in your journal or on a separate sheet of paper.

The Battle of Plattsburgh

While the British were attacking Washington and Baltimore, they sent a second force to invade the United States from Canada. The Governor of Canada led 10,000 British troops southward to Lake Champlain. The safety of his invasion force depended on British control of the lake.

Thomas Macdonough commanded American ships in Lake Champlain. His ships had fewer guns than British ones, so he placed them in the harbor of Plattsburgh so that they could swing rapidly to the side to fire their cannons on the British. As the British ships sailed into the harbor, Macdonough's ships swung into action just as he had planned. They destroyed the British ships and killed their commander. Without control of the lake, the British troops were forced to turn back to Canada.

Henry Clay John Quincy Adams

The Negotiations at Ghent

By this time, British and American representatives were already discussing peace terms in Ghent, a town in Europe. **Henry Clay** and **John Quincy Adams** (the son of John Adams) were two of the Americans in this negotiation. The British hoped that sending their experienced troops from Europe to North America would give them a string of victories. These would allow them to dictate the terms of the peace settlement. The British demanded that they keep land in Maine and upstate New York to protect Canada. They also proposed creating a large new country for Native Americans, to be located between Canada and the United States.

News of their defeat at Plattsburgh and failure to take Baltimore forced the British negotiators to give up these demands. The two sides finally agreed to keep their borders the same as they had been before the war. A treaty was signed on December 24, 1814. The issue of the impressment of sailors was never resolved and was left out of the treaty. But impressment was no longer a problem since the war in Europe was over.

The Battle of New Orleans

A final attempt by Britain to use its naval power to win a decisive victory took place in the South. A British fleet carried 7,500 troops to the Gulf of Mexico for an attack on New Orleans. The British force landed after the peace treaty was signed at Ghent but no one knew this at the time. The troops began marching towards the city. On January 8, 1815, they came up against a force of Americans commanded by **General Andrew Jackson**.

Jackson had defeated the Creek Indians in Georgia and had marched to New Orleans, where he took command of the city's defenses. He was helped by city residents,

Battle of New Orleans

Andrew Jackson

including free blacks and the pirate Jean Lafitte.

As the British approached, they saw that on one side of Jackson's forces was the swamp and on the other side was the Mississippi River. The British had no choice but to attack or retreat. The British charged. In half an hour they lost half their men to American cannon and musket fire. Jackson became a hero and Americans had the feeling they had won the war.

The Hartford Convention

The New England states had never supported the war. They had opposed the declaration of war in Congress. During the war, they felt that their businesses were being hurt and refused to send their militia. The Governor of Massachusetts invited all the New England states to send representatives to a convention. The delegates met in Hartford, Connecticut, in December 1814. Some members proposed secession (*leaving the Union*), but they were a minority. Members of the Hartford Convention published resolutions calling for an end to the "Three-fifths Compromise." They declared that New England had the right to assert its authority over unconstitutional laws. Shortly after their convention, news was received that a peace treaty had been signed and that Jackson had defeated the British at New Orleans. The Federalists were viewed as traitors, and the Hartford Convention became the final blow to the Federalist Party.

The Convention of 1818

The War of 1812 was the last war between the United States and Britain. This was because both countries continued in talks to work out their differences. In 1817, they agreed that neither of them should have warships or fortifications on or around the Great Lakes. In the Convention of 1818, the British agreed to let Americans continue fishing off the coasts of Newfoundland and Nova Scotia in Canada. These rights were especially important to New England fishermen. The convention also defined the northern border of the Louisiana Purchase. It left open the question of the northern border of the Oregon Territory.

This is an example of foreign policy.

Consequences of the War of 1812

1. American nationalism rose. People took pride in their country. The victory over Britain at the battle of New Orleans made Americans especially proud.
2. Native American power in the Northwest Territory was destroyed.
3. Both the United States and Canada had successfully defended themselves. Americans considered the War of 1812 a "Second War of Independence."
4. The Federalist Party was disgraced. Its actions at the Hartford Convention appeared unpatriotic. The party collapsed.
5. American manufacturers benefited. When people could not get British goods, they bought American manufactured products instead.

The Historian's Apprentice

1. Do you think the War of 1812 was a worthwhile conflict? Or was declaring war a mistake? Discuss this with a partner and share your ideas with the class.
2. Make your own illustrated timeline of the period from the Embargo of 1807 to the Battle of New Orleans in 1815. Include events leading up to the war as well as of the war itself.
3. Make your own video or give an oral presentation on the causes, course and consequences of the War of 1812.

The "Era of Good Feelings"

How do you feel when your school team wins a game—especially when many people predicted that it would lose? Most people feel good. That is exactly how most Americans felt after the War of 1812. They felt so good that the next ten years became known as the "**Era of Good Feelings**." During these years, people from all sections of the country felt proud to be American.

The collapse of the Federalist Party put a temporary end to party differences. Although the Democratic-Republican Party became the only party, it accepted many Federalist ideas. People were eager to promote the national interest. After the War of 1812, the government introduced a new protective tariff, created a new national bank, and continued building a "national road." The Supreme Court strengthened federal power, while the President asserted American power in the Western Hemisphere.

Each branch of government can check another's powers through the system of checks and balances.

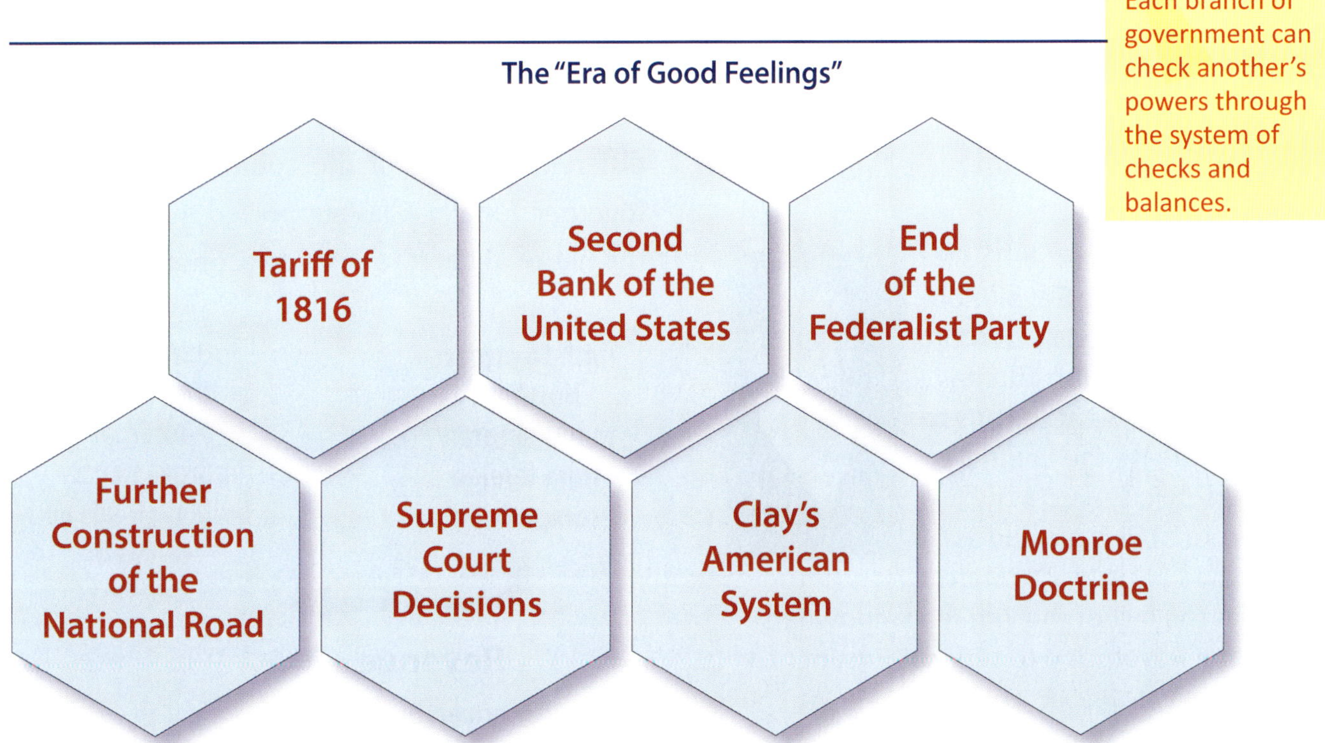

The Tariff of 1816

British warehouses were piled high with unsold goods. With the war over, Americans feared they would be flooded with cheap British imports. To help American manufacturers, Madison proposed a protective tariff. Even Southerners like John C. Calhoun supported it.

The Second Bank of the United States (1816)

The first national bank ended in 1811. Madison had been against the bank and did not try to renew its charter. But during the War of 1812, it became difficult to conduct the war without a national bank. In 1816, Madison proposed the Second Bank of the United States. Congress approved the bank and gave it a charter for the next twenty years.

The End of Party Differences

The war and the Hartford Convention had destroyed the Federalist Party. In the Presidential election of 1816, the Federalist candidate won only Massachusetts and two small states. In the 1820 election, there was no Federalist candidate at all. Americans threw party differences aside and united behind James Monroe, who was elected President in 1816. All Americans were now Democratic-Republicans.

The National Road and Internal Improvements

Just as Americans needed a strong central government, they needed good roads and canals. In 1806, Congress voted to build the **National Road**. It was to go westward from Cumberland, Maryland. Construction began in 1811. By 1818, the road reached Wheeling (today, in West Virginia). In May 1820, Congress voted to extend the National Road to St. Louis on the Mississippi River.

Henry Clay's "American System"

Henry Clay, the popular congressman from Kentucky, proposed greater cooperation between the different sections of the country. His "**American System**" was based on keeping a high tariff to protect the manufacturers of the Northeast. Revenue from the tariff could then be used to pay for "**internal improvements**"—building roads and canals in the West. Clay believed that such cooperation would tie the different sections of the country more closely together. Finally, Clay supported the creation of the national bank to provide economic stability.

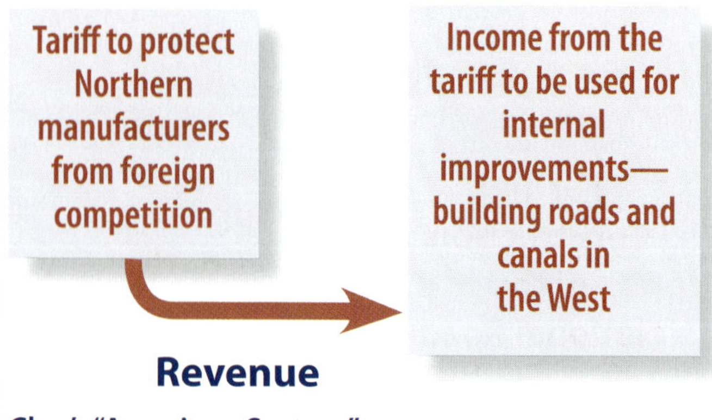

Clay's "American System"

James Monroe (1758–1831) had fought in the Revolution and was wounded at Trenton. He studied law with Thomas Jefferson and went to Paris to help negotiate the Louisiana Purchase. He served as Governor of Virginia and as Madison's Secretary of State. He was the last of the Virginia landowners from the Revolution to serve as President of the United States.

The Adams-Onís Treaty (1819)

During the "Era of Good Feelings," Americans added Florida to the United States. The United States actually took over Florida in three stages.

In 1810, Americans took some of West Florida, claiming this was part of the Louisiana Purchase. During the War of 1812, an American force marched into the Mobile region and took more of West Florida. This gave the United States control of rivers flowing south from the future states of Mississippi (1817) and Alabama (1819) into the Gulf of Mexico.

Florida from Pensacola to the Atlantic coast still belonged to Spain. In 1818, General Andrew Jackson marched across the border into Spanish Florida in pursuit of Seminole Indians. Jackson captured the fort at St. Marks, where he raised the American flag. Jackson accused two British residents he found there of arming Indians against American settlers and promptly hanged them. Next, Jackson marched west and occupied the town of Pensacola. Spain protested against Jackson's actions in Florida but was facing revolutions in Mexico and South America. It had no resources left to fight the United States.

Jackson's actions were wildly popular with most Americans. Monroe and John Quincy Adams, his Secretary of State, decided to support Jackson rather than condemn him. Adams wrote to Spain that Jackson had been forced to enter Florida because Spain itself was unable to keep order there. Adams demanded that Spain either "place a force in Florida adequate at once to the protection of her territory" or give Florida to the United States. He complained that Florida had become a place that gave shelter to "every enemy, civilized or savage, of the United States."

With no way to resist the United States, the Spanish government agreed to give up Florida. Adams negotiated a treaty with Luis de Onís, the Spanish minister in Washington, D.C. The United States paid off $5 million in debts owed by Spain to American citizens. The United States also recognized that Texas belonged to Spain and was not part of the Louisiana Territory. In exchange, Spain gave Florida to the United States. The treaty was not fully ratified (*approved*) until 1821, and the transfer took place in February 1821.

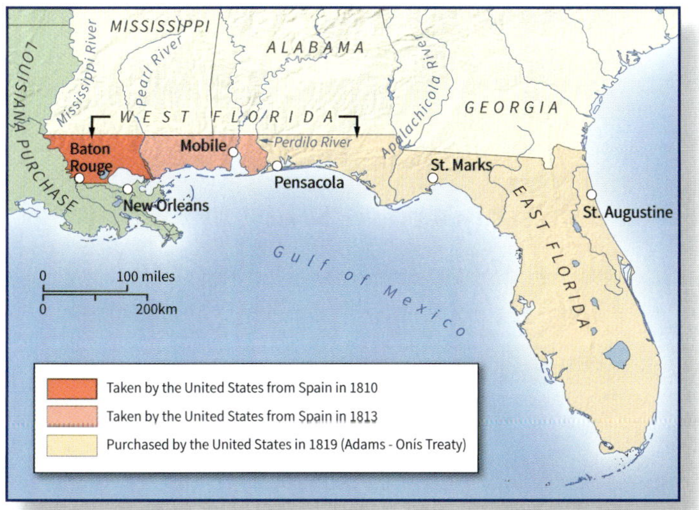

The "Panic of 1819"

Americans experienced hard times during an economic downturn in 1819, known as the "Panic of 1819." The **recession** (*economic downturn*) was caused by several factors. State banks had issued paper money that had little value. The national bank needed gold and silver to pay banks in Europe that had lent money for the Louisiana Purchase. Europeans had a good harvest and were buying fewer American crops. Prosperity had led many Americans to buy land or make other investments that now fell in value. The Second National Bank reduced its loans and stopped accepting paper notes from local banks. The recession lasted more than three years. The Panic of 1819 created bitter feelings towards the new bank.

The Supreme Court hears cases on disputes between states and appeals concerning the Constitution.

The Supreme Court: *McCulloch v. Maryland* (1819)

This case dealt with the Second National Bank. In this decision, Chief Justice John Marshall once again increased the power of the federal government.

Factual Background

State banks were unhappy with the national bank. Two years after Congress created the Second National Bank, Maryland placed a special tax on it. James McCulloch, the head of the Baltimore branch of the national bank, refused to pay the tax. Maryland sued the national bank in its own state courts. Maryland's courts found the bank to be unconstitutional and subject to the state tax. The bank appealed to the U.S. Supreme Court.

The Lawsuit

The case raised two issues:

1. Was the national bank constitutional?
2. Did a state have the power to tax the bank or any other federal agency?

The Decision

1. Chief Justice John Marshall found that the bank was indeed constitutional for the same reasons Hamilton had stated back in 1791. The "Necessary and Proper" Clause of the Constitution (also known as the "Elastic" Clause) gave Congress the power to pass any law that helped it exercise its listed powers. Congress had to collect taxes, hold onto money, and be able to borrow money. The bank helped it perform all these tasks. The creation of the bank was therefore permitted by the "Necessary and Proper" Clause.
2. Marshall said that if Maryland had the power to tax the bank, it could destroy it: "If the states may tax the bank, to what extent shall they tax it, and where shall they stop? An unlimited power to tax involves, necessarily, a power to destroy." Such a power would end the supremacy of federal law over state law. Therefore, Maryland could not tax the bank.

Based on the Supremacy Clause of the Constitution, federal law is superior to any conflicting state law.

Significance

This decision greatly strengthened federal power over the states. It also increased the power of Congress by recognizing that Congress had "implied powers" based on the "Necessary and Proper" Clause.

The Historian's Apprentice

Your class should pretend it is the Supreme Court hearing "oral argument" on *McCulloch v. Maryland*. Your teacher should appoint students as Supreme Court Justices, attorneys for each side, reporters and observers. The attorneys for each side should present their arguments and the Justices should ask questions. Reporters and observers should take notes. Afterwards, the Justices should deliberate and reach a decision. The outcome could be different from the actual one reached in 1819, but it should be justified by good reasons.

The Missouri Compromise (1820)

Americans felt a spirit of national unity during the "Era of Good Feelings." The truth, however, was that the country was becoming deeply divided. The divisions were less between political parties than between geographic sections of the country. Northern states had abolished slavery and were becoming industrialized. In Southern states, slavery and the plantation economy were booming.

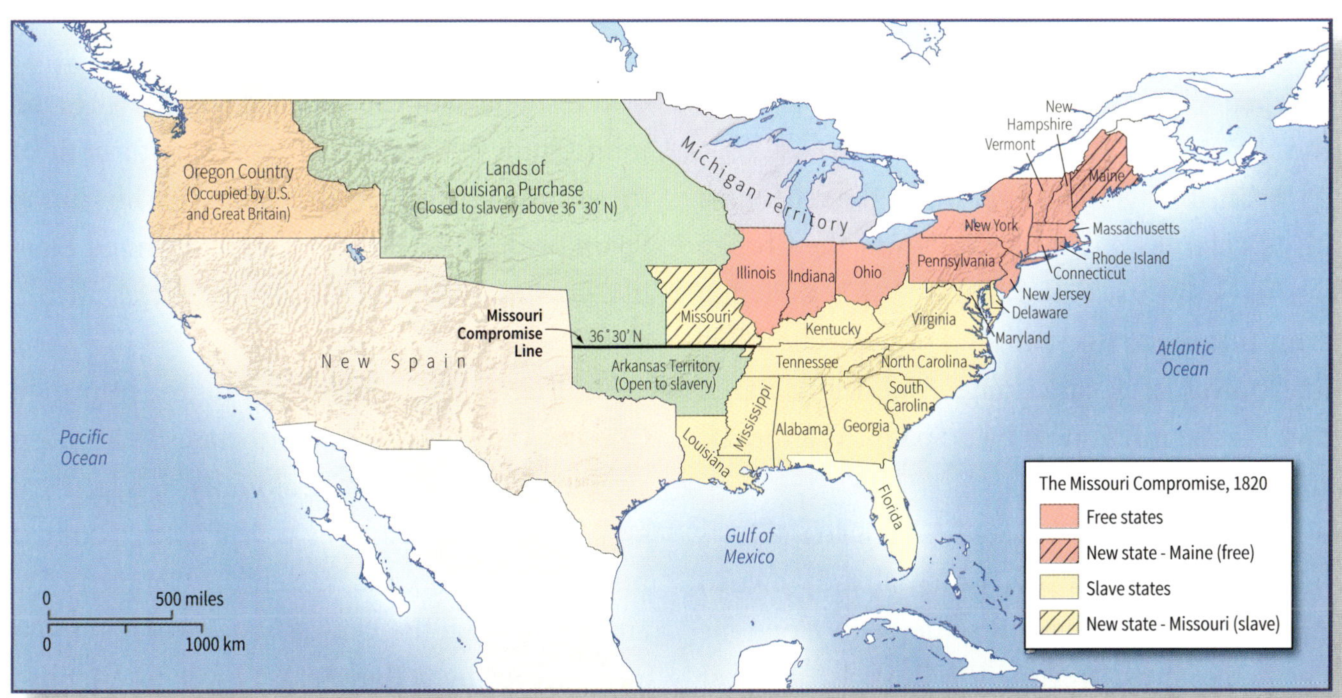

Population of the United States

Year	Whites	Free African Americans	Enslaved Persons
1790	3,172,444	59,557	697,624
1800	4,306,446	108,435	893,602
1810	5,862,073	186,446	1,191,362
1820	7,862,166	233,634	1,538,022

Source: US Census Bureau, *A Century of Population Growth*

The Northwest Ordinance had prohibited slavery in the Northwest Territory. Should slavery similarly be prohibited in the lands of the Louisiana Purchase? Louisiana had already been admitted as a slave state in 1812. In 1819, Missouri's population was large enough to apply for statehood. It was another place where slavery already existed.

In 1819, the balance in the Senate between "free states" (*states where slavery was prohibited*) and "slave states" (*states where it was permitted*) was exactly equal. Northern states therefore did not want to admit Missouri as another slave state. This would have upset this balance.

Henry Clay, who became known as the "Great Compromiser," finally came up with a solution. Maine, which was part of Massachusetts but separated from it by other states, would be admitted as an independent free state. Missouri could then be admitted as a slave state. This would keep the existing balance between free and slave states.

In addition, Clay proposed that slavery should be prohibited in the Louisiana Territory above the latitude line 36° 30' North except for in the State of Missouri itself. This was the southern border of Missouri and became known as the "Missouri Compromise" line. Congress approved Clay's plan and the "Missouri Compromise" kept the country at peace.

The Monroe Doctrine (1823)

In the early 1800s, the spirit of the American and French Revolutions spread to Mexico and South America. Spanish colonists demanded independence, while Spain was weakened by the Napoleonic Wars.

Spanish attempts to put down the rebellions in its colonies failed. A revolution then broke out in Spain itself in 1820. In 1823, a French army marched into Spain and restored the absolute power of Spain's king. Americans feared that France might next help Spain to restore its rule in Latin America.

There was also a threat to American interests in the Far West. Russia, which already owned Alaska, was planning new settlements along the Pacific coast of Oregon. The Russian Emperor announced that other countries would not be permitted to land their ships or bring merchants to this coast.

President Monroe and his Secretary of State, John Quincy Adams, had to deal with both of these problems. They did not want to annoy Spain before the United States had gained Florida. So, they delayed recognizing Spain's former colonies as independent.

In March 1822, President Monroe informed Congress that independent states had been established in Mexico, Colombia, Chile, Peru and Argentina. Just over a year later, Monroe made another bold statement to Congress. He announced that the United States would oppose any attempt by a European power to establish

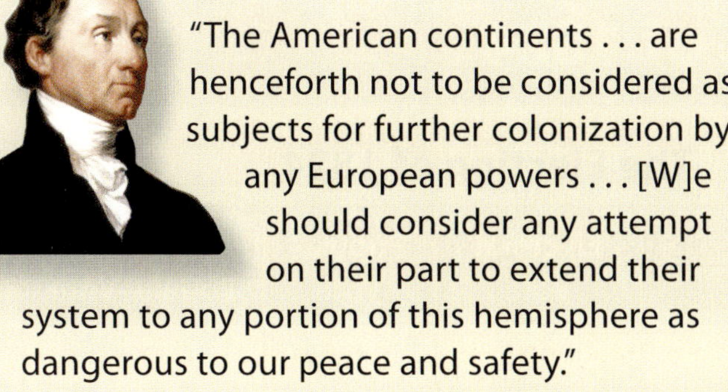

"The American continents . . . are henceforth not to be considered as subjects for further colonization by any European powers . . . [W]e should consider any attempt on their part to extend their system to any portion of this hemisphere as dangerous to our peace and safety."

—President James Monroe, December 2, 1823

new colonies or to restore rule over colonies that had achieved their independence. Monroe's main points were these:

1. The Western Hemisphere was no longer open to new colonies.
2. The United States would not interfere in European affairs.
3. Any attempt by European powers to establish new colonies or to restore their control over former ones in the Western Hemisphere would be viewed as an "unfriendly act" by the United States.

Monroe's message was a warning to Spain and France not to restore Spain's rule over its former colonies in Latin America. It was likewise a warning to Russia not to create new colonies along the Pacific coast. This policy became known as the **Monroe Doctrine**.

The Historian's Apprentice

1. Nationalism is love of one's country and people. It has been a powerful force in history. How did the Monroe Doctrine demonstrate the nationalist feelings of the "Era of Good Feelings?"
2. Your teacher should divide your class into groups. Each group should research one Latin American country that achieved independence during this period. Groups can use the Internet or the school library for their research. Each group should then make an oral presentation to the class with a summary of its findings.
3. Choose any one of the topics you have studied from the "Era of Good Feelings." Research more information about it from the Internet or your school library. Then make an oral presentation to your class sharing what you have learned.

The Election of 1824

In 1824, the Presidential election seemed to be wide open. The "Founding Fathers" who had played leading roles in the birth of the United States had either passed away or were too old to serve. It was a moment in history when a new generation was ready to take over. The official **caucus** (*a group of Congress members*) of the Democratic-Republican Party nominated William Crawford, but different sections of the party put up their own candidates. All four men were Democratic-Republicans, but they came from different parts of the country.

The Election of 1824

Candidate	Electoral Vote	Popular Vote	Percent of Popular Vote
Andrew Jackson	99	153,544	43%
John Quincy Adams	84	108,740	31%
William Crawford	41	46,618	13%
Henry Clay	37	47,136	13%

Source: Historical Statistics of the United States

In the election, Andrew Jackson received the most popular votes and the most electoral votes. However, he did not have quite enough electoral votes to win the election. That meant the election had to be decided in the House of Representatives, where each state had one vote. The Constitution stated that the House could consider only the three candidates with the most electoral votes. In 1824, these were Jackson, Adams and Crawford. Crawford, however, was badly affected by a stroke he had in 1823.

Today, a candidate needs 270 electoral votes to win.

Henry Clay was Speaker of the House. He exercised great influence over its members. Clay threw his support behind Adams. For example, Kentucky, Missouri and Ohio had cast their electoral votes for Clay. In the House all three states now voted for Adams. This helped Adams to win the election.

William Crawford

A member of Monroe's Cabinet, selected by the Congressional caucus and supported by Jefferson and Madison. He came from the South.

John Quincy Adams

The son of John Adams and Secretary of State under Monroe. He actually wrote most of the Monroe Doctrine. He represented the Northeast.

Andrew Jackson

The popular hero of the Battle of New Orleans. He came from the West.

Henry Clay

The "Great Compromiser" from Kentucky. Like Jackson, he represented the West.

Shortly afterwards, Adams appointed Clay as his Secretary of State. Clay's appointment made Jackson furious. He accused Adams and Clay of making a "corrupt bargain." Jackson believed the election had been stolen from the American people. From that moment on, Jackson and his supporters began campaigning to defeat Adams in the next election. The spirit that had united the country during the "Era of Good Feelings" was beginning to break down.

The Presidency of John Quincy Adams

John Quincy Adams was a distinguished diplomat and a scholarly man. He was the son of a famous President. He had lived in Europe and spoke several foreign languages. Some people found him to be rather cold and unfriendly.

As President, Adams continued the policies of the "Era of Good Feelings." Adams supported Clay's "American system." The federal government began construction of several important canals and extended the Cumberland Road. Adams also wanted to create a national university and to give more support to art and science. He favored a high protective tariff to protect American industry. He was friendly to the Indians. He also made sure the government paid off much of the national debt.

Jackson's supporters opposed most of Adams' proposals. They still felt bitter about the election of 1824. That election cast a long shadow over Adams' Presidency. In the end, Adams did not achieve as much as he had wanted. Like his father, he ended up serving only one term.

While John Quincy Adams was President, his father John Adams passed away. It was on July 4, 1826—fifty years to the day since the signing of the Declaration of Independence. In old age, Adams had resumed his friendship with Jefferson. The two men wrote each other often. On his deathbed, Adams' last words were: "Thomas Jefferson still survives." In fact, 500 miles to the south, Thomas Jefferson had died on the very same day.

The Historian's Apprentice

1. Look online or in your school library to find out more about the Presidency of John Quincy Adams. Write a paragraph describing his goals and accomplishments.
2. John Quincy Adams did not have a majority of the popular vote in 1824. This weakened his Presidency. Do you think our system of choosing the Presidency should be replaced? Should we eliminate the Electoral College and just choose the candidate with the most popular votes? Why or why not?

Name:________________________________

Complete the chart below on the War of 1812.

Causes	Course	Consequences

Complete the concept ladder below by adding your own descriptions and explanations.

The "Era of Good Feelings"

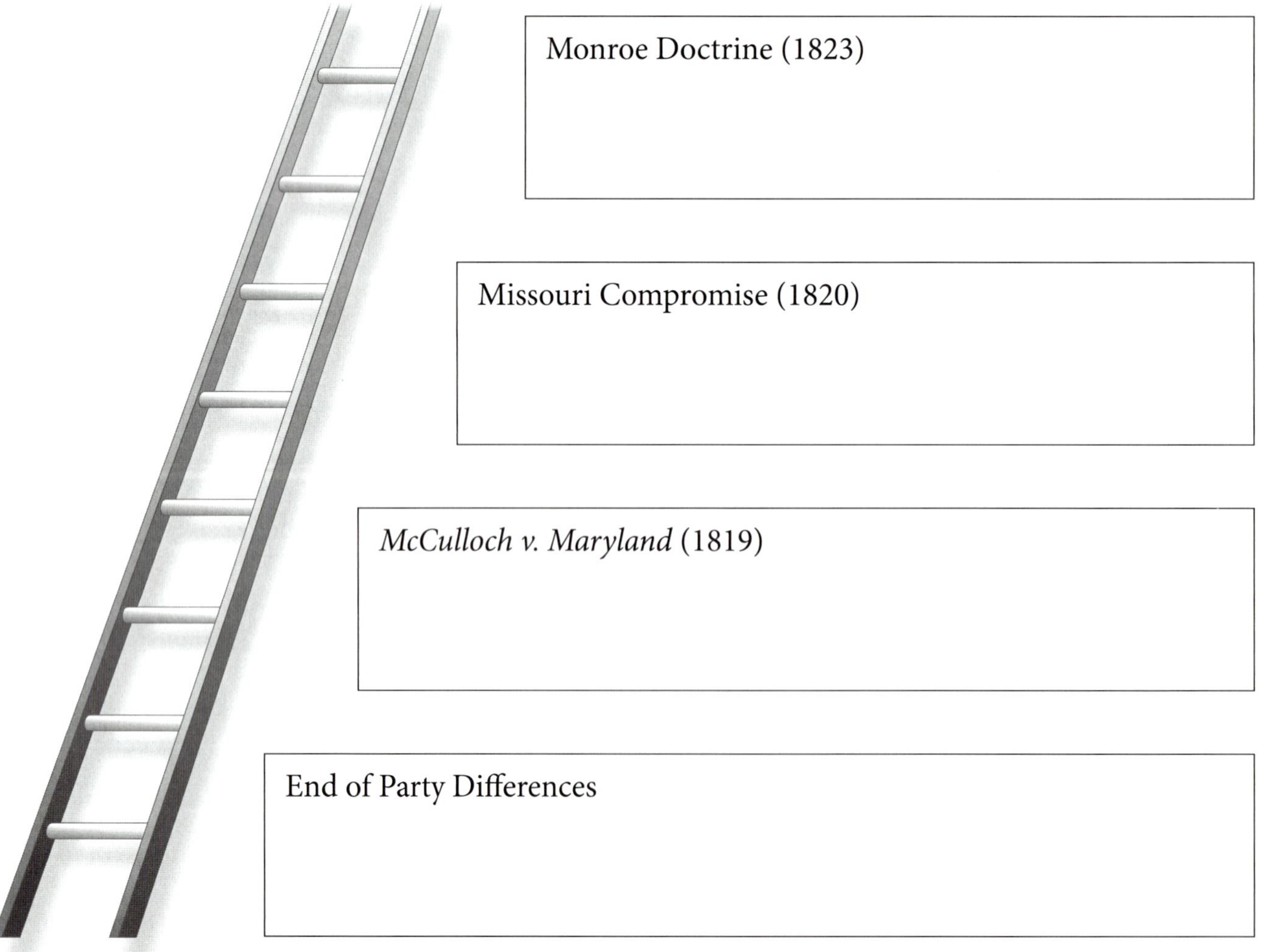

Chapter Review Cards

Overview of the War of 1812

- In 1809, **James Madison** became President.
- The **War of 1812** was fought between the United States and Great Britain. The British also had Indian allies. The war lasted from 1812 to 1815. Some have called it the "Second American War for Independence" because the Americans defended their rights against British interference.
- A peace treaty was signed in Europe in December 1814 before the last battle took place.

The Major Causes of the War of 1812

1. Americans Blamed the British for Indian Attacks in the Northwest Territory

- Chief Tecumseh and his brother, "**The Prophet**," tried to unite all Indian tribes against Americans. They resented losing so much land to white settlers. They argued no tribe had the right to surrender Indian lands.
- Their attempts at uniting Indian tribes ended when Governor William Henry Harrison defeated the "Prophet" in the **Battle of Tippecanoe** (1811) and burned down Prophetstown. **Chief Tecumseh** fled to Canada.
- Americans blamed the British for supplying the Indians with arms. Harrison found the Indians had British guns.

2. The British Blockade of Europe Interfered with American Shipping

- American relations with the British also worsened because of economic warfare during the Napoleonic Wars. Britain and France each tried to block the other's trade.
- American merchants were caught in the middle. The United States stayed neutral in the war. Jefferson had placed a total **embargo** on all overseas trade in 1807. The **Non-Intercourse Act of 1809** prohibited trade with Britain and France but allowed it with other nations.
- In 1810, Congress permitted trade with both Britain and France but stated that if either country lifted its restrictions on American trade, then the United States would prohibit trade with the other. Napoleon promised to lift restrictions on American trade and Congress placed a new ban on trade with Britain.

3. British Impressment of American Sailors

- The British were stopping American ships at sea to seize deserters from the British Royal Navy. This process was called **impressment**.
- Many of the sailors that the British seized were not British deserters at all but simply American sailors.

4. American War Hawks Desire to Annex Canada

- The "**war hawks**" in Congress, including Henry Clay and John C. Calhoun, were pushing for America to take Canada from Britain.

The Course of the War

- In 1812-1813, the Americans tried to invade Canada using three different land routes. All their attempts failed.
- American naval forces proved to be much more effective in fighting the British.
- In 1813, **Commander Oliver Perry** defeated British ships in the **Battle of Lake Erie**. Perry gained control of Lake Erie, forcing British troops to leave Fort Detroit. William Henry Harrison attacked the retreating British troops and killed Chief Tecumseh in this battle.
- In 1814, France surrendered to Britain and the war in Europe ended. This freed British troops for the war in North America. The British planned attacks on the United States through Canada and by water in Chesapeake Bay and at New Orleans.
- In August 1814, British troops burned public buildings in Washington, D.C., including the White House and the Capitol. **Dolley Madison** helped protect records and valuables from the White House.
- The British decided to attack Baltimore but their land forces retreated when they saw the city's strong defenses. Instead, the British navy attacked Fort McHenry at the entrance to the harbor. American lawyer **Francis Scott Key** watched the entire battle as a prisoner in a British ship. He was so overjoyed at the sight of the American flag still flying the next morning that he wrote the poem, "**The Star-Spangled Banner**." His poem later became our national anthem.
- On Lake Champlain, U.S. Commander Macdonough prepared to defend against a British invasion from Canada. He defeated British ships at the **Battle of Plattsburgh**, forcing British troops to retreat.
- A third British force was sent to New Orleans. British troops attacked New Orleans in 1815 because news of the peace (signed in December 1814) had not yet reached America. **General Andrew Jackson** successfully organized the defense of the city and became a national hero by defeating the British attackers.

The End of the War

- The United States and Britain signed a peace treaty in Ghent in December 1814. They kept the original borders of Canada and the United States. Because of American victories, the British had to give up their plans to take more territory or to create a new Indian nation between the United States and Canada.
- During the **Hartford Convention** of 1815, Federalist delegates from New England states discussed the effects of the war on their businesses. A few delegates even proposed to leave the United States. Soon after the convention, the peace treaty was signed and these Federalists were branded as unpatriotic.
- In 1817, the United States and Britain agreed not to have large warships or fortifications on the Great Lakes. In the **Convention of 1818**, the British allowed Americans to keep their fishing rights off the coasts of Newfoundland and Nova Scotia in Canada. Control of the Oregon Territory remained shared by the British and Americans.

The "Era of Good Feelings"

- As a result of victory against the British, Americans felt very proud to be American. This period became known as the "Era of Good Feelings."
- The Federalist Party was shamed and dissolved a few years after the Hartford Convention, leaving a one-party America. In the Presidential election of 1816, most Americans voted for **James Monroe** and soon all Americans were Democratic-Republicans.
- Congress approved the **Tariff of 1816**, to protect American manufacturers from British goods.
- Congress also approved creation of the **Second Bank** of the United States. In *McCulloch v. Maryland* (1819), the Supreme Court upheld the constitutionality of the national bank on the basis of the power of Congress to pass laws it felt were "necessary and proper" to carry out its enumerated powers. The Court also ruled that states did not have the power to tax federal agencies.
- The federal government also supported "internal improvements" such as roads. In 1811, construction had already begun for the **National Road**. This road was to go west from Maryland.
- Speaker of the House **Henry Clay** supported a high tariff to support American manufacturers in the Northeast. He proposed to use funds from the tariff for internal improvements in the West such as the building of roads and canals. This model became known as Clay's "**American System**."
- After Andrew Jackson's occupation of parts of Florida, Spain agreed to give Florida to the United States in the **Adams-Onís Treaty** (1819).

The Missouri Compromise

- In 1819, Missouri applied for statehood as a "slave" state. This would have upset the balance in the Senate between "slave" and "free" states. There were 11 of each.
- Henry Clay came up with a successful compromise. Missouri entered as a "slave" state and Maine entered as a new "free" state.
- Slavery was also forbidden in the Louisiana Territory north of the southern boundary of Missouri—except in Missouri itself.

The Monroe Doctrine

- In the 1820s, Latin American countries were fighting for their independence. There was concern that France might help Spain crush these revolutions. Russia also claimed part of the Pacific coast.
- In 1823, President Monroe issued the **Monroe Doctrine**. It stated that the United States would not allow European powers to start new colonies or restore rule over former ones that had achieved independence. It also said the U.S. would not interfere with European affairs.

The Election of 1824 and the Presidency of John Quincy Adams

- In the election of 1824, Andrew Jackson received the most popular and electoral votes.
- Jackson did not have enough electoral votes to win, and the House of Representatives decided the winner. Henry Clay used his influence in the House of Representatives in favor of **John Quincy Adams**. Adams then chose Henry Clay to be his Secretary of State.
- Jackson and his supporters were furious. They accused Adams and Clay of a "corrupt bargain" and vowed to beat Adams in the next election.
- During his Presidency, President John Quincy Adams paid off much of the government debt and provided funds for the construction of several important canals.
- Because of the strong opposition from Jackson's supporters, Adams did not accomplish everything he wanted to do.

The War of 1812 and the "Era of Good Feelings"

Presidency of James Madison (1809–1817)

- Election of 1808
- Non-Intercourse Act (1809)
- Tecumseh and Prophet try to unite tribes
- Battle of Tippecanoe (1811)

"Era of Good Feelings"

- Period of national unity
- Federalist Party ends, leaving one party
- Tariff of 1816
- Second Bank of the United States
- Presidency of James Monroe (1817–1825)

McCulloch v. Maryland (1819)

- Court upholds constitutionality of the national bank. States cannot tax federal agencies

Adams-Onís Treaty (1819)

- After Andrew Jackson's occupation of part of East Florida, Spain gives Florida to the United States for payment of debts

The War of 1812

Causes

- British impressment of American sailors
- Americans blame British for Indian attacks
- American "war hawks" want to invade Canada

Course of the War

- Americans try to invade Canada but fail
- American ships do well in battles against British ships

Battle of Lake Erie (1813)

- Oliver Perry defeats British ships
- British leave Fort Detroit
- Tecumseh killed

- War ends in Europe and British send more troops in 1814
- "Burning of Washington" by British; Dolley Madison saves valuables
- British fail to take Baltimore—Francis Scott Key's "Star Spangled Banner"
- British invasion through Lake Champlain stopped at Plattsburgh
- British attack on New Orleans stopped by General Andrew Jackson
- Hartford Convention—Federalist delegates oppose the war
- Treaty of Ghent ends the war

Missouri Compromise (1820)

- National unity maintained by admitting Missouri as a slave state and Maine as a free state
- No other slavery permitted in Louisiana Purchase above Missouri Compromise Line

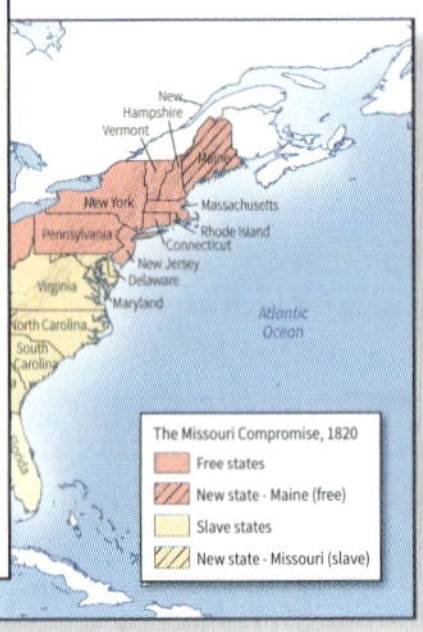

Monroe Doctrine (1823)

- United States will not allow European powers to start new colonies or restore rule over former ones that have achieved independence

Presidency of John Quincy Adams

- Nationalist program
- Jackson accused Adams and Clay of a "corrupt bargain"

Consequences of the War

- American independence upheld
- Northern manufacturers benefit
- Collapse of Federalist Party

What do you know?

SS.6.A.4.1

1. Why did some Americans consider the War of 1812 the "Second War for American Independence"?

   A. American citizens continued to protest against British taxes.

   B. The British burned public buildings in the new capital city of Washington, D.C.

   C. The United States and Great Britain never previously signed a treaty ending the Revolutionary War.

   D. The British were stopping American ships and arming hostile Indians, showing disrespect for the United States.

SS.6.A.4.1

2. The diagram below describes an event in American history.

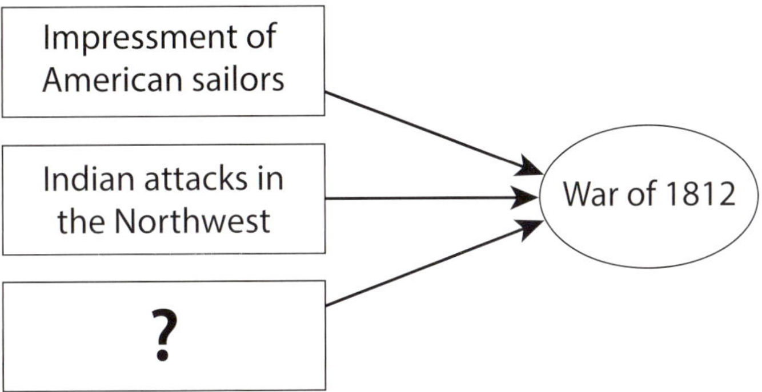

   Which statement best completes the diagram?

   A. British wanted New Orleans.

   B. British attacked the United States.

   C. "War hawks" in Congress wanted Canada.

   D. British refused to trade with America.

SS.6.A.4.1

3. What was an important consequence of the War of 1812?

   A. The federal government was weakened.

   B. American Indians were removed from the southeastern United States.

   C. Americans began ordering more finished goods from Northeastern manufacturers.

   D. Americans began trading more with France than Great Britain for their manufactured goods.

SS.6.A.4.1

4. The cartoon below was published in 1813. It shows George III of Great Britain and President James Madison. John Bull was the nickname for England.

Based on the cartoon, which statement best describes the artist's feelings?

A. The artist fears that Great Britain is too powerful for the United States.

B. The artist believes that the present war offers the best time for the United States to conquer Canada.

C. The artist is pleased that several American ships have defeated British ones in the first year of the war.

D. The artist feels it is unfair to fight the British at a time when they are also at war with Napoleon in Europe.

SS.6.A.4.13

5. The excerpt below is from Article I, Section 8 of the U.S. Constitution.

> *The Congress shall have Power ... To make all Laws which shall be necessary and proper for carrying into Execution the foregoing Powers . . .*

Which landmark Supreme Court case was decided on the basis of this excerpt?

A. *Marbury v. Madison (1803)*

B. *McCulloch v. Maryland (1819)*

C. *Gibbons v. Ogden (1824)*

D. *Dred Scott v. Sandford (1857)*

SS.6.A.4.1

6. The cartoon below was published in 1812. The man in the red uniform is a British officer. The man in the blue uniform is an American soldier. The top line reads: "A scene on the frontiers as practiced by the humane British and their worthy allies."

With which statement would the cartoonist most likely agree?

A. The United States and Britain should find a way to end the war.

B. British officers have been responsible for Indian attacks on Americans.

C. An independent Indian nation should be created between Canada and the United States.

D. The "war hawks" in Congress have exaggerated the involvement of Britain in Indian attacks.

SS.6.A.4.8

7. What was the goal of Henry Clay's "American System" in the 1820s?

A. to gradually eliminate slavery

B. to obtain United States control of Canada

C. to strengthen the United States to resist foreign invaders

D. to encourage greater cooperation between different sections of the country

SS.6.A.4.1

8. Which statement summarizes the main idea of the Monroe Doctrine (1823)?

A. Foreign nations cannot form alliances with the United States.

B. There is a barrier between European nations and the United States.

C. The United States will protect the continents of Europe and Africa.

D. The United States will protect the Western Hemisphere from further European colonization.

SS.6.A.4.17

9. The map below shows Florida during the period 1810 to 1819.

Which event contributed most to the changes shown on this map?

A. the signing of the Treaty of Ghent in 1815

B. Andrew Jackson's victory in the Battle of New Orleans

C. the Haitian Revolution ending Napoleon's plans for an American empire

D. Andrew Jackson's entry into Spanish Florida in pursuit of Seminole Indians

SS.6.A.4.2

10. How did the Missouri Compromise (1820) treat the balance of power between free and slave states in the U.S. Senate?

A. It kept the balance by letting Maine enter as a free state and Missouri as a slave state.

B. It let the North have two more Senators in exchange for a harsher Fugitive Slave Law.

C. It let the North have two more Senators but kept the "Three-fifths" Compromise in the House of Representatives.

D. It required a Constitutional amendment for any further changes in the balance of free and slave states in the Senate.

Part 3
When Americans Expanded, Prospered and Divided

Some Events that Took Place between 1828 and 1877

Thousands of Cherokee Indians died along the Trail of Tears.

Americans went to war with Mexico and gained the lands of the Mexican Cession.

The factory demand for cotton led to an increase in slavery in the South.

William Lloyd Garrison began publishing an abolitionist newspaper, demanding an end to slavery.

The spread of railroads connected major American cities.

South Carolina fired on Fort Sumter in Charleston Harbor, starting the Civil War.

General Lee surrendered to General Grant at Appomattox, ending four years of bloody Civil War.

President Abraham Lincoln was assassinated just after the surrender.

CANADA
The United States in 1830
Oregon Territory (shared with Great Britain)
Unorganized Territory
Michigan Territory
Michigan Territory
New Hampshire
Vermont
Maine
Massachusetts
New York
Rhode Island
Connecticut
Pennsylvania
New Jersey
Delaware
Maryland
Illinois
Indiana
Ohio
Virginia
Missouri
Kentucky
North Carolina
Tennessee
South Carolina
Arkansas Territory
Mississippi
Alabama
Georgia
Louisiana
Florida Territory
Atlantic Ocean
Gulf of Mexico
MEXICO
Pacific Ocean
CUBA
Caribbean Sea
The Northwest (or "West")
The Northeast (or "East")
The South (slave-holding states)
Claimed areas
0
500 miles
0
1000 km

CHAPTER 11 Andrew Jackson and the Age of Reform

SS.6.A.4.8 Describe the influence of individuals on social and political developments of this era in American history.

SS.6.A.4.9 Analyze the causes, course and consequences of the Second Great Awakening on social reform movements.

SS.6.A.4.13 Explain the consequences of landmark Supreme Court decisions (*McCulloch v. Maryland* [1819], *Gibbons v. Odgen* [1824], *Cherokee Nation v. Georgia* [1831], and *Worcester v. Georgia* [1832]) significant to this era of American history.

SS.6.A.4.14 Examine the causes, course, and consequences of the women's suffrage movement (1848 Seneca Falls Convention, Declaration of Sentiments).

SS.6.A.4.15 Examine the causes, course, and consequences of literature movements (Transcendentalism) significant to this era of American history.

SS.6.A.4.16 Identify key ideas and influences of Jacksonian democracy.

SS.6.A.4.17 Examine key events and peoples in Florida history as each impacts this era of American history.

SS.6.A.4.18 Examine the experiences and perspectives of different ethnic, national, and religious groups in Florida, explaining their contributions to Florida's and America's society and culture during the Territorial Period.

(continues next page)

Names and Terms You Should Know

Political party
Election campaign
Democratic Party
Party nominating convention
Party platform
Candidate
"Jacksonian Democracy"
Property qualifications
Public official
Rotation of officeholders
"Spoils system"
Equality
Veto

Raw materials
Renew
Charter
Recession
Tariff
Congress
State legislature
Compact of states
Convention
Ordinance
Nullification
Treason
Authorize
Proclamation

Compromise
Reform
Abolish
Abolition
Public education
Temperance
Compulsory
Exclude
Grievances
Women's rights
Suffrage
Voting rights
Civil disobedience

Alignment to Grade 7 Civics Standards

SS.7.C.2.8 Identify America's current political parties, and illustrate their ideas about government.

SS.7.C.2.9 Evaluate candidates for political office by analyzing their qualifications, experience, issue-based platforms, debates, and political ads.

SS.7.C.2.10 Examine the impact of media, individuals, and interest groups on monitoring and influencing government.

SS.7.C.2.13 Examine multiple perspectives on public and current issues.

SS.7.C.3.3 Illustrate the structure and function (three branches of government established in Articles I, II, and III with corresponding powers) of government in the United States as established in the Constitution.

SS.7.C.3.8 Analyze the structure, functions, and processes of the legislative, executive, and judicial branches.

Florida "Keys" to Learning

1. During the period of "Jacksonian Democracy," states abolished property qualifications for voting. All adult white males gained the right to vote. New campaign methods were developed. Jackson started the Democratic Party. Party nominating conventions began selecting candidates and making party platforms.

2. Jackson favored rotating officeholders. He dismissed top government officials and appointed his own supporters. Some people called this the "spoils system."

3. In 1830, Jackson proposed the Indian Removal Act, forcing all Indian tribes to relocate west of the Mississippi.

4. Georgia passed laws requiring the Cherokee Indians to leave. In *Cherokee Nation v. Georgia* (1831), Chief Justice John Marshall concluded the Cherokee tribe was not an independent foreign state and the Court had no authority over the case. In *Worcester v. Georgia* (1832), he ruled that Georgia state officials had no right to enter Cherokee lands. In 1838, federal troops forced the Cherokee from their homes. About 4,000 Cherokee died on the "Trail of Tears."

5. Jackson saw the Second Bank of the United States as representing elite interests. He vetoed a renewal of its charter and won the election of 1832 against supporters of the bank. In 1833, he withdrew government funds from the bank.

6. John C. Calhoun believed the federal union was a "compact" of states and that each state had the right to nullify (*cancel*) federal laws within its borders or to secede. In the Webster-Hayne debate, Daniel Webster argued the federal union was a union of the American people. States had no right to nullify federal laws or secede.

7. In 1832, Congress passed a new tariff. South Carolina objected and passed the Ordinance of Nullification. Congress authorized Jackson to use force against the state. The crisis ended when South Carolina withdrew its ordinance.

8. The Second Great Awakening encouraged greater emotion in religion. Participants applied Christian values to social issues. Preachers became active in the abolitionist and temperance movements.

9. In 1826, the American Temperance Society was formed against alcoholic beverages.

10. Christian preachers taught that slavery was a sin and encouraged the abolitionist movement. William Lloyd Garrison started *The Liberator* in 1831 and helped form the Anti-Slavery Society in 1833.

11. Dorothea Dix persuaded state legislatures to build state hospitals for the treatment of the mentally ill.

12. Horace Mann spread the "Common School" movement, which promoted state-tax funded schooling for children of all backgrounds with professional training for teachers.

13. In 1848, Elizabeth Cady Stanton and Lucretia Mott held the Seneca Falls Convention for women's rights. It approved Stanton's "Declaration of Sentiments."

14. Ralph Waldo Emerson rejected traditional religion. He found God in nature and inside each of us. Henry David Thoreau developed the idea of civil disobedience.

15. The period 1830–1860 was a golden age for American literature.

On a clear, crisp morning in March 1829, Andrew Jackson took the oath of office as President in front of the U.S. Capitol. He was surrounded by a crowd of more than 20,000 people. Jackson left the Capitol riding on a white horse. He trotted up Pennsylvania Avenue until he reached the White House. His new home was already filled with a bustling crowd. Visitors included Washington high society dressed in their finest clothes, Western frontiersmen in buckskin, and factory workers from the Northeast. Everyone wanted a glimpse of the new President.

Jackson's Inauguration

People entered and left the White House with dirty boots. Some guests accidentally knocked into the furniture and broke the White House china. White House staff moved the punch bowls, ice cream, and cake being served to visitors to the lawn to reduce the crowd inside. Jackson himself left for a nearby hotel.

The contrast with President Washington's inauguration forty years earlier could not have been greater. Jackson's election was seen as a victory for the "common man." By inviting the public to the White House, Jackson emphasized that the Presidency belonged to the people. In this chapter, you will learn how Jackson reached the White House and how America changed during his Presidency.

The Democratic Party is one of the two major political parties in the United States today.

The Presidency of Andrew Jackson

Jackson felt that Adams had stolen the 1824 election with Clay's help. In 1828, Jackson and Adams fought another bitter campaign. Both sides made strong personal attacks. Jackson was determined that the election would not be stolen again. His supporters organized clubs, public meetings, and torchlight parades. They printed thousands of pictures of General Jackson on his horse. His troops had once called Jackson "Old Hickory" because they said he was as tough as old hickory wood. His supporters now formed "Hickory Clubs" across the nation. Jackson's supporters also created their own new political party—the **Democratic Party**. It is the direct ancestor to the Democratic Party we have today.

Far more people voted in 1828 than four years earlier. This time Jackson won a clear majority of both the popular vote and the Electoral College. Sadly, his victory was accompanied by personal tragedy. His wife died a few weeks after his election. Jackson blamed her death on the stress from personal attacks by Adams and Clay.

Citizens can evaluate candidates by reading their political advertisements, listening to debates and learning about their platforms.

Election of 1828

Candidate	Electoral Vote	Popular Vote	Percent of Popular Vote
Andrew Jackson	178	647,286	56%
John Quincy Adams	83	508,064	44%

Source: Historical Statistics of the United States

Who Was Andrew Jackson?

Andrew Jackson's father died before he was born. As a boy, he carried papers for the Patriot army during the American Revolution. Both he and his brother were captured and held as prisoners. When Andrew refused to clean the boots of a British officer, his hand was slashed by the swing of a British sword. Andrew and his brother caught smallpox while being held by the British. His brother died. His other brother died in battle. His mother caught cholera while caring for American prisoners-of-war on British ships. She also died, leaving young Andrew an orphan. His entire family was wiped out by the Revolution. Young Jackson worked at odd jobs before studying law and becoming a lawyer on the frontier. He attended the Tennessee state convention in 1796 and became the state's first member in the U.S. House of Representatives. Later, Jackson became one of Tennessee's U.S. Senators as well as a member of the Tennessee Supreme Court. Jackson bought former Indian lands and became one of the founders of the city of Memphis. He also bought a large plantation for himself near Nashville. He became commander of the Tennessee militia. When the War of 1812 broke out, Jackson led militia forces against the Creek Indians. At the Battle of Horseshoe Bend, Jackson's soldiers killed hundreds of Creeks. Jackson forced the Creeks to give over millions of acres of land. In 1815, he became the hero of New Orleans. In 1818, his actions created the crisis that led Spain to give Florida to the United States.

"Jacksonian Democracy"

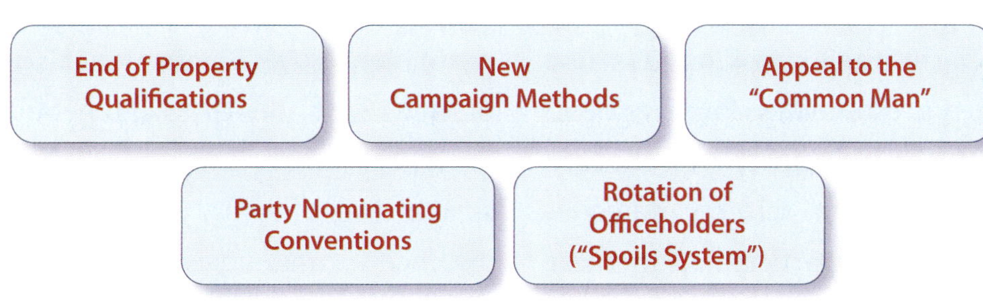

The 15th Amendment later expanded voting rights to adult males of all races: "The right of citizens of the United States to vote shall not be denied . . . on account of race . . ."

Characteristics of Jacksonian Democracy

Andrew Jackson believed in a strong Presidency. He saw the President as the only public official representing all the citizens of the United States.

During Jackson's two terms in office, the United States became more democratic. Historians often refer to these developments as "**Jacksonian Democracy**."

In these years, state governments were changing their requirements for voting. When the United States was founded, states had **property qualifications**. Only those with a certain amount of property could vote. In the 1820s, states were ending these requirements. By 1828, all adult white males could already vote in ten states. This meant ordinary workers and farmers could now influence national elections.

The Historian's Apprentice

Not everyone was happy with these democratic changes. The paragraph below is from an editorial in the *New York Journal of Commerce*:

> "*By throwing open the polls to every man that walks, we have placed the power in the hands of those who have neither property, talents, nor influence in other circumstances and who require in their public officers no higher qualifications than they possess themselves.*"

Why did the editors of this journal oppose ending property qualifications for voting?

With ordinary working people voting, the nature of politics changed. Candidates had to reach out more. There was no television, radio, or Internet. Political parties had to rely on newspaper articles, pamphlets, rallies, and meetings to get their message across. As methods of transportation and communication improved, it became possible to get more people involved in the political process. Jackson tried to appeal to these new voters—farmers, workers, and craftsmen. He became the champion of the "common man." Although he had become a rich slaveholder, he had worked his way up from poverty.

In the past, party leaders in Congress had chosen their party's candidates for President. During the 1830s, the first **party nominating conventions** were held to select candidates. Ordinary party members participated in these public conventions. The conventions chose candidates and made up party **platforms** (*changes the party hoped to make*). The Democratic Party held its first national convention in Baltimore in May 1832. Andrew Jackson was its candidate.

The Rotation of Officeholders—the "Spoils System"

During the election campaign of 1828, Jackson's enemies had pointed to his lack of experience in public office. They argued that he was not qualified to be President.

Jackson felt many officeholders stayed too long in government. They either became corrupt—using their power to benefit themselves—or they ignored public needs. Jackson favored the **rotation** (*changing*) of officeholders. He believed ordinary people should be able to fill the offices of government for a time. Then a new group of citizens should take their place. This would give more citizens actual experience participating in government. It would also make government more responsive to public needs. Finally, it would prevent the rise of a group of permanent government officials who were out of touch with the American people.

After Jackson was elected, he dismissed several top officials. Some of them had been in office for many years. Jackson appointed his own supporters in their place. Some called this the "spoils system" because it treated offices as spoils. In ancient times, the soldiers of a victorious army had rewarded themselves by taking riches from cities they conquered. These were called the "spoils of war." Jackson never used the term "spoils system" himself. In fact, he left most public officials in place. But he did change many more officeholders than previous Presidents had done.

The Historian's Apprentice

"The duties of all public officers are . . . so plain and simple that men of intelligence may readily qualify for their performance. . . .

I cannot but believe that more is lost by the long continuance of men in office than is generally to be gained by their experience. . . .

There are . . . few men who can for any great length of time enjoy office and power without being more or less under the influence unfavorable to the faithful discharge of their public duties."

—Andrew Jackson in his first Address to Congress (1829)

Make your own two-column chart listing the advantages and disadvantages of Jackson's rotation of officeholders, or "spoils system."

A Frenchman named **Alexis de Tocqueville** visited the United States in 1831. He described the practices of "Jacksonian Democracy" in his book *Democracy in America* (1835). Tocqueville believed that American social conditions had caused the expansion of democracy. Americans had achieved greater social equality than anywhere else. "It is impossible to believe that equality will not eventually find its way into the political world as it does everywhere else." Greater social equality was leading to more democratic politics.

Alexis de Tocqueville and a page from *Democracy in America*

Jackson and Internal Improvements: The Maysville Road Veto

In 1830, Congress passed a bill to provide money for building a road from Lexington to Maysville, Kentucky. The road was to be part of the system of roads connected to the National Road. It would also help connect Kentucky to the Ohio River. The proposal was typical of the internal improvements supported during the "Era of Good Feelings."

President Jackson vetoed the bill. Since the new road was being built in only one state, he said federal money should not be spent on it. Some historians think he may have opposed the road simply because Henry Clay recommended it as part of his "American System." Others see his veto as a defense of states' rights.

The President has the power to veto bills from Congress. A veto can be overridden by a 2/3 vote of members present in each house of Congress.

Jackson and the Indian Removal Act

Jackson grew up on the frontier. He had commanded troops against Creek and Seminole Indians. He feared that Indian tribes might cooperate with a foreign power like Britain or Spain. While Indians had been forced off the Northwest Territory, many tribes still remained in the South. Jackson wanted to move all Indian

Locations of Indians in the Southeast before the Indian Removal Act

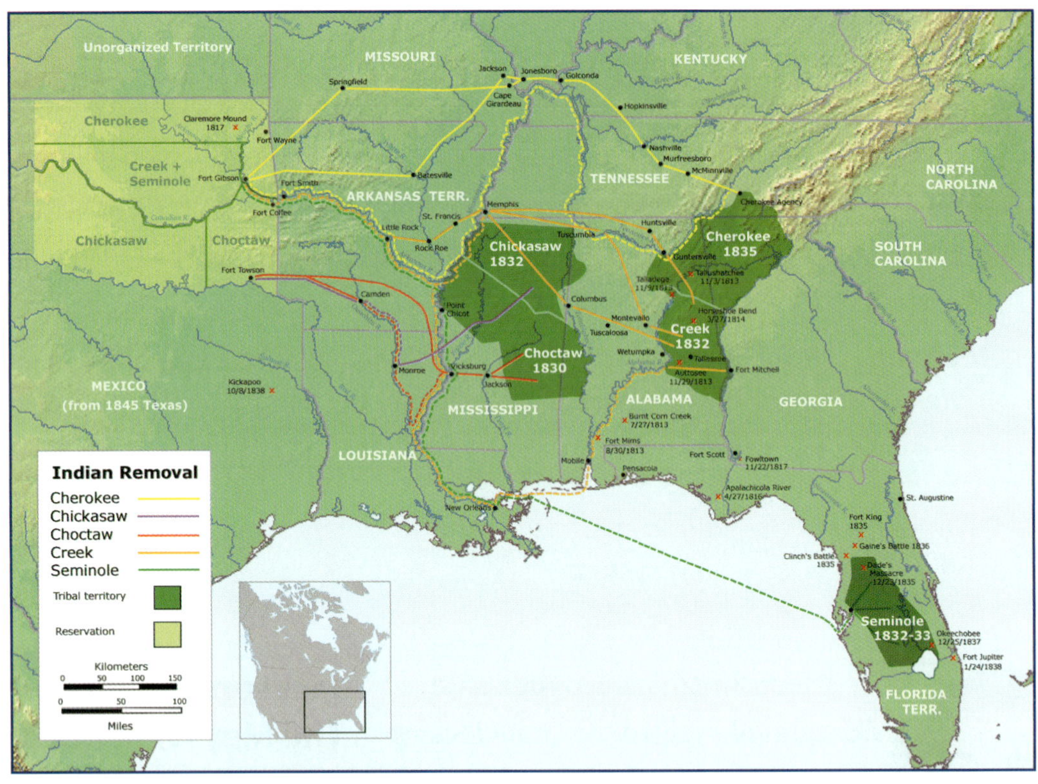

Leaders of several different tribes that were removed

Cherokee

Creek

Seminole

Chickasaw

Choctaw

Members of the Choctaw tribe in Louisiana during relocation

tribes to west of the Mississippi River in order to give their lands to white settlers.

In 1830, Jackson proposed the **Indian Removal Act** to Congress. Under this act, the Cherokee, Creeks, Choctaws, Chickasaws, Seminoles and all other tribes would be forced to relocate to lands reserved for them west of the Mississippi.

The Historian's Apprentice

In presenting the Indian Removal Act to Congress, Jackson listed these benefits:

"It will place a dense and civilized population in large tracts [*areas*] of country now occupied by a few savage hunters. By opening the whole territory between Tennessee on the north and Louisiana on the south to the settlement of whites it will incalculably strengthen the southwestern frontier. . . . It will relieve the whole state of Mississippi and the western part of Alabama of Indian occupancy, and enable those states to advance rapidly in population, wealth, and power.

It will separate the Indians from immediate contact with settlements of whites; free them from the power of the states; enable them to pursue happiness in their own way and under their own rude institutions; will retard [*slow down*] the progress of decay, which is lessening their numbers, and perhaps cause them gradually, under the protection of the government, and through the influence of good counsels, to cast off their savage habits and become an interesting, civilized and Christian community."

—Andrew Jackson, Address to Congress, December 6, 1830

1. Which of the reasons listed above was most important to Jackson? Why?
2. How, according to Jackson, would the proposed act benefit the Indians?
3. Imagine you are a member of Congress in 1830–1831. Write a short speech for or against this proposed act.
4. Which evidence in this passage suggests that Jackson may have been biased against Indians?
5. How do you think American society would have developed if Jackson had not forced Native American tribes to move west of the Mississippi River?

Most of the tribes agreed to move west, including the Choctaw, Creek, and Chickasaw. A small group of Indians led by **Chief Black Hawk** resisted during the "Black Hawk War." They were defeated in August 1832.

The **Cherokee** Indians also resisted removal. They relied on the American system of law rather than armed resistance.

The Cherokee lived in Georgia, North Carolina, Tennessee, and South Carolina. They considered themselves a "civilized" tribe. One of their chiefs, Sequoyah, even created a special alphabet for their language with 86 letters. The Cherokee had their own written constitution, elected their own officials, and published

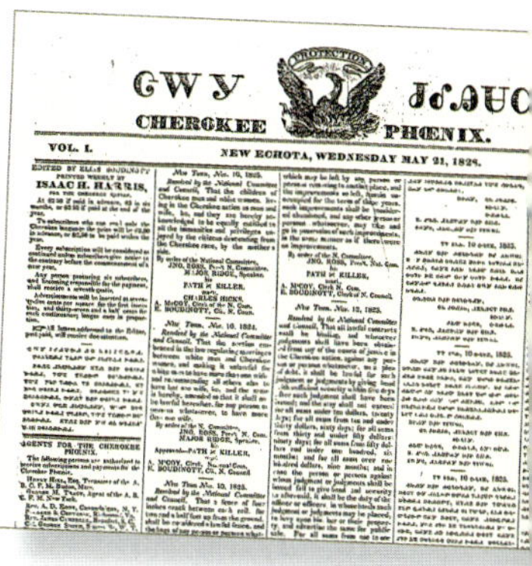

ᏣᎳᎩ CHEROKEE PROTECTION PHŒNIX.

VOL. I. NEW ECHOTA, WEDNESDAY MAY 21, 1828.

Cherokee-language newspaper

After they surrendered, **Chief Black Hawk** and other chiefs were imprisoned. Then a surprising thing happened. Rather than punish Black Hawk, Jackson had Black Hawk and the other chiefs taken by steamboat and railroad to several large American cities in the East. The chiefs were greeted by huge crowds. Black Hawk was even sent to Washington, D.C., to meet with President Jackson. Jackson wanted the Indian chiefs to see just how large and powerful the United States really was. Black Hawk later told his story to an American interpreter (*someone who translates*). His autobiography was published as a book and became a best seller. In the last years of his life, Black Hawk tried to promote peace between Indians and white settlers.

their own newspaper. They could not believe that their towns would be torn down and their people uprooted.

The State of Georgia passed its own laws requiring the Cherokee Indians to leave the state. White settlers were especially eager to claim these lands after gold was discovered there in 1829.

The Cherokee Indians challenged Georgia's removal order in the U.S. Supreme Court. The Cherokee claimed they were protected by several treaties. In the case of *Cherokee Nation v. Georgia* (1831), Chief Justice John Marshall ruled that the Cherokee tribe was a "dependent" nation. As a "dependent" nation, the tribe had a special relationship with the federal government. But since the Cherokee Indians were not an independent "foreign state," the Supreme Court had no authority to decide the case.

The Supreme Court is the highest court of the land and can hear appeals related to the Constitution.

A law can be challenged as "unconstitutional" (against the Constitution).

The Supreme Court: *Worcester v. Georgia* (1832)

The next year, the Supreme Court ruled on a second case concerning the Cherokee Indians and the State of Georgia. At this time, several American missionaries were living among the Cherokee. Some of them even advised the Cherokee to resist removal. In 1830, Georgia passed a new law. It said that any white person who wanted to live among the Indians needed a special license from the governor.

Samuel Worcester was one of the missionaries living with the Cherokee. Georgia officials entered Cherokee lands to arrest him. They sent Worcester to prison for four years for breaking the new law. Worcester sued the State of Georgia for his release. The Cherokee Indians helped pay his legal fees.

In this case, John Marshall ruled that the Georgia law was unconstitutional. Because the Cherokee tribe was a "dependent" nation, Georgia state officials had no right to enter Cherokee lands without their permission: "The Cherokee Nation is a distinct community, occupying its own territory . . . in which Georgia laws can have no force."

Jackson disagreed with Marshall's decision. He believed the Cherokee Indians should either submit to state authorities or move out of the state.

Despite Marshall's ruling, Jackson still wanted to move the Cherokee tribe west of the Mississippi. He concluded a treaty with a small group of Cherokee leaders in 1835. The new treaty gave the Cherokee two years to leave their homes to move to Oklahoma. Cherokee leaders representing most of the tribe rejected the treaty. They even appealed to the U.S. Senate asking them not to ratify it. Eventually all of their efforts ended in tragedy. In the late spring of 1838, federal troops appeared on their lands to take them to "Indian" territory (Oklahoma). They were first taken to guarded camps. Then groups of about a thousand each were forced to make the long journey in the fall and winter. About a fourth of them died from hunger and cold on the tragic march known as the **"Trail of Tears."** The State of Georgia gave their former lands to white settlers.

Jackson's "War" on the Bank

Much of Jackson's time as President was spent attacking the Second Bank of the United States. Jackson saw the bank as representing a small privileged elite, which took unfair advantage of government favors.

This is another example of a Presidential veto—one of the powers of the executive branch.

General Jackson Slaying the Many Headed Monster

Jackson had a great hatred for the bank. He blamed the bank for his own money troubles during the "Panic of 1819." Within months of becoming President, Jackson accused the bank of failing to create a stable currency. Despite the Supreme Court's ruling in *McCulloch v. Maryland*, Jackson said the bank was unconstitutional. The president of the bank, Nicholas Biddle, feared the bank's charter would not be renewed in 1836. He tried to reach a compromise with Jackson but failed.

Henry Clay persuaded Congress to vote to renew the bank's charter in 1832, before the old charter ran out. Jackson vetoed the bill. Renewal of the bank's charter became the central issue of the election of 1832. Jackson was running for his second term. Clay and other opponents of Jackson formed a new political party called the Whigs. They made fun of Jackson's overbearing and dictatorial ways. The cartoon to the right shows him as "King Andrew." Clay became the Whig candidate. He was Jackson's opponent in the election.

King Andrew

Jackson's Democratic Party held its first nominating convention that year. Jackson believed that his party represented ordinary American farmers and workers against the "monied interest"—the wealthy bankers and investors who favored the bank.

The Election of 1832

Candidate	Political Party	Electoral Vote	Popular Vote	Percent of Popular Vote
Andrew Jackson	Democratic	219	687,502	56%
Henry Clay	Whig	49	530,189	44%

Source: Historical Statistics of the United States

Jackson again won a landslide victory. After his re-election, he took further steps against the bank. In 1833, he suddenly ordered the withdrawal of all of the federal government's funds from the bank. Jackson moved these funds into state banks. This caused the bank to collapse even before its charter ended. In fact, the bank had served many useful purposes. Without it, there was little control over state banks, which printed too many bank notes. The result was another **recession** (*economic downturn*) in 1837, just after Jackson left office.

The Historian's Apprentice

Andrew Jackson told Congress the following during his "war" with the bank:

"It is to be regretted that the rich and powerful too often bend the acts of government to their selfish purposes. Distinctions in society will always exist under every just government. . . . [W]hen the laws undertake to add to these natural and just advantages artificial distinctions, to grant . . . exclusive privileges, to make the rich richer and the potent more powerful, the humble members of society—the farmers, mechanics and laborers—who have neither the time nor the means of securing like favors to themselves, have a right to complain of the injustice of their Government . . . "

1. How did this speech and Jackson's "war" on the bank show his concern for the "common man"?
2. Was Jackson right to oppose the bank? Were Americans better off with or without it?

A bill goes through a long process to become a law. To become a law, a majority of both houses of Congress must approve it.

The Tariff and the Nullification Crisis

Another important issue that Jackson faced was the tariff issue. This led to a crisis that could have ended in civil war.

The Tariff of Abominations

A few months before the election of 1828, a bill for a new tariff came before Congress. It proposed tariffs on raw materials needed by manufacturers as well as on manufactured goods. It raised rates above 60%. The sponsors of the bill actually hoped it would be rejected by the Northeast and that no tariff would be passed at all. To their surprise, the bill passed. Southerners and some members from New England

The Supreme Court can declare laws unconstitutional. This is an example of checks and balances.

voted against it, but it had the support of the West, the Mid-Atlantic states, and most of New England. Southerners called the new law the "Tariff of Abominations." (An *abomination* is something that disgusts us.)

Calhoun and Nullification

In 1828, John C. Calhoun was Vice President. Twelve years earlier, he had supported the protective tariff of 1816. Since that time, Calhoun had become very concerned about the future of the South. He turned against the tariff, which favored the North. He even decided that the tariff was unconstitutional because it so clearly favored one section of the country over another.

Calhoun became the leading spokesman for states' rights. He secretly published an essay that argued that the federal union was a "compact" of states. Each state therefore had the right to **nullify** (*cancel*) a law within its borders if it thought the law was unconstitutional. A state also had the right to **secede** (*break away*) from the union. Calhoun's essay was called *South Carolina Exposition and Protest*. (An "exposition" is an explanation.)

The Webster-Hayne Debate

In January 1830, the Senate debated whether the sale of public lands in the West should be temporarily stopped. In the debate, Southern and Northern Senators battled for the support of the West. Senator Hayne of South Carolina brought up the tariff issue. He argued in favor of Calhoun's "nullification" theory. Senator Daniel Webster of Massachusetts argued against it. Webster told Congress that the federal union was not a "compact" of states. It was a union of the American people. States therefore did not have the right to nullify a law or to leave the union. Moreover, it was not the role of states to decide if a law was constitutional. That job, Webster said, belonged to the U.S. Supreme Court. Webster ended his speech with a striking declaration. He called for "Liberty and Union, now and forever, one and inseparable." Americans could not have one without the other.

John C. Calhoun	Daniel Webster
1. The union was a **compact** of states (an association by agreement).	1. The union was the creation of the American people as a whole.
2. Any state can **nullify** a federal law within its borders if it believes the law is unconstitutional.	2. States cannot nullify federal law.
3. States can leave the union at any time.	3. States cannot leave the union.

Jackson Makes His Views Known

Andrew Jackson was a Southerner and slave owner. He was a known supporter of states' rights. Calhoun hoped that Jackson would support his views. Instead, Jackson remained silent on the matter. Calhoun and his supporters wished to encourage Jackson to give them his public support. In April 1830, Jackson, Calhoun, and other important leaders attended a dinner in honor of Thomas Jefferson's birthday. Calhoun made a series of toasts. Finally, it was Jackson's turn to make one of his own. All the guests fell silent and turned their eyes towards the President as he spoke. "The federal union," Jackson said as he raised his glass, "It must be preserved!"

With these words, everyone knew that Jackson opposed Calhoun's ideas on nullification. Calhoun replied with his own toast: "The union—next to our liberty, most dear." He continued: "May we all remember that it can only be preserved by respecting the rights of the states."

South Carolina's Ordinance of Nullification

In 1832, Congress passed a new tariff. Its rates were lower than those of the Tariff of Abominations, but South Carolina still objected to it. The citizens of South Carolina held a special state convention. The convention passed the **Ordinance of Nullification**. This *ordinance*, or law, declared that the Tariff of 1832 was unconstitutional. Therefore, the state would not enforce it. South Carolina further threatened to **secede** (*leave*) from the union if the federal government tried to make it collect the tariff duties. Calhoun resigned as Vice President in December 1832.

Jackson's Response

President Jackson responded to the crisis at once. He called South Carolina's Ordinance of Nullification an act of treason (*the crime of betraying one's country*). He sent warships to the harbor of Charleston, the main city of South Carolina. Congress passed a **Force Bill** authorizing Jackson to use military force against the state. Jackson published a "Proclamation to the People of South Carolina." He warned its citizens that the nullification power they claimed was "incompatible with the existence of the Union" and that he was prepared to use force.

Faced with this threat, South Carolina quickly stepped down. The state withdrew its ordinance. Henry Clay suggested a compromise in which tariffs were gradually reduced over the next ten years. Congress quickly approved his proposal. In this way, bloodshed was avoided.

The Historian's Apprentice

1. Discuss your answers to the following two questions with a partner. Then share your ideas with your class.
   - Do you think Jackson handled the crisis effectively?
   - Are there any lessons in how Jackson dealt with the nullification crisis for leaders today?
2. Would you consider Jackson a "good" or a "bad" President? Make a chart or graphic organizer showing both his accomplishments and drawbacks. Consider his impact on democratic politics, internal improvements, Indian resettlement, the national bank, and the preservation of the union.
3. Andrew Jackson believed in the political and legal equality of white adult males of all backgrounds and incomes. This was a great step forward in the march towards equality. Yet Jackson had no respect at all for Native Americans or African Americans. He also did not look on women as equals. Was he advanced in his views if we judge him by the standards of his time? Or could he have done more to reform society and promote equality? Discuss your views with a partner and share your ideas with the class.

The Age of Reform

The period of Jackson's Presidency is sometimes called America's first "Age of Reform." Reformers wanted to raise the nation's morals and spread Christian values. In the 1820s and 1830s, people believed reform could be achieved through private and voluntary efforts. During these years, a large number of reform societies appeared. These social movements were just as important as the changes in politics.

The Second Great Awakening

Behind these new reform movements were deep religious forces. The "**Second Great Awakening**" began in the early 1800s and reached its peak in the 1830s. Like the First Great Awakening, it encouraged greater emotion and enthusiasm in religion. People examined their own lives to see if they would be "saved" and go to Heaven.

During the Second Great Awakening, Protestant "revival" meetings took place in frontier areas such as Tennessee, Kentucky, Ohio, and upstate New York. In many of these areas, there were no permanent preachers or churches. Traveling preachers went from place to place. They attracted large audiences from many nearby communities. Women were especially active in the Second Great Awakening.

Hundreds of people gathered outside in the open air at special "camp meetings." They listened to preachers and sang hymns. Different ministers preached and sang until late into the night. As the meeting continued, the sermons became more emotional and the audience grew more excited. People might jerk their heads, roll on the ground, or dance for hours.

Those who participated in the Second Great Awakening tried to apply Christian values to social issues. Preachers emphasized that each

individual had a personal responsibility to help end sinful practices and promote God's will. They saw reform as an important part of God's plan. Some hoped to make the world a better place in order to bring the return of Jesus (the "Second Coming") sooner. These Christians believed that slaveholding and drinking strong alcoholic beverages were serious sins. Many of them became active in reform movements.

Lyman Beecher was a popular Protestant minister in Boston. He helped organize the American Temperance Society, which opposed the use of alcoholic beverages. Beecher also founded a famous religious school for preachers in Ohio. His son, Henry Ward Beecher, was another important preacher and social

Charles Grandison Finney (1792–1875) was a leading preacher during the Second Great Awakening. He taught that people could save themselves if they had the will to do so. In his twenties, Finney had been studying law. Finney had a spiritual experience that led to his "conversion" to Christianity. He felt God's love moving through his body like a wave of electricity. Finney gave up law to become a preacher. He introduced "New Measures" in his preaching. Finney asked women to pray aloud in prayer meetings. He asked listeners to stand up and make public pledges when they felt ready to become born-again Christians. Finney used informal, common language in his prayers and sermons. His "free church movement" had an open-door policy in which anyone could come into his church. An "Anxious Bench" was set aside for those souls who felt especially troubled. Finney's preaching had a radical impact. In 1830, he gave a series of 98 sermons in Rochester, New York—a boomtown along the Erie Canal. His sermons were so popular that half the shops in the town were closed.

In 1835, some of Finney's students took him to Oberlin College in Ohio. This was the first American college to offer education to women and African Americans on equal terms with white men. Finney became a professor and later the president of Oberlin. He was a prominent **abolitionist** (*someone working to abolish slavery*). He encouraged his wife to help with his activities and he also promoted women's rights.

reformer. His daughter, Harriet Beecher Stowe, was a famous abolitionist and the author of *Uncle Tom's Cabin* (1852).

The Temperance Movement

In the early 1800s, the average American drank almost three times as much alcohol as today. Cheap whiskey made from corn was very popular. Reformers believed that heavy drinking was bad for health and morals. People blamed heavy drinkers for ruining their families' lives and for committing crimes. In 1826, Lyman Beecher started the American Temperance Society. Within five years, it had almost 200,000 members. Members made a pledge not to drink strong alcoholic beverages like whiskey. Temperance groups spread quickly across the West and South. In the 1840s, they began asking states to pass laws against alcoholic beverages. In 1846, Maine became the first state to limit alcoholic drinks. In 1851, it banned them altogether.

The Abolitionist Movement

The 13th Amendmer
later abolished slave

During the Second Great Awakening, Christian preachers taught that slavery was a sin. These preachers became early leaders in the **abolitionist movement**—the movement to *abolish*, or end, slavery. Free African Americans, such as the minister Theodore S. Wright, Sojourner Truth, and Frederick Douglass, were also important abolitionists.

In 1831, **William Lloyd Garrison** began publishing his abolitionist journal, *The Liberator,* in Boston. Garrison called for an immediate end to slavery and its horrors.

In December 1833, Garrison met with other abolitionists in Philadelphia to form the **Anti-Slavery Society.** A third of its founders were Quakers. New anti-slavery societies soon sprang

The Historian's Apprentice

"My name is 'LIBERATOR'! I propose

To hurl my shafts at freedom's deadliest foes! . . .

I am determined, at every hazard, to lift up the standard of emancipation in the eyes of the nation, *within sight of Bunker Hill and in the birth place of liberty* . . .

I am aware that many object to the severity of my language; but is there not cause for severity? I *will be* as harsh as truth, and as uncompromising as justice. On this subject, I do not wish to think, or speak, or write, with moderation. . . . I am in earnest—I will not equivocate—I will not excuse—I will not retreat a single inch—**AND I WILL BE HEARD**."

—William Lloyd Garrison, first issue of *The Liberator* (January 1, 1831)

1. Why did Garrison refer to Bunker Hill?
2. In 1831, would you have favored an immediate or gradual end to slavery? Why?

up across the North. They mailed pamphlets, printed articles and sent petitions to Congress against slavery. A few abolitionists even stopped eating sugar or wearing cotton clothes because these products were made by slaves.

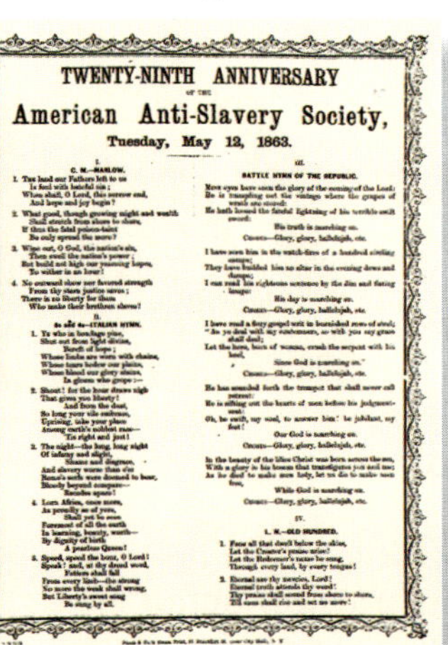
TWENTY-NINTH ANNIVERSARY OF THE American Anti-Slavery Society, Tuesday, May 12, 1863.

In the 1830s, abolitionists also mailed anti-slavery flyers to the South. Southern post offices refused to deliver them, fearing they might lead to a slave rebellion. President Jackson, himself a slaveholder, supported the post office in this policy.

Being an abolitionist could be dangerous, even in the North. In 1834, a mob attacked abolitionists' homes in New York City. In 1835, William Lloyd Garrison spoke at Harvard University. He was chased by an angry crowd and almost killed. In 1847, abolitionist publisher Elijah Lovejoy was murdered in Illinois by a mob that broke into his warehouse.

Prison Reform

The Constitution safeguards people's basic rights. We enjoy more rights today than Americans did in 1830.

In the early 1800s, American prisons were also in need of reform. Criminals were punished by beating, whipping, or being thrown in jail. There was no belief, as today, that prisoners should be reformed so that they could safely return to society.

In Jackson's day, jails were often just one large room. Debtors, the mentally ill and older children might be thrown in jail alongside dangerous criminals. Prisons were usually dirty and unhealthy places. Many were old buildings once used for a different purpose. Prisoners might have no opportunity to talk with other prisoners or to exercise. They could be charged for their food.

Reformers tried to change these conditions. They looked at crime as a social problem and tried to treat its causes. They passed new laws to keep debtors out of jail. They built special reform schools for children who had committed crimes, rather than putting them together with adult prisoners.

Instead of putting all prisoners in a large common room, New York State began putting prisoners in separate cells. Prisoners worked together during the day, but they slept alone at night. Other states began to copy this example.

American prison reform became so well known that the French government sent Alexis de Tocqueville here to study it. That is why Tocqueville originally came to the United States.

The Treatment of Mental Illness

In the 1830s, people with serious mental illness could be thrown in a prison or "mad house." They could be locked up, tied up, or beaten. There was little understanding of mental illness and how it should be treated.

Dorothea Dix was a school teacher who volunteered to teach in a women's prison in Massachusetts in 1841. She was shocked to see inmates whose only crime was mental illness. Many had been locked up and were dressed in rags or even naked. Dix made a detailed investigation of mentally ill people in Massachusetts prisons. Her research took two years to complete. Then she wrote a report for the state legislature. She complained that the mentally ill were placed in "cages, closets, [and] stalls." They were "chained, naked, beaten with rods and [whipped] into obedience." Dix persuaded the state legislature to change its policies. The state built a special addition to the state hospital for the treatment of the insane.

Soon Dix was invited to inspect prison conditions in other states. She proposed a system of federal hospitals for the insane. Congress approved her proposal, but President Franklin Pierce vetoed it. Dix continued to work in other states. Her reports led many states to build special hospitals for patients with mental illnesses.

Education: The "Common School" Movement

The rise of industry and the growing number of Americans living in cities created an urgent need for a better system of American education. There was no uniformity anywhere. In many states, children received no formal schooling at all. In others, they went to school but children of all ages were placed together in the same classroom.

In Massachusetts, **Horace Mann** believed that the state should have free and compulsory (*required*) elementary education for all children—both boys and girls. In 1837, Mann was appointed as the secretary to the state's new Board of Education. He reorganized the state's entire educational system. Mann also began making annual reports. Mann's program became known as the "Common School" movement because he believed that all children should attend the same common schools. Mann felt that children from all social classes and backgrounds would benefit from being mixed together.

Principles of Mann's "Common School" Movement

1. The state should use tax money to pay for elementary schools. School should be free for all families.
2. School should be compulsory for younger children.
3. Children of all backgrounds should be in the same common schools.
4. Schools should not be religious.
5. Teachers should receive professional training.

The Historian's Apprentice

1. What is the relationship between public education and democracy?
2. Which ideas of the "Common School" movement do you see as still influential today?

The 19th Amendment later gave women the right to vote.

Women's Rights

In the early nineteenth century, American women did not enjoy the same rights as men. They could not vote. They could not get a higher education. They could not have a professional career in medicine, law, or religion. Often a woman had no choice in selecting her husband. Once a woman did marry, her property and any money she earned belonged to her husband, not herself.

Lucretia Mott

Elizabeth Cady Stanton

This is an example of how citizens can influence public policy.

Some women in the abolitionist movement became active in the struggle for women's rights. Sarah Grimké published *Letters on the Equality of the Sexes and the Condition of Women* in a Massachusetts newspaper in 1837. Ernestine Rose moved from Europe to America in 1836. She gave lectures on both abolition and women's rights. In 1838 she sent a petition to the New York State legislature demanding property rights for married women.

Lucretia Mott and **Elizabeth Cady Stanton** were both abolitionists. Mott was a Quaker. Stanton was active in the temperance movement. The two women met by accident at an international abolitionist conference in England in 1840. The men at the conference voted to exclude (*keep out*) the women delegates. Mott, Stanton, and other women were sent behind a curtain to listen as observers. William Lloyd Garrison, who was also there, was so angry that he joined the women in protest. This experience made Stanton and Mott turn their attention to women's rights.

It took them several years, but Mott and Stanton finally organized a convention for women's rights at Seneca Falls in upstate New York in 1848. This was the town where Stanton lived. Several hundred people attended their **Seneca Falls Convention**. The famous abolitionist Frederick Douglass was one of many speakers. Stanton wrote a "**Declaration of Sentiments.**" She read it aloud at the convention. She based much of it on the Declaration of Independence.

The Declaration included a list of women's grievances. One of the most important was that women did not have the right to vote, yet they had to submit to the decisions of a government that did not represent them.

A hundred people at the convention signed the Declaration. The demand for the right to vote—known as **suffrage**—would become the main focus of the women's rights movement in the coming years. But in 1848, many women reformers were willing to put their grievances aside for a time while they put all their efforts into the slavery question.

> We hold these truths to be self-evident: that all men and women are created equal; that they are endowed by their Creator with certain inalienable rights; that among these are life, liberty, and the pursuit of happiness; that to secure these rights governments are instituted, deriving their powers from the consent of the governed . . .
>
> The history of mankind is a history of repeated injuries and usurpation on the part of man toward woman, having in direct object the establishment of an absolute tyranny over her. To prove this, let facts be submitted to a candid world.
>
> —*The Declaration of Sentiments* (1848)

The Historian's Apprentice

1. Make a poster for women's rights in 1848.
2. Using the Internet, read "*The Declaration of Sentiments.*" Make a list of the grievances it includes and present your list to a small group or your entire class. Then discuss which of these grievances were the most important.
3. Women reformers were divided over whether to focus on their own rights or on abolition in the years before the Civil War. If you had been a reformer in 1848, what would have been your view?

Literary and Artistic Movements

Literary and artistic movements also had a great impact on American life in these years. Even today, many people believe some of the greatest works of American literature were written in this period.

Ralph Waldo Emerson began his life as a Protestant minister. He stopped preaching when his twenty-year-old wife died in 1831. His grief was too great. Emerson went on a tour of Europe. In Paris, he was very moved by the arrangement of plants in the city's gardens. He came to the belief that everything in nature was connected. When Emerson returned to America, he wrote "Nature," a famous essay that had a great impact on writers and artists. Emerson abandoned religion as it was understood by most people. Instead, he felt that truth could be found by looking at the natural world. To truly understand nature, Emerson said, we have to separate ourselves from society. We have to go to a place of untamed nature on our own and see it with our very own eyes. We have to look at the stars, the ocean, or a group of trees and appreciate their beauty without being distracted by other concerns—"if a man would be alone, let him look at the stars." Then the beauty of nature will simply take us away. We will realize that we are actually a part of nature ourselves. God, Emerson believed, was not revealed in Bible stories. God could only be experienced in nature. God is in nature and also within each of us.

The same year that Emerson published "Nature," he started the "Transcendental Club." Emerson and other **Transcendentalists** believed we should not be influenced by what others think of us. Instead, we have to look inside ourselves for our own true principles. Inside each of us is our own individual "genius" or spirit.

Emerson's views had a great influence on other writers and painters. His student, **Henry David Thoreau**, developed the idea of **civil disobedience**—that we should refuse to obey laws we think are immoral. Thoreau spent a night in jail rather than pay a tax he thought would help promote the spread of slavery. Emerson also encouraged the work of the famous poet **Walt Whitman**.

Novelists **Nathaniel Hawthorne** and **Herman Melville** were also influenced by Emerson. Hawthorne was Emerson's neighbor in Concord in the 1840s. He wrote best-selling novels that looked at America's Puritan past. His books *The Scarlet Letter* (1850) and *The House of Seven Gables* (1851) dealt with the themes of love, sin, jealousy, and guilt. Herman Melville became a friend of Hawthorne's in the 1850s. Melville's stories and novels, such as *Benito Cereno* (1855) and *Moby-Dick* (1851), dealt with themes like slavery, the whaling industry, and life at sea. Many readers consider these among the best American novels ever written.

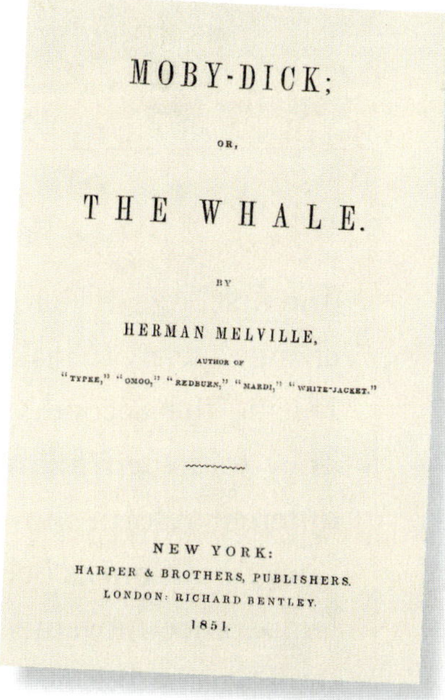
MOBY-DICK;

OR,

THE WHALE.

BY

HERMAN MELVILLE,

AUTHOR OF

"TYPEE," "OMOO," "REDBURN," "MARDI," "WHITE-JACKET."

NEW YORK:
HARPER & BROTHERS, PUBLISHERS.
LONDON: RICHARD BENTLEY.
1851.

Title page of Moby-Dick

Artists were also greatly affected by Emerson's love of nature as well as by the Romantic painters of Europe. The artists of the **Hudson River School** painted giant landscapes. They glamorized the American wilderness. They painted tiny, isolated human figures against

In the woods, we return to reason and faith. There I feel that nothing can befall me in life, — no disgrace, no calamity . . . which nature cannot repair. . . . I am nothing; I see all; the currents of the Universal Being circulate through me; I am part or particle of God. . . . I am the lover of uncontained and immortal beauty. . .

—Ralph Waldo Emerson, *Nature*

How do you feel when you go into nature—looking at the woods, a beach, or the stars?

scenes of giant cliffs, trees, or mountains. They showed magnificent lakes, rivers, and waterfalls. In their paintings, the sky is often shown with sun rays breaking through puffy clouds or patches of bright blue. These stunning visions illustrated Emerson's belief that God can be found in the beauty of nature.

Albert Bierstadt, *Among the Sierra Nevada Mountains*

The Historian's Apprentice

1. Imagine a conversation between Ralph Waldo Emerson and Charles Grandison Finney. What do you think they would talk about? Select a partner in your class. One of you should pretend to be Emerson and the other should be Finney. Then have a conversation.
2. Research a major American writer or painter who worked in the period 1830-1850. How did the events and ideas of those times influence their works? Write a short paper or prepare an oral presentation for your class.

America's First "Age of Reform"

The first "Age of Reform" was an important era of American history. Reform is any attempt to change society to make it better. Religious forces were behind many of these reform movements. During the Second Great Awakening, Protestant preachers ______________________. They told their followers that ______________________. There were many different reform movements. Each of these movements was an example of civic participation. Abolitionists believed that ______________________. Supporters of the temperance movement wanted to ______________________. Dorothea Dix worked to improve conditions for ______________________. Horace Mann was the leader of the "Common School" movement. Mann urged states to ______________________. Lucretia Mott and Elizabeth Cady Stanton held a convention at Seneca Falls in 1848 in support of ______________________.

The chart below lists some of the main events during the Presidency of Andrew Jackson and the Age of Reform. Create your own illustrated timeline using some of these events. Decide on the theme of your timeline and create a title. Then, choose those events that relate to your theme. Finally, make your own illustrations.

May 1828	"Tariff of Abominations"
Nov 1828	Jackson elected as President
March 1829	Inauguration of Jackson
April 1830	Toasts at Jefferson Day Dinner
May 1830	Jackson signs Indian Removal Act
Sept 1830	Charles Grandison Finney's Rochester Revival
Jan 1831	William Lloyd Garrison starts *The Liberator*
March 1831	*Cherokee Nation v. Georgia*
March 1832	*Worcester v. Georgia*
July 1832	Congress passes bill to renew bank charter; Jackson vetoes bank bill
July 1832	Jackson signs Tariff of 1832
Nov 1832	Jackson re-elected; South Carolina passes Ordinance of Nullification
March 1833	Jackson signs Force Bill; Compromise Tariff of 1833; South Carolina repeals Ordinance of Nullification
June 1833	Jackson removes federal funds from Second Bank of the US
Dec 1835	A group of Cherokees sign treaty with Jackson
Sept 1836	Emerson publishes "Nature"
March 1837	Jackson leaves Washington; Martin Van Buren becomes President
June 1837	Horace Mann becomes Secretary of Board of Education
Summer 1838	US Army begins rounding up Cherokee Indians, starting the "Trail of Tears"; they begin their march that winter
Sept 1838	Frederick Douglass escapes from slavery
March 1841	Dorothea Dix visits women's prison in Massachusetts
July 1848	Seneca Falls Convention for Women's Rights
March 1850	Nathaniel Hawthorne publishes *The Scarlet Letter*
Nov 1851	Herman Melville publishes *Moby-Dick*

Name:________________________________

Explain how the names and terms in each box are related.

Political party	Election campaign
Party nominating convention	Party platform

Indian Removal Act	Dependent nation
Cherokee v. Georgia	Trail of Tears

Tariff	Ordinance
Nullification	Compact of States

Veto	Bank of the United States
Charter	Monopoly

Women's rights	Suffrage
Abolitionist	Temperance

Chapter Review Cards

The Election of 1828

- In 1828, Adams and Jackson fought another bitter campaign. It was the first modern election campaign. More people voted in 1828 than in the previous election.
- Jackson and his supporters formed the **Democratic Party** in 1828.
- Jackson won a majority of both the popular vote and the Electoral College.

"Jacksonian Democracy"

- Jackson believed in a strong Presidency. He believed the President was the only public official representing all citizens.
- The United States was becoming more democratic. States abolished **property qualifications** for voting. In many states, all adult white males had the right to vote. Millions of workers and farmers could now vote. Jackson represented the "common man."
- Candidates had to reach out more to voters. Political parties relied on newspaper articles, pamphlets, rallies, and meetings to get their message to voters.
- During the 1830s, the **first party nominating conventions** were held to select candidates. The conventions chose candidates and made up party **platforms**. Jackson's **Democratic Party** held its first national convention in 1832.
- Jackson felt officeholders stayed too long in government and favored the **rotation** of officeholders. He dismissed several top government officials and appointed his own supporters in their place. Some called this the "**spoils system**."

Jackson and the Indian Removal Act

- In 1830, Jackson proposed the **Indian Removal Act**. This forced remaining Indian tribes to relocate west of the Mississippi. His aim was to separate Indians from whites and also to take their lands.
- Indians led by **Chief Black Hawk** resisted during the "Black Hawk War." They were defeated in 1832.
- The State of Georgia passed laws requiring the Cherokee Indians to leave the state. The Cherokee challenged these laws in the case of ***Cherokee Nation v. Georgia*** (1831). Chief Justice John Marshall concluded that the Cherokee tribe was a "dependent" nation. Because they were not an independent "foreign state," the Supreme Court had no authority to decide the case.
- In 1830, Georgia passed a law that a white person needed a special license from the governor to live among the Indians. Missionary Samuel Worcester was arrested and sent to prison for breaking this law. Worcester sued the State of Georgia. In the Supreme Court case, ***Worcester v. Georgia*** (1832), Marshall ruled that the state law was unconstitutional. Georgia state officials had no right to enter Cherokee lands.
- In 1836, Jackson signed a treaty with a small group of Cherokee. It gave them two years to leave their homes to move to Oklahoma. The majority of Cherokee rejected the new treaty.
- In 1838, federal troops appeared on their lands to take them to "Indian" territory in Oklahoma. They ended up moving in the cold winter. About 4,000 of them died on what is known as the "**Trail of Tears**."

Jackson's "War" on the Bank

- Jackson saw the **Second Bank of the United States** as representing the interests of a wealthy, privileged minority in the Northeast. Congress voted to renew the bank's charter in 1832. Jackson vetoed this bill.
- Jackson felt that his Democratic Party represented farmers and workers against the "monied interest" that favored the bank. Jackson won a landslide victory in 1832 against Clay and the Whig Party, who favored the bank.
- In 1833, Jackson withdrew government funds from the bank. He ended the bank's effectiveness even before its charter came to an end.
- The bank had prevented state banks from printing too many bank notes. Its end led to a **recession**.

The Tariff and the Nullification Crisis

- The Tariff of 1828 was so high it became known as the "**Tariff of Abominations**."
- Vice President **John C. Calhoun** believed the tariff was unconstitutional because it favored the North over the South. Calhoun published an essay, *South Carolina Exposition and Protest*. He argued that the federal union was a "compact" (or agreement) of states. Each state therefore had the right to **nullify** (cancel) a law within its borders if it thought the law was unconstitutional. A state also had the right to **secede** from the union.
- In the **Webster-Hayne Debate** of 1830, Senator Hayne of South Carolina argued in favor of Calhoun's "nullification" theory. Senator **Daniel Webster** of Massachusetts argued that the federal union was a union of the American people. States therefore did not have any right to nullify a law or leave the union: "Liberty and union—one and inseparable."
- In 1832, Congress passed a new tariff law. South Carolina objected and passed the **Ordinance of Nullification**. It said the tariff was unconstitutional and that it would not enforce it. The state also threatened to **secede** (leave) from the union. Jackson called the ordinance an act of treason and sent warships to Charleston. Congress passed a **Force Bill**, authorizing Jackson to use military force against the state. South Carolina withdrew its ordinance. Clay came up with a compromise tariff, gradually reducing rates.

The Second Great Awakening

- The **Second Great Awakening** encouraged greater emotion and enthusiasm in religion. Preachers held "camp meetings," especially in frontier areas. Participants tried to apply Christian values to social issues.
- Preachers emphasized that each person had a responsibility to help end sinful practices and promote God's will. They saw reform as an important part of God's plan and became active in the abolitionist and temperance movements.
- **Charles Grandison Finney** (1792–1875) was a leading preacher during the Second Great Awakening. Finney used informal language in his sermons. His "free church movement" had an open-door policy in which anyone could come and sit anywhere in his church. He was a prominent **abolitionist** and also promoted women's rights.

The Temperance Movement

- In 1826, Presbyterian minister Lyman Beecher founded the American Temperance Society in Boston.
- Temperance, against drinking alcoholic beverages, became very popular.
- In the 1840s, supporters began asking states to ban the sale of alcoholic beverages.

The Abolitionist Movement

- Christian preachers taught that slavery was a sin. Many became leaders of the **abolitionist movement**, along with free African Americans such as Theodore S. Wright, Sojourner Truth, and Frederick Douglass.
- In 1831, **William Lloyd Garrison** published the first issue of his journal, *The Liberator*, which called for an immediate end to slavery.
- In 1833, Garrison and others formed the **Anti-Slavery Society** in Philadelphia. New anti-slavery societies appeared across the North. They printed articles and sent petitions to Congress against slavery.

Prison Reform

- Reformers saw crime as a social problem. They passed laws keeping debtors out of jail. They built special reform schools for children who committed crimes.
- New York State started putting prisoners in separate cells. Prisoners worked together during the day and slept alone at night.

Mental Illness

- **Dorothea Dix** conducted a two-year study of the mistreatment of the mentally ill in Massachusetts state prisons. She presented a report to the state legislature. Dix persuaded the state legislature to build a state hospital to treat the mentally ill.
- Dix continued her work in other states. Her work led to the further building of special hospitals for patients with mental illnesses.

Education Reform

- **Horace Mann** believed that states should provide free and compulsory elementary education to all children—both boys and girls. In 1837, as Secretary to the new Board of Education, Mann reorganized the Massachusetts education system and started giving annual reports.
- His program became known as the **"Common School" movement**. Mann believed: states should use tax money to pay for schooling; children of all backgrounds should be in the same schools; schools should not be religious; and teachers should receive professional training.

Women's Rights

- Women could not vote, receive higher education, or have professional careers. They often had no choice whom they married. Once married, their property belonged to their husbands in most states.
- Female abolitionists became active in the struggle for women's rights. In 1848, **Elizabeth Cady Stanton** and **Lucretia Mott** organized a convention for women's rights at Seneca Falls, New York. Here, Stanton read her "**Declaration of Sentiments**." Based on the Declaration of Independence, it demanded equal rights for women, especially the right to vote (**suffrage**).

Ralph Waldo Emerson and the Transcendentalists

- **Ralph Waldo Emerson** rejected traditional religion. He found God in nature and inside each of us. Emerson had a great influence on writers and artists. His student **Henry David Thoreau** developed the idea of **civil disobedience**. He refused to obey laws he thought were immoral.
- The period 1830–1860 was a golden age for American literature and art. Nathaniel Hawthorne and Herman Melville wrote in this period. American painters were greatly influenced by Emerson and by Romanticism. They painted large canvases glorifying the American wilderness.

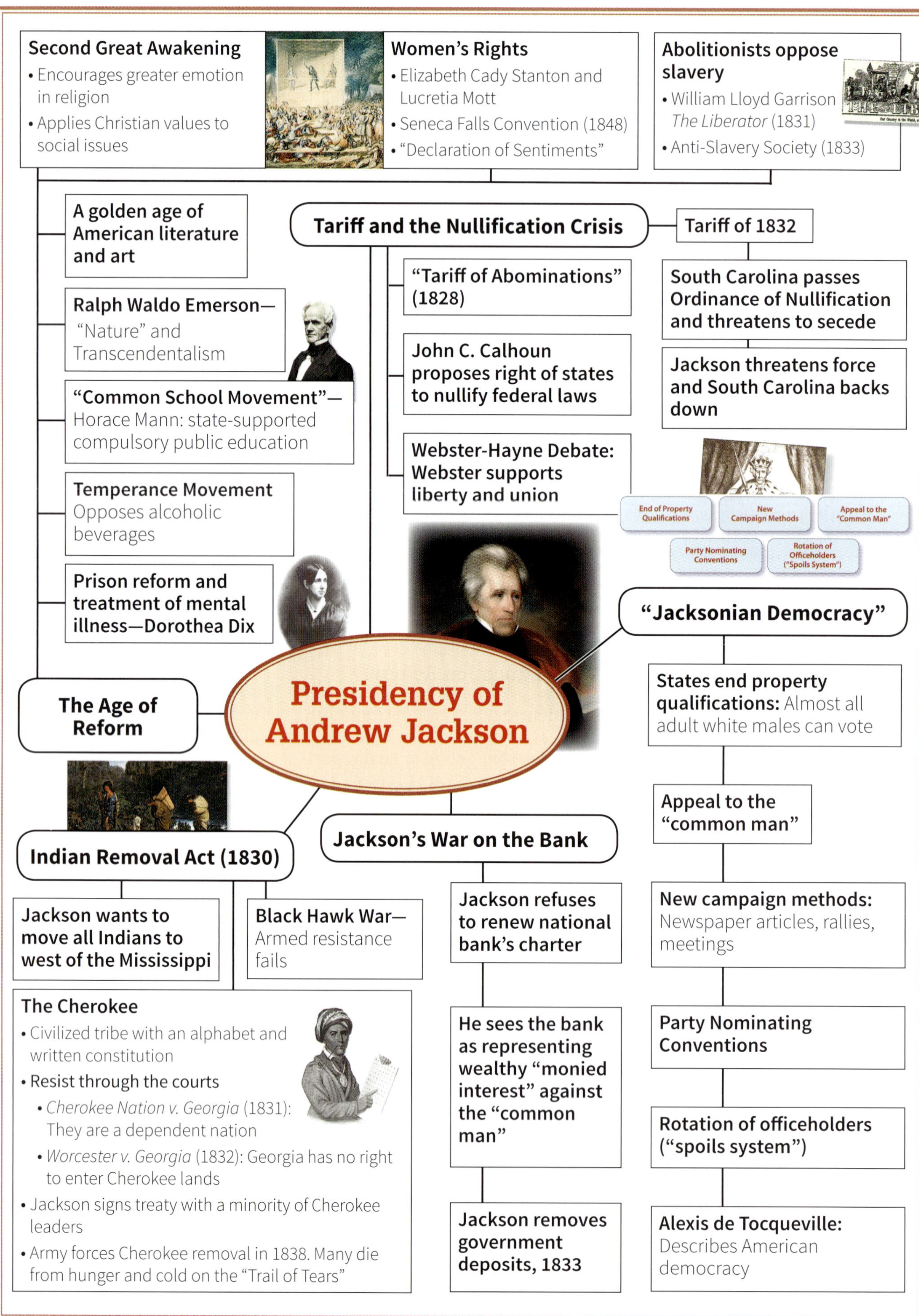
Second Great Awakening
• Encourages greater emotion in religion
• Applies Christian values to social issues
Women's Rights
• Elizabeth Cady Stanton and Lucretia Mott
• Seneca Falls Convention (1848)
• "Declaration of Sentiments"
Abolitionists oppose slavery
• William Lloyd Garrison The Liberator (1831)
• Anti-Slavery Society (1833)
A golden age of American literature and art
Ralph Waldo Emerson—"Nature" and Transcendentalism
"Common School Movement"—Horace Mann: state-supported compulsory public education
Temperance Movement Opposes alcoholic beverages
Prison reform and treatment of mental illness—Dorothea Dix
The Age of Reform
Tariff and the Nullification Crisis
"Tariff of Abominations" (1828)
John C. Calhoun proposes right of states to nullify federal laws
Webster-Hayne Debate: Webster supports liberty and union
Tariff of 1832
South Carolina passes Ordinance of Nullification and threatens to secede
Jackson threatens force and South Carolina backs down
End of Property Qualifications
New Campaign Methods
Appeal to the "Common Man"
Party Nominating Conventions
Rotation of Officeholders ("Spoils System")
Presidency of Andrew Jackson
"Jacksonian Democracy"
States end property qualifications: Almost all adult white males can vote
Appeal to the "common man"
New campaign methods: Newspaper articles, rallies, meetings
Party Nominating Conventions
Rotation of officeholders ("spoils system")
Alexis de Tocqueville: Describes American democracy
Indian Removal Act (1830)
Jackson wants to move all Indians to west of the Mississippi
Black Hawk War—Armed resistance fails
The Cherokee
• Civilized tribe with an alphabet and written constitution
• Resist through the courts
• Cherokee Nation v. Georgia (1831): They are a dependent nation
• Worcester v. Georgia (1832): Georgia has no right to enter Cherokee lands
• Jackson signs treaty with a minority of Cherokee leaders
• Army forces Cherokee removal in 1838. Many die from hunger and cold on the "Trail of Tears"
Jackson's War on the Bank
Jackson refuses to renew national bank's charter
He sees the bank as representing wealthy "monied interest" against the "common man"
Jackson removes government deposits, 1833

What do you know?

SS.6.A.4.16

1. In 1828, Andrew Jackson was elected President by a large majority of voters. Which change in American politics contributed to his victory?

   A. The Federalist Party had dissolved.

   B. The Electoral College had been abolished.

   C. Political candidates refused to campaign actively for office.

   D. Many states had recently ended their property qualifications for voting.

SS.6.A.4.16

2. Based on these headlines, what conclusion can be made about Andrew Jackson's Presidency?

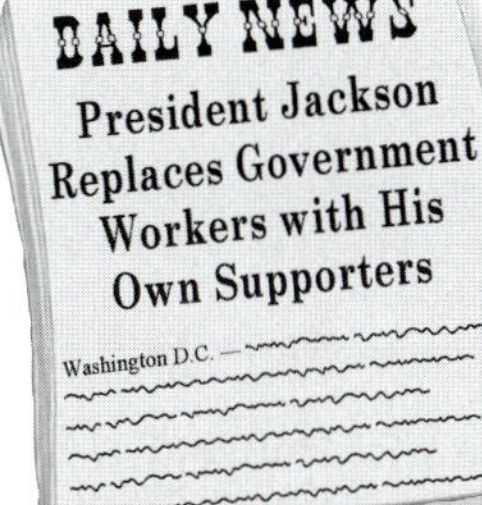

   A. Jackson was weak in dealing with domestic issues.

   B. Jackson was reluctant to use force to carry out his policies.

   C. Jackson expanded the role of the President in domestic affairs.

   D. Jackson believed Congress should have more power than the President.

SS.6.A.4.9

3. The passage below is from Dorothea Dix's "Report to the Massachusetts Legislature" in 1843.

   . . . I come to place before the legislature of Massachusetts the condition of the miserable, the desolate, and the outcast. I come as an advocate of men and women who are helpless, forgotten, and mentally ill. I come to demand change in conditions against which even the most unconcerned would react with horror.

   What was the outcome of reports by Dix such as the one above?

   A. an expansion of women's right to vote

   B. greater support for the abolitionist movement

   C. new laws banning the sale of alcoholic beverages

   D. the construction of new facilities for those with mental illness

SS.6.A.4.16

4. The cartoon below was published by Thomas Nast in 1877. It shows a statue of President Andrew Jackson.

Which legacy of President Jackson is addressed in the cartoon?

A. the rotation of officeholders in government

B. the removal of the Cherokee Indians to Oklahoma

C. the preservation of the Union in the Nullification Crisis

D. the destruction of the Second Bank of the United States

SS.6.A.4.16

5. How did President Jackson defend the system shown in the cartoon?

A. He explained that this system would increase the power of the federal government.

B. He asserted that permanent public officials were more likely to be corrupt than temporary ones.

C. He stated that those who had worked hard to elect a candidate deserved to receive some payback.

D. He claimed he needed to reward his supporters with public offices in order to hold his political party together.

SS.6.A.9

6. How did the "Second Great Awakening" promote social reform?

A. Participants believed that conditions on Earth could not be improved.

B. Participants grew tired of religion and became social reformers instead.

C. Participants wanted to apply Christian ethics to important social issues.

D. Participants were no longer concerned with their own personal salvation.

SS.6.A.4.16

7. The statement below was made to Congress by President Andrew Jackson in 1830.

> *The . . . speedy removal [of the Indians] . . . will place a dense and civilized population in large tracts of land now occupied by a few savage hunters . . . What good man would [not] prefer a country . . . filled with all the blessings of liberty, civilization, and religion?*

Based on the statement, which conclusion can be made about President Jackson's view of lands occupied by Indians?

A. He believed white settlers and Indians could successfully use these lands together.

B. He believed the Indians had destroyed the soils of these lands, which were of little value.

C. He believed white settlers would make better use of these lands than the Indians had done.

D. He believed Indian lands were not useful to white settlers and the Indians should be left alone.

SS.6.A.4.13

8. The excerpt below is from the Supreme Court's decision in *Worcester v. Georgia* in 1832.

> *The Cherokee nation . . . is a distinct community, occupying its own territory . . . which the citizens of Georgia have no right to enter but with the assent [agreement] of the Cherokee themselves . . .*

Why did this ruling fail to protect Cherokee ownership of their lands?

A. A majority of Cherokee leaders agreed to leave Georgia.

B. Georgia had already given their lands away to white settlers.

C. Congress proposed a constitutional amendment that overturned this decision.

D. The ruling did not affect relations between the Cherokee nation and the federal government.

SS.6.A.4.9

9. Which statement identifies the goal of the temperance movement?

A. The sale of alcoholic beverages should be outlawed.

B. African Americans should no longer be held in slavery.

C. Conditions in prisons and hospitals should be improved.

D. Factory workers should receive better pay for shorter hours.

SS.6.A.4.1

10. Why did the migration of Cherokee Indians become known as the "Trail of Tears"?

    A. The Cherokee lost their hunting and fishing skills and had to change their lifestyles.

    B. Most Americans did not agree with the removal of the Cherokee Indians and protested against it.

    C. The Cherokee were unhappy because they knew they would not get their lands back from Georgia.

    D. Soldiers forced the Cherokee to leave their lands and thousands of them died on the long, cold journey to the west.

SS.6.4.16

11. The table below lists several events just before and during the Presidency of Andrew Jackson.

May 1828	Tariff of Abominations
December 1828	John C. Calhoun's Exposition and Protest
January 1830	Webster-Hayne Debate
May 1830	President Jackson's Toast to the Union
July 1832	Tariff of 1832
November 1832	South Carolina's "Ordinance of Nullification"
December 1832	President Jackson's "Proclamation to the People of South Carolina"
March 1833	Force Bill
March 1833	South Carolina repeals Ordinance of Nullification

Which conflict did these events concern?

A. large vs. small states

B. Congress vs. the President

C. states' rights vs. federal supremacy

D. Northern bankers and merchants vs. the "common man"

SS.6.A.4.14

12. The excerpt below is from the Declaration of Sentiments, approved by the Seneca Falls Convention in 1848.

> *Resolved, that all laws which prevent woman from occupying such a station in society as her conscience shall dictate, or which place her in a position inferior to that of man, are contrary to the great precept of nature and therefore of no force or authority.*

Based on this excerpt, which laws were the signers of the Declaration of Sentiments protesting?

A. laws giving rights to men but not to women

B. laws forcing the migration of the American Indians

C. laws requiring the return of "fugitive slaves" to the South

D. laws making it difficult for workers to organize into unions

SS.6.A.4.8

13. The statement below was written by Horace Mann in 1848.

> *Education . . . is a great equalizer of the conditions of men . . . [I]t prevents being poor.*

Based on this statement, which goal did Mann believe public education should achieve?

A. a society in which poor as well as rich children enjoy opportunities

B. a society in which there are no cultural differences between ethnic groups

C. a society in which slavery is preserved in the South without spreading to the North

D. a society in which the wealthiest and best educated citizens maintain control over government

SS.6.A.4.15

14. Which statement expresses an important belief of Ralph Waldo Emerson and other Transcendentalists?

A. We must obey the law even if we think it is immoral.

B. Social reform will speed God's "Second Coming" back to Earth.

C. God's work is revealed in the wonders of the natural world.

D. Art and literature are usually not worth the effort they take to create.

SS.6.A.4.8

15. The box below lists several influential American women in the nineteenth century.

Elizabeth Cady Stanton Lucretia Mott Susan B. Anthony

How did these women gain national prominence?

A. They opposed abolitionist activities.

B. They led labor unions to fight for better wages.

C. They participated in church revivals and started the temperance movement.

D. They encouraged women to fight for economic independence and the right to vote.

SS.6.A.4.9

16. The timeline below shows events related to education.

1817	Thomas Galludet establishes the first school teaching deaf children to read and write.
1821	Emma Willard opens one of the first academies offering advanced education to women.
1833	Oberlin College starts the first coeducational classes.
1837	Horace Mann is appointed Secretary to the Massachusetts Board of Education.
1839	Horace Mann starts the first teacher-training institute.

Which conclusion can be drawn from this timeline?

A. Most teachers were well educated in 1839.

B. Every American citizen could read and write by 1839.

C. Few educational changes took place in the early 1800s.

D. Educational opportunities for Americans expanded in the 1820s and 1830s.

SS.6.A.4.9

17. How did the Second Great Awakening encourage the abolitionist movement?

A. Most participants decided to give up drinking alcoholic beverages.

B. Protestant preachers declared that the practice of slavery was sinful.

C. Defenders of slavery pointed to numerous examples of slavery in the Bible.

D. Ministers argued that slaves were better treated than factory workers in the North.

CHAPTER 12 An Expanding America: Manifest Destiny and the West

SS.6.A.4.1 Examine the causes, course, and consequences of United States westward expansion and its growing diplomatic assertiveness (War of 1812, Convention of 1818, Adams-Onís Treaty, Missouri Compromise, Monroe Doctrine, Trail of Tears, Texas annexation, Manifest Destiny, Oregon Territory, Mexican American War/Mexican Cession, California Gold Rush, Compromise of 1850, Kansas Nebraska Act, Gadsden Purchase).

SS.6.A.4.2 Describe the debate surrounding the spread of slavery into western territories and Florida.

SS.6.A.4.3 Examine the experiences and perspectives of significant individuals and groups during this era of American history.

SS.6.A.4.4 Discuss the impact of westward expansion on cultural practices and migration patterns of Native American and African slave populations.

SS.6.A.4.17 Examine key events and peoples in Florida history as each impacts this era of American history.

SS.6.A.4.18 Examine the experiences and perspectives of different ethnic, national, and religious groups in Florida, explaining their contributions to Florida's and America's society and culture during the Territorial Period.

(continues next page)

Names and Terms You Should Know

Expansion
Population
Province
Official
Self-Government
Mission
Dictator
Convention
Declaration of Independence
Annex

Annexation
Manifest Destiny
Humanitarian
Strategic
Multiple Perspectives
Negotiate
Mexican-American War
Treaty of Guadalupe Hidalgo
Mexican Cession
Mexicanos

California Gold Rush
Boom town
Immigrants
Seminoles
Black Seminoles
Seminole Wars
Osceola
Chief Billy Bowlegs
Statehood
State Constitution
Preamble

Alignment to Grade 7 Civics Standards

SS.7.C.2.1 Define the term "citizen," and identify legal means of becoming a U.S. citizen.

SS.7.C.2.13 Examine multiple perspectives on public and current issues.

SS.7.C.3.3 Illustrate the structure and function (three branches of government established in Articles I, II, and III with corresponding powers) of government in the United States as established in the Constitution.

SS.7.C.3.13 Compare the constitutions of the United States and Florida.

SS.7.C.4.3 Describe examples of how the United States has dealt with international conflicts.

Florida "Keys" to Learning

1. In the northeast of Mexico, Texas had few settlers and was threatened by Indian attacks. The Mexican government agreed to let Stephen Austin and other *empresarios* (land agents) bring families to Texas from the United States.

2. The Mexican government saw that the Anglo-American settlers were not adopting the Mexican way of life. In 1830 it passed a law against any more settlers from the United States.

3. The settlers in Texas were angry about the new restriction. In 1835, fighting began between the settlers and the Mexican government.

4. General Santa Anna took a large army from Mexico to Texas. He led a brutal attack on Texans defending the Alamo. He also executed settlers who surrendered at Goliad.

5. A Texas convention declared independence from Mexico. Sam Houston led a surprise attack on Santa Anna at San Jacinto. Santa Anna was captured and forced to agree to Texas independence.

6. At first, American leaders feared a war with Mexico and refused to annex Texas. Northern states did not want to add another slave state.

7. In 1844, Democratic candidate James Polk made the annexation of Texas the focus of his campaign.

8. Polk believed in Manifest Destiny—the belief that it was the fate of Americans to take over the entire continent.

9. Polk was elected by a landslide. Congress invited Texas to join the United States and Texas became a new state.

10. In 1845, the Oregon Territory was being shared by Britain and the United States. Polk proposed to divide it. Eventually, it was divided by extending the line between the United States and Canada. Americans received present-day Washington and Oregon.

11. Polk next set out to take California and New Mexico from Mexico. He used a dispute over the border of Texas as an excuse to start a war.

12. The Mexican-American War lasted from 1846 to 1848. U.S. forces invaded Mexico and occupied Mexico City. The Treaty of Guadalupe Hidalgo gave the United States half of Mexico's territory. The "Mexican Cession" included the future states of California, Utah, Arizona, and Nevada, and parts of Colorado and New Mexico. In 1853, the United States acquired the Gadsden Purchase from Mexico for $10 million.

13. Most Mexicans on these lands chose to remain and become U.S. citizens. Mexicanos made valuable contributions to American culture, especially to ranching methods, foods, music, language, and architecture.

14. In 1848, gold was discovered in California. Many newcomers arrived during the "Gold Rush," including immigrants from China.

15. The Mormons emigrated to the Great Salt Lake in Utah.

16. Florida had been a safe place for Seminole Indians and escaped slaves ("Black Seminoles") under Spanish rule. Many of its free black residents fled to Cuba when the United States acquired it.

17. Andrew Jackson was Florida's first U.S. governor. The territory's capital alternated between Pensacola and St. Augustine until a new capital was established at Tallahassee.

18. Conflicts over land led to three Seminole Wars. Eventually all the Seminoles left Florida except for a few hundred warriors who fled to the Florida Everglades.

19. By 1845, when Florida became a state, its population had grown to 70,000 people.

In childhood we grow bigger as we get older. In the early nineteenth century, the young American republic was also growing. The United States was growing in *area* as it expanded westward. And the nation was growing in *population*, as the number of people living in the United States increased. In this chapter, you will learn how the United States was growing in this period.

Growth of the United States, 1820–1850

Year	Total Population	Enslaved Population	Area in Square Miles
1820	9,638,453	1,538,202	1,749,462
1830	12,860,702	2,009,043	1,749,462
1840	17,063,353	2,487,355	1,749,462
1850	23,191,876	3,204,313	2,969,640

The Historian's Apprentice

1. Based on the table in the upper right, in which of these decades did the United States grow in land area? By what percentage did it increase?
2. By what percentage did the United States increase in total population between 1820 and 1850?
3. Which grew at a faster rate in this period (from 1820 to 1850): America's total population or its enslaved population?

"Gone to Texas"

From the time of the thirteen colonies, Americans who fell on hard times or who just wanted new opportunities knew they could pick themselves up and move farther west. Americans also knew their children or grandchildren might one day move westward. This made America different from the countries of Europe.

Americans had crossed the Appalachian Mountains, filled the Ohio River Valley, and spilled over into the rest of the Northwest Territory. To the South, they had pushed out the Cherokees and other Indian tribes and filled Georgia and the new states of Mississippi and Alabama. In the 1820s, one area that became attractive to some settlers was not a part of the United States at all. It was a province of Mexico.

When Mexico became independent in 1821, it was as large as the United States. Texas was its most northeastern part. Mexican officials knew that this area had few people. They wanted to fill it with settlers for defense against Indian raids. Mexican officials were therefore happy to sign an agreement with **Stephen Austin**, an American, who had offered to act as an *empresario*. An *empresario* was an agent who brought families to settle in Mexico in return for land. Austin brought 300 families from the United States to the fertile area between the Colorado and Brazos Rivers. The settlers

Stephen Austin

promised to become Mexican citizens, to follow the Roman Catholic faith, and to obey Mexico's laws against slavery.

Austin's colony was highly successful. Soon other *empresarios* brought more Anglo-American settlers to the region. However, these settlers did not adopt the Catholic faith. Some even brought slaves with them. The Mexican government realized that the settlers were not adopting Mexican ways and that they were increasing in numbers. They felt the settlers posed a future risk to Mexico. The government therefore passed a law against any more Americans coming into Texas. The new law also required settlers to pay higher taxes on goods coming from the United States.

The Anglo-American settlers in Texas protested bitterly. They sent Stephen Austin to Mexico City to speak to the Mexican government on their behalf. Their demands were rejected and Austin was thrown in jail for more than a year. Shortly after Austin returned to Texas in 1835, fighting broke out between the settlers and the Mexican government. The Texans seized control of the city of San Antonio. They demanded greater self-government although they still did not seek total independence. The Texans appointed **Sam Houston**, a friend of Andrew Jackson and a former Governor of Tennessee, to command their small army.

Sam Houston

"Remember the Alamo!"

General Santa Anna had recently seized power in Mexico City, becoming a **dictator** (*a ruler with absolute power*). He was in no mood to give in to the colonists' demands. Early in 1836, he marched north with 6,000 troops to restore order to Texas.

General Santa Anna

A small number of Texans had been left guarding the former mission of San Antonio, known as the **Alamo**. A *mission* is a group of religious buildings once built by Spanish priests for converting, teaching, and housing Indians. Soon they found themselves surrounded by thousands of Mexican troops. William Travis, commander of the Alamo, sent out a proclamation seeking reinforcements: "I shall never surrender or retreat," he declared. "I am determined . . . to die like a soldier who never forgets what is due to his own honor and that of his country—victory or death."

Santa Anna pounded the Alamo with cannon fire for almost two weeks. On the morning of March 6, 1836, the Mexican army finally attacked. More than a thousand Mexican troops died in the battle, which lasted a little more than an hour. But the Alamo was taken. Its 189 defenders were killed. At nearby Goliad, another force of 400 armed Texans surrendered to Mexican forces. Santa Anna ordered them all to be shot as traitors, although sixty of them escaped.

Just days before the Alamo was taken, a convention of Texans announced their independence from Mexico. Their Declaration of Independence borrowed phrases from the American Declaration of 1776.

Meanwhile, Sam Houston had been drilling his army and preparing for an attack. In late April, Santa Anna took part of his army to capture the leaders of the new Texas government. Houston saw his chance. He was able to surprise Santa Anna's soldiers at **San Jacinto** while they were taking an afternoon nap. Santa Anna himself was captured. Houston spared the general's life but demanded that Mexico withdraw its troops and recognize the independence of Texas. Santa Anna agreed to his terms.

Sam Houston battles Santa Anna at San Jacinto

The Texans immediately invited the United States to **annex** their territory. Much to their surprise, they were turned down. President Martin Van Buren and the U.S. Congress feared that the annexation of Texas might bring a war with Mexico. Northern states also did not want to bring another slave state into the union. Texas was forced to stay independent as the "Lone Star Republic."

James Polk and Manifest Destiny

Texas remained an independent country for eight years. Then the question of its annexation became an issue again in the Presidential election of 1844. Henry Clay and the Whig Party still opposed annexation. The Democratic candidate, **James Polk,** made annexation the focus of his campaign. Polk also demanded control of the Oregon Territory, which the United States had been sharing with Britain.

Polk believed in **Manifest Destiny**. He thought that it was the destiny, or *fate*, of the United States to stretch across the North American continent from the Atlantic to the Pacific. American acquisition of Texas and Oregon was an important part of his plan.

Polk won a landslide victory in the 1844 election. Most American voters believed—along with Polk—that it was their nation's "Manifest Destiny" to extend across the continent.

Soon after Polk's election, Congress passed a resolution inviting Texas to become part of the United States. Texans held a special convention and quickly accepted. In December 1845, Texas was admitted as the 28th state.

James Polk

Manifest Destiny

Manifest Destiny had several aspects. There were religious, humanitarian, strategic, economic, and political reasons for it.

Religious: Many Americans believed it was God's will that they should spread from coast to coast.

Humanitarian: Americans felt they had a responsibility to civilize the Indians by spreading Christianity, democracy, and American values.

Strategic: The United States would become more secure against future foreign attacks.

Economic: The American economy would become stronger. Americans would gain land and natural resources. They would have plenty of space to grow.

Political: The United States would establish a strong, prosperous democratic republic that would serve as a shining example for the rest of the world.

The Oregon Territory

Oregon had once been home to Indians and fur traders. In 1842, hundreds of American settlers began taking wagon trains along the **Oregon Trail** from the Missouri River to the fertile Willamette Valley of Southern Oregon. The trail allowed settlers to ride in covered wagons with large wheels. Hundreds of thousands of settlers eventually passed along this route. The trail was dangerous because it crossed the Rocky Mountains. Many brave pioneers lost several family members to cold, hunger, or disease while making the trip.

The Convention of 1818 had given the United States and Great Britain joint ownership of the entire Oregon Territory. Polk proposed to divide the territory in two by extending the line that already existed between Canada and

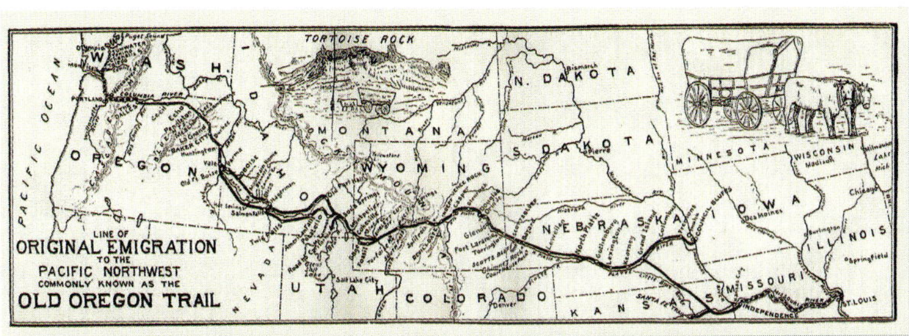

Old Oregon Trail

the United States to the east. When the British turned down his proposal, Polk demanded *all* of the Oregon Territory, right up to the latitude line of 54° 40′N (the southern border of Russian Alaska). His supporters adopted the slogan, "Fifty-four forty or Fight!" The British backed down and both sides finally agreed to Polk's original offer to divide the Oregon Territory at 49°N latitude. This extended the existing border between Canada and the United States westward to the Pacific. It gave Americans the future states of Washington, Oregon and Idaho, while Britain kept British Columbia. The peaceful resolution of this dispute was good news because Americans were already at war in the south.

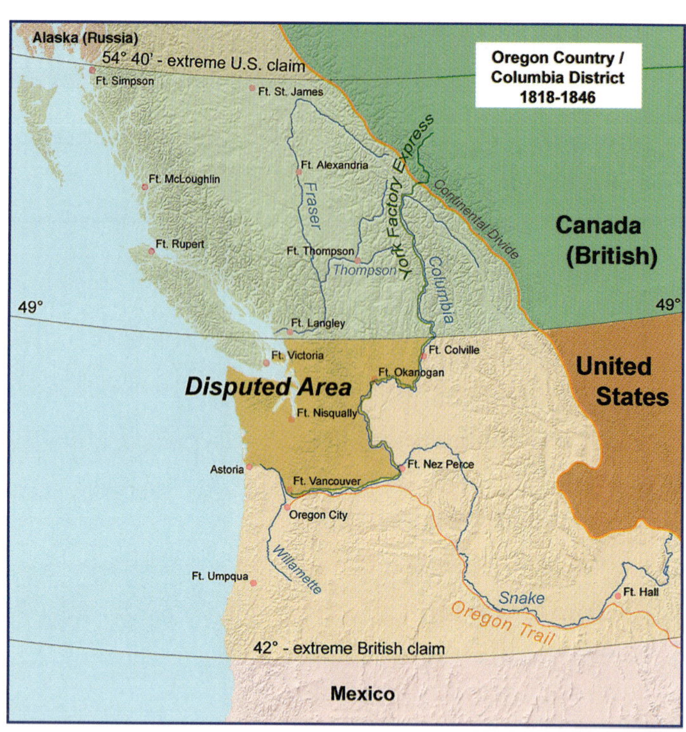

The Mexican-American War

President Polk was already thinking of other ways to add more territory to the United States. Polk had his eyes on the Mexican provinces of Upper California and New Mexico. He knew these northern borderlands were underpopulated and far from the center of Mexican national life in Mexico City, just as Texas had been.

There was also a small dispute about the border between Texas and Mexico. Now that Texas was part of the United States, this border had to be clearly defined. Mexicans believed their border with Texas was the Nueces River. Americans claimed that it was farther south at the Rio Grande. Polk sent troops into the contested area between the two rivers. From the Mexican point of view, Americans had entered Mexican soil. Some believed Polk's true purpose was not to settle the border dispute at all but to start a new war.

When Mexicans finally fired on American troops, Polk immediately asked Congress for a declaration of war. Americans were confident that defeating Mexico would be easy. Mexicans felt they were defending their way of life against an aggressive neighbor. The war actually lasted for almost two years.

Only Congress can declare war. This enumerated power belongs only to Congress.

The Historian's Apprentice

Ulysses S. Grant was one of the soldiers who crossed the Nueces River under General Zachary Taylor.

> "We were sent to provoke [*cause*] a fight, but it was essential that Mexico should commence [*start*] it. It was very doubtful whether Congress would declare war [unless] Mexico should attack our troops . . . Accordingly, preparations were begun for moving the army to the Rio Grande."
>
> —Ulysses S. Grant

1. Based on this passage, what was Grant's view of the reasons for the U.S. occupation of this area?
2. Consider this issue from multiple perspectives. "Multiple perspectives" refers to other points of view. What was the Mexican view of the U.S. occupation of the area between the Rio Grande and the Nueces River? What was the American view of the occupation?

General Zachary Taylor had commanded the troops that first crossed the Nueces. These troops now pushed further south, becoming the first invasion force into Mexico. A second force headed west through New Mexico, one of the territories Polk hoped to annex. A naval force was also sent to the Pacific coast to claim California.

U.S. forces quickly occupied these border provinces. Their successes, however, could not persuade the Mexican government to agree to surrender territory to the United States.

President Polk decided to send General Winfield Scott with an invasion force into the heart of Mexico. Scott was the general who had supervised the first steps of the Cherokee removal. Now he sailed with his army to Vera Cruz on the coast of Mexico. Scott attacked the city with cannon fire. Then he landed his troops and began the march along the "National Road" towards Mexico City. It was the same route Cortés had taken 300 years earlier.

U.S. troops in Mexico

The Historian's Apprentice

1. Why did President Polk turn to Congress to ask for a declaration of war?
2. Did the President have the power to start a war without the approval of Congress? Explain your answer.

Mexicans were unsure how to cope with these events. No one in the government was willing to give up territory to the United States. General Santa Anna, who had been sent into exile, returned to take charge of the nation's defenses. All Mexicans rallied around the former dictator. But Santa Anna failed to listen to his advisers and made several costly mistakes. Instead of patiently waiting for Scott's army, he marched his men quickly northward to surprise Taylor. Santa Anna's men were exhausted by their long march and were unable to defeat Taylor's smaller force. Santa Anna then marched his army quickly back to Mexico City. He tried to ambush Scott's army but failed to place cannons on the highest ground and lost another major battle.

General Winfield Scott

Every time Scott thought he had finally beaten Santa Anna, however, Santa Anna was able to raise new forces, demonstrating the patriotism of the Mexican people. When all attempts to negotiate failed, Scott finally prepared to attack Mexico City itself. Santa Anna and what was left of his army quietly withdrew from the city. Santa Anna went back into exile. With the surrender of the capital, a new Mexican government entered into negotiations with an American diplomat who had been sent with Scott.

A treaty was signed in February 1848 at Guadalupe Hidalgo near Mexico City. In the **Treaty of Guadalupe Hidalgo**, Mexico gave up half of its territory to the United States, including the present states of California, Utah, Arizona, and Nevada, and parts of Colorado and New Mexico. The United States paid $15 million to Mexico for this territory, known as the **Mexican Cession**. The Rio Grande was recognized as the border between Texas and Mexico.

The Mexican Cession raised an important question. Would these new territories later be admitted as free or slave states? You will learn more about this issue in Chapter 14.

The Gadsden Purchase

In 1853, the United States purchased an additional piece of land from Mexico for $10 million. Congress thought this area might be used for a southern railway route to the Pacific. The deal was arranged by James Gadsden, U.S. Ambassador to Mexico, and became known as the **Gadsden Purchase**.

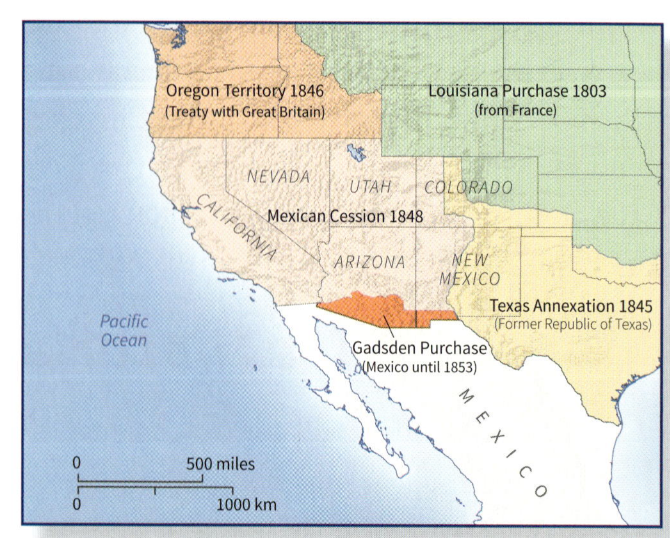

Territories of Western U.S.

The Mexicanos

There were as many as 80,000 Mexican citizens, or **Mexicanos**, living in the territories that the United States gained after the Mexican-American War. The Treaty of Guadalupe Hidalgo gave them the right to stay where they lived and to choose U.S. citizenship. Most of them did so. Although they were promised they would be able to keep their property, U.S. courts often demanded that they prove their ownership. They usually did not have the documents the courts required and lost their lands. In the area around Santa Fe, the Mexicanos remained a large proportion of the population and kept more of their lands than in California.

These Mexicanos made many important cultural contributions to the United States. They taught ranchers how to round up and control cattle. They also taught them how to raise and herd sheep. They taught miners how to pan for gold. Mexicano farmers were experts at irrigation. They contributed foods such as corn tortillas, words such as "barbecue" and "ranch," music, and unique styles of architecture. Under Mexican law, married men and women shared their property as part of a community. Most of the U.S. territories that came out of the Mexican Cession adopted the Mexican principles of community property law.

The California Gold Rush

One of the most important areas that the United States acquired in 1848 was California, a long stretch of land along the Pacific coast. California had first been settled by Spanish priests who built missions to convert the Indians. The Mexican government had then given out land grants to turn parts of California into ranches. Some Anglo-American settlers had also moved there, and there was growing trade as ships brought goods to Monterey and other seaports.

Advertisement for San Francisco

During the Mexican-American War, American settlers in California declared their independence from Mexico. U.S. warships arrived, claiming California for the United States.

The United States took over California at an especially lucky time. In January 1848, gold was discovered in the foothills of the Sierra Nevada Mountains, about 150 miles from the city of San Francisco on the Pacific coast. News of the discovery led thousands, known as the "Forty-Niners," to sail to California or to cross overland in order to pan for gold. Miners put mud from the river in a pan with water. Because gold is heavier than other stones or dirt, they shook the pan

gently so that any gold dust or nuggets would fall to the bottom.

So many people came to California at this time that people spoke of the California "**Gold Rush**." Almost a hundred thousand people came to California looking for gold in 1849 alone. They arrived by sea and by land. **Boom towns** (*towns enjoying sudden prosperity*) sprang up overnight. Almost all of the miners and other arrivals were men. Many of the newcomers were immigrants from other countries, including China. The merchants who supplied the miners made fortunes by charging the miners high prices for their goods.

Chinese **immigrants** (*people who come to a country to live*) faced special prejudice. In 1852, a special tax was placed on non-citizens who were mining. The tax was half of what an average miner made. Chinese arrivals were not permitted to become citizens so the tax was mainly aimed at them. Many Chinese left mining to open restaurants, laundries, and stores. By then, there were thousands of Chinese living in California.

The Gold Rush lasted only a few years. Afterwards large mining companies took over. But California's population still continued to grow. By 1850, the population of California was 93,000. The territory was ready to apply for statehood. One third of its residents were living in one city, San Francisco.

The admission of California as a free state would have upset the balance between free and slave states in the United States Senate. Eventually the problem was solved with the Compromise of 1850. You will learn more about that compromise in Chapter 14.

Chinese immigrants mining for gold

Many California cities started as mining camps.

The Southwest

Unlike the eastern part of the United States, much of the territory in the Mexican Cession was dry and mountainous. Some of this territory had already been explored by Americans. **Zebulon Pike** had explored the Southwest between 1806 and 1807, at the time of Lewis and Clark's journey. Pike was sent to explore the southern part of the Louisiana Purchase and to find the source of the Red River. Pike went west to the Rocky Mountains. Pike's Peak, one of the highest mountains in the Rocky Mountains, is named after him. His expedition then went south into New Mexico where they were captured by Spanish soldiers. Pike was quickly released, but was killed not long after in the War of 1812.

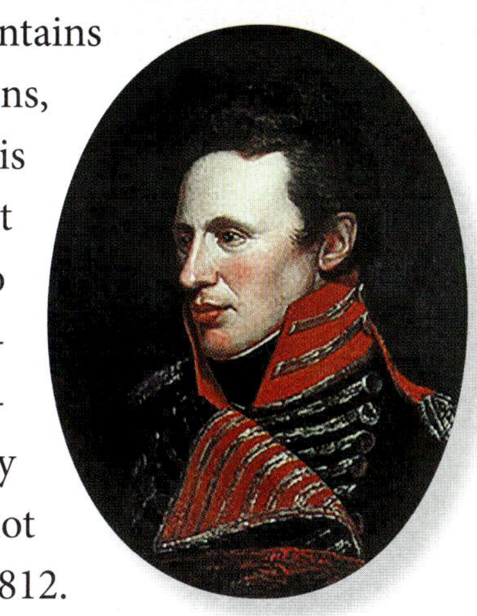

The Mormons in Utah

Utah was another area that was settled soon after the Mexican-American War. This area became home to the Mormons (Church of Latter Day Saints). The Mormons were a religious group that formed in upstate New York during the Second Great Awakening. Joseph Smith, their founder, said he had been presented with a new holy book, *The Book of Mormon*, by an angel. The Mormons planned to build their own community, a "New Jerusalem." They moved first to Ohio, then to Missouri, and finally to Illinois, where Smith was killed. **Brigham Young** became the next leader of the Mormons. He successfully brought the Mormons in covered wagons across the dry lands of the Great Basin to the Great Salt Lake, where they settled in 1847.

The Story of Florida: From Territory to Statehood

The history of Florida provides a good example of how the United States expanded. It shows how a new territory slowly became a part of the nation.

The transfer of Florida from Spain to the United States was delayed for almost two years before Spain approved the Adams-Onís Treaty of 1819. The treaty finally went into effect in February 1821. Andrew Jackson became the first American governor of Florida in July 1821. Jackson only held the post a few months before he resigned.

A New Capital for Florida

At first, the capital of the Florida Territory went back and forth each year between St. Augustine, the capital of East Florida, and Pensacola, the capital of West Florida. Finally in 1823, the governor of the territory decided to look for a new capital between the two cities. **Tallahassee** was chosen. The territorial council first met in the new capital as early as November 1824. A two-story brick capitol building was completed in 1826.

Seminoles and Black Seminoles

When Florida first became part of the United States, it was a home to Seminole Indians and free runaway slaves. The escaped slaves lived alongside Seminole communities and were known as "**Black Seminoles**." Florida had provided a haven for free blacks ever since the Spanish government had built **Fort Mose** in Saint Augustine in 1738. That fort had been built for runaway slaves from British colonies who agreed to become Catholics. The Spanish government saw this as one way to defend its territory from the British to the north. Later, Fort Mose became a place where slaves stopped who were trying to escape to the Bahamas or Mexico.

In the treaty with Spain, the United States promised to respect the legal status of blacks in Florida who had been free under Spanish rule. Hundreds of these free blacks still fled to Cuba before Florida became part of the United States. Despite the treaty, the Florida Territorial Council limited the rights of free blacks.

New Settlers Arrive

There were fewer than 8,000 white settlers and slaves in Florida in 1821. Wagon trains brought settlers from Georgia and South Carolina with their slaves. The new settlers built plantations, especially in Middle Florida, where cotton was grown. Further south, their plantations grew sugar cane. Other settlers came to Florida to raise cattle, harvest timber, or plant citrus orchards. The Florida "**crackers**" were less wealthy farmers who came for cheap land. Still others were attracted by Florida's tolerance for religious differences. Florida included Catholics, Protestants, and Jews such as David Levy Yulee, who later became the first Jewish U.S. Senator.

Jacob Summerlin was known as the "King of the Crackers." He rounded up wild cattle on the Florida grasslands and drove them to the Gulf to be sent to Cuba. The term "cracker" may have come from their cracking their long whips.

By the 1830s, the Florida Territory had more than 35,000 white settlers and enslaved people. By the time Florida became a state in 1845, its population was 70,000. Forty percent of those were enslaved people without any rights.

The Seminole Wars

When Florida became part of the United States, the most important issue facing the new territory was the future of the Seminole Indians. In 1823, James Gadsden—who later arranged the Gadsden Purchase—was sent by the federal government to negotiate with the Seminole chiefs. Gadsden signed the **Treaty of Moultrie Creek** with them. The Seminole leaders agreed to move to a large reserve of four million acres set aside for them in the center of Florida. The Seminoles moved to their new lands and lived peacefully for several years. However, the reserved lands were not fertile and within a few years the Seminoles found they had very little to eat. They began fighting with nearby settlers and returning to their old lands in north Florida. White settlers wanted the Seminoles out of Florida. In 1832, Gadsden was sent back to negotiate a new agreement with the Seminoles. He persuaded a few of their chiefs to sign a new treaty in which they agreed to move farther west. This time, however, most of the chiefs refused to sign the treaty. The situation was ripe for war.

In 1834, government officials in Florida began asking Seminole leaders when they planned to move. Most replied they did not plan to move at all. In December 1835, Seminoles killed two government officers near Ocala, Florida. They also attacked U.S. soldiers near Bushnell, Florida. These attacks led to the **Second Seminole War**, which lasted almost seven years. Zachary Taylor, who would later fight in Mexico, commanded the U.S. forces. General Winfield Scott also participated. The Indians were greatly outnumbered but they were led by great fighting chiefs and leaders such as Osceola, Coacoochee ("Wildcat"), Tiger Tail, Alligator, Arpeika, Thlocco (the Prophet), Billy Bowlegs, and Micanopy.

Osceola, a young warrior, had a British father and an Indian mother. He was not a chief but he became known for his daring and leadership. He was strongly against giving up lands and moving any farther west.

This illustration depicts the massacre of white settlers by Seminoles and escaped slaves.

A governor leads a state or territory just as the President leads our nation. A governor heads the executive branch at the state level.

In 1837, Osceola went to see U.S. Major General Thomas S. Jesup for talks under a white flag of truce. Despite the white flag, Jesup had Osceola arrested. Osceola died a few months later in prison. Jesup similarly captured Chief Coacoochee, who also came under a white flag of truce. Jesup captured other Seminole chiefs but still could not end the war. By 1841, there were only a few hundred Seminole warriors left in Florida. Almost four thousand Seminole Indians had already moved west. A peace was finally arranged, giving the remaining warriors a reservation of 6,700 square miles in Florida.

By the 1850s, there were again pressures from white settlers to remove the few remaining Seminoles. The Seminole warriors at that time were led by **Chief Billy Bowlegs**. Rather than agreeing to move, Bowlegs and his warriors chose to fight. This led to the **Third Seminole War**. In 1856, they made fifteen raids and killed twenty-eight settlers. In 1857, federal troops found Billy Bowlegs' village hidden in the swamps. They burned down the Seminoles' houses and took their food. Bowlegs and his warriors finally agreed to move to lands reserved for them west of the Mississippi. They also received money from the federal government for making the move. About 200 Seminoles still refused to agree and escaped into the Florida Everglades.

Florida's Constitution and Admission to Statehood

During the territorial period, Florida's governors worked hard to gain statehood. The first step was writing a state constitution.

In 1838, the territorial council called for a convention to write a constitution and a bill of rights. The convention met and finished its work by December that same year. Most of the provisions of Florida's first state constitution were borrowed from the constitutions of other Southern states. The first article provided a "Declaration of Rights." The second article established that the state's government would be divided into three branches: legislative, executive, and judicial. The third article described the powers and responsibilities of the Governor of Florida.

David Levy Yulee, Florida's territorial representative to the U.S. Congress, persuaded Congress to approve the admission of Florida as the 27th state in March 1845. Florida was admitted as a slave state while Iowa was admitted as a free state the following year. This kept the existing balance between free and slave states in the U.S. Senate.

The Historian's Apprentice

You may recall that a "preamble" is an introduction, especially to an important document. The Preamble to the Florida Constitution of 1838 began as follows:

> We, the People of the Territory of Florida, by our Delegates in Convention, . . . having and claiming the right of admission into the Union, as one of the United States of America, consistent with the principles of the Federal Constitution, . . . in order to secure to ourselves and our posterity the enjoyment of all the rights of life, liberty, and property, and the pursuit of happiness, do mutually agree, each with the other, to form ourselves into a Free and Independent State, by the name of the State of Florida.

Discuss the answers to the following questions with a partner and then share your views with the rest of your class:

1. From which documents did the beginning of this Preamble borrow some of its language?
2. Why does a state need a constitution?
3. How does a state constitution differ from the federal constitution?

In less than five years, the United States had expanded all the way to the West Coast—taking Texas, Oregon, and the Mexican Cession (California and the American Southwest). But gaining new land was only one way in which America grew in these years. Americans also expanded their economy. You will learn about that in the next chapter.

Name:________________________________

Describe the relationships between the terms and phrases and their significance in the concept boxes below.

Manifest Destiny	Humanitarian
Economic	Religious

James Polk	Annexation of Texas
Oregon Territory	Mexican-American War

Treaty of Guadalupe Hidalgo	Mexican Cession
Gadsden Purchase	Mexicanos

California	Gold Rush
"Forty Niners"	Chinese immigrants

Seminoles	Black Seminoles
Tallahassee	Crackers

Chapter Review Cards

The United States Grows Westward

- The United States grew significantly in size during the period 1840–1850.
- During this period of expansion, the United States gained the present-day states of Texas, Washington, Oregon, California, Utah, Arizona, and Nevada and parts of Colorado and New Mexico.

The Texas Revolution

- When Mexico gained its independence in 1821, much of its northern territory was still unsettled. **Texas** was its most northeastern part. The area had few settlers and was threatened by Indian attacks.
- The Mexican government agreed to let **Stephen Austin** and other *empresarios* (*land agents*) bring families to Texas from the United States. These American settlers promised to become Mexican citizens and to follow the Mexican way of living—practicing Roman Catholicism and prohibiting slavery.
- The settlers did not become Catholics and some brought slaves. The Mexican government saw that its Anglo-American settlers were not adopting the Mexican way of life. In 1830, it passed a law against any more settlers coming from the United States.
- The settlers in Texas were angry at the new restrictions. They sent Stephen Austin to Mexico City, but the Mexican government imprisoned Austin for a year. In 1835, fighting began between the settlers and the Mexican government. The settlers captured the city of San Antonio.
- **General Santa Anna** took a large army to Texas. He led a brutal attack on those Texans defending the mission outside San Antonio known as the **Alamo**. He also executed Texas settlers who surrendered at **Goliad**.
- In March 1836, a Texas convention declared independence from Mexico. A few months later, **Sam Houston** led a surprise attack on Santa Anna at **San Jacinto**. Santa Anna was captured and forced to agree to Texas independence.
- Texans asked to join the United States, but the President and Congress refused because they feared war with Mexico. Northerners did not want another slave state. Texas became the "Lone Star Republic."

Manifest Destiny

- "**Manifest Destiny**" was the term used for the belief held by many Americans in the 1840s that it was the **destiny**, or fate, of the United States to expand from the Atlantic to the Pacific.
- There were several reasons behind Americans' belief in Manifest Destiny. Many Americans believed it was God's will that they should spread their form of Christianity and democracy. Many also felt they had a responsibility to "civilize" the American Indians. They wanted to make the United States stronger by obtaining more land and resources. They also wanted to make the country more secure by keeping foreign powers out of the continent.

The Presidency of James Polk

- **James Polk** was a strong believer in Manifest Destiny. Polk made the annexation of Texas the focus of his campaign in 1844 and was elected President.

Annexation of Texas

- Congress invited Texas to join the United States right after Polk's election.

Oregon Territory

- Since 1818, the United States had been sharing the **Oregon Territory** with Britain. Many American pioneers had taken the **Oregon Trail** by covered wagon to settle in Oregon.
- President Polk proposed that Britain and the United States divide the territory by extending the line between Canada and the United States from the east. Britain at first rejected his proposal. Polk then demanded the entire Oregon Territory (up to 54° 40′ N).
- The British finally agreed to Polk's original proposal. This gave the United States the present-day states of Washington and Oregon. Britain kept British Columbia.

The Mexican-American War

- President Polk next set out to seize California and New Mexico from Mexico.

The Texas Border Dispute

- He used the dispute with Mexico over the border of Texas as an excuse to start a war.
- Mexico claimed the border was the **Nueces River** and the United States claimed it was the **Rio Grande**. Polk sent U.S. troops into the disputed territory. When Mexicans finally fired on U.S. troops, Polk asked Congress for a declaration of war.

The Course of the War

- Americans thought they would win the war quickly but in fact it lasted almost two years.
- U.S. forces quickly took New Mexico and the U.S. Navy was sent to California. **Zachary Taylor** pushed beyond the Rio Grande into northeastern Mexico.
- Despite U.S. victories, Mexican leaders refused to give up any territory to the United States. Polk sent **General Winfield Scott** with an invasion force to capture Mexico City. Scott landed at Vera Cruz and marched to Mexico City.
- General Santa Anna, who had been in exile, came back to defend his country. However, he made a series of mistakes and lost several battles to Taylor and Scott. Santa Anna and his army finally withdrew from Mexico City, which was occupied by American forces.

The Treaty of Guadalupe Hidalgo

- Mexican leaders agreed to the **Treaty of Guadalupe Hidalgo** (1848).
- Mexico gave up about half of its territory, known as the "**Mexican Cession**"—territory from the border of Texas all the way west to the Pacific Ocean. The Mexican Cession included the future states of California, Utah, Arizona, and Nevada, and parts of Colorado and New Mexico. It almost doubled the size of the United States.
- The United States paid Mexico $15 million for this large area.
- Mexicans living in these territories, known as **Mexicanos**, were given the option to stay or to leave. Most stayed. Mexicanos also had the opportunity of becoming U.S. citizens. Many of them lost their lands when they could not produce the ownership documents required by American courts.
- Mexicanos made valuable contributions to American culture, especially to ranching methods, foods, music, language, and architecture.

The Gadsden Purchase

- In 1853, U.S. Ambassador James Gadsden arranged for the United States to pay Mexico $10 million in exchange for a section of land that became known as the **Gadsden Purchase**. Americans wanted this land for a future railroad.

The California Gold Rush

- In 1848, gold was discovered at the foothills of the Sierra Nevada Mountains.
- Many people moved westward in the movement known as the "**Gold Rush**." In 1849 alone, as many as 100,000 people went by land and sea to California to find gold. **Boom towns** sprang up overnight.
- A large group of these early miners were Chinese immigrants. These Chinese immigrants faced much prejudice. In 1852, a special tax was placed on non-U.S. citizen miners, which mainly applied to Chinese immigrants. Many of them left mining to start their own local businesses in California.

The Mormons in Utah

- The **Mormons** (or Church of Latter Day Saints) were a religious group that was founded in upstate New York during the Second Great Awakening.
- Joseph Smith, their founder, said he had been presented with a new holy book, *The Book of Mormon*, by an angel. The Mormons planned to build their own community, a "New Jerusalem." They moved from New York to Ohio, then to Missouri and Illinois, before moving further west.
- In 1847, the Mormons crossed the Great Basin by covered wagon and settled by the Great Salt Lake in present-day Utah.

The Story of Florida

- Under Spanish rule, Florida was a safe place for **Seminole Indians** and for African Americans who had escaped from slavery (sometimes known as "**Black Seminoles**"). **Fort Mose** was built by Spain in 1738 for free blacks escaping from the British colonies. Many black residents fled to Cuba when Florida became part of the United States. Those who remained in Florida lost many of their rights.

New Territorial Capital

- Florida came under American rule in 1821. Andrew Jackson was its first U.S. governor, although he resigned after a few months.
- The capital alternated between Pensacola and St. Augustine until a new capital was chosen between the two at **Tallahassee**.

Settlers

- Settlers came to Florida from nearby Southern states. Some brought slaves. "**Crackers**" were less wealthy farmers who came for cheap land. The term may come from the cracking of whips by those who rounded up cattle on Florida's grasslands.

Seminole Wars

- There were still many Seminole Indians in Florida. Under the **Treaty of Moultrie**, they were given a large reserve in the middle of Florida. The land was not fertile and after a few years, conflicts arose between the Seminoles and white settlers.
- Most Seminole leaders rejected a new treaty, leading to the **Second Seminole War**. The Seminoles were outnumbered and **Osceola** and **Chief Coacoochee** were captured through the trickery of General Thomas Jesup. In 1841, a new treaty was signed that promised 6,700 square miles of Florida to the Seminoles.
- The **Third Seminole War** broke out when the Seminole Indians were once again pressured by white settlers to give up land. Chief Billy Bowlegs led raids on white settlers. When the U.S. Army found and destroyed his main Seminole village, Bowlegs and others agreed to move to lands reserved for them farther west. A few hundred Seminoles disagreed and escaped into the Florida Everglades.

Statehood for Florida

- A constitutional convention was held in 1838.
- Florida's first **state constitution** borrowed from other Southern state constitutions. It had a bill of rights and created a state government with three separate branches. Its preamble began with "We, the People . . ." like the U.S. Constitution.
- When Florida finally became an official state in 1845, its population was 70,000 people. About 40 percent of them were enslaved.
- Florida was admitted as a slave state. To maintain the balance between free and slave states in the U.S. Senate, Iowa was admitted as a free state the following year.

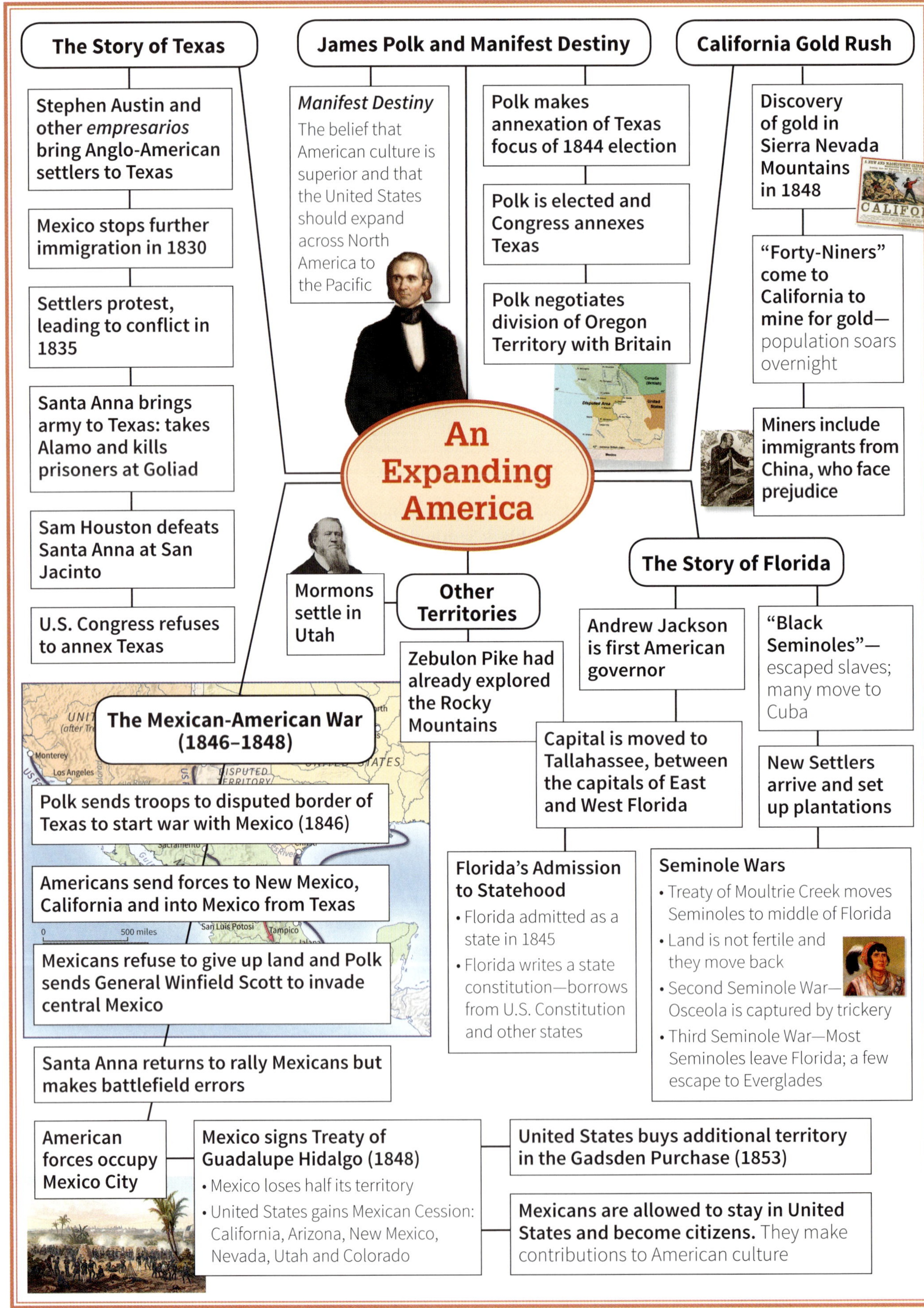
An Expanding America
The Story of Texas
Stephen Austin and other *empresarios* bring Anglo-American settlers to Texas
Mexico stops further immigration in 1830
Settlers protest, leading to conflict in 1835
Santa Anna brings army to Texas: takes Alamo and kills prisoners at Goliad
Sam Houston defeats Santa Anna at San Jacinto
U.S. Congress refuses to annex Texas
James Polk and Manifest Destiny
Manifest Destiny
The belief that American culture is superior and that the United States should expand across North America to the Pacific
Polk makes annexation of Texas focus of 1844 election
Polk is elected and Congress annexes Texas
Polk negotiates division of Oregon Territory with Britain
California Gold Rush
Discovery of gold in Sierra Nevada Mountains in 1848
"Forty-Niners" come to California to mine for gold—population soars overnight
Miners include immigrants from China, who face prejudice
Other Territories
Mormons settle in Utah
Zebulon Pike had already explored the Rocky Mountains
The Story of Florida
Andrew Jackson is first American governor
"Black Seminoles"—escaped slaves; many move to Cuba
Capital is moved to Tallahassee, between the capitals of East and West Florida
New Settlers arrive and set up plantations
Florida's Admission to Statehood
• Florida admitted as a state in 1845
• Florida writes a state constitution—borrows from U.S. Constitution and other states
Seminole Wars
• Treaty of Moultrie Creek moves Seminoles to middle of Florida
• Land is not fertile and they move back
• Second Seminole War—Osceola is captured by trickery
• Third Seminole War—Most Seminoles leave Florida; a few escape to Everglades
The Mexican-American War (1846–1848)
Polk sends troops to disputed border of Texas to start war with Mexico (1846)
Americans send forces to New Mexico, California and into Mexico from Texas
Mexicans refuse to give up land and Polk sends General Winfield Scott to invade central Mexico
Santa Anna returns to rally Mexicans but makes battlefield errors
American forces occupy Mexico City
Mexico signs Treaty of Guadalupe Hidalgo (1848)
• Mexico loses half its territory
• United States gains Mexican Cession: California, Arizona, New Mexico, Nevada, Utah and Colorado
United States buys additional territory in the Gadsden Purchase (1853)
Mexicans are allowed to stay in United States and become citizens. They make contributions to American culture

What do you know?

SS.6.A.4.1

1. The passage below was written by John Quincy Adams in 1811.

The whole continent of North America appears to be [meant] by Divine Providence to be peopled by one nation, speaking one language, professing one general system of religious and political principles, and accustomed to [the same] social usages and customs. For the common happiness of them all, for their peace and prosperity, I believe it is indispensable [essential] that they should be associated in one federal Union.

Which view is expressed in this passage?

A. support for freedom of the seas

B. opposition to the extension of slavery

C. belief in America's Manifest Destiny

D. resistance to Indian attacks in the Northwest Territory

SS.6.A.4.1

2. In the 1840s, how did the United States and Great Britain resolve their disagreement over control of the Oregon Territory?

A. The United States sent troops to occupy the disputed territory.

B. They resolved the dispute peacefully by dividing up the territory.

C. They created a new territory for Indians to occupy the disputed area.

D. Americans had a "Second War for Independence" against the British.

SS.6.A.4.1

3. The excerpt below was part of a message delivered by President James Polk to Congress in 1846.

We have tried every effort at restoring harmony. The cup of tolerance had been exhausted even before the recent information from the frontier of the Del Norte. But now, after repeated menaces, they have passed the boundary of the United States, have invaded our territory and have shed American blood upon American soil. [They have] proclaimed that hostilities have begun, and that the two nations are now at war.

How did Polk make use of the dispute described in this message?

A. He entered into a war with Mexico to increase the size of Texas.

B. He entered into a war with Mexico to obtain New Mexico and California.

C. He used the threat of a war with Mexico to prevent the annexation of Texas.

D. He used the threat of a war with Mexico to silence abolitionist critics of his policies.

SS.6.A.4.1

4. Below are the different views of two historians on the Mexican-American War (1846–1848).

You Can't Stop Progress	U.S. Mobilization was an Outright Attack
The United States was often referred to as a "go-ahead" nation, a "go-ahead" people with the locomotive as a symbol . . . The Mexican-American War was an example of this boundlessness and reform spirit—a quest for a better place for the nation. —Robert Johanssen, an American historian	[T]he mobilization of the U.S. army was an outright attack on Mexico . . . [T]he Mexican government [acted to] protect the border. . . between the Rio Grande and the Nueces River. —Jesus Velas-Marquez, a Mexican historian

Which conclusion can be drawn from these views?

A. Americans' belief in their right to expand was seen as a threat by Mexicans.

B. The United States was interested in progress, but Mexico was greedy for land.

C. The proposed Mexican-U.S. border affected rights to precious mineral resources.

D. Americans were trying to build new railroads, but the Mexican government was blocking their progress.

SS.6.A.4.1

5. The print below shows U.S. troops fighting on the outskirts of Mexico City in August 1847.

Why did President Polk send U.S. troops on the mission shown in this print?

A. The Mexican army had previously invaded the United States.

B. President Polk planned to place a group of friendly Mexican politicians in power.

C. The Mexican government refused to surrender its northern provinces already occupied by U.S. troops.

D. American public opinion wanted revenge on Mexico for atrocities committed during the Texas War for Independence.

SS.6.A.4.1

6. Which event led to a rapid increase in the population of California in 1849–1850?

   A. the construction of a canal across Panama

   B. the discovery of gold in the foothills of the Sierra Nevada Mountains

   C. massive immigration by Chinese refugees escaping rebellions in China

   D. completion of a transcontinental railroad between Missouri and California

SS.6.A.4.1

7. The map below provides information about regions added to the United States.

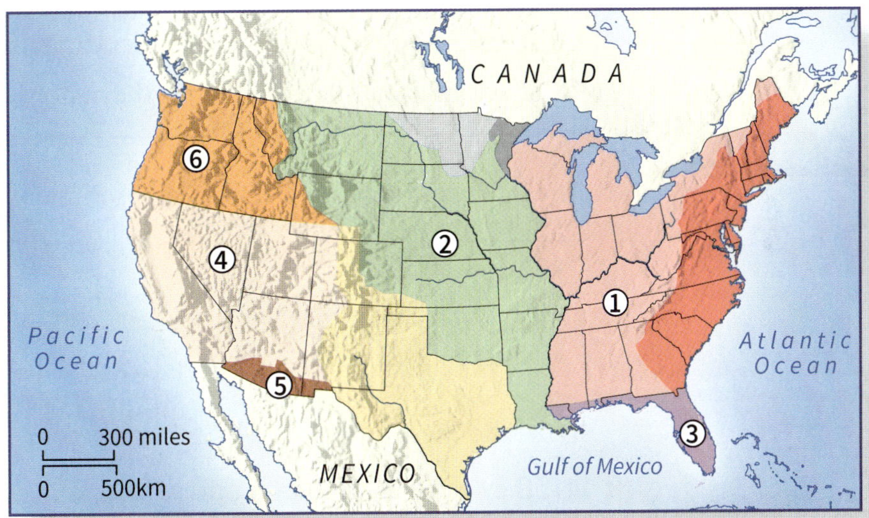

   Based on the map, which region was transferred to the United States by the Treaty of Guadalupe Hidalgo at the end of the Mexican-American War?

   A. Region 1

   B. Region 2

   C. Region 3

   D. Region 4

SS.6.A.4.1

8. Based on the map above, which region did the United States purchase from Mexico for possible construction of a transcontinental railroad along a southern route?

   A. Region 3

   B. Region 4

   C. Region 5

   D. Region 6

SS.6.A.4.18

9. Who were the "Black Seminoles"?
   - **A.** Seminole Indians who occupied land with rich, dark soil
   - **B.** a group of Seminole warriors who participated in the Black Hawk War
   - **C.** formerly enslaved African Americans who escaped into Spanish Florida
   - **D.** a small band of Seminole Indians who refused to abandon their lands and escaped into the Everglades

SS.6.A.4.17

10. Why was the capital of Florida moved to Tallahassee?
    - **A.** It was the largest city in Florida.
    - **B.** It was on territory claimed by Alabama.
    - **C.** It was midway between the former capitals of East and West Florida.
    - **D.** It was midway between the northern border and southern tip of Florida.

SS.6.A.4.18

11. The information below lists several prominent individuals.

    - Osceola
    - Chief Coacoochee
    - Chief Billy Bowlegs

    What did these individuals have in common?
    - **A.** They were arrested by Andrew Jackson.
    - **B.** They resisted relocation to west of the Mississippi.
    - **C.** They led their people in the migration westward.
    - **D.** They refused to take up arms against the United States.

SS.6.A.4.17

12. How were the preamble of Florida's first state constitution and the preamble to the Constitution of the United States similar?
    - **A.** Both included a bill of rights.
    - **B.** Both began with the phrase "We the People."
    - **C.** Both listed the purposes of the federal government.
    - **D.** Both contained direct quotations from the Declaration of Independence.

SS.6.A.4.3

13. Which group was permitted to seek U.S. citizenship under the terms of the Treaty of Guadalupe Hidalgo?
    - **A.** Cubans
    - **B.** Seminoles
    - **C.** Mexicanos
    - **D.** former slaves

CHAPTER 13 The Industrial Revolution and its Consequences: North and South

SS.6.A.4.3 Examine the experiences and perspectives of significant individuals and groups during this era of American history.

SS.6.A.4.5 Explain the causes, course, and consequences of the 19th century transportation revolution on the growth of the nation's economy.

SS.6.A.4.6 Identify technological improvements (inventions/inventors) that contributed to industrial growth.

SS.6.A.4.7 Explain the causes, course, and consequences (industrial growth, subsequent effect on children and women) of New England's textile industry.

SS.6.A.4.10 Analyze the impact of technological advancements on the agricultural economy and slave labor.

SS.6.A.4.11 Examine the aspects of slave culture including plantation life, resistance efforts, and the role of the slaves' spiritual system.

SS.6.A.4.13 Explain the consequences of landmark Supreme Court decisions (*McCulloch v. Maryland* [1819], *Gibbons v. Odgen* [1824], *Cherokee Nation v. Georgia* [1831], and *Worcester v. Georgia* [1832]) significant to this era of American history.

(continues next page)

Names and Terms You Should Know

- Economy
- Technology
- Industrial Revolution
- Textiles
- Loom
- Factory
- Steam engine
- Interchangeable parts
- Transportation Revolution
- Canal
- Steamboat
- *Gibbons v. Ogden* (1824)
- Railroad
- Mass-produced goods
- Cotton gin
- Plantation
- Resistance
- Underground Railroad

Alignment to Grade 7 Civics Standards

SS.7.C.2.13 Examine multiple perspectives on public and current issues.

SS.7.C.3.12 Analyze the significance and outcomes of landmark Supreme Court cases . . .

SS.7.C.3.4 Identify the relationship and division of powers between the federal government and state governments.

Florida "Keys" to Learning

1. The Industrial Revolution began in the British textile industry. New machines used water and steam power to make thread and cloth. These machines were placed in factories, where workers labored many hours without rest.

2. Samuel Slater came to America and built the first textile factory here in 1793. He employed entire families in the "Rhode Island System." In 1814, Francis Lowell and his partners built a large factory in Massachusetts. They hired young unmarried women who lived in company boarding houses. This became known as the "Lowell System."

3. Eli Whitney introduced the use of interchangeable parts. All parts of a product were cut from the same machine and had the same shape and size.

4. Americans also experienced a transportation revolution. The Erie Canal, completed in 1825, connected the Hudson River with Lake Erie. It dramatically reduced the cost of shipping goods from the Great Lakes to New York City. Other states began building their own canals.

5. John Fitch built the first steamboat. Robert Fulton and his business partner opened the first successful commercial steamboat operation in 1807.

6. In the case of *Gibbons v. Ogden* (1824), Chief Justice John Marshall ruled that moving people affects commerce. Congress, not the states, therefore had the power to regulate it.

7. The first American railroad opened in 1830. By 1860, all major U.S. cities were connected by railroad.

8. In the 1840s, Samuel Morse invented an improved telegraph. It permitted instant communication over long distances.

9. The rise of industry and the transportation revolution increased the population of Northern cities. Farm workers and immigrants moved to towns and cities to find work.

10. In 1793, Eli Whitney invented the cotton gin. It pulled seeds out of raw cotton. The cotton gin increased the demand for Southern cotton and caused slavery to spread.

11. Most cotton was grown by slaves on Southern plantations. Only a few thousand Southerners actually owned more than a hundred slaves. Enslaved people had no rights. They were treated as property, bought and sold by others in auctions. The threat of whipping and other punishments forced them to work.

12. Enslaved people developed their own culture. African traditions survived in many slave communities. Slaves added new elements, such as the Christian faith.

13. People resisted the demands of slavery: they often did not work as hard as they could. Less often, they might strike an overseer or try to escape. Punishments for such actions were severe. In 1831, Nat Turner even led an unsuccessful rebellion of slaves in Virginia.

14. Northern abolitionists helped organize escape routes for slaves, known as the Underground Railroad. Leading abolitionists included escaped slaves. Frederick Douglass published an autobiography that described his experiences in slavery. Sojourner Truth preached against slavery. Harriet Tubman helped so many escape by the Underground Railroad that she became known as "Moses."

In the last chapter, you learned how the United States increased in size as it expanded westward. In this chapter you will learn how Americans also expanded their **economy**—the amount of goods and services they produced.

America's Economy Expands

Between the time that Captain John Smith landed in Jamestown and the American Revolution began, **technology**—the ways of making and doing things—improved but not in a dramatic way. Captain John Smith would have felt very comfortable visiting the home of George Washington at Mount Vernon in 1775. People still traveled by horse. Machines relied on human strength, animal power, or running water. To read at night still required a candle or a lamp with oil. Thread, cloth, and clothes were still all made by hand. But if Smith had returned just 50 years later in the 1830s, he would have been truly astonished. New inventions were changing almost every aspect of daily life. There were turnpikes, canals, steamboats, trains, factories, and factory-made cloth. Cities were crowded with people. We call this period of rapid technological improvement the "**Industrial Revolution**." The world entered a period of rapid change from which it has never really left. In this section, you will learn how these changes began and how they affected people's ways of doing things.

The Industrial Revolution

The Industrial Revolution actually began in Great Britain in the 1700s. The British already had many advantages. They had an extensive overseas empire, which included the American colonies. They were shipping and trading goods all over the world. They had a powerful middle class that valued hard work, good ideas, and making money from business. Britain was separated just enough from Europe to be saved from the worst effects of Europe's many wars. The British also had many valuable natural resources, including wood, coal, and fast-running streams. Everything was in place for what was about to come.

Handloom weaver

The Industrial Revolution began in the **textile industry**—the industry that makes our thread, cloth, and clothing. For thousands of years, people had taken wool, flax, or cotton and twisted it into thread (or yarn) by hand or by using a spinning wheel. Then they used handlooms to weave these threads together, crisscrossing them to make cloth.

In 1764, an English weaver had the idea of attaching several spindles (rods) together to one wheel. A person could then turn the wheel and make thread on several spindles at once. Three years later, another English inventor had the idea of connecting this new textile machinery

A series of mechanized looms

to waterpower. The running water could turn a large waterwheel. The wheel could then turn hundreds of spindles making thread at once. The machines were housed in "textile mills." These were the first **factories**—places where people came together to work.

A third invention made all this machinery work even better. James Watt built an improved steam engine in the 1760s. This machine heated water until it turned to steam. The steam pressed a piston that was tightly fitted inside a cylinder, moving it forward. When the piston was pushed forward, it uncovered a hole for the steam to escape. Pressure from the other side pushed the piston back into the cylinder. The motion of the piston could be used to drive machines in factories. Because the steam engine could be placed at any location, factories could be located in towns—close to workers—rather than next to streams.

Other inventions made it easier to weave thread into cloth. British inventors developed the first power looms by the 1790s. These looms were driven by steam power.

With all these new machines, the way that work was organized also changed. Workers had once made thread and cloth at home. Often they were farmers who did some spinning or weaving to earn extra money. Now workers had to work in a factory. They were watched and had to keep working for long hours without a break. Their work was repetitious and monotonous (*always the same*). The workers had no other income and depended on their wages to buy food and meet their needs. When the factory owner didn't need them, they were out of work and could starve.

The new British factory system was the wonder of the world. But the British did not want to share their ideas. They passed strict laws preventing anyone from taking away the plans for building the new textile machines or mills.

A steam engine

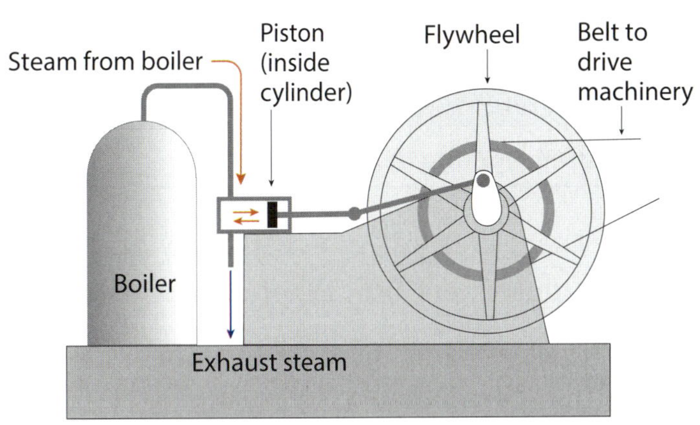

How it works

The Industrial Revolution Comes to America

Samuel Slater was born in England in 1768. At ten years old, he began working in an English textile mill that used waterpower and that had all the new machines. Slater became an apprentice to the factory owner and learned how the machines worked. Slater later moved to America. In 1793, he opened a textile mill with an American partner in Rhode Island. Their factory was an instant success. Slater hired local families to work in his mill, including both parents and children. Children might be given special jobs, like fixing machinery in tight spaces with their small hands. Using entire families as textile workers became known as the "**Rhode Island System**."

Children working in a textile factory.

Slater's mill was soon copied by others. By 1810, there were fifty factories making cotton thread in the United States. The Embargo of 1807 greatly increased the demand for American-made goods. **Francis Cabot Lowell** was from Massachusetts. He decided that Americans should become more independent in manufacturing. Lowell went to England and Scotland in 1810. He spent two years touring factories. Lowell returned to the United States and formed a manufacturing company with partners in 1814. They built a large factory in Massachusetts. Their machines ran on waterpower. They had power-driven spinning machines and looms. All the steps for turning raw cotton into finished cloth took place at their factory under one roof.

Rather than hiring entire families, Lowell and his partners hired young unmarried women as their factory workers. They came from New England farming families and were from 15 to 35 years old. These women lived in boarding houses provided by Lowell's company close to the factory. The women were paid lower wages than men received at the time. Their work hours were long but they were also provided with classes and social activities. They even published their own newspaper. Many of the women found the entire experience more enjoyable than doing farm work in a village. This became known as the "**Lowell System**." Lowell himself died in 1815, but his partners continued. They built an entire town for their female factory workers and named it after Lowell.

As the prices for cotton cloth dropped, more people could afford to buy cotton clothes. Demand rose. Cotton clothes had once been a luxury for the rich, but now ordinary people could wear them. The rising demand for cotton cloth led

CONSTITUTION OF T
Lowell Factory Girls As

PREAMBLE.

manufacturers to produce even more of it. Factories began turning out thousands of yards of cotton cloth each day.

Other Inventors and Their Inventions

The success of the textile industry encouraged other inventors and **entrepreneurs** (*people who start or invest in new businesses*). **Eli Whitney** was an inventor from New England. He introduced the use of **interchangeable parts**. This meant all the parts of a product were cut from the same machine and had the same shape and size. One identical part could be substituted for another. Broken parts could be easily replaced. Interchangeable parts meant that goods could be made more quickly using tools and machines. Machines and mechanical devices (like guns and clocks) could be more easily repaired.

Whitney gave a demonstration of interchangeable parts to President John Adams in 1801. He brought ten muskets. Whitney took them apart and mixed all the parts up. Then he put ten guns back together. It did not matter if the same part found its way back into the same gun, because the parts were interchangeable. The members of Congress were so impressed that they ordered Whitney's guns.

The use of factory production spread from textiles to other products. Instead of making most things themselves, Americans began buying mass-produced goods made in factories.

The Number of Factory Workers in the United States	
1820	350,000
1860	2,000,000

The Transportation Revolution: Americans on the Move

In the early nineteenth century, Americans went through a transportation revolution that was just as important as the changes in manufacturing.

At the time of the American Revolution, Americans were connected by trails and dirt roads. During spring rains, these roads often became impossible to pass. In summer, they were dry and dusty. They had holes and stones. Travelling by horse, stagecoach, or wagon was often uncomfortable. Early attempts to cover roads with logs were not very successful.

Private companies began building better private roads known as **turnpikes**. They paved their roads with stone and gravel for a better road surface. They also built bridges over waterways. The turnpike company then charged users a fee. The fee was collected at special tollgates found along the length of the road. Inns and taverns were also built along the turnpike, where travelers could eat and rest. Most turnpikes were short distances and many turned out not to be profitable. State governments were often involved. Pennsylvania gave money to more than fifty turnpike and bridge companies. By 1830, there were five thousand miles of turnpikes in the United States.

The Canal "Craze"

In the early 1800s, travel by water was easier and cheaper than travel by land. People used flatboats, rafts, barges, or ships with sails to carry goods to distant places. A **canal** is a human-made waterway. Canals are usually dug to bring natural waterways together that are not

already connected by water. After the War of 1812, Americans entered a great canal-building period. Canals were expensive to dig. Almost all of them were paid for by state governments.

In 1816, the New York State Legislature approved a bill to build the **Erie Canal.** This waterway was to connect the Hudson River with Lake Erie. Work began in 1817. Most of the workers who dug the canal were Irish Americans. There were no power tools in those days, so all the work had to be done by hand or with the help of oxen. The work was hard and slow. Men had to shovel earth to dig a ditch that was 363 miles long. The canal was finally completed in 1825. The Erie Canal was not deep or wide. It had a series of locks to take into account how the height of the land changed. Flatboats moved up and down the canal, pulled by horses that walked on a pathway alongside it. The effect of the canal on shipping costs was dramatic. The cost of shipping a ton of wheat from Buffalo (on Lake Erie) to New York City fell from $100 to $10.

A lock on the Erie Canal

Cities along the Erie Canal such as Rochester and Buffalo grew rapidly in size. Other smaller canals were built that connected to the Erie Canal. Midwestern states like Ohio also benefited. Farmers could load their crops anywhere on the Great Lakes, send them across Lake Erie to Buffalo, have them carried by flatboat along the Erie Canal, and then ship them down the Hudson River. The Erie Canal was so successful that other states began building their own canals, connecting key cities and waterways.

Steamboats

The "canal craze" was just one step in the transportation revolution. The invention of the steam engine also affected transportation. Once engineers were able to build a steam engine that was small and powerful enough, it could be used to power a boat. Today, computer engineers keep designing computers that are smaller and more powerful. Two hundred years ago, inventors and engineers were doing the same thing with steam engines. They kept making them better and more powerful.

John Fitch, an American, was the first person to have the idea of using a steam engine to power a boat. His boat actually had two steam engines. Each engine moved three oars on one side of the boat. Fitch demonstrated his steamboat to members of the Constitutional Convention in August 1787, while they were having a break. Fitch obtained a **patent** for his design (*a license*

A model of Fitch's steam-powered boat

from the federal government to be the only one to use an invention for a period of time). But Fitch never received the right to be the only one to offer steamboat travel. In fact, he was never able to turn his invention into a successful business.

Robert Fulton was more fortunate. He went to live in England and France, where he came up with all kinds of ideas for inventions for boats and canals, including plans for a submarine. After he returned to the United States, Fulton put one of Watt's steam engines on a boat and used it to turn a paddle wheel. The paddles moved the boat along the water. Fulton and his business partner were able to get **monopoly rights** from the New York State Legislature for running steamboats along the Hudson River. This meant they were the only ones with the right to run a steamboat on the river. They began the country's first successful commercial steamboat operation in 1807. Their steamboat ran up and down the Hudson River between New York City and Albany.

Robert Fulton's steamboat with side paddle wheels

Unlike boats with sails, a steamboat did not depend on wind or the weather. It also could go upstream against the current as well as downstream. Designs kept improving and steamboats became even bigger. By 1835, there were more than 300 steamboats moving up and down rivers in Western states alone.

The Supreme Court: *Gibbons v. Ogden* (1824)

The invention of the steamboat led to another famous Supreme Court decision by Chief Justice John Marshall. This case had to do with "interstate commerce"—commerce between states.

Factual Background

Robert Fulton and his partner had received the right from New York State to be the only ones to operate a steamboat on the Hudson River for several years. They had a **monopoly right**. Gibbons bought this right from them. Ogden had a different license from the U.S. Congress to operate boats along the U.S. coast. Ogden began a ferry service between New York City and New Jersey using a steamboat. Gibbons tried to stop Ogden's ferry service. He said it violated his monopoly from New York State. Ogden disagreed. He said Congress had the right to give him a license because Congress had the power to "regulate interstate commerce."

Question

The Constitution gave Congress the right to "regulate interstate commerce." Was the movement of people by a ferry part of "interstate commerce"?

Decision

Marshall said that we may think of "commerce" as trade in goods, but moving people affects commerce as well. He said Congress had the power to determine the rules for commerce between states, including "navigation" in general. Because Congress had the right to regulate "interstate commerce," individual states could not also regulate it. That would create too many conflicting rules. Therefore, Ogden's license from Congress gave him the right to run the ferry across the Hudson from New York to New Jersey.

Significance

The case greatly increased the power of Congress to make laws that affect interstate commerce. It also meant that state governments could not create monopolies limiting interstate commerce. This helped open up the country to the transportation revolution. The number of new steamboats on American rivers increased after the decision.

The regulation of interstate commerce is an enumerated power of Congress. Enumerated powers are specific powers given to Congress.

The Historian's Apprentice

1. Do you agree with Marshall's decision?
2. Should individual states be allowed to regulate interstate commerce along with the federal government? Why or why not?

Railroads

The transportation revolution was far from over. British inventors wanted to use steam power for travel on land as well as on water. They placed a steam engine on a wagon with wheels. The wagon moved along iron rails. The rails were kept together by planks of wood and hammered into place along a flat bed of gravel. The railroad was born.

Once again, this invention went from Britain to the United States. The first American railroad opened in 1830, while Andrew Jackson was President. This railroad, the Baltimore and Ohio Railroad, connected Baltimore with the Potomac River. Later it was extended all the way to the Ohio River.

The spread of railroads was at first slow because they were so expensive to build. But unlike canals and boats, railroads could be built almost anywhere. Trains kept getting faster and more efficient as engineers improved the design of their locomotives. Train travel was also more comfortable than other forms of travel. Trains were large enough for passengers to move around. The federal government also began giving land to railroad companies that laid down new tracks. Between 1850 and 1860, the amount of railroad track tripled in the United States. Smaller railroads were often merged

Miles of Railroad Track in the United States

Year	Miles
1830	23
1835	1,098
1840	2,818
1845	4,633
1850	9,021
1855	18,374
1860	30,626

together. For example, the New York Central Railroad brought several smaller railroad companies together in 1853. This railroad ran parallel to the Erie Canal. By 1860, all major U.S. cities were connected by railroad.

The Telegraph

The spread of railroads was further helped by the invention of the telegraph. This invention used electromagnetism to instantly send messages across wires over long distances. **Samuel Morse**, an American painter, developed a better telegraph and a code using dots and dashes in the 1840s. With his "Morse Code," operators could send messages along telegraph wires. People could immediately find out election results or the prices of goods in other parts of the country. They could learn if a train or boat had arrived or if it had been delayed. With railroads, steamboats, and telegraphs, Americans were better connected than they had ever been before.

A telegraph key

Northern Cities

The rise of industry and the transportation revolution increased the number of people living in Northern cities. Farm workers moved to towns and cities to find work in factories or to provide services for other people living there. Northern cities were also filled with immigrants in the 1840s and 1850s, especially immigrants from Ireland and Germany. In Ireland, a disease killed most of the potatoes that people lived on. People were dying of famine and hundreds of thousands of Irish left for the United States. They filled cities like New York and Boston. Germans came too, especially to escape political troubles in 1848 or to find new economic opportunities.

A meeting of the New York Central Railroad's investors

The Historian's Apprentice

Your teacher should divide your class into small groups. Each group will be assigned one of the inventors in the chart below. Your group should research additional information about the inventor's life and accomplishments. Include any important obstacles that the inventor had to overcome. Each group should then present the results of its research in a video or oral presentation to the rest of the class, or in the form of a poster about the inventor's life.

Inventor	Accomplishment
John Fitch (1743–1798)	A clockmaker and inventor who learned about steam engines and decided to add a steam engine to a boat to pull a series of oars. He built and demonstrated the first steamboat in 1787 and then ran it briefly in 1790, but could not get enough money to continue.
Robert Fulton (1765–1815)	An American painter and inventor who went to live in England and France. He developed designs for canals, steamboats, a submarine, and torpedoes. He brought the first Watt steam engine back to the United States, where he set up a company that received a monopoly from the New York Legislature for steamboat travel up and down the Hudson River. His steamboat, the Clermont, began trips between New York City and Albany in 1807. It took 32 hours to travel 150 miles.
Eli Whitney (1765–1825)	An American inventor who helped develop the system of interchangeable parts for guns, which became standard for all industries. Interchangeable parts are pieces that are identical. While visiting a plantation in Georgia, Whitney also invented the cotton gin, a machine that could be used to pull the seeds out of raw cotton.
Samuel Slater (1768–1835)	An apprentice in an English textile mill who came to the United States to build the first factory here. Slater introduced the new cotton spinning machinery invented in England. He has been called the "Father of the American Industrial Revolution."
Francis Cabot Lowell (1775–1817)	An American who studied in British factories for two years; he returned to build the first factory in the United States turning raw cotton into cloth using powered machinery. His Lowell factory set the standard for American textile manufacturers.
Samuel Morse (1791–1872)	An American painter who developed a commercially successful electromagnetic telegraph system using his "Morse Code," which used dots and dashes. His telegraph made it possible to communicate instantly over long distances.
Cyrus McCormick (1809–1884)	The son of an inventor, in 1834 he developed an improved mechanical reaper pulled by horses. He continually improved its design over the following years.
Isaac Singer (1811–1875)	An inventor who developed an improved sewing machine that was easier and faster to use. Singer made it possible to sew cloth together into clothes more quickly.
Elijah McCoy (1844–1929)	McCoy was born to fugitive slaves in Canada. His family returned to the United States when he was five years old. He moved to Scotland to become an apprentice and a mechanical engineer. He returned to the United States where he invented different devices for steam engines and other machines to lubricate themselves (*adding oil or grease to run more smoothly with less friction*).

The South and Slavery

The Industrial Revolution affected the South just as much as it affected the North and West. Northern factories needed raw materials. Textile mills turned raw cotton into finished cloth. But where did all this raw cotton come from? The answer was the South, where cotton was planted, grown, harvested, cleaned, packed, and shipped by the forced labor of enslaved African Americans.

The Cotton Gin

In 1792, the inventor **Eli Whitney** had just graduated college. He was visiting a plantation in Georgia when he noticed slaves picking seeds from cotton by hand. Whitney thought he had a better idea. He designed a box with a handle that turned. Around the handle were spikes. The spikes pulled the cotton through the teeth of a comb attached to the opposite side of the box. The cotton was pulled through the comb while the seeds were blocked by its teeth and dropped out. Whitney called his machine a cotton engine. It became known as the **cotton gin**. With a cotton gin, workers could clean cotton fifty times faster than they could by hand.

A cotton gin

The Spread of Slavery

In the 1790s, many people predicted that slavery would gradually die out. The soil where slaves grew tobacco and other cash crops was becoming exhausted. Whitney's invention of the cotton gin actually caused slavery to spread. With the cotton gin, the kind of cotton that could be grown in the South with short fibers and many seeds could easily be cleaned and prepared. Soon most of the factories in Britain and the United States were using cotton from Southern plantations. The warm climate and rich fertile soil, especially in the newer states of Mississippi and Alabama, were perfect for growing cotton. One acre of land in South Carolina could grow as much as 300 pounds of cotton in a single season. In Alabama, an acre might grow 800 or 1,000 pounds. By 1860, three-quarters of the world's supply of cotton came from the Southern United States.

Most plantations grew cotton but some grew other cash crops. Along the coasts of Georgia, Louisiana, and South Carolina, plantation owners grew rice. In Virginia, Kentucky, and Missouri, they still grew tobacco. In Louisiana, plantation owners grew sugar cane. These cash crops were so profitable (*made so much money*) that plantation owners often bought much of their food from other farmers, including farmers in the Northwest who shipped their crops down the Mississippi River.

Plantation Life

Only a few thousand Southerners actually owned more than a hundred slaves. Most white Southerners owned no slaves at all. But slavery still influenced every aspect of Southern life. Many people earned their incomes by selling goods or services to plantation owners or by shipping their cotton and other cash crops.

On small farms, slaves might work alongside their owners. Large plantation owners had **overseers** (*people who supervise workers*). These large plantations were self-sufficient communities. Each large plantation was actually like a village with a main house, slaves' quarters, a blacksmith's shop, barns, a smokehouse, and other buildings. Skilled slaves acted as craftspeople and could make almost anything that was needed. Others worked as household servants for the plantation owner and his family.

An owner and a slave

Frederick Douglass escaped from slavery in Maryland and became a famous abolitionist. He describes the plantation where he had once been enslaved in the passage below.

That plantation is a little nation of its own, having its own language, its own rules, regulations and customs. . . There are no conflicting rights of property, for all the people are owned by one man; and they can themselves own no property.

[H]ere were a great many houses . . . There was the little red house, up the road, occupied by Mr. Sevier, the overseer. A little nearer to my old master's, stood a very long, rough, low building, literally alive with slaves, of all ages, conditions and sizes. This was called "the Long Quarter." Perched upon a hill, across the long green, was a very tall, dilapidated, old brick building . . . now occupied by slaves, in a similar manner to the Long Quarter. Besides these, there were numerous other slave houses and huts, scattered around in the neighborhood, every nook and corner of which was completely occupied. . . .

Besides these dwellings, there were barns, stables, store-houses, and tobacco-houses; blacksmiths' shops, wheelwrights' shops, coopers' shops—all objects of interest; but, above all, there stood the grandest building my eyes had then ever beheld, called, by every one on the plantation, the "Great House." This was occupied by Col. Lloyd and his family. . . . The great house was surrounded by numerous and variously shaped out-buildings. There were kitchens, wash-houses, dairies, summer-houses, green-houses, hen-houses, turkey-houses, pigeon-houses, and arbors, of many sizes and devices, all neatly painted, and altogether interspersed with grand old trees . . .The great house itself was a large, white, wooden building, with wings on three sides of it. In front, a large portico [*porch*], extending the entire length of the building, and supported by a long range of columns, gave to the whole establishment an air of solemn grandeur.

—Frederick Douglass, *My Bondage and My Freedom* (1855)

The Historian's Apprentice

1. Make your own drawing or map of this plantation based on the description on the previous page.
2. Why were there such differences in the types of buildings found on this plantation?

The Life of a Slave

Most of the slaves on Southern plantations worked as field hands. Life for these slaves was extremely hard. The plantation bell sounded before the sun rose. Slaves had to rise early and work all day in the fields until sunset. After dark they still had other chores. Many worked up to 18 hours a day for six days a week. The only days off were Sundays, when slaves enjoyed recreation and went to church.

Harvesting cotton

Workers were controlled by the threat of brutal physical punishment. Overseers carried rawhide leather whips. They cracked their whips as slaves worked in gangs or individually picking cotton. Any violation, like taking a rest or not picking enough cotton, could be punished with a severe whipping. Slaves could be branded, chained, or worse. Overseers were usually paid by how much they made their slaves produce. Most had no sympathy at all for how the slaves felt as human beings.

The Historian's Apprentice

Solomon Northup was a free African American who was kidnapped and sold into slavery. He described plantation life in his book *Twelve Years a Slave*. His story was later made into a movie, which received the Academy Award for Best Picture in 2013. In the passage below, a "hand" is an enslaved field worker.

When a new hand . . . is sent for the first time to the field, he is whipped up smartly and made for that day to pick as fast as he can possibly. At night it is weighed, so that his capability in cotton picking is known. He must bring in the same weight each night following. If it falls short, it is considered evidence that he has been laggard [*slow*], and a greater or less number of lashes is the penalty.

An ordinary day's work is two hundred pounds [of cotton]. A slave who is accustomed to picking is punished if he or she brings in a less quantity [*amount*] than that. . . .

The hands are required to be in the cotton field as soon as it is light in the morning, and, with the exception of ten or fifteen minutes, which is given them at noon to swallow their allowance of cold bacon, they are not permitted to be a moment idle [*at rest*] until it is too dark to see, and when the moon is full, they often times labor till the middle of the night. They do not dare to stop even at dinner time, nor return to the quarters, however late it be, until the order to halt [*stop*] is given by the driver [*overseer*].

The day's work over in the field, the baskets are "toted," or in other words, carried to the gin-house, where the cotton is weighed. . . . This done, the labor of the day is not yet ended, by any means. Each one must then attend to his respective chores. One feeds the mules, another the swine [*pigs*], another cuts the wood, and so forth; besides, the packing is all done by candlelight. Finally, at a late hour, they reach the quarters, sleepy and overcome with the long day's toil. . . .

Read the passage above and discuss your answers to the following questions with a partner. Then share your answers with the class.

1. If you had been a slave, do you think you would have been able to survive such hard manual work?
2. If you had been an overseer, do you think you would have been able to treat other people so cruelly?
3. How could people who otherwise believed in liberty and human rights, like George Washington and Thomas Jefferson, have permitted such a system?
4. Do conditions like this still exist anywhere in the world today? If they do, do we have any responsibility to do something about it? Explain your opinion.

Most slaves lived in simple wooden cabins of one or two rooms, often with dirt floors. They had no furniture and usually slept on piles of rags or straw. Each week, slaves were usually given some bacon, molasses, and corn meal for making hominy grits or corn bread. Some were permitted to grow their own vegetables. They were responsible for making their own meals in the few hours when they were not working for the plantation owner. Twice a year, they might be given linen clothes, or clothes of coarse cloth made in Northern factories especially for slaves. The slaves also received shoes, which often did not fit. Some slaves preferred to go barefoot.

A slave family in the 1860s

The 13th Amendment abolished slavery.

The Legal Status of Enslaved People

Enslaved people had no rights. They were treated as property, not human beings. They were bought and sold by others in auctions. In many Southern states, it was even against the law to teach a slave to read and write. Slaves could not marry without the permission of their masters. A slave owner could break up families by selling slaves from the same family to other owners. Female slaves might be sexually abused.

Family members were sold separately to different buyers—probably never to meet again

With the end of the slave trade and the growing demand for cotton, the price of enslaved persons rose dramatically. Their hard work for no pay is what made plantation agriculture so immensely profitable. Wealthy Southerners had little interest in investing in factories or improvements in transportation because all their extra money went into buying land and slaves. This made it even more unlikely that Southerners would be willing to abolish slavery—the "**peculiar** (*unusual*) **institution**" of the South.

Slave Culture

A "culture" is a way of life. Although enslaved people were kept under strict control, they developed their own culture. This helped them survive the hardships of slavery. A unique slave culture began developing just as soon as the captured Africans were being carried across the Atlantic Ocean in slave ships. In Africa, these people had belonged to different tribal groups. They spoke different languages. Now, they found themselves together with a new common identity. In America, they were defined by their race and by their common experience of slavery, not by their tribe.

Unknown to plantation owners, African traditions survived in many slave communities. African priests continued to play a role. Memories of an African homeland where they had once lived in freedom were handed down from one generation of slaves to the next. Circles had a special meaning in many African societies, and slaves might form circles with other slaves for celebration or recreation. Dancing and music were other ways in which African traditions were kept alive in new surroundings. Stories told at night as slaves gathered around a campfire were sometimes based on oral traditions from Africa. Often, these stories included tales of betrayal reminding the slaves of those African chiefs who had cruelly sold them into slavery.

On the plantations, the slaves added new elements to older African traditions. They adopted

Dancing was a part of slave culture

the Christian faith, even though their churches were influenced by African practices and beliefs. They found comfort in the story of Moses, who led his people out of slavery. The slaves created new families and developed strong family ties. They performed their own marriages. In some cases, these marriage ceremonies were based on older African rituals. Family ties were so strong that most runaway slaves were actually trying to reunite with family members or loved ones who had been sold off to other owners.

The Historian's Apprentice

If you found yourself in an unjust and life-threatening situation surrounded by violence, and you were asked to work under horrible conditions, what would you do?

How Slaves Resisted

Enslaved African Americans resisted slavery in a number of ways. The most common way was by simply not working as hard as they could. Slaves might be uncooperative or pretend to be ignorant. Less often, slaves might strike back at their overseer or owner, or try to escape. The punishments for such actions could be very severe.

The very strongest form of resistance was rebellion. In August 1831, a slave named **Nat Turner** led a group of seventy slaves in a revolt in Virginia. Turner knew how to read and write, and he believed that he was receiving visions from God. After seeing a solar eclipse, he began preparing for an uprising to end slavery across the South. With a group of about seventy other slaves, Turner went from house to house freeing slaves and killing any white people they came across. Turner's group killed about sixty whites, including women and children. Eventually they were stopped by a militia force. More than fifty of the rebels were caught and hanged. Several hundred other slaves were killed in acts of violence. Nat Turner was captured two months later. Turner was tried and hanged. His rebellion caused a wave of fear among Southern slaveholders.

The Underground Railroad

Northern abolitionists helped organize escape routes for slaves. These routes were known as the "**Underground Railroad**." This was not a real railroad at all but a group of secret meeting points, escape routes, and safe places known as "stations." The stations were often barns, church cellars, or caves. Slaves usually travelled at night in small groups from station to station. "Stationmasters" gave them food. Those who led the escaping slaves were known as "conductors." Many of the stationmasters and conductors were actually African-American ministers, Quakers,

A station along the Underground Railroad

or free blacks. The Underground Railroad took the slaves to free states or north to Canada.

Because of the problem of runaway slaves, Congress passed a series of fugitive slave laws. These gave slave owners the right to have their "property"—the escaped slaves—returned. Slave catchers went to Northern states to track down and capture runaway slaves so that they could claim a reward.

Leading African-American Abolitionists

Some of the African Americans who escaped from slavery became famous abolitionists. Three of the most famous were Frederick Douglass, Sojourner Truth and Harriet Tubman.

Frederick Douglass (1818–1895)

Frederick Douglass was a slave in Maryland. The wife of his owner taught him the alphabet and he learned to read. He was twenty when he escaped by disguising himself as a free black sailor and taking a train and steamboat to Philadelphia. He next moved to Massachusetts, where he married and became a preacher and an abolitionist. Douglass became friends with William Lloyd Garrison and began telling about his experiences as a slave at abolitionist meetings. In 1845, he published *Narrative of the Life of Frederick Douglass, an American Slave*, which was an instant success. At the time, many whites believed that African Americans were somehow an inferior race. Frederick Douglass' brilliant writing and speaking style demonstrated to all that this was not true. Douglass went to Ireland and England in 1846 so that he would not be reclaimed by his former owner. British supporters raised the money needed to buy his freedom. Douglass returned to the United States where he started publishing an abolitionist newspaper, *The Northern Star*. He supported equality not only for African Americans but also for women. He was also a strong believer in public education. He thought that having a good education was worth even more than having the right to vote.

Sojourner Truth (1797–1883)

Sojourner Truth was not a Southern slave. She was actually born in slavery in upstate New York at a time when the state was gradually abolishing slavery. Truth was sold to a series of different owners. When she fell in love with a slave from a nearby farm, this young man was beaten so badly that he died. In 1826, Truth finally escaped. It was only one year before the final abolition of slavery in New York. One of her young children was sold illegally to an owner in Alabama. She filed a claim in court and won her son back. She became the first African-American woman to win a court case against a white man. In 1843, she had a deep religious experience. She adopted the name "Sojourner Truth" and began preaching against slavery. She also became friends with William Lloyd Garrison. In 1850, he published her book, *The*

Narrative of Sojourner Truth: A Northern Slave. In 1851, she gave a famous speech in which she demanded equal rights for women as well as for African Americans.

Harriet Tubman (1822–1913)

Tubman was born a slave in Maryland. She was often beaten and whipped as a child. She escaped to Philadelphia in 1849, but she later returned to Maryland several times to rescue other members of her family. Later, Tubman became one of the most daring conductors of the Underground Railroad. She led so many slaves to freedom that she became known as "Moses." She wore many disguises and carried a revolver. She also gave many abolitionist speeches. When the Civil War broke out, she worked for the Union army and conducted raids to free slaves.

The Historian's Apprentice

1. Select one of these three abolitionists. Conduct your own research to find out more about his or her life. Then pretend to be that individual and give a short speech to your class about your life experiences and why slavery should be abolished.
2. In April 2016, the U.S. Treasury announced its plans to replace Andrew Jackson on the front of the twenty-dollar bill ($20) with Harriet Tubman. Jackson will still be on the back of the bill. If these plans are not changed, the new twenty-dollar bill will go into use in 2020. Do you support this change? Write a paragraph in your journal or on a separate sheet of paper giving your opinion.

Name:___________________________________

Review the list of names and terms below.

Samuel Slater	Plantation	Underground Railroad
Robert Fulton	"Rhode Island System"	Eli Whitney
Cotton gin	Overseer	John Fitch
Erie Canal	Steam engine	Resistance
Steamboat	"Lowell System"	Whipping
Sojourner Truth	Abolitionists	Turnpikes
Francis Cabot Lowell	Factory	
Frederick Douglass	Nat Turner	

Now sort the items on the list above into the following three columns

Industrial Revolution	Transportation Revolution	Slavery and the South

Imagine that you come from a village in New England. You are now a female worker in a Lowell factory in 1830. Write a letter to a member of your family or a friend telling them what your life is like. Some facts you might want to consider are these:

- You wake up at 4:30 am in the morning, start work at 5:00 am, and finish work at 7:00 pm in the evening.
- You have a half-hour breakfast break at 7:00 am, and half-hour for lunch at noon.
- The factory where you work carries out several processes. It turns raw cotton into cloth under one roof.
- The machines where you work use waterpower. They are loud and noisy. They also create cotton fibers and dust.
- You agree to follow company regulations.
- You live in a company boarding house with other young women.
- The boarding house is made of brick. You sleep in a room with three other women. Each room has its own fireplace. Sometimes two women share a bed. You have become close friends with your roommates, who also come from New England farms.
- The boardinghouse has a "keeper" who makes evening meals for you.
- You attend church on Sundays.
- You listen to lectures and take classes given in the company hall.
- You write for the mill workers' newspaper, the *Lowell Offering*.

Imagine that it is 1840 and you live on the cotton plantation shown in this map. You might be an enslaved worker, an overseer, or an owner. Write a short description of the plantation and your daily life. Use information from the map and the chapter to write your description.

Chapter Review Cards

The Industrial Revolution

- The **Industrial Revolution** introduced new ways of making things. It organized work in factories and used new sources of energy like water and steam.
- The Industrial Revolution began in Great Britain with a series of inventions for the **textile industry**. The spinning jenny attached several spindles (rods) together to one wheel. A person could turn the wheel and make thread on several spindles at once. An English inventor connected this new textile machinery to waterpower. These machines were housed in "textile mills," which became the first **factories**.
- In the 1760s, James Watt built an improved **steam engine**. Factories using steam power could be located in towns—close to workers—rather than next to streams. By the 1790s, British inventors also developed the first steam-powered looms, weaving thread into cloth.
- Workers no longer worked at home but in factories. They were watched and worked many hours without rest. Factory work was repetitious and monotonous. Workers depended on their wages to buy food. When the factory owner didn't need them, they were out of work and might even starve.

The Industrial Revolution Comes to America

- The British passed strict laws preventing anyone from taking away the plans for building the new textile machines or factories. **Samuel Slater**, an apprentice in an English textile mill, came to the United States and built the first U.S. factory in Rhode Island. Slater and his partners employed entire families in their factory, including children. This became known as the "**Rhode Island System**."
- The **Embargo of 1807** greatly increased the demand for American-made goods. By 1810, fifty factories were making cotton thread in the United States.
- In 1814, **Francis Cabot Lowell** formed a manufacturing company. Lowell built a large factory in Massachusetts, which used power-driven spinning machines and looms. Lowell's factory could turn raw cotton into cloth.
- Lowell hired young unmarried women as factory workers. They lived in boarding houses provided by Lowell's company. Lowell provided his women workers with classes and social activities. This became known as the "**Lowell System**."
- The success of the textile industry encouraged other inventors and **entrepreneurs** (people who start or invest in new businesses).
- New England inventor **Eli Whitney** introduced the use of **interchangeable parts**. This meant all the parts of a product were cut from the same machine and had the same shape and size, making the repairing of machines quicker and easier.
- The use of factory production spread from textiles to other products. Instead of making most things themselves, Americans began buying **mass-produced goods** made in factories.

The Transportation Revolution

- In the early nineteenth century, Americans went through a **transportation revolution**.

Roads

- Private companies began building better private roads, known as **turnpikes**. The turnpike company charged users a fee, which was collected at special tollgates.

Canals

- After the War of 1812, Americans entered a great canal-building period. A **canal** is a human-made waterway, usually dug to connect natural waterways.
- In 1816, the New York State legislature approved a bill to build the **Erie Canal**. This connected the Hudson River with Lake Erie. Work began in 1817 and was completed in 1825. The effect of the canal on shipping costs was dramatic. The cost of shipping a ton of wheat from Buffalo (on Lake Erie) to New York City fell from $100 to $10. Midwestern farmers could send their crops to Northeastern cities. Other states copied New York's example by building their own canals.

Steamboats

- American **John Fitch** was first to design a boat powered by steam engine.
- **Robert Fulton** put one of Watt's steam engines on a boat and used it to turn a paddle wheel. Fulton and his business partner obtained **monopoly** (exclusive) **rights** from the New York State Legislature for running steamboats along the Hudson River. They opened the first successful commercial steamboat operation in 1807. Steamboats could move easily upstream (against the current) as well as downstream and did not depend on the weather like sailboats.

Railroads

- British inventors placed a steam engine on a wagon with wheels that moved along iron rails held together by planks of wood. The railroad was born.
- This invention went from Britain to the United States. The first American railroad, connecting Baltimore and the Potomac River, opened in 1830.
- The federal government began giving land to railroad companies that laid down new tracks. Between 1850 and 1860, the amount of railroad track tripled in the United States. By 1860, all major U.S. cities were connected by railroad.

The Telegraph

- In the 1840s, American painter **Samuel Morse** developed a better telegraph. He used a code made up of dots and dashes. The code became known as "Morse Code." It permitted instant communication between cities.

Gibbons v. Ogden (1824)

- In the case of ***Gibbons v. Ogden*** (1824), the U.S. Supreme Court ruled on the meaning of "interstate commerce."
- Gibbons had bought Fulton's monopoly rights for steamboat travel on the Hudson River. Ogden had a federal license for coastal trade and started a ferry service between New York City and New Jersey.
- Gibbons sued Ogden. He argued that Ogden's ferry service violated his monopoly from New York State.
- Ogden claimed Congress had the right to give him a license because Congress had the power to "regulate interstate commerce."
- Chief Justice John Marshall ruled that moving people affects commerce and Congress has the power to regulate it. Because Congress has the power to regulate "interstate commerce," individual states cannot also regulate it. Ogden's license from Congress therefore gave him the right to run a ferry across the Hudson from New York to New Jersey.
- The case increased the power of Congress in regulating "interstate commerce." It prevented state governments from creating monopolies that would have limited interstate commerce.

The Increasing Size of Northern Cities

- The rise of industry and the transportation revolution increased the population of Northern cities. Farm workers moved to towns and cities to find work in factories or to provide services for other people living there.
- Northern cities were filled with Irish and German immigrants in the 1840s and 1850s. In Ireland, a disease killed most of the potato crop, causing a famine. Germans came to escape political troubles in 1848 or to find new economic opportunities.

The Cotton Gin and the Spread of Slavery in the South

- In 1793, inventor **Eli Whitney** designed the **cotton gin**. This machine could pull the seeds out of raw cotton. It made it possible to use Southern-grown cotton in textile factories.
- The increased demand for raw cotton from British and Northern factories combined with the invention of the cotton gin caused slavery to spread.
- Most Southern plantations grew cotton, but in some areas they grew other cash crops: rice, tobacco, and sugar cane.
- Only a few thousand Southerners actually owned more than a hundred slaves. Large plantation owners had **overseers** (people who supervise workers). These large plantations were self-sufficient communities. Forced labor planted, harvested, cleaned and packed raw cotton for shipment north or to Britain.
- On smaller farms, slaves might work alongside their owners.

The Status of Enslaved People

- Enslaved people had no rights. They were treated as property, bought and sold by others in auctions.
- Slaves could not lawfully marry without the permission of their masters. A slave owner could break up families by selling slaves from the same family to other owners. Female slaves might be sexually abused.
- In many Southern states, to teach a slave to read and write was against the law.
- With the end of the slave trade and the growing demand for cotton, the price of enslaved persons rose. Wealthy Southerners had little interest in investing in factories or improvements in transportation because all their extra money went into buying land and slaves. This made it even more unlikely that Southerners would be willing to abolish slavery—the "**peculiar institution**" of the South.

Slave Culture

- Although enslaved people were kept under strict control, they developed their own culture. In Africa, these people had belonged to different tribal groups and spoke different languages. In America, they were defined by their race and by their common experience of slavery.
- African traditions survived in many slave communities. Slaves added new elements to older African traditions, often adopting the Christian faith.
- Although lawful marriage was usually forbidden, slaves often performed their own marriage ceremonies. Runaway slaves were most often attempting to rejoin spouses or family members.

How Slaves Resisted

Enslaved people resisted the demands of slavery in many ways:

- Slaves would not work as hard as they could.
- Slaves might be uncooperative or pretend to be ignorant.
- Less often, slaves might strike back at their overseer or owner, or even try to escape. The punishments for such actions could be very severe.
- In August 1831, **Nat Turner** believed that God was sending him visions to end slavery across the South. He led a group of seventy slaves in a rebellion in Virginia. They went from house to house, freeing slaves and killing white people in the process. They were eventually stopped by state militia. Turner was caught and hanged.

The Underground Railroad

- Northern abolitionists helped organize escape routes for slaves. These routes were known as the "**Underground Railroad.**" Places where slaves hid were called "stations." Those that guided them were "conductors." Most travel took place at night.
- Congress passed a series of **fugitive slave laws**. These laws gave slave owners the right to have their "property" the escaped slaves returned. Slave catchers went to Northern states to capture runaway slaves in exchange for a reward.

Leading African-American Abolitionists

Frederick Douglass (1818–1895)

- Douglass escaped from slavery by disguising himself as a free black sailor and taking a train and steamboat to Philadelphia.
- He moved to Massachusetts, where he became a preacher and an abolitionist. In 1845, he published *Narrative of the Life of Frederick Douglass, an American Slave*, which was an instant success.
- Douglass went to Ireland and England in 1846 to avoid being reclaimed by his former owner. British supporters raised the money needed to buy his freedom. Douglass returned to America where he started publishing an abolitionist newspaper, *The Northern Star*.

Sojourner Truth (1797–1883)

- She was born a slave in upstate New York. In 1826, one year before the abolition of slavery in New York, she escaped slavery.
- One of her young children was sold illegally to an owner in Alabama. She filed a claim in court and won her son back.
- In 1843, she had a deep religious experience and adopted the name "Sojourner Truth". She began preaching against slavery. In 1850, her friend William Lloyd Garrison published her book, *The Narrative of Sojourner Truth: A Northern Slave.*

Harriet Tubman (1822–1913)

- She escaped to Philadelphia in 1849. She returned to Maryland several times to rescue members of her family. She became a conductor of the Underground Railroad.

The Industrial and Transportation Revolutions

In the 19th century, new inventions led to revolutions in industry and transportation. Samuel Slater built the first American ____________________. He introduced new British machinery for spinning raw cotton into ____________________.

John Fitch built the first ____________________. It used a steam engine to pull oars. Later, ____________________ began running the first commercially successful ____________________. It went up and down the Hudson River. Other inventors used steam engines to move carts along iron rails. This invention led to the ____________________. This made it easier for farmers to ship their crops.

In 1793, Eli Whitney invented the ____________________ while visiting a plantation in Georgia. This invention made it easier to remove seeds from ____________________. Plantation owners could grow more ____________________ to sell to factories. The increased demand for this crop encouraged the spread of ____________________ throughout the South.

The Industrial Revolution and its Consequences: North and South

The Industrial Revolution Comes to America
- Samuel Slater builds a factory in Rhode Island
- "Rhode Island System" uses whole families as employees
- Francis Lowell builds factory in Massachusetts to turn raw cotton into cloth under one roof
- The "Lowell System": Young, unmarried women live in company boardinghouses and have activities, but also long hours at work

Gibbons v. Ogden (1824)
- U.S. Supreme Court expands the definition of "interstate commerce"

The Transportation Revolution

Turnpikes

Canals
- Erie Canal—completed in 1825
- Makes transport of goods from Great Lakes to New York City much cheaper
- Other states copy its example

Steamboats
- Can travel upstream
- John Fitch's steamboat
- Robert Fulton—first commercially successful steamboat (1807)

Railroads
- By 1860, major cities are connected

Telegraph
- Morse code
- Instant communication

Northern Cities Grow

The Industrial Revolution
New machines use water and steam power to make textiles in factories

Other Inventors
- Eli Whitney promotes use of interchangeable parts
- Factory production spreads from textiles to other goods

The South and Slavery
Southerners grew raw materials for factories

The Cotton Gin
- Invented by Eli Whitney in 1793
- Removes seeds from raw cotton
- Increases need for slave labor

Plantation Life
- Each plantation is a self-sufficient community
- Owner lives in large mansion
- Slaves live in cabins with dirt floors
- Owners use overseers to supervise and punish slaves

The Experience of Slavery
- Slaves are forced to work or severely punished
- Slaves develop their own culture
- Slaves resist slavery
- The Underground Railroad helped slaves to escape
- Nat Turner led a slave rebellion in 1831
- Some escaped slaves became important abolitionists in the North
  - ★ Frederick Douglass
  - ★ Sojourner Truth
  - ★ Harriet Tubman

What do you know?

SS.6.A.4.7

1. The graph below shows the urban population of the United States from 1800 to 1850.

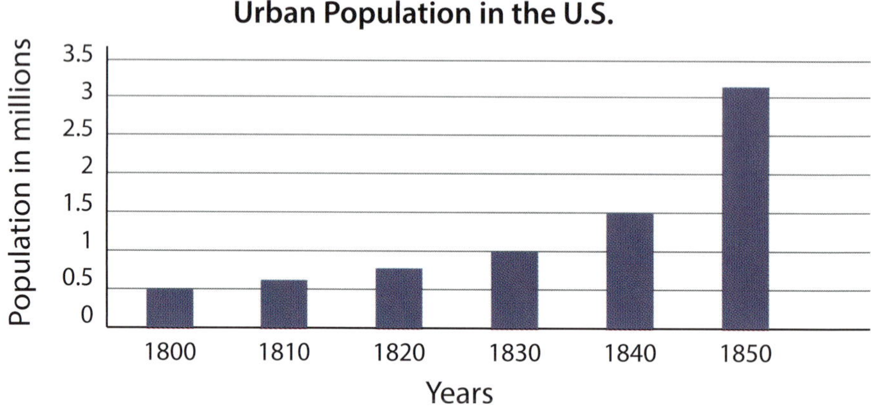

Which conclusion can be drawn from the information in the graph?

A. By 1850, more than half of all Americans lived in cities.

B. Urban populations increased as the new factory system spread.

C. Most of America's large cities were in the western part of the country.

D. Urban growth was largely a result of the arrival of new immigrants from Europe.

SS.6.A.4.6

2. How did the invention of the steam engine contribute to economic growth?

A. Steam power made machines and factories safer to operate.

B. Farms needed more workers to operate new agriculture machines.

C. Manufacturers benefited from the power generated by waterwheels.

D. Factories could be built and operated away from sources of running water.

SS.6.A.4.6

3. How did technological improvements in the early 1800s influence American manufacturing?

A. The use of child labor in manufacturing decreased.

B. New machines produced goods more quickly and cheaply.

C. Fewer people worked in manufacturing because of new machines.

D. Skilled craftsmen used new tools to make more handmade goods than factories could produce.

SS.6.A.4.6

4. During the early 1800s, what was an important impact of improvements in technology?

A. The use of child labor decreased.

B. New machinery was used to produce more goods.

C. More goods were produced by small family businesses.

D. Skilled craftsmen made goods faster than factories could produce them.

SS.6.A.4.6

5. The passage below is from an application for a town charter in Webster, Massachusetts.

> *This territory was . . . very thinly inhabited until the waterpower provided by the river and a large natural pond attracted the manufacturers. After that, it began to flourish vigorously.*

Based on the passage, which conclusion can be drawn about the impact of geography on the growth of towns?

A. When manufacturers built factories and hired workers, nearby towns grew.

B. The demand for laborers declined as more factories were built near rivers.

C. Manufacturers were often forced to relocate their factories because of a lack of workers.

D. Urban populations decreased because of the noise and pollution caused by the first factories.

SS.6.A.4.7

6. The Venn diagram below compares features of the Rhode Island System and Lowell System.

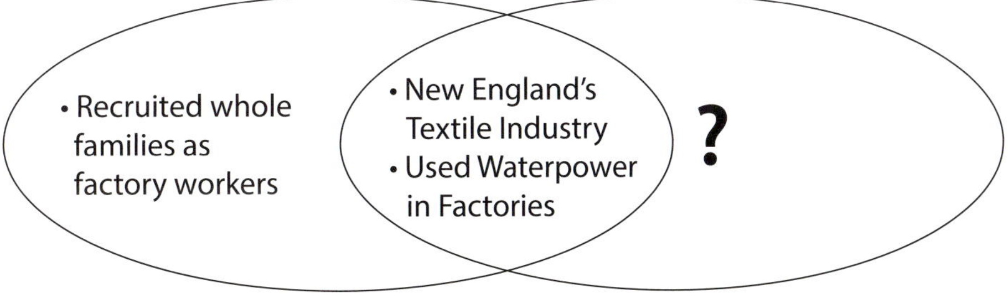

Which feature completes the Venn diagram?

A. recruited children as factory workers

B. recruited young men as factory workers

C. recruited young women as factory workers

D. recruited older men and women as factory workers

SS.6.A.4.7

7. Which inventions made it possible for factories to produce textile goods more quickly and cheaply?

A. Locomotive and telegraph

B. Spinning jenny and power loom

C. Mechanical reaper and steamboat

D. Interchangeable parts and assembly line

SS.6.A.4.7

8. The passage below is from a newspaper advertisement in the early 1800s.

> *Do you know a family of children, girls or boys, from 7 to 12 years of age, with a parent or parents not in well-off circumstances? A widow would be preferred. They are to live near one of our cotton mills, so that the children may work in them and the parents may perhaps be employed.*

Based on the passage, which conclusion can be drawn?

A. New American industries depended on immigrant families to work in their factories.

B. Factories needed workers so badly they provided child care so that parents could work.

C. Parents were encouraged to work so that their children could attend school near the factory.

D. Factory owners preferred to employ children so they could pay them a lower wage than adults.

SS.6.E.2.1

9. How did Elijah McCoy contribute to America's industrial growth?

A. He introduced innovations he had seen in Scotland.

B. He invented a better and less expensive sewing machine.

C. He invented devices that enabled steam engines to lubricate themselves.

D. He invented a method for transmitting messages instantly across an electric wire.

SS.6.A.4.5

10. How did Robert Fulton's *Clermont* affect major inland waterways in the United States?

A. It made Southern waterways as profitable as those in the North.

B. It re-introduced slavery along the Ohio River to help ship goods.

C. It showed a practical way to ship goods upstream as well as downstream.

D. It created a new transportation system for settlers west of the Mississippi River.

SS.6.A.4.5

11. What impact did the development of canals have on the United States in the early1800s?

  A. They led to a decline in American exports to European countries.

  B. They caused New York City to lose its position as a manufacturing center.

  C. They helped the Midwest to become a major center of American textile production.

  D. They made it easier for Midwestern farmers to ship their crops to cities in the Northeast.

SS.6.A.4.10

12. The information below describes key characteristics of an important invention.

> - This invention made it possible for one slave to do the work of several, producing large quantities of clean cotton fiber each workday.
> - This invention turned cotton into the most important cash crop grown in the South and America's most valuable export.
> - This machine revitalized African-American slavery in the South as a profitable institution.

  Which invention had these characteristics?

  A. Eli Whitney's cotton gin

  B. Isaac Singer's sewing machine

  C. Samuel Slater's textile machinery

  D. Cyrus McCormick's mechanical reaper

SS.6.A.4.10

13. Which sentence describes how American society was affected by Eli Whitney's cotton gin?

  A. It led Northern factories to move to Southern states.

  B. It encouraged the spread of slavery in much of the South.

  C. It made Americans less dependent on imports from Great Britain.

  D. It encouraged Southern farmers to grow a greater diversity of crops.

SS.6.A.4.11

14. How did plantation owners ensure that enslaved people worked hard on their land?

  A. They paid higher wages to their best workers.

  B. They paid workers based on how much cotton or other crops they produced.

  C. They only gave food to the families of workers who produced a certain amount of crops.

  D. They used overseers and the threat of physical punishment for those who did not produce enough.

SS.6.A.4.11

15. The headline below describes an event in U.S. history.

DAILY OBSERVER

AUGUST 12, 1831

Nat Turner Leads Slave Revolt!

Richmond, Virginia —

What was the impact of the event described in the newspaper headline?

A. Thousands of enslaved people across the South rose up in rebellion.

B. The President of the United States issued the Emancipation Proclamation.

C. The rebellion was crushed but Southern slaveholders feared future revolts.

D. Two competing governments—free and slave—were established in Kansas.

SS.6.A.4.11

16. The information below lists the actions of enslaved people in the South in the early 1800s.

- Not working as hard as they could
- Striking back at an overseer or owner
- Escaping with the Underground Railroad
- Conducting their own secret ceremonies and traditions

Which title describes this list?

A. Ways in which African Americans contributed to plantation life

B. Ways in which African Americans resisted the demands of slavery

C. Ways in which African Americans preserved traditional African culture

D. Ways in which African Americans blended old and new to create a new culture

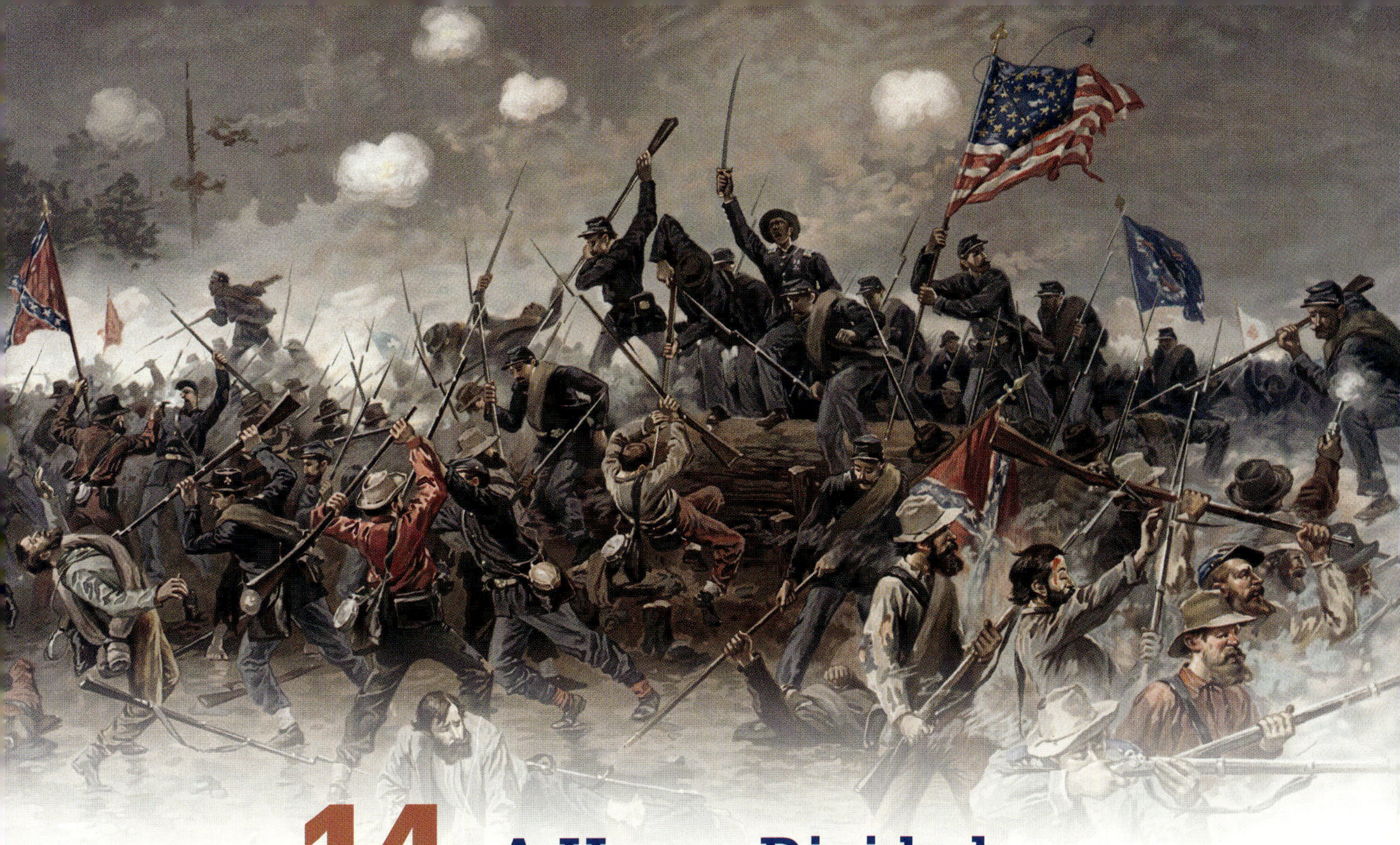

CHAPTER 14 A House Divided: The Story of the Civil War

SS.6.A.5.1 Explain the causes, course, and consequence of the Civil War (sectionalism, slavery, states' rights, balance of power in the Senate).

SS.6.A.5.2 Analyze the role of slavery in the development of sectional conflict.

SS.6.A.5.3 Explain major domestic and international economic, military, political, and socio-cultural events of Abraham Lincoln's presidency.

SS.6.A.5.4 Identify the division (Confederate and Union states, Border states, western territories) of the United States at the outbreak of the Civil War.

SS.6.A.5.5 Compare Union and Confederate strengths and weaknesses.

SS.6.A.5.6 Compare significant Civil War battles and events and their effects on civilian populations.

SS.6.A.5.7 Examine key events and peoples in Florida history as each impacts this era of American history.

Names and Terms You Should Know

Sectionalism

Abolitionists

Compromise

Popular sovereignty

Republican Party

Dred Scott Decision

Citizenship

Lincoln–Douglas Debates

Secession

Conscription

Suspension of Writ of *Habeas Corpus*

Emancipation Proclamation

Alignment to Grade 7 Civics Standards

SS.7.C.2.1 Define the term "citizen" and identify legal means of becoming a citizen.

SS.7.C.2.5 Distinguish how the Constitution safeguards and limits individual rights.

SS.7.C.2.8 Identify America's current political parties, and illustrate their ideas about government.

SS.7.C.3.7 Analyze the impact of the 13th, 14th, 15th, 19th, 24th and 26th Amendments on participation of minority groups in the American political process.

Florida "Keys" to Learning

1. The Civil War had several causes, including sectionalism, slavery, differing views of states' rights, and the balance of power in the Senate.

2. Sectionalism describes the loyalty many Americans felt towards their own geographic region—the North, South or West—rather than to the country as a whole.

3. The North saw the rise of manufacturing; the West had independent farmers growing food and raising livestock; the South grew cash crops for export, such as cotton and rice, and remained dependent on the use of slave labor.

4. Abolitionists wanted to end slavery. Supporters of slavery argued that Southern slaves were better treated than Northern factory workers.

5. Americans disagreed on whether slavery should spread westward. A series of compromises at first seemed able to resolve the issue. Under the Missouri Compromise (1820), Missouri became a slave state and Maine became a free state. Slavery was not otherwise to be permitted in the lands of the Louisiana Purchase above a certain line (36°30′ N). In the Compromise of 1850, California was admitted as a free state and a stricter fugitive slave law was enacted.

6. This system of compromise broke down with the passage of the Kansas-Nebraska Act (1854), "Bleeding Kansas" (1855–1856), the *Dred Scott* decision (1857), and John Brown's raid (1859).

7. In the Presidential election of 1860, Democrats were divided. Republican candidate Abraham Lincoln won the election with only 39% of the popular vote. He received no electoral votes from the Southern states. South Carolina and six other Southern states immediately seceded (*withdrew from the Union*). The seceding states formed the Confederate States of America.

8. In his inaugural address, Lincoln called on Southern states to remain in the Union. He promised not to end slavery in the South. When he sent supplies to Fort Sumter in Charleston Harbor, South Carolina fired on the fort. This act started the Civil War. Rather than fight fellow Southerners, four more states seceded.

9. The North had many advantages: a larger population, greater revenues, more railroad lines and factories, and naval power. The South had its military traditions and the fact that white Southerners were fighting to preserve (*keep*) their way of life. The existence of a large number of enslaved Southerners created a degree of uncertainty.

10. In the early campaigns, the South stopped attempted Northern invasions. However, it could not successfully advance into the North itself. The North relied on its naval power to strangle the South. It imposed a naval blockade of the Atlantic coast and gradually took control of the Mississippi River.

11. In September 1862, Lincoln issued the Emancipation Proclamation. It announced the emancipation (*freeing*) of slaves in states still in rebellion on January 1, 1863.

12. The turning point of the war was reached in 1863. The North defeated Southern forces at Gettysburg and General Ulysses S. Grant captured Vicksburg. Lincoln put Grant in command of Union forces. Grant aimed at destroying Confederate forces and their sources of support. Sherman's "March to the Sea" further divided the South and destroyed farms, towns and railroad lines.

13. In April 1865, General Robert E. Lee surrendered to Grant at Appomattox. Less than a week later, President Lincoln was assassinated.

14. The Civil War ended slavery, preserved the Union, and strengthened the federal government.

In the last chapter, you learned how different sections of the country developed different lifestyles. These led to disagreements over key issues. In this chapter you will learn how these differences finally led to war in 1861. It was a war of brother against brother, and sister against sister. Families were divided based on whether members lived in the North or the South. More Americans were killed in this war than in any other. The wounds left by the Civil War took many years to heal.

Causes of the Civil War

There were several reasons why Americans finally went to war in 1861. These included sectionalism, slavery, states' rights, and the balance of power in the U.S. Senate.

Sectionalism

By 1850, the nation was divided into three sections. Each section had its own interests and ways of life.

- The South had slavery—its "peculiar (*unusual*) institution"—long after slavery had ended in the North. The invention of the cotton gin and the increased demand for raw cotton from factories led to an expansion of slavery in the South. As many as four million people—about one-third of the entire population of the South— were enslaved African Americans. Most of them worked on the large plantations of the wealthiest Southern landowners.
- The Northwest was made up of small, independent farmers. It became the "bread basket" of the United States. Its farmers grew grain that was shipped by river and canal to the Northeast and the South.
- The Northeast became the center of American manufacturing and trade.

These economic and social differences led to the rise of "sectionalism." *Sectionalism* describes the strong loyalty that many Americans felt to their own "section" of the country. Often this was greater than their loyalty to the nation as a whole.

People in each section wanted policies favorable to their interests. Northerners wanted high tariffs to protect their manufactured goods from

Economic Specialization in the United States in 1850

Section	Population in 1850	Leading Economic Activities
Northeast (9 states)	9 million	Manufacturing (textiles, ironwares, and machinery), shipping, small farms, and fishing
South (14 states)	9 million (including about 4 million slaves)	Small farms and large plantations using slave labor to grow cash crops like cotton, tobacco, rice, and sugar for export
Northwest (6 states)	5 million	Family farms on fertile lands produced wheat and livestock for sale in the Northeast and South

British competition. Southerners opposed high tariffs because they sold raw cotton to Britain and wanted to buy cheap British imports. Northerners favored an active federal government. Southerners wanted as little federal interference as possible.

Important National Issues, 1820–1850

	North	South	West
Protective Tariff	Yes	No	Yes
National Bank	Yes	No	No
Federal Financing of Roads and Canals	Yes	No	Yes
Cheap Federal Land	No	Yes	Yes
Extension of Slavery to New Territories	No	Yes	No

States' Rights

Southerners were strong supporters of states' rights. They argued that the states had created the federal government by ratifying the Constitution. Because each state had joined the Union voluntarily, it also had the power to withdraw if it wished.

Northerners took a different view. They held the view expressed by Daniel Webster in the Webster-Hayne debate. They saw the Constitution as the work of the American people as a whole. Its preamble begins with "We the People," not with the names of individual states. States therefore did not have the right to leave the Union whenever they pleased.

Slavery

The most explosive issue facing Americans was slavery. Abolitionists saw slavery as a great moral evil that had to be ended.

Harriet Beecher Stowe's book *Uncle Tom's Cabin* (1852) greatly added to the sense of moral outrage. Stowe was the daughter of Protestant minister Lyman Beecher. Her book on slavery focused on the fugitive slave law and stirred the nation's conscience. It also inspired a play that toured Northern cities. Abraham Lincoln called Stowe the woman who had caused the war.

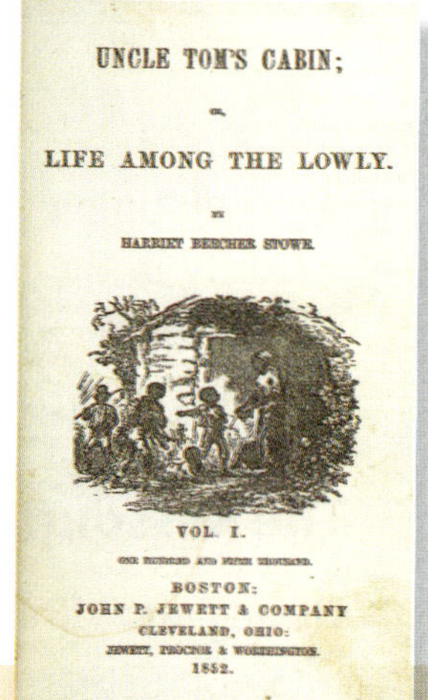

Uncle Tom's Cabin

Stowe's novel tells the story of a friendly old slave named Uncle Tom. He is abused by his new owner, Simon Legree. Legree hates Tom because Tom will not beat other slaves. Tom encourages another slave, Cassy, to run away. Legree has Tom killed when he will not reveal where Cassy has gone.

Pro-slavery Southerners argued that African Americans were inferior and actually better off as slaves. They claimed that Southern slaves were better treated than factory workers in the North. They further argued that suddenly freeing millions of slaves would bring widespread disorder and violence.

The Balance of Power in the United States Senate

Congress has two houses: the House of Representatives and the Senate.

When the United States took land from Mexico, it raised a new question: Would the territories of the Mexican Cession be admitted as slave or free states? This would affect the balance of power in the Senate. Southerners were especially determined to maintain that balance. The Senate was their main weapon for defending slavery against

Slave and Free States in the U.S. Senate

Year	1789	1800	1821	1837	1846	1848	1850	1858	1861
Free States	5	8	12	13	14	15	16	17	19
Slave States	8	9	12	13	15	15	15	15	15

the more populous North, which already had a majority in the House of Representatives. Many Northerners, however, were horrified at the thought of slavery spreading further.

The Missouri Compromise (1820)

During the "Era of Good Feelings," Americans were able to preserve (*keep*) the balance in the Senate through careful compromise. When Missouri applied for admission as a slave state, there were exactly eleven free states and eleven slave states. Neither side wanted to give the other a majority in the Senate. A compromise was finally worked out:

- Missouri was admitted as a slave state.
- Maine was admitted as a free state.
- Except in Missouri itself, slavery was not to be allowed in the Louisiana Territory above the southern border of Missouri, known as the "Missouri Compromise" line (36°30′ N).

When Florida was admitted as a slave state, Iowa was admitted as a slave state a year later. The admission of Texas (slave state) was balanced by Wisconsin (free state).

The Compromise of 1850

A crisis occurred when California applied for admission as a free state. This would again have upset the balance in the Senate. Once more, a careful compromise was worked out. Both Henry Clay and Illinois Senator Stephen Douglas helped to arrange it:

- California was admitted as a free state.
- The rest of the Mexican Cession was divided into two territories: New Mexico and Utah. The system of "popular sovereignty" was to be applied to them. People living in those territories would decide for themselves whether or not they

"Popular sovereignty" means that the people govern themselves.

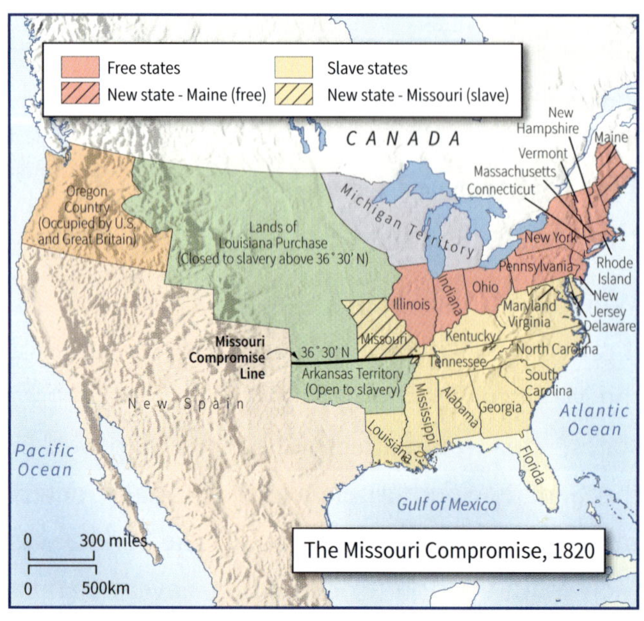

The Missouri Compromise, 1820

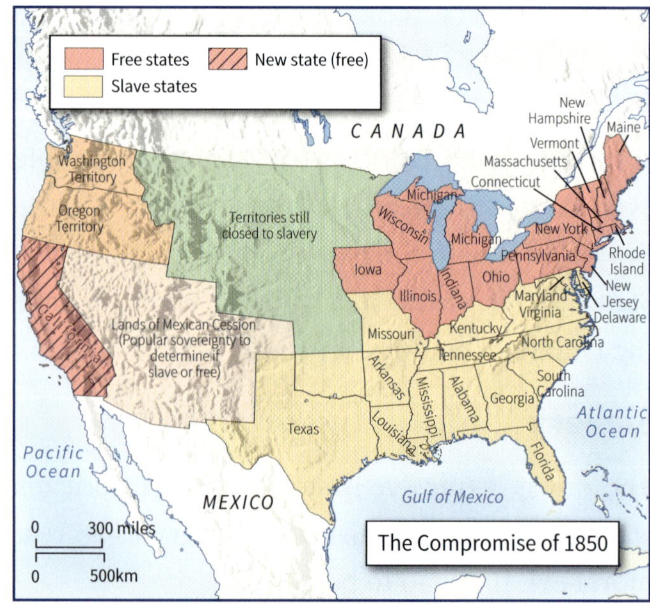

The Compromise of 1850

would permit slavery. This left open the possibility of more slave states.

- Slavery was also allowed to continue in Washington, D.C. However, slaves could no longer be bought and sold there.
- A stricter fugitive slave law was passed. The new law required states in the North to provide more help to Southerners trying to recover their runaway slaves. This new fugitive slave law was greatly resented in the North.

The admission of California as a free state did end the balance of free and slave states in the Senate. However, the fact that popular sovereignty would be applied to the rest of the Mexican Cession meant there was hope for Southerners that the balance would be restored in the future. In the meantime Southerners had gained other benefits from the compromise, such as the stricter fugitive slave law.

The Breakdown of Compromise and the Road to War

These careful compromises began falling apart in 1854 with the Kansas-Nebraska Act.

The Kansas-Nebraska Act (1854)

In 1854, Senator Stephen Douglas introduced the Kansas-Nebraska Act. Douglas wanted to win Southern support for a railroad line from the Midwest to California. He could only win the support he needed in a crucial Senate committee by overturning the Missouri Compromise.

The Kansas-Nebraska Act divided the Nebraska Territory, a part of the Louisiana Purchase, into two smaller territories: Nebraska and Kansas. The act then repealed the Missouri Compromise by applying the principle of "popular sovereignty" to both of these territories. This meant slavery might again be possible above the "Missouri Compromise" line in the Louisiana Purchase, where it had been prohibited for more than thirty years.

Douglas argued that "popular sovereignty" offered the most democratic way of resolving the slavery question. He thought it would remove the issue from national politics. Instead of the federal government deciding who could have slavery, people in territories would decide for themselves. Many Northerners were shocked.

Birth of the Republican Party (1854)

The **Republican Party** was formed in 1854 in direct response to the Kansas-Nebraska Act. Republicans opposed the extension (*spread*) of slavery to any new territories. They could accept slavery where it was, but they could not see it spread any further.

The Republican Party is one of the two major political parties in the United States today.

"Bleeding Kansas" (1855–1856)

The issue of whether Kansas would have slavery in the future was to be decided by popular vote. Both pro-slavery and anti-slavery forces tried to influence the outcome. Each side brought in its own group of settlers. By 1855, two rival state governments for Kansas had formed. One was pro-slavery and the other was against slavery.

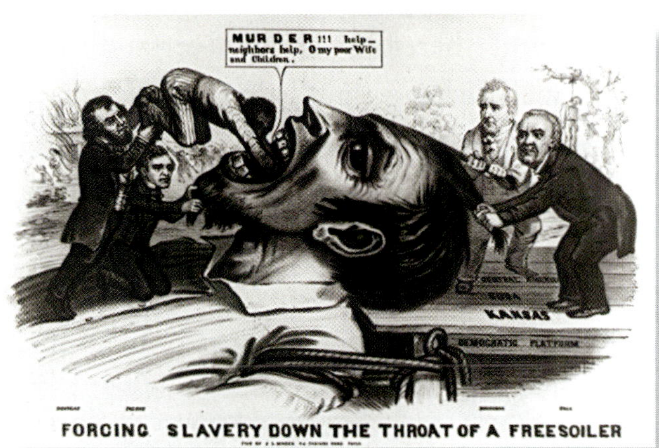

The federal government eventually had to send in troops to restore order.

Violence in the Senate

Violence even reached the U.S. Senate in May 1856. In one of his speeches, Senator Charles Sumner of Massachusetts threw insults at Senator Butler of South Carolina. A few days later, Butler's nephew beat Sumner unconscious with a gold-tipped walking cane on the floor of the Senate.

The *Dred Scott* Decision (1857)

The U.S. Supreme Court tried to resolve the problem of slavery with its decision in the case of *Dred Scott v. Sandford*. Dred Scott was a Missouri slave. Scott lived with his owner, an army officer, for several years in Illinois, a free state. They had also been in a northern territory where slavery was prohibited. During this time, Scott married another slave and had two children. After the Scotts returned with their owner to Missouri, they sued for their freedom. They claimed that they had lived in a free state and were no longer slaves. The Scotts were actually freed in 1850, but the Missouri Supreme Court reversed the decision. The Scotts then appealed their case to the United States Supreme Court. Scott's wife dropped out of the suit to make the case easier. Five years later, the Supreme Court reached its decision. Chief Justice Roger Taney ruled that because Dred Scott was an African American, he was not a U.S. citizen. Therefore, he had no right to sue in federal court.

The 14th Amendment later stated that all persons born or naturalized in the United States are citizens of the United States.

The Historian's Apprentice

The **Dred Scott** decision turned a light on the question of citizenship. What is a citizen? What does citizenship mean to you? Although Scott was born in this country, the Court held he had no rights of citizenship. Why was that so important?

According to the Chief Justice Taney, a slave was not a person at all but a piece of property that belonged to someone else.

The slaveholder, on the other hand, was a citizen and therefore enjoyed certain rights. These included the right to own property. On these grounds, the Supreme Court also held that the prohibition of slavery in northern territories by the Missouri Compromise had been unconstitutional. Congress did not have the right to take away a slaveholder's property or to limit his property rights.

"[African Americans] had no rights which the white man was bound to respect; and [an African American] might justly and lawfully be reduced to slavery for his benefit. He was bought and sold and treated as an ordinary article of merchandise, whenever profit could be made by it. [Referring to language in the Declaration of Independence] it is too clear for dispute, that the enslaved African race were not intended to be included, and formed no part of the people who framed and adopted this declaration. . . ."

—Chief Justice Taney,
Dred Scott v. Sandford (1857)

This ruling by Chief Justice Taney and the Justices of the U.S. Supreme Court, a majority of whom came from the South, raised a storm of protest across the North. Fortunately for Dred Scott, his owners freed him two months after the decision was announced.

The Historian's Apprentice

Your class should pretend it is putting Chief Justice Roger Taney on trial for his opinion in *Dred Scott v. Sandford*. Did Taney and the other Justices of the Supreme Court act fairly and reasonably in reaching their decision? Did they follow the U.S. Constitution, based on the views of that time? Should they have reached a different decision?

The Lincoln-Douglas Debates (1858)

Abraham Lincoln was a lawyer on the Illinois frontier and a former Congressman. He was the candidate of the new Republican Party for U.S. Senator from Illinois in the 1858 election. His opponent in the election was Senator Stephen Douglas, author of the Kansas-Nebraska Act.

Lincoln and Douglas held a series of debates for voters across Illinois. Douglas accused Lincoln of being an abolitionist who believed in racial equality. Lincoln replied that he thought African Americans had basic rights and that slavery was wrong. He argued that Douglas' approach would one day end by extending slavery to all states.

The public learns about candidates' stands on issues and their party platforms by listening to debates.

Abraham Lincoln

Stephen Douglas

John Brown's Raid on Harpers Ferry (1859)

John Brown was a white abolitionist. He moved to "Bleeding Kansas," where he fought and killed pro-slavery agitators.

Brown later drew up plans for launching slave revolts across the South. He even told Frederick Douglass and Harriet Tubman about his plans. In 1859, Brown captured a federal **arsenal** (*place where weapons are kept*) in Harpers Ferry, Virginia. Brown believed this news would cause revolts across the South. Not a single slave joined Brown's uprising. His tiny force was soon overwhelmed by U.S. troops. Brown was hanged two months later. His attempt to stir the slaves to revolt failed but still inspired fear among Southern whites.

TREASON!

All TRUE CHRISTIANS who believe in "Immortality through Jesus Christ alone," are requested to pray for

CAPT. JOHN BROWN,

who now is under sentence of death, and is to be hung next month for righteousness sake, and doing justly with his fellow man, his country and his God.

By request of one who loves the Truth, and feels for the man that is to die a martyr to it. J.

John Brown

The Election of Abraham Lincoln

In the Presidential election of 1860, the Republican Party nominated Abraham Lincoln. Democrats were divided. Southern Democrats nominated Vice President John C. Breckinridge. Northern Democrats nominated Stephen A. Douglas. Another new party, the Constitutional Union, was made up of Southerners who supported the Union. They nominated John Bell. With all these candidates, the national vote was greatly divided. Lincoln was able to win the election with only 39% of the popular vote. Not a single Southern state gave its electoral votes to Lincoln.

The Secession of the South

As soon as Lincoln was elected, South Carolina announced its **secession** from the Union. Six other Southern states, all from the "Deep South," quickly followed. Although they seceded, Southern leaders still hoped to avoid war. They wanted to create a separate nation of slaveholders and slaves, with an economy based on exporting cash crops from slave labor. They had no desire for a war with the United States. President James Buchanan declared that the Southern states had no right to secede. But he also felt that he had no power stop them. Meanwhile, the Southern states organized themselves into a new nation, calling themselves the "**Confederate States of America**." They drew up their own constitution and elected their own President, **Jefferson Davis**. In his inaugural address, Davis emphasized that Southerners had the right to choose their own government and way of life. Because they had no designs of aggression, he hoped the two nations—the Confederacy and the Union—could live side-by-side in peace.

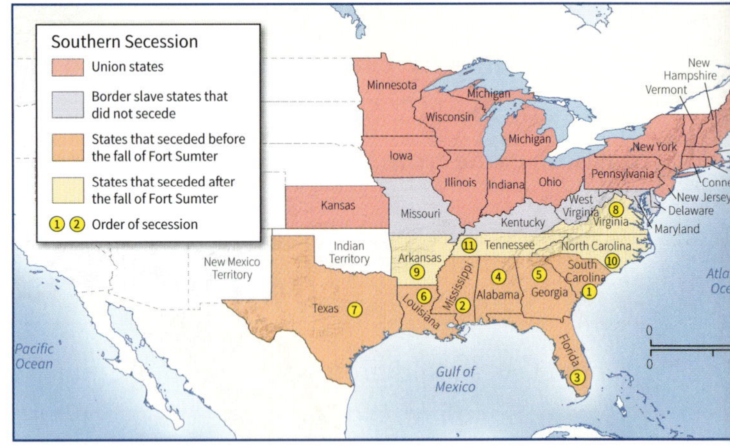

Jefferson Davis

In his own inaugural address, Lincoln tried to calm the fears of white Southerners. He pledged not to interfere with slavery where it already existed. But he also said he would not allow the secession of states. Lincoln hoped a show of firmness would avoid bloodshed. He was willing to go to war if necessary to bring the Southern states back to the Union: "[T]he Union of these states," he declared, "is perpetual," and "no state can lawfully get out of the Union."

The Shots Fired at Fort Sumter

Once South Carolina had seceded, the problem arose of what to do with federal forts and federal property located in that state. President Lincoln sent food supplies to **Fort Sumter**, a federal fort in Charleston, South Carolina. Forces of the new Confederate States of America fired on Fort Sumter on April 12, 1861. Lincoln called on all states to supply **militia** (*citizen troops*) to help put down the rebellion. Those Southern states that had not seceded were now

Fort Sumter under fire by Confederate forces

forced to choose sides. Should they secede or fight against another Southern state? Virginia and three other Southern states joined the Confederacy rather than fight other Southerners.

The border states of Maryland, Delaware, Kentucky, and Missouri stayed loyal to the Union. This was not accidental. Lincoln did not want Washington, D.C., to be totally surrounded by Confederate states. He also did not want Southerners to be able to reach the Ohio River through Kentucky. So he sent federal troops into those border states that were tottering between the Union and the Confederacy. In Maryland, the mayor of Baltimore and other secessionists were thrown into jail. In Missouri, federal troops challenged state militia and forced the governor, who favored secession, to flee. Meanwhile, West Virginia broke off from Virginia to form a new state loyal to the Union.

Once blood was shed, the frustrations of the past thirty years quickly came to the surface. In both the North and the South, people welcomed the outbreak of war as a great release and as an opportunity to demonstrate their own superiority. Most people thought their side would win quickly and easily. Unfortunately, they were wrong.

The Course of the Civil War

Union and Confederate Strengths and Weaknesses

Advantages of the North

When the Civil War began, the North had many advantages. It had a population of 22 million, compared to only 6.5 million free persons in the South. The North was more industrialized with more railroads, factories, mines, roads, and canals than the South. Its factories could produce more arms and ammunition. The North had more coal, iron, gold, and other natural resources than the South.

In 1862, when Southern leaders wanted to build a steam engine for one of their ships, they were surprised to learn there wasn't a single factory in the South that could do it. The Southern economy was completely dependent on its exports of a few cash crops. The North had merchant ships and control of the U.S. Navy, while the South had almost no navy at all.

Finally, the South was home to a large slave population, which created great uncertainty. Would the slaves help their owners or would they start their own uprisings to assist the North?

Advantages of the South

White Southerners still had some advantages. Most important of all, they were defending their own way of life. They believed they were more motivated than Northerners. They had a strong military tradition and many gifted military commanders, including **Robert E. Lee** and **"Stonewall" Jackson**. Both had studied at the U.S. Military Academy in West Point and had served in the Mexican-American War. Lee came from a famous Virginian family. The South also had wealth from its exports of cotton and other cash crops. Because of their trade relations with Britain and France, Southerners thought those countries would be friendly to them. Finally, thc population of the South was spread out over a vast area, making it difficult to conquer.

Military Strategies

General Winfield Scott, the general who had invaded Mexico in 1847, suggested the basic Northern strategy. This became known as the "**Anaconda Plan**." Scott intended to strangle the South as an Anaconda snake might do. He proposed to do this by setting up a naval blockade of Southern ports. Then he proposed to use Northern naval power to seize control of the Mississippi and divide the Confederacy in two. Scott optimistically hoped his plan could succeed with little bloodshed. Lincoln believed that the North should take advantage of its greater resources by attacking the South at several places at once.

For their part, Southerners had no desire to conquer the North. They simply hoped to defend themselves against Northern attacks. Once they showed Northerners that the war could not be won easily, Southern leaders expected public opinion in the North to turn against it. Southern leaders also hoped to receive support from those foreign countries that relied on Southern cotton.

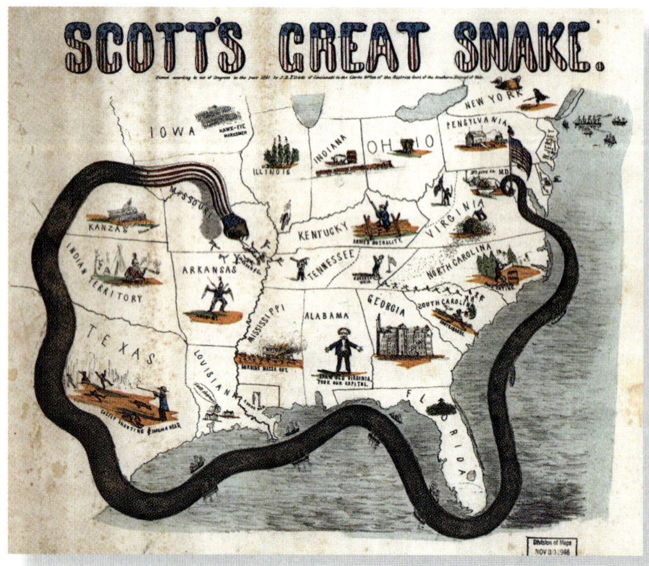

The "Anaconda Plan"

Once the war began, Lincoln acted quickly. He immediately ordered a naval blockade of the South. He also introduced military **conscription** (*obligatory service*). This was the requirement that all able-bodied men serve in the army. It is sometimes known as the "draft." In those days, a rich person could hire a substitute to take his place if he were drafted.

The Obligations of Citizenship

Today, men are not required to serve in the military, but they must register with the Selective Service when they reach 18 years of age. They should be ready to serve if the nation ever calls on them. This is one of the obligations of U.S. citizenship.

Lincoln also suspended the right to apply for a **writ of *habeas corpus***. This is a right guaranteed to us in peacetime by the U.S. Constitution. It gives us the right to ask a federal court to order the release of anyone who has been wrongly imprisoned.

Finally, Lincoln began issuing paper money to pay for wartime expenses.

The First Campaigns

The first campaign took place in the area separating Washington, D.C., and Richmond, Virginia, the capital of the Confederacy. The two cities were not far apart. Many people thought the war would be over quickly if one of these two national capitals were captured. A Northern army marched south towards Richmond. Its soldiers were inexperienced and untrained, but the public pressure to act quickly was great.

The Northern army faced Confederate forces at the **Battle of Bull Run** (July 1861). Spectators from Washington, D.C., came to picnic and watch the battle. They were not used to the horrors of war.

The Southerners stood firm. "Stonewall" Jackson's troops had the most casualties, but they kept the Confederate army from yielding to the North. Unknown to the Union generals, the Confederates reinforced their army with troops brought by train. The battle turned in favor of the Confederates. Union soldiers and the spectators fled for their lives.

The Monitor and the Merrimack

The Monitor and the Merrimack

In March 1862, the Civil War saw the world's first battle between two iron-covered steamships. The Confederates built their ship, the *Virginia*, using the remains of the *Merrimack*. The ship was covered with iron plates two-inches thick. Confederates hoped the ship would be able to destroy wooden ships and break the Union blockade. Northerners learned of this plan and built their own iron-covered ship, the *Monitor*. This ship had a circular top with a large cannon, which turned. The *Virginia* was finished in February 1862. It began sinking Union ships in early March. Then suddenly the *Monitor* appeared. The two ships fired on each other in a battle for several hours and then withdrew.

Neither side was the victor. A few months later, the Confederates sank the *Virginia* when they could not hold onto the port of Norfolk. The *Monitor* sank in an accident. Their battle was important because it showed what battleships would be like in the future.

McClellan's Advance on Richmond

The Civil War was mainly fought in two separate areas—the west and the east. In the west, Union forces took control of the area where the Ohio River flows into the Mississippi. In April 1862, the U.S. Navy then had a spectacular victory against the South. It captured New Orleans, the South's largest port. Federal troops farther north began pushing southward along the Mississippi River.

In the east, Lincoln appointed a new commander, **General George McClellan**, after the disaster at Bull Run. McClellan quickly created and trained a Union army of 100,000 men. He made sure his men were well supplied and well fed. He carefully fortified Washington, D.C. As commander, McClellan was well loved by his troops. In April 1862, McClellan took the offensive. He sailed a large army south into Chesapeake Bay and the York River in order to march northward to the capital of the Confederacy at Richmond. A second army remained north to protect Washington, D.C.

McClellan excelled at training and supplying his men, but was too afraid to risk his army in actual combat. He was convinced that the Confederates had twice as many soldiers as he did, when actually it was the opposite. So he hesitated, giving the Confederates time to organize their resistance. Heavy rains reduced the dirt roads to mud, making his advance difficult.

McClellan was very organized. He had graduated near the top of his class at West Point, trained as an engineer, fought in the Mexican-American War, and had been sent by the army to Europe to observe fighting in the Crimean War. McClellan had then left the army to become a railroad executive.

McClellan finally began his march northward. His troops eventually got as far as six miles from Richmond. His men could even hear the town's church bells. Then General Lee and Stonewall Jackson attacked. Fighting lasted seven days. Confederate losses were greater than Union ones, but the Union advance was stopped. McClellan retreated.

Lee next ordered Stonewall Jackson to attack the Union army to the north. It was under the command of General John Pope. Lee also marched north and joined Jackson. They attacked Pope's army in the Second Battle of Bull Run in August 1862. Union troops retreated to Washington, D.C. President Lincoln finally dissolved Pope's army. This moment was the high point of the Confederacy—the time when it seemed most likely that the South would win the war.

The Confederate Advance into Maryland and the Battle of Antietam

In September 1862, Lee advanced into Maryland with over 50,000 men. Southern leaders thought Maryland, as a slaveholding state, would welcome the arrival of Confederate troops. Lee planned to cut the railroad line supplying Washington, D.C. He hoped to turn public opinion in the North against the war. He also needed supplies from farms in Maryland for his half-starved troops. Finally, a victory in the North might encourage the British to support the Confederacy.

Problems arose soon after the invasion. Some Confederate troops refused to join the invasion since they were only willing to defend the Confederacy. Others left because they were without shoes and Maryland had hard roads. Most people in Maryland opposed the Southerners rather than being friendly.

Lincoln put McClellan in command of the army around Washington. A copy of Lee's battle plans, wrapped around three cigars, was captured by Union forces. This told McClellan exactly what Lee was going to do. McClellan learned Lee had divided his forces. Still, McClellan did not act on this information for 18 hours.

Forces under Lee and McClellan fought each other in the cornfields of **Antietam** on September 17, 1862. This battle was the bloodiest single day of the war. Union casualties (*killed, injured,*

Artillery at the Battle of Antietam

and missing) were 12,400, of whom 2,100 were killed. Confederate casualties were 10,320, of whom 1,550 were killed. There were as many American deaths on the battlefield that day as in the entire American Revolution. Lee eventually withdrew. McClellan failed to follow up his victory by chasing Lee's army.

The Emancipation Proclamation

At first, Lincoln had not wanted to say that slavery had been a cause of the war. This might have cost the North the support of the **border states**—Delaware, Maryland, Kentucky, Missouri, and West Virginia. These states still permitted slavery but had stood by the Union.

Frederick Douglass and other abolitionists, however, wanted to use the war to end slavery. They felt there could be no better time. Many slaves were leaving their plantations. Equally important, Lincoln feared that Britain and France might help the Confederacy.

For all these reasons, Lincoln decided to issue the **Emancipation Proclamation** on September 22, 1862, just days after the Battle of Antietam. To "emancipate" means to free or liberate. The Emancipation Proclamation did not free all slaves and its effects were not immediate. It freed all slaves in states still in rebellion on January 1, 1863. The Proclamation did not free any slaves in the border states loyal to the Union. This meant that Lincoln was not actually freeing any slaves at all in areas where the federal government was in control. Some questioned whether the President even had the power under the Constitution

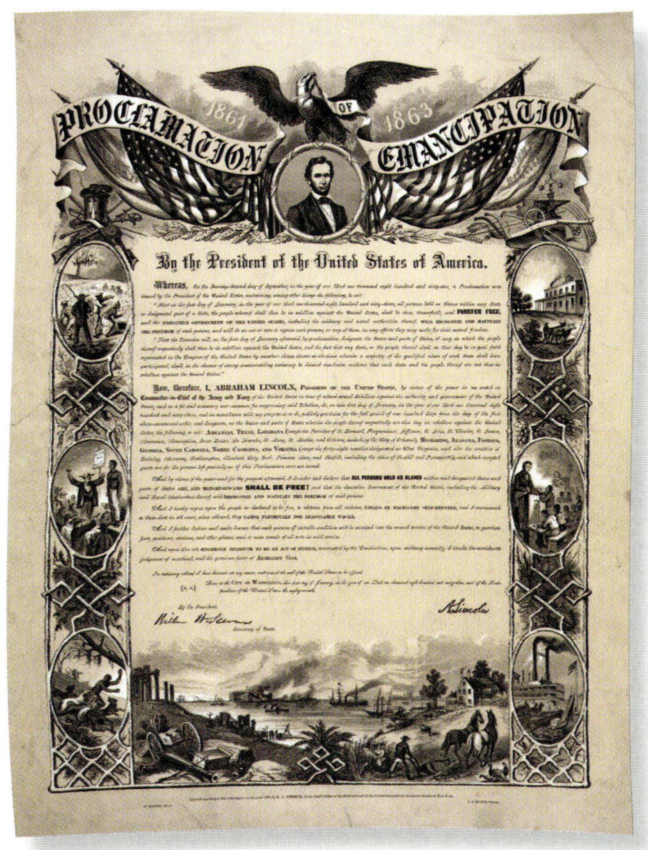
PROCLAMATION 1861 OF 1863 EMANCIPATION

By the President of the United States of America.

The Emancipation Proclamation

to free slaves. Later the issue was resolved by the Thirteenth Amendment, which ended slavery. You will learn about that in the next chapter.

The Emancipation Proclamation turned the war into a contest over slavery. It encouraged slaves in the South to leave their plantations to join the Union army. It also kept Britain and France from helping the Confederacy.

The Union began recruiting African-American troops for combat. These included the brave fighters of the **54th Massachusetts Regiment**. Almost half its men were wounded or killed in their attack on Fort Wagner in South Carolina. The regiment also covered the Union retreat at the Battle of Olustee in Florida.

Gettysburg and Vicksburg: The Turning Point of the War

Lincoln dismissed McClellan and appointed several other generals. None of them, however, could defeat Robert E. Lee. In the spring of 1863, Lee again tried to bring the war to the North. He advanced into Pennsylvania. If he could wage war in the North, Lee thought Northern public opinion would force Lincoln to seek peace.

> "They are in position and I am going to whip them or they are going to whip me."
>
> —General Lee at Gettysburg, July 2, 1863

Instead, Lee's forces were defeated at the **Battle of Gettysburg** in July 1863. The Union commander carefully chose positions that his men could defend. Then he waited for Lee to launch his attacks. On the third day of the battle, both sides were on ridges (*hills*) on the opposite sides of a level field. Lee thought his cannons had weakened the Union lines. He ordered General

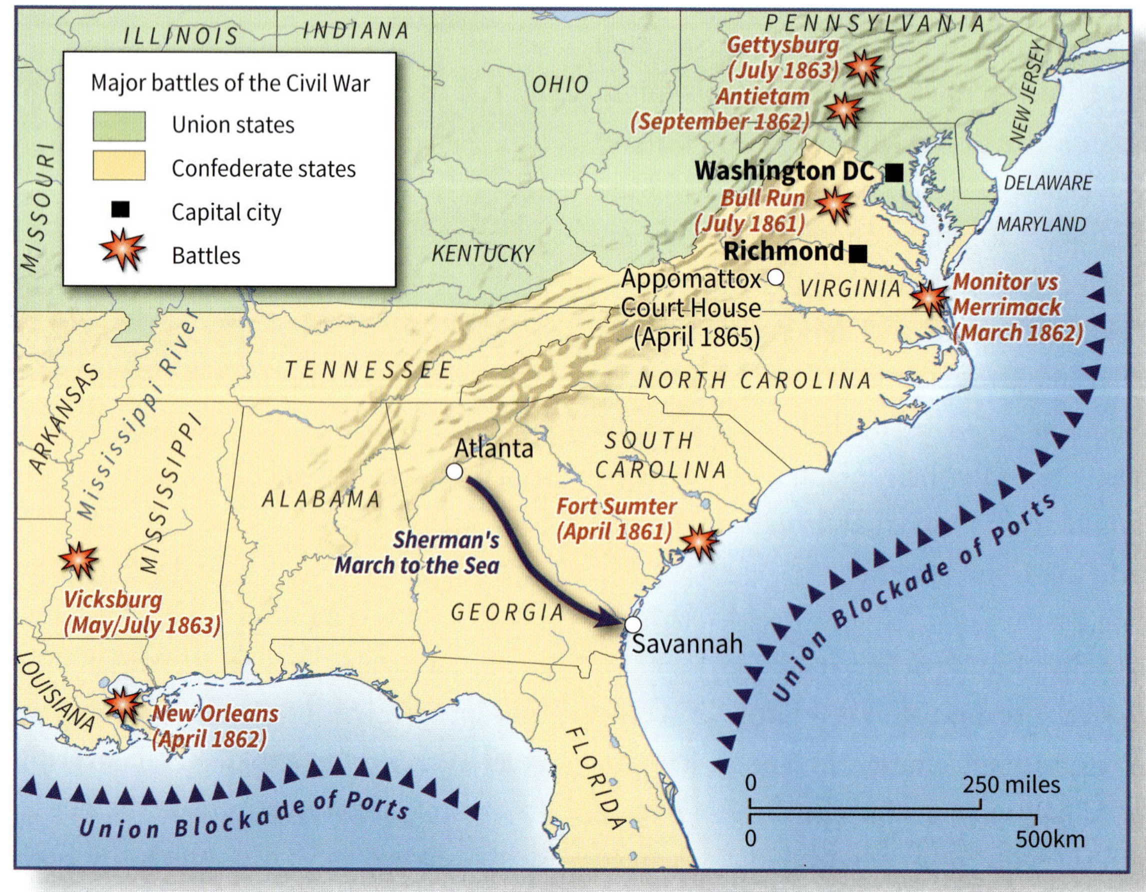

Pickett to make a desperate charge across the field. Pickett's charge ended in the slaughter of his men. More than 50,000 troops on both sides were injured or killed in the three days of battle. Lee lost one third of his army. He retreated and never advanced into the North again. It was the turning point of the war.

The Historian's Apprentice

Lincoln honored Union losses in his famous **Gettysburg Address**. The following is part of the speech that Lincoln gave at Gettysburg:

> Four score and seven years ago our fathers brought forth on this continent a new nation, conceived in liberty, and dedicated to the proposition that all men are created equal. Now we are engaged in a great civil war, testing whether that nation, or any nation, so conceived and so dedicated, can long endure.
>
> We are met on a great battlefield of that war. We have come to dedicate a portion of that field, as a final resting place for those who here gave their lives that that nation might live. . . .
>
> The brave men, living and dead, who struggled here, have consecrated [*blessed*] it, far above our poor power to add or detract. . . . It is rather for us to be here dedicated to the great task remaining before us—that from these honored dead we take increased devotion to that cause for which they gave the last full measure of devotion—that we here highly resolve that these dead shall not have died in vain—that this nation, under God, shall have a new birth of freedom—and that government of the people, by the people, for the people, shall not perish [*disappear; be destroyed*] from the earth.
>
> —Abraham Lincoln, *The Gettysburg Address* (November 19, 1863)

- What was the "new birth of freedom" to which Lincoln referred?
- Why do you think this speech has become so famous?

The day after the Battle of Gettysburg was over, **General Ulysses S. Grant** took **Vicksburg**, farther to the west. Grant only captured this fortress after a bitter two-month bombardment. Residents had been living in caves and dirt bunkers with almost nothing to eat.

> "We have spent the last two nights in a cave, but tonight I think we will stay at home. It is not safe, I know. . . . In one of the hospitals where some of the wounded had just undergone operations, a shell exploded and six men had to have limbs amputated [*cut off*]."
>
> —Emma Balfour, resident of Vicksburg (1863)

Grant's victory gave the North control over the entire Mississippi River Valley. It divided the Confederacy in two.

Ulysses S. Grant introduced the idea of "hard war." He ordered General Sheridan to follow and fight a Confederate army "to the death." He ordered General Sherman to "get into the interior of the enemy's country as far as you can [and make] all the damage you can against their war resources."

General Grant and the Final Year of the War

In March 1864, Lincoln appointed General Grant as his supreme commander. Grant aimed at destroying the Confederate army. He also wanted to destroy its supplies.

Grant began a new campaign to take Richmond in May 1864. He marched with 120,000 troops into the woodlands of northeastern Virginia. Lee had just over 60,000 troops but was able to delay Grant's advance. In the Battle of the Wilderness, soldiers could barely see one another because of the smoke from burning trees. After more than 40 days, Grant and Meade, (the victor at Gettysburg) attacked Lee at Cold Harbor. They had nearly twice as many men as Lee but still lost the battle because Lee had so carefully prepared his defense.

Unlike earlier Union generals, Grant didn't give up. Suddenly the Union army disappeared from Lee's sight. In fact, Grant took his men across the James River and marched past the Confederate army towards Petersburg, a city controlling key railroad lines and roads to Richmond. Petersburg was well fortified. Grant surrounded the city and cut off all food and supplies, just as he had at Vicksburg. The Union army enjoyed plenty of food and supplies while the citizens of Petersburg starved.

Meanwhile, Grant ordered **General William Tecumseh Sherman** to march from western Georgia to Atlanta and then all the way to the coast. During **Sherman's "March to the Sea,"** Union forces looted and burned farms. They tore up railroad lines, and even burned down the city of Atlanta. Sherman's goal was to destroy all the places that might give support or supplies to the Confederate army. His march through Georgia had devastating effects on civilians. They lost their homes, belongings, and sometimes their loved ones. His march further divided the territory of the Confederacy. From Savannah on the coast, Sherman then turned north to spread destruction across South Carolina.

Just as Sherman was seizing crops, tearing up farms and railroad lines, and burning cities in Georgia, General Philip Sheridan was doing the same in Virginia's Shenandoah Valley, an important source of food for the Confederate army.

General Sherman

Lincoln's Re-election

In the early years of the war, it seemed that Lincoln might not be re-elected for a second term. His opponent in the Presidential election of 1864 was the former commander of Union forces: General George B. McClellan. But with Sherman's capture of Atlanta, Lincoln was able to win re-election and continue the war.

The Blue and the Gray: Soldiers in the Civil War

When the war began in 1861, most soldiers were volunteers with little knowledge of the military. They often enlisted with their friends and formed companies together. They had to learn to march together, to load and fire their rifles, to cook their food, and to set up tents. A few officers had experience in the Mexican-American War but most had no experience at all. Later in the war, soldiers were conscripted (*required to serve*).

Early volunteers wore their own clothes. After confusion at the Battle of Bull Run, Union soldiers were supplied with standard blue uniforms. Confederate soldiers wore uniforms of gray.

For most of the war, Union soldiers enjoyed a steady supply of food. Each carried a canteen, cup, knife, fork, frying pan, coffee can and lantern in his knapsack. Although Southern farms grew food, they often had no way of bringing it to their soldiers. Confederate soldiers therefore sometimes went hungry. In general, soldiers ate salted meat, coffee, and "hardtack" (*a hard biscuit*). The hardtack had to be dipped in coffee or broken up and mixed with water. They also received flour, beans, potatoes and dried vegetables. Soldiers might seize fresh vegetables and livestock from farms they passed on their march.

The armies of the Civil War were young. The average age of a soldier was only 24 years old. Many soldiers were only in their teens. Drummer boys could be even younger. Soldiers in the Union army were most often farmers, factory workers or immigrants. Soldiers in the Confederacy were often farmers or students.

At first the war seemed like a great adventure. But after the Battle of Bull Run, attitudes changed. Hardships increased such as long marches, hunger, disease, and the terror of battle.

Weapons were more deadly than in earlier wars. **Rifling** is a way of placing grooves along the inside barrel of a gun. It causes the bullet to spin as it leaves the rifle. This makes a rifle much more accurate than a musket. During the Civil War, soldiers stood in lines or ran into each other as in earlier wars, but their weapons were much more accurate. The result was that many more people were injured or killed.

Imagine you are a soldier in the Civil War. Your officers order you to attack. A drummer boy sounds the beat. You and your fellow men begin walking towards the enemy. As you get closer, you start to run. Then you stop from time to time to load your rifle, aim and fire. Meanwhile, the soldiers you are attacking have formed two lines. One line is made up of soldiers who are kneeling and loading their weapons. The other stands, aims and fires. In the background there are cannons firing, the smell of gunpowder and lots of smoke. The bodies of injured and dead soldiers begin to clutter the field.

Doctors and nurses played a critical role in the war. For the first time, the wounded were carried to tents that served as hospitals. Doctors took out bullets and **amputated** (*cut off*) limbs. They did not know to wash their hands or sterilize their instruments, so many died of infection. But a large number miraculously survived. And twice as many soldiers died from disease as from wounds in battle.

Lee surrenders to Grant at Appomattox

The assassination of President Lincoln

Surrender at Appomattox

By 1865, Confederate forces were shrinking. Confederates did not have enough food, supplies, or guns. They were feeling the effects of the blockade and of the harsh strategy of Generals Grant and Sherman.

After being surrounded for ten months, Petersburg finally surrendered on April 2, 1865. This meant that Lee could no longer defend the Confederate capital of Richmond. President Jefferson Davis and the government fled. The Confederates burned down parts of the city rather than let the Union army get their supplies. Abraham Lincoln went to visit the former Confederate capital on April 4, 1865, just after its capture. He was surrounded by thankful freed slaves.

Lee still hoped to escape southwards and join Confederate forces in North Carolina. But his escape route was cut off by another Union victory. On April 9, 1865, Lee finally surrendered to Grant at **Appomattox Court House**, ending the Civil War. The Confederate army lay down its arms. Some thought that the Confederate officers would be imprisoned for treason, but Grant saluted Lee and offered his army generous terms. Grant gave food to the hungry Confederate soldiers and demanded only that they give up their weapons, take an oath not to fight against the United States, and go home. Confederate soldiers could even take their horses back to their farms. Their officers were allowed to keep their side arms. Northerners and Southerners were countrymen again.

Less than one week later, President Lincoln was assassinated at Ford's Theatre in Washington, D.C., by the actor John Wilkes Booth.

Appomattox Court House was the name of the town that had the court house for Appomattox County. Lee didn't surrender to Grant in the court house but in the living room of the home of Wilmer McLean. McLean had moved to Appomattox in search of quiet after his house in Manassas had been used as Confederate headquarters in the First Battle of Bull Run.

The Civil War in Florida

In 1860, Florida had just over 140,000 people. Two-fifths of them were slaves. The state's economy centered on growing cotton and cutting down trees for lumber. Both activities used slave labor. On January 10, 1861, a constitutional convention was called by Florida's General Assembly. The convention adopted an Ordinance of Secession by a vote of 62 to 7. Florida thus seceded from the United States. Former Governor Richard Call denounced (*condemned*) secession. The following month, Florida joined the Confederate States of America.

Civil War battles in Florida

For much of the war, the North controlled Florida's coastline to enforce its blockade of the South. This prevented Florida from sending food and guns to Confederate forces. Union troops occupied Fort Pickens near Pensacola. They made the fort their headquarters in Florida for most of the war. Federal forces also invaded and seized Apalachicola, Cedar Keys, Fernandina, Jacksonville, St. Augustine, and Tampa. Floridians sometimes ran the Union blockades. They landed goods from Cuba and the Bahamas in the many bays and waterways of Florida.

Confederate General Robert E. Lee had hoped to hold on to the interior of Florida as a source of crops and cattle for the South. A number of battles were fought in the state. In 1864, 5,200 Confederate troops led by General Joseph Finnegan defeated 5,500 Union soldiers at the **Battle of Olustee**. Further Confederate victories followed at Gainesville, Cedar Keys, and the **Battle of Natural Bridge**. Confederate forces in Florida consisted mainly of younger boys and older men. Many of the slaves in Florida remained loyal to their owner. They stayed to help their owners' wives manage their properties and nurse the wounded. The war in Florida lasted until May 10, 1865, when Tallahassee was occupied by Union troops.

The Consequences of the War

The Civil War ended slavery, preserved the Union, and strengthened the power of the federal government. It showed that states did not have the right to leave the Union. It greatly increased the political and economic power of the North. Finally, it led to the loss of more than 600,000 lives and destroyed much of the South.

The Historian's Apprentice

1. Make a chart or poster summarizing the effects of the Civil War. Consider its political, economic, and social effects.
2. Research a military or civilian leader during the Civil War. Present your findings in an oral presentation to the class or in a written report.
3. In your opinion, were the consequences of the Civil War worth the bloodshed?

1. Imagine you are a "Yankee" (Union) or a "Rebel" (Confederate) soldier in the Civil War. Write a letter to a member of your family about what you have experienced. Include one of the battles or events discussed in this chapter—Bull Run, Antietam, the Emancipation Proclamation, Gettysburg, Vicksburg, Olustee, or the surrender at Appomattox Court House.

2. Suppose you have been invited to speak at Abraham Lincoln's funeral. Describe some of the challenges faced by this President and his accomplishments.

3. Imagine the United States never went to war with the South. What would the United States and Confederate States of America be like today?

Chapter Review Cards

Causes of the Civil War

The Civil War was the most destructive war in American history. It had several causes:

- **Sectionalism**: Many Americans felt greater loyalty to their section—the North, South, or West—than they did to the nation as a whole. Each section had different economic interests. For example, Northerners favored high tariffs on imported manufactured goods. Southerners opposed them.
- **States' Rights**: Many Southerners were strong supporters of states' rights. They believed the states had created the Union and had the right to leave the Union if they desired.
- **Slavery**: Abolitionists wanted to end slavery. **Harriet Beecher Stowe's** popular book, *Uncle Tom's Cabin* (1852), added to the outrage against slavery. Southern slaveholders argued that enslaved African Americans were actually better off than Northern factory workers.
- **The Balance of Power in the Senate**: In the early 1800s, the number of slave and free states in the Senate was equal. Since the North had a larger population, Southerners looked to the Senate to prevent the North from abolishing slavery or passing other laws unfavorable to the South.

The Question of the Extension of Slavery to New Territories

- New territories gained from the Louisiana Purchase and Mexican Cession posed an important problem. Would these territories become free or slave states?
- Most Northerners did not want to see slavery extended to new territories. Most Southerners feared being outnumbered by free states if slavery did not spread.

The Missouri Compromise (1820)

- Missouri was admitted as a slave state and Maine was admitted as a free state, keeping the balance of free and slave states in the Senate equal.
- Slavery was prohibited in the Louisiana Purchase north of 36°30′N outside of Missouri.

The Compromise of 1850

- California was admitted as a free state.
- The sale of slaves was banned in Washington, D.C., although slavery itself was permitted there.
- A tougher fugitive slave law was passed, requiring the return of runaway slaves.
- "Popular sovereignty" was to be applied to the slavery question in the rest of Mexican Cession—local voters would decide for themselves whether to permit slavery.

The Breakdown of Compromise

Kansas-Nebraska Act (1854)

- This act applied popular sovereignty to determine the slavery question in the remaining territories of the Louisiana Purchase. It thus reopened the slavery issue in these territories, overturning the Missouri Compromise.

Birth of Republican Party (1854)

- Many Northerners were outraged. The Republican Party formed to oppose any spread of slavery.

"Bleeding Kansas" (1855–1856)

- Anti-slavery and pro-slavery settlers violently contested control of the Kansas Territory.

Violence in the Senate

- Senator Charles Sumner was beaten by a cane in the U.S. Senate.

***Dred Scott v. Sandford* (1857)**

- The U.S. Supreme Court ruled that **Dred Scott**, an enslaved African American, was not a citizen and had no right to sue in court. The Court also ruled that Congress had no right to forbid slavery in the territories. This decision overturned the Missouri Compromise and all other Congressional compromises. It was highly unpopular in the North.

Lincoln-Douglas Debates (1858)

- **Abraham Lincoln** and **Stephen Douglas** debated the issue of the extension of slavery in debates across Illinois for election as U.S. Senator. Douglas proposed local "popular sovereignty" on the issue and Lincoln opposed any extension of slavery.

John Brown's Raid on Harpers Ferry (1859)

- **John Brown**, a white abolitionist, attacked a federal arsenal in Virginia, hoping to stir up slave revolts throughout the South. Slaves failed to respond and Brown was defeated and executed.

The Election of Lincoln and the Secession Crisis

Presidential Election of 1860

- The Democrats were divided, helping Republican candidate **Abraham Lincoln** to win the election with 39% of the popular vote and no electoral votes at all from Southern states.

Secession

- South Carolina immediately **seceded**. Six other Southern states quickly followed.
- They formed the **Confederate States of America**. **Jefferson Davis** was elected as its President.
- Four states of the Upper South, including Virginia, seceded after the war broke out.

The Border States

- The **border states** of Maryland, Delaware, Kentucky and Missouri stayed in the Union even though they had slaves. West Virginia broke off from Virginia to stay in the Union.

The Attack on Fort Sumter

- Lincoln sent supplies to **Fort Sumter**, a federal fort in Charleston Harbor. Confederate forces fired on the fort on April 12, 1861, starting the Civil War.
- Lincoln called on all states to send militia forces. This is when the Upper South finally seceded and the border states stayed loyal to the Union.

The Advantages of the North and South

Advantages of the North

- The North had a larger population, more industry and resources, and a powerful navy.
- The border states remained with the Union.
- Northerners had a gifted leader in Abraham Lincoln. He took active measures to defend the Union.

Advantages of the South

- The South had several talented generals, such as **Robert E. Lee** and **"Stonewall" Jackson**, and a strong military tradition.
- Southerners were fighting for their own way of life. They did not have to conquer the North--just defend themselves from Northern attacks.
- Southerners also hoped to get support from Britain and France, who purchased their cotton and other cash crops.
- Enslaved African Americans in the South created some uncertainty.

Military Strategies

- **The North**: Lincoln imposed a naval blockade on the South. General Winfield Scott suggested that the North strangle the South with the "**Anaconda Plan**," blockading its harbors and dividing the South in two along the Mississippi River.
- **The South**: Southerners hoped to defend themselves until Northern public opinion tired of the war.

The Course of the War: Early Battles

- In the early battles, each side tried to capture the other's capital city to win the war quickly. Northerners advanced but were defeated in the first major battle at **Bull Run**.
- General McClellan's plan to capture Richmond failed because he delayed too long in starting his attack.
- The bloodiest day of the war was during the **Battle of Antietam** (September 17, 1862), when the Union army stopped Lee's advance into Maryland.

The Emancipation Proclamation (1862)

- Lincoln issued the **Emancipation Proclamation** in September 1862, freeing all slaves in states still in rebellion on January 1, 1863. This did not apply to border states.
- The Emancipation Proclamation kept Britain and France from allying with the Confederacy, met the demands of abolitionists like Frederick Douglass, allowed the North to help slaves escaping from the South, and gave a new moral dimension to the war.
- There was a question whether the President really had the right to free the slaves. Later the **Thirteenth Amendment** ended slavery.

The Course of the War: Later Battles

The Monitor and the Merrimack

- The Confederates built a ship covered in iron to attack wooden ships and break the Union blockade. The Union army built its own iron-clad ship, the *Monitor*. The two iron-clad ships faced each other in March 1862. The battle was a draw. Later each ship was damaged and sank. The battle pointed to the future of naval warfare.

The Turning Point of the War: Gettysburg and Vicksburg

- General Lee tried to bring the war to the North again by crossing over into Pennsylvania in 1863. His troops were defeated at the **Battle of Gettysburg** (July 1863).
- Lincoln later gave the **Gettysburg Address** on the battlefield.
- The same week as the battle, **General Ulysses S. Grant** captured **Vicksburg** on the Mississippi River. This gave the North control of the Mississippi River Valley and divided the Confederacy.

The Final Year

- Lincoln made Grant the Union commander in March 1864. Grant marched a large army towards Richmond. Lincoln was re-elected as President in November 1864.
- **General William Tecumseh Sherman** waged a war against the resources of the Confederate army. Sherman marched through Georgia, dividing the Confederacy further. During **Sherman's "March to the Sea,"** his forces burned down Atlanta and other towns and farms and tore up railroad tracks.

The Surrender at Appomattox

- When General Lee could no longer defend the Confederate capital at Richmond, he surrendered to Grant at **Appomattox Court House** in April 1865, ending the war.
- Later the same week, President Abraham Lincoln was assassinated.

Florida in the Civil War

- Florida seceded and joined the Confederacy.
- Florida was valued for its cattle and food supplies.
- The **Battle of Olustee** was fought in the north of Florida in 1864. The African-American **54th Massachusetts Regiment** covered the Union retreat.

The Consequences of the Civil War

- The Union was preserved (*kept*).
- Slavery was abolished.
- There was a tremendous loss of life and destruction of property. More than 600,000 people were killed. More Americans died in this war than in any other.
- The power of the federal government was increased.
- The political and economic power of the North was increased.

The Civil War

Causes

- Sectionalism
- Slavery
- Westward expansion
- States' rights
- Balance of power in the Senate

Breakdown of Compromise

- Missouri Compromise
- Compromise of 1850
- *Uncle Tom's Cabin*
- Kansas–Nebraska Act
- "Bleeding Kansas"
- *Dred Scott* decision
- Lincoln-Douglas Debates
- John Brown's raid

Secession and War

- Election of President Lincoln (1860)
- Secession of Southern states
- Birth of Confederacy
- Shots fired at Fort Sumter

Course of the Civil War

- Greater population and resources of North
- "Anaconda Plan"
- North blockades and divides South
- Bull Run
- Monitor vs. Merrimack
- Antietam
- Emancipation Proclamation
- Gettysburg and Vicksburg
- Sherman's March to the Sea
- Surrender at Appomattox

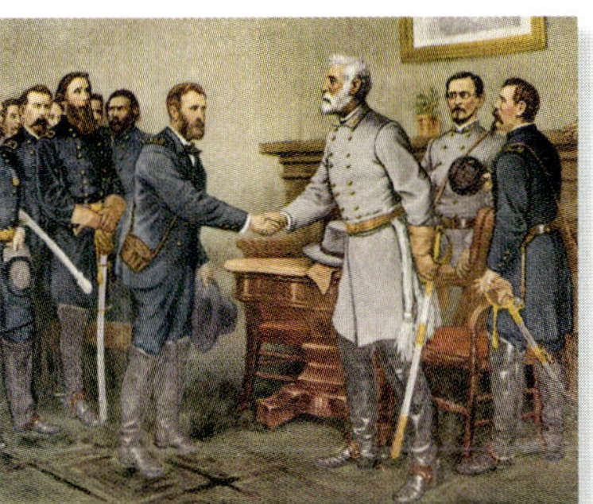

Consequences

- Union preserved
- Slavery abolished
- Great loss of life and property
- Federal government strengthened

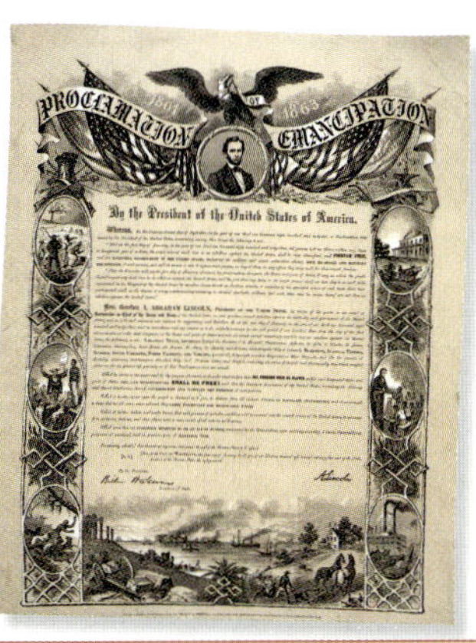

What do you know?

SS.6.A.5.2

1. The poster below was printed after the passage of the Fugitive Slave Act of 1850.

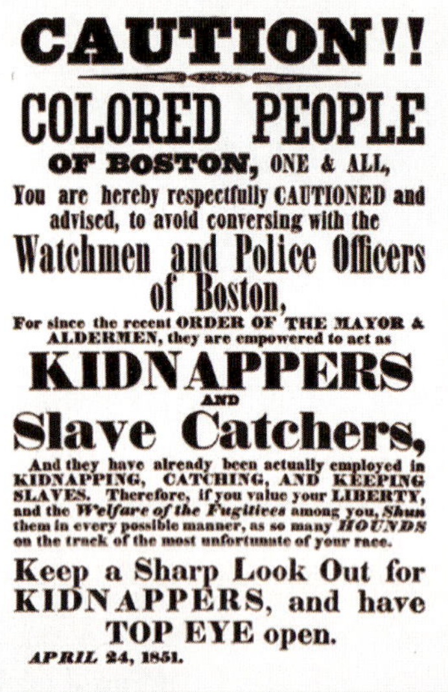

Based on the poster, which conclusion about the Fugitive Slave Act can be drawn?

A. It required all Southerners to catch their runaway slaves.

B. It asked police officers in the North to help catch runaway slaves.

C. It never became a concern for free African Americans in the North.

D. Its main purpose was to send free African Americans into slavery in the South.

SS.6.A.5.1

2. Which states' rights issue led directly to the Civil War?

A. whether states could modify federal tariff rates

B. whether states could secede from the United States

C. whether individual states could sign treaties with foreign nations

D. whether state governments could redraw Congressional districts

SS.6.A.5.2

3. What was a consequence of the Kansas-Nebraska Act (1854)?

A. It created the same number of slave and free states.

B. It closed the New Mexico and Utah Territories to future slavery.

C. It made slavery possible in territories previously closed to slavery.

D. It rejected the use of popular sovereignty to resolve the slavery issue.

SS.6.A.5.1

4. The diagram below describes events that contributed to the outbreak of the Civil War.

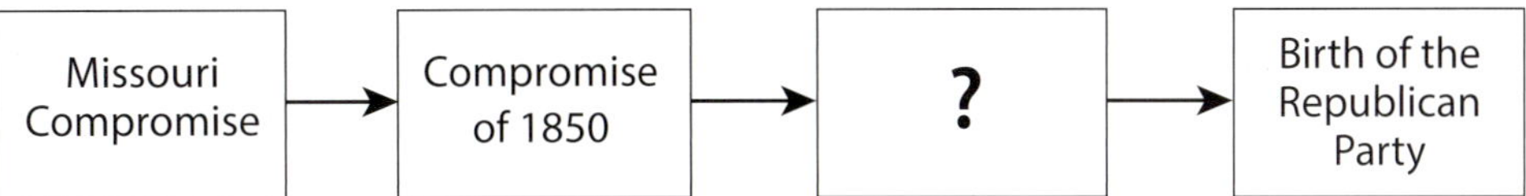

Which event completes the diagram?

A. *Dred Scott v. Sandford*

B. Kansas-Nebraska Act

C. Lincoln-Douglas debates

D. John Brown's raid on Harpers Ferry

SS.6.A.5.2

5. The illustration below is from Harriet Beecher Stowe's *Uncle Tom's Cabin* (1852). The caption says: "Eliza comes to tell Uncle Tom that he is sold and that she is running away to save her child."

What was the purpose of this illustration in the book?

A. to show the importance of slavery to the Southern economy

B. to make readers sympathize with slaves struggling to gain freedom

C. to help readers realize that slaves need the direction of their masters

D. to show that Southern slaves were better off than Northern factory workers

SS.6.A.5.6

6. Which Civil War battle was a turning point because Confederate losses were so high that General Robert E. Lee never advanced into the North again?

A. Bull Run

B. Antietam

C. Vicksburg

D. Gettysburg

SS.6.A.5.1

7. The excerpts below are from the Inaugural Addresses of Presidents Abraham Lincoln and Jefferson Davis in 1861.

Inaugural Address of Abraham Lincoln	Inaugural Address of Jefferson Davis
I hold that . . . the Union of these States is perpetual [*lasting forever*] . . . Continue to execute all the express provisions of our National Constitution, and the Union will endure [*last*] forever . . . . no State upon its own . . . can lawfully get out of the Union.	Our present condition . . . illustrates the American idea that governments rest upon the consent of the governed, and that it is the right of the people to alter or abolish governments . . . [A] peaceful appeal to the ballot-box declared that so far as [Southerners] were concerned, the government created by [the Constitution] should cease to exist [*come to an end*].

On which issue do President Lincoln and President Jefferson Davis disagree in these excerpts?

A. states' rights

B. the continuation of slavery

C. enforcement of the Fugitive Slave Act

D. the balance of power between slave and free states

SS.6.A.5.4

8. Which border states permitted slavery but stayed loyal to the Union during the Civil War?

A. Iowa, Illinois, Indiana, Ohio

B. Maryland, Delaware, Kentucky, Missouri

C. South Carolina, Mississippi, Florida, Alabama

D. Virginia, North Carolina, Tennessee, Arkansas

SS.6.A.5.6

9. The information below lists the characteristics of an important individual in the Civil War.

- Graduated from West Point
- Fought in the Mexican War
- Served as a leader of Confederate troops
- Defeated at Gettysburg
- Surrendered at Appomattox Court House

Which leader is described by these characteristics?

A. Robert E. Lee

B. Ulysses S. Grant

C. Stonewall Jackson

D. William Tecumseh Sherman

SS.6.A.5.5

10. The table below compares the strengths and weaknesses of the Union and Confederacy.

	Union	Confederacy
Strengths	◆ Larger population ◆ More factories, mines and railroads ◆ Powerful navy ◆ More natural resources	◆ Highly motivated to defend their way of life ◆ Talented military commanders ◆ Active trade with Britain and France
Weaknesses	◆ Division of public opinion about the war	◆ Smaller population ◆ Weak navy ◆ **?**

Which sentence completes the table?

A. Most white Southerners thought slavery was wrong.

B. Jefferson Davis was a very unpopular President.

C. Southern soldiers did not have the support of the countryside.

D. Presence of a large number of enslaved people created uncertainty.

SS.6.A.5.1

11. How did the Civil War affect the economy of the North?

A. It caused a severe depression.

B. It led to rising unemployment rates.

C. It promoted increased industrialization.

D. It reduced the demand for agricultural goods.

SS.6.A.5.3

12. The diagram below gives the reasons for an event during Abraham Lincoln's Presidency.

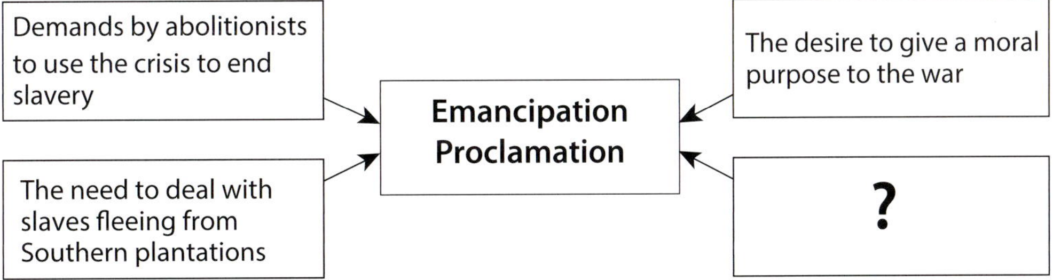

Which phrase completes the diagram?

A. The need to end slavery in the border states

B. The need to prevent Britain from helping the South

C. The need to strengthen the powers of the President

D. The need to lift the naval blockade for humanitarian reasons

SS.6.A.5.6

13. The photograph below shows General Sherman's troops destroying railroad tracks in Georgia.

What was the purpose of this action?

A. to punish Southerners for owning slaves

B. to prepare the ground for an improved railroad line

C. to make it difficult for Confederates to supply their troops

D. to keep the soldiers occupied while waiting for the next battle

SS.6.A.5.5

14. The table below provides data on casualties of the Civil War.

Casualties of the Civil War

	Union Troops	Confederate Troops
Total Troops	1,566,678	1,082, 119
Wounded	275,175	194,000*
Died of Wounds	110,070	94,000
Died of Disease	249,458	164,000

Source: Garraty and McCaughey, *The American Nation*, Harper and Row, 1987
*Shelby Foote, *The Civil War, A Narrative, Vintage Books*, 1986

Which conclusion is supported by the data in the table?

A. More soldiers died from disease than from wounds.

B. The Civil War had more casualties than any other war.

C. The Union army had better doctors than the Confederacy.

D. The Confederacy lost the war because its army had more fatalities.

CHAPTER 15 The Reconstruction Era

SS.6.A.5.8 Explain and evaluate the policies, practices, and consequences of Reconstruction (presidential and congressional reconstruction, Johnson's impeachment, Civil Rights Act of 1866, the 13th, 14th, and 15th Amendments, opposition of Southern whites to Reconstruction, accomplishments and failures of Radical Reconstruction, presidential election of 1876, end of Reconstruction, rise of Jim Crow laws, rise of Ku Klux Klan).

SS.6.C.1.1 Identify the constitutional provisions for establishing citizenship.

SS.6.C.1.6 Evaluate how amendments to the Constitution have expanded voting rights from our nation's early history to present day.

SS.6.C.2.1 Evaluate and compare the essential ideals and principles of American constitutional government expressed in primary sources from the colonial period to Reconstruction.

SS.6.E.2.3 Assess the role of Africans and other minority groups in the economic development of the United States.

(continues next page)

Names and Terms You Should Know

Thirteenth Amendment
"Black Codes"
Civil Rights Act of 1866
Fourteenth Amendment
Fifteenth Amendment
Naturalized Citizens
Right to Vote
Presidential Reconstruction
Impeachment
Radical Reconstruction
Ku Klux Klan
Literacy tests
"Grandfather clauses"
Poll taxes
"Jim Crow" laws
Segregation
Plessy v. Ferguson
Nineteenth Amendment
Twenty-fourth Amendment
Twenty-sixth Amendment

Alignment to Grade 7 Civics Standards

SS.7.C.2.1 Define the term "citizen," and identify legal means of becoming a U.S. citizen.

SS.7.C.3.5 Explain the constitutional amendment process.

SS.7.C.3.7 Analyze the impact of the 13th, 14th, 15th, 19th, 24th, and 26th amendments on participation of minority groups in the American political process.

SS.7.C.3.12 Analyze the significance and outcomes of landmark Supreme Court cases including, but not limited to . . . *Plessy v. Ferguson* . . .

Florida "Keys" to Learning

1. Americans faced many challenges during Reconstruction. Southern states had to be readmitted into the Union. Freed slaves had to be educated. The South had to rebuild its war-torn economy.

2. President Lincoln proposed to treat the South leniently (*not harshly*). But he was assassinated in April 1865. The next President, Andrew Johnson, came from a Southern state. He began pardoning most former Confederates.

3. One of the most important issues was the future of the "freedmen"—the former slaves. How would four million people, suddenly freed from slavery, find work and enter into public life? The federal government set up the Freedmen's Bureau, with offices throughout the South, to help the freedmen adjust and to set up schools to educate them.

4. Southern state legislatures had to accept the end of slavery, but passed "Black Codes," based on older slave codes. These limited the civil rights and freedom of movement of the freedmen.

5. Republicans in Congress were outraged by the election of former Confederates to Congress and by the passage of the Black Codes in the South. Republicans passed the Civil Rights Bill, granting the freedmen civil rights. This federal law later became the basis for the Fourteenth Amendment.

6. Congress also passed its own program for Reconstruction, dividing the South into five districts—each occupied by the Union army. Former Confederate leaders lost their political rights, while the freedmen were given the right to vote.

7. The Republicans in Congress impeached President Johnson. He was "impeached" (accused) in the House of Representatives, but the Senate failed to remove him from office.

8. During Reconstruction, three amendments were added to the Constitution. The Thirteenth Amendment abolished slavery. The Fourteenth Amendment guaranteed all citizens the "equal protection of the laws" and "due process." The Fifteenth Amendment prohibited any denial of voting rights on the basis of race.

9. During Reconstruction, freedmen, carpetbaggers, and scalawags held power in Southern governments. For the first time, African Americans were elected to government office.

10. Reconstruction governments built roads and schools and took steps towards racial equality. However, after Northern troops were withdrawn, Southern states started passing segregation laws in the late 1870s.

11. Southerners developed a new economy during Reconstruction. Former slave-owners often did not have money to pay laborers. The freedmen did not have land. Many former slaves became sharecroppers, giving a share of their crops to the landowner in exchange for use of the land. Other freedmen became tenants, and soon owed debts to their landlords (often their former masters).

12. After the end of Reconstruction, Southern state governments passed "Jim Crow" laws. These required racial segregation (the separation of "white" and "colored") in public places. These laws were upheld by the U. S. Supreme Court in *Plessy v. Ferguson* (1896). The Ku Klux Klan also terrorized African Americans and prevented them from exercising their rights. Southern state governments introduced literacy tests and poll taxes to keep African Americans from voting.

13. Later constitutional amendments expanded the right to vote to other groups. The 19th Amendment gave it to women, the 24th Amendment ended poll taxes, and the 26th gave it to all those who were 18 years of age or older.

When the Civil War ended, much of the South had been destroyed. White Southerners had fought for years for a cause that lost. Slavery was abolished. There was no way for Southerners to return to the way things had been before the war.

The Challenges of Reconstruction

The next twelve years were known as the **Reconstruction Era.** To "reconstruct" means to rebuild. During Reconstruction, Americans had to face several political, economic, and social challenges.

Political Challenges

1. How should the Southern states be readmitted into the Union?
2. Does the President or Congress have the power to readmit them?
3. Should former Confederate leaders be permitted to **participate** in public life, or should they be excluded (*kept out*)?
4. Should the **freedmen** (*formerly enslaved people*) be permitted to participate in public life? If so, how should they be prepared for **civic participation**?

Social Challenge

5. How could the freedmen be helped?

Economic Challenges

6. How could the economy of the South be rebuilt?
7. How should the economy of the South be reorganized without slavery?

Many historians believe the Reconstruction Era was a time of great promise. Unfortunately, America's leaders failed to bring the former slaves into American society on a fair and equal basis.

Early Plans for Reconstruction

Even before the war had ended, people started thinking about Reconstruction. A special "**Freedmen's Bureau**" was created by Congress in March 1865. The goal of this federal agency was to help the former slaves adjust to freedom. An **agency** is a government office or department that deals with specific problems or provides specific services.

An office of the Freedmen's Bureau

In his second Inaugural Address, President Lincoln announced his plans for Reconstruction. He did not want to treat the South harshly. Instead, he proposed to act with kindness—"with malice (*bitterness, bad feelings*) toward none, with charity for all." Once 10 percent of the voters of a Southern state pledged allegiance to the Union and agreed to the Emancipation

Proclamation, Lincoln planned to readmit that state back into the Union.

The Thirteenth Amendment

In April 1864, the Senate proposed the **Thirteenth Amendment**, which prohibited slavery. Lincoln's Emancipation Proclamation had ended slavery, but not in all states. It also was unclear whether the President actually had the authority to end slavery. The Thirteenth Amendment made the abolition of slavery clear and absolute. The proposed amendment passed the House in January 1865. It was ratified (*approved*) by the states before the end of the year.

The two-step process to amend the Constitution is long and difficult. It has only been amended 27 times.

The Thirteenth Amendment

Neither slavery nor involuntary servitude, except as a punishment for crime whereof the party shall have been duly convicted, shall exist within the United States, or any place subject to their jurisdiction.

The Historian's Apprentice

1. Why was the Thirteenth Amendment necessary when Lincoln had issued the Emancipation Proclamation?
2. Who deserves credit for ending slavery: Lincoln, Congress, or the American people? Why?
3. What is meant by "involuntary servitude"?

Presidential Reconstruction

President Lincoln was assassinated in April 1865. His Vice President, Andrew Johnson, now became President. Johnson was a former slaveholder from Tennessee, a Southern state that had joined the Confederacy. Johnson came from a poor family. He had always resented the wealthiest slaveholders.

In the months before the new Congress assembled, Johnson had complete control over Reconstruction. Many thought Johnson might impose harsh conditions on Southern states. He refused, for example, to give a general pardon to all former Confederate leaders.

President Andrew Johnson

f the expressed powers of the President
right to grant pardons for federal crimes.
oes not affect impeachments.

Under the U.S. Constitution, the President has the power to **pardon** (*release from punishment*) people who have committed federal crimes.

However, Johnson soon began giving thousands of individual pardons. He let former Confederates regain their properties as well as their rights of citizenship.

Johnson hoped that relations between the North and the South would improve quickly. He recognized new Southern state governments run by former Confederate leaders. As a Southerner, Johnson came under the suspicion of many Northerners. They thought he was being too sympathetic to the South.

The Black Codes

With Johnson as President, white Southerners became more daring. In new elections, they elected their former Confederate leaders, including several generals and colonels, to represent them in Congress. Southern states also passed new "**Black Codes**." These codes were based on the slave codes of the past. Each Southern state wrote its own code, but they all had some things in common. They prevented "persons of color" from exercising the **rights and duties of citizenship**, including voting, serving on juries, holding office, and serving in the state militia. The freedmen were not able to exercise any of these rights and duties. The Black Codes also had rules for freedmen's marriages and labor contracts (*agreements*). "Such persons are *not* entitled to social and political equality with white persons," announced the South Carolina Black Code of 1865.

Finally, the Black Codes made it illegal for freedmen to travel freely or to leave their jobs. Each freedman had to show that he or she had work during the current year. This forced former slaves to remain on the same plantations. Black workers could even be whipped for showing disrespect to their employers—usually their former owners. African-American children were "apprenticed" to white employers, and black convicts were turned over to white employers for hard labor. The whole aim of the "Black Codes" was to keep Southern society as it had been before the war, despite the abolition of slavery.

U.S. citizens enjoy rights but they also have responsibilities and obligations. One responsibility is that citizens should be informed. An example of an obligation is that citizens must obey the law.

Bills vetoed by the President can still become law if Congress overrides the veto by a 2/3 vote in each house.

Radical Reconstruction

People in the North were furious when former rebel leaders were elected in Southern states. They were equally shocked at the Black Codes. The victory in the Civil War itself seemed to be in danger. Congress refused to accept former Confederate leaders as members. Moderate Republicans joined hands with the "**Radical Republicans**." The Radical Republicans believed that African Americans should be given full political and civil equality. Radical Republicans soon became the most powerful group in Congress.

The Radical Republicans passed the **Civil Rights Bill of 1866**. It made freedmen U.S. citizens. It also outlawed discrimination based on race. President Johnson vetoed this bill, but the Radical Republicans were able to override his veto. The Radical Republicans also passed their own bill for Reconstruction in the South. They divided the South into five districts. Each district was governed by the U.S. Army and placed under **martial law**.

The Fourteenth Amendment

Congress passed the Civil Rights Act of 1866 over President Johnson's veto. But what if the U.S. Supreme Court decided that the act was unconstitutional? To protect the law against this threat, Congress rewrote it as a new amendment. Congress then proposed this amendment—the **Fourteenth Amendment**—to the states for ratification.

Types of Law

Laws are the rules that we all must live by. Did you know that there are different types of law?

Criminal laws tell us which actions are crimes. People who are convicted for committing those crimes are punished by society.

Civil laws establish rules for how people should treat one another in business and in private life. For example, the civil law has rules for enforcing contracts. It also has rules for making those who cause careless accidents pay for the damage they have caused.

Martial law is military law. Under martial law, people are tried by military courts (known as courts-martial) and have to follow military rules. These rules are much stricter than other forms of law.

The Fourteenth Amendment prevented state governments from denying African Americans and other minorities the rights of citizenship. These rights included the right to a fair trial and to the "equal protection of the laws."

The Fourteenth Amendment overturned the earlier *Dred Scott* decision. The amendment begins by defining what a citizen is. It states that anyone who is born in the United States is an American citizen. Because Dred Scott was born in the United States, he would have been a citizen under this amendment.

The Fourteenth Amendment also provided for "**naturalized** citizens." These are immigrants in the United States who become citizens. The amendment did not set up the steps of the naturalization process. That was left for Congress to do.

To become a ***naturalized*** *citizen* today, a person must be eighteen years old, live in the United States for five years, pass a test on U.S. history and government, and take an oath of allegiance.

The Fourteenth Amendment

Section 1.

All persons born or naturalized in the United States, and subject to the jurisdiction thereof, are citizens of the United States and of the State wherein they reside. No State shall make or enforce any law which shall abridge the privileges or immunities of citizens of the United States; nor shall any State deprive any person of life, liberty, or property, without due process of law; nor deny to any person within its jurisdiction the equal protection of the laws.

Word Helper

jurisdiction = authority

reside = live

abridge = limit

privileges = benefits, rights

immunities = freedoms

deprive = take away

due process of law = fair procedures

equal protection of the laws = equal treatment under the law

What Is Citizenship?

A **citizen** is a member of the community with rights and responsibilities. **Obligations** are things citizens must do, such as pay taxes, respect the law, and register with the Selective Service. Southern states had tried to take away these rights and responsibilities from their African-American citizens. The purpose of the Fourteenth Amendment was to protect those rights from actions by state governments.

The Historian's Apprentice

Who is a "citizen" under the Fourteenth Amendment? Read the language of the Fourteenth Amendment above. Under this amendment, do you think women were entitled to vote? Using the Internet, conduct research on **Susan B. Anthony**. She was a friend of Elizabeth Cady Stanton and a leader in the struggle for women's rights. Anthony tried to vote in 1870 on the basis of the Fourteenth Amendment. She claimed that she was a U.S. citizen entitled to the privileges of citizenship. However, the judge told her that she could not vote because she was a woman. Would you have agreed with the judge in this case? Give at least two reasons for your answer.

Finally, the Fourteenth Amendment defined the rights of citizens. These included the right to "due process" and to "the equal protection of the laws." This means the government cannot imprison us or take away our property without fair, just, and open procedures. It also means that we are all treated as equals under the law.

To be readmitted to the Union, each Southern state had to ratify the Fourteenth Amendment. The right of former Confederate leaders to hold elected office was also taken away. These changes had a great impact on the make-up of Southern state governments.

The Impeachment of President Andrew Johnson

President Johnson opposed the policies of the Radical Republicans. But in the 1866 Congressional elections, Northern voters supported them. In fact, the Radical Republicans increased the number of seats they had in Congress.

The Radical Republicans next passed a law that limited the President's power to dismiss his own Cabinet members. President Johnson refused to obey this law. He saw it as a clear violation of the separation of powers.

The separation of powers and system of checks and balances are two principles of the Constitution.

Impeachment of the President

The U.S. Constitution has a two-step process for removing the President from office. First, the President must be "impeached" in the House of Representatives. Second, the President is tried by the Senate. If two-thirds of the Senate approve, then the President is removed.

When the President refused to obey this law, Congressional leaders attempted to remove him from office through the process of **impeachment**.

President Johnson was successfully impeached by the House of Representatives in February 1868. When he was tried in the Senate, however, the Radical Republicans failed to get enough votes to remove him. Johnson was the first President ever to be impeached. Later that year, General Ulysses S. Grant was elected as the next President of the United States.

The impeachment trial of President Andrew Johnson

The chart below compares the early views on Reconstruction of the President, the Southern states, and the Radical Republicans in Congress.

	President Andrew Johnson	Southern States	Radical Republicans
Who should control the readmission of Southern states?	The President		The U.S. Congress
When should Southern states be readmitted?	Immediately, so long as they support the Union and the end of slavery	Immediately, with each state in charge of its own affairs	Only when most citizens in the state agree to support the Union and African-American citizens are given their full civil and political rights
Should former Confederate leaders be punished?	Almost all Southern rebels are individually pardoned by the President	No punishment for former Confederate leaders	Confederate leaders should be punished and all who served in the Confederacy should lose their political rights
Should the freedmen be allowed to vote?	Johnson recommends that state governments give voting rights to educated freedmen and African-American veterans, but he refuses to force them to do so	No	Yes

The Historian's Apprentice

1. Make an illustrated timeline showing the development of Presidential and Congressional policies for Reconstruction.
2. Pretend your class is the U.S. Senate in May 1868. It must decide whether to remove President Andrew Johnson from office. One team should present the grounds for his removal. A second team should defend his actions. Then put his removal from office to a vote. Members of the "Senate" should write a paragraph explaining how they voted. Did President Johnson narrowly survive impeachment in your classroom, as he did in 1868?
3. Write a paragraph on whether you think President Johnson's impeachment was justified. Examine the grounds for impeachment in the U.S. Constitution. For what reasons do you believe a President should be impeached?

The Fifteenth Amendment

Shortly after Grant's election, the Radical Republicans proposed the Fifteenth Amendment to protect the rights of African-American voters. The amendment was ratified in 1870. It guaranteed the right to vote to adult males of all races.

The Fifteenth Amendment

The right of citizens of the United States to vote shall not be denied or abridged by the United States or by any State on account of race, color, or previous condition of servitude.

Radical Reconstruction in the South

During Radical Reconstruction, state governments in the South came under the control of new groups. These included new arrivals from the North known as "**carpetbaggers**." This was a term of abuse used by Southern newspapers. It meant that the Northerners were able to fit all of their belongings into a few bags made of carpet, and that they came to exploit (*take advantage of*) the South. In reality, many Northerners came for idealistic reasons, especially to help the freedmen. The new Reconstruction governments in the South also included "**scalawags**"—white Southerners who had opposed the Confederacy. Finally, much of the Southern electorate in the Reconstruction Era was made up of new African-American voters.

For the first time, African Americans had the opportunity to participate as citizens in Southern state governments. Over six hundred freedmen served as state legislators during the Reconstruction Era (1865–1877). Sixteen African Americans sat in the U.S. Congress during Reconstruction. There was an African-American Governor of Louisiana and an African-American U.S. Senator from Mississippi. African Americans filled

A cartoon of a carpetbagger

many posts in state governments. In South Carolina, African Americans became a majority of the state legislature. They chose an African-American Speaker of the House.

The Reconstruction governments had many accomplishments. They created new systems of public schools in Southern states. They passed laws against racial discrimination. They encouraged investment in railroads.

Reconstruction governments also had some weaknesses. They had financial difficulties. Some were guilty of the corruption typical of the time, such as taking bribes. They never won the support of most white Southerners. White Southerners resented Northern interference. They refused to see their former slaves as social equals.

Reconstruction governments were unable to provide the freedmen with the tools they needed to fight this prejudice. Freedmen had no land or wealth. They gained nothing for all their years of work as slaves. They had been unable to get an education, and they could not catch up in just twelve years. Without providing black Southerners with economic security and without changing the attitudes of white Southerners, Reconstruction policies were bound to fail.

The Historian's Apprentice

1. Imagine that you are an African-American freedman, a Northern "carpetbagger," or a white Southern "scalawag." Write a paragraph for a local newspaper giving your views on Reconstruction in your state.
2. In a small group, select a Southern state during the Reconstruction Era. Find out more information from the Internet and your school library about Reconstruction government in that state. Then create a newspaper from the time period for that state in which you report on some of the events taking place. Or prepare a PowerPoint presentation about events in the state you have researched and share your presentation with the rest of the class.

The Economics of Reconstruction: The "New South"

One of the main challenges of Reconstruction was to repair the economy of the South. Without slave labor, the old plantation system could not be restored. Some plantation owners were forced to sell off part of their lands. Most plantation owners entered into **sharecropping** arrangements with their former slaves. The landowner provided a cabin, a mule, tools, and a plot of land to farm. In return, the "sharecropper" gave a share of his crop to the landowner. Most freedmen became sharecroppers. A few became tenant farmers. Tenant farmers rented land from the landowner but provided their own tools and provisions. Very few freedmen became landowners themselves.

Sharecroppers

African-American men could also serve in the U.S. Army. For example, the "Buffalo Soldiers" were African-American troops who fought in the Indian Wars on the Great Plains after the Civil War.

Some Southerners saw the end of slavery as beneficial to the South. They thought the South could now develop a stronger economy. It could start growing different types of crops and carry out more of its own manufacturing. They called this the "New South." The farming of new crops like fruits and vegetables was added to the growth of traditional cash crops like cotton, tobacco, rice, and sugar. Most important of all, more railroads, cotton mills, and steel furnaces were built in the South. More people moved into Southern cities. Although manufacturing in the South was still not as much as in the North, it became much greater than in pre-Civil War times. Most people, however, continued to work at growing cash crops for export such as cotton. Immense quantities of raw cotton and other raw materials were still needed by the factories of the Northeast and Britain.

Reconstruction Comes to an End

The Reconstruction Era came to a sudden end in a surprising way. It was the outcome of a disputed Presidential election.

In 1876, the election contest was between Republican candidate Rutherford B. Hayes and Democratic candidate Samuel Tilden. Tilden won the popular vote but did not have quite enough votes in the Electoral College.

The election results were disputed in Oregon and three Southern states: Florida, Louisiana, and South Carolina. If all twenty disputed votes went to Hayes, he would win the election. Tilden needed only one more vote to win. A special Congressional commission was formed to decide the disputed votes. In the end, a compromise was worked out. The Congressmen gave all of the disputed electoral votes to Hayes. In return, Hayes promised to withdraw Northern troops from the South, ending Reconstruction.

President Hayes removed all Northern troops from the South in 1877. Local governments then came back under white Southern rule. Former Confederate leaders began voting and running for office. Southern state legislatures took steps to prevent African-American citizens from voting or enjoying the other rights of citizenship. Most of the gains African Americans had made during Reconstruction were taken away.

Reasons for the Failure of Reconstruction

There were several reasons why Reconstruction failed to achieve equality for African Americans.

A Legacy of Racism

White Americans in the North as well as the South failed to recognize African Americans as equals. Centuries of prejudice stood in the way.

The Economic Dependence of African Americans

Reconstruction governments failed to divide up plantations and give freedmen their own plots of land. This meant black Southerners remained dependent on their former owners. Sharecroppers and tenants needed to use the landowner's land to survive. Many tenants quickly fell into debt to their landlords, creating a system of **debt peonage** (*they owed the landlord their labor until they paid off their debt*). To protect their economic livelihoods, most African Americans in the South stopped defending their political rights.

Freedmen Lacked Education and Political Experience

Before the Civil War, it had been against the law to teach slaves to read and write. Most of the freedmen had no formal education. This weakened their ability to compete with whites.

White Terrorism

The **Ku Klux Klan** was a secret society of Southern whites, formed after the Civil War. Klan members terrorized African Americans who attempted to stand up for their rights. Klan members disguised themselves with white hoods at night. They visited the homes of African Americans and beat them or killed them. A "**lynching**" was a brutal hanging by a crowd of people. African Americans who tried to vote might be lynched. The white Southerners who committed these crimes were never charged. Southern sheriffs, judges, and juries were all white.

Loss of Northern Interest

Reconstruction governments were established right after the Civil War. Northerners wanted to assert their control of the South after a hard-fought conflict. After the twelve years of Reconstruction, most Northerners lost interest in events in the South. They also needed the raw cotton and other crops grown in the South for their factories.

The Aftermath of Reconstruction: The Segregated South

Despite the promise of the Reconstruction Era, most African Americans in the South did not enjoy voting rights or the equal protection of the laws for another century.

African Americans in Southern States Lose Their Voting Rights

The Fifteenth Amendment had guaranteed African Americans the right to vote. But after Reconstruction ended, this right was taken away. Southern legislators passed special laws to prevent African Americans from voting:

Literacy Tests: **Literacy** (*the ability to read*) was not a constitutional requirement for voting. Southern states started asking voters to pass a literacy test before they could vote. Literacy tests were made more difficult for African Americans. White citizens were often excused from this requirement.

Poll Taxes: These were special taxes that had to be paid before voting. Poor African Americans could not afford them. They often had to be paid long in advance and could not be paid on the day of the election.

"**Grandfather Clauses**": These laws allowed people qualified to vote at the beginning of 1867, or their descendants, to vote without passing a literacy test or paying a poll tax. Poor whites didn't need to meet the new requirements. Only

The Voting Rights Act of 1965 attempted to remedy the denial of voting rights that occurred after Reconstruction ended.

The 24th Amendment abolished this practice, once used by Southern states to deny African Americans the right to vote.

poor African Americans did, because almost no African Americans had been qualified to vote in the South in January 1867. "Grandfather clauses" were finally declared unconstitutional by the U.S. Supreme Court in 1915.

As a result of these steps, white Southerners took control of Southern state governments and Southern representation in Congress. For the next hundred years, white Southerners voted for the Democratic Party. Republicans were blamed for the Civil War and Reconstruction. This led to what was known as the "Solid South" in national elections.

Racial Segregation: The "Jim Crow" Laws

Southern states also passed laws **segregating** (*separating*) blacks from whites. Whites and blacks attended different schools, rode in separate railway cars, ate in different restaurants, used different public bathrooms and water fountains, and sat on different public benches. These segregation laws were known as "**Jim Crow" laws**. "Jim Crow" laws denied black citizens equal opportunities and rights. They reinforced racial hatred and gave the false message that one race was somehow better than another.

The Supreme Court upheld these segregation laws in 1896 in the case of *Plessy v. Ferguson*.

This decision was later overturned by *Brown v. Board of Education* in 1954. The Court then ruled that racial segregation in public schools violated the "Equal Protection" Clause of the 14th Amendment.

Homer Plessy was seven-eighths white and only one-eighth African American. To test Louisiana's new "Jim Crow" law, Plessy bought a first-class train ticket. He then entered a "whites only" railroad car. Plessy was arrested and tried by the state courts. Plessy claimed that the law denied his rights under the Fourteenth Amendment. The case reached the U.S. Supreme Court. The Court upheld Louisiana's practice of racial segregation in *Plessy v. Ferguson* (1896). It ruled that racial segregation by a state was permitted so long as the state offered "separate but equal" facilities to both races. Black facilities were supposed to be as good as white ones, but could be separate.

Homer Plessy

The Historian's Apprentice

1. Imagine you are an attorney arguing the case of *Plessy v. Ferguson* in the U.S. Supreme Court. Give a five-minute presentation of your ideas, either for Plessy or for the State of Louisiana.
2. Make a slide show showing surviving photographs of daily life in the segregated South between 1877 and 1917.

The Later Expansion of Voting Rights

In 1877, many groups in America still had no right to vote. These included women, minority groups, and people who were old enough for military service but not old enough to vote. Over time our democracy has expanded. Different groups have fought for the right to vote and succeeded in obtaining it. A series of important constitutional amendments have expanded voting rights to reach all Americans.

Nineteenth Amendment (1920)	"The right of citizens of the United States to vote shall not be denied or abridged by the United States or by any State on account of sex."	This amendment gave women the right to vote. It was achieved after almost a century of activity by the women's rights movement.
Twenty-fourth Amendment (1964)	"The right of citizens of the United States to vote in any primary or other election for President or Vice President, for electors for President or Vice President, or for Senator or Representative in Congress, shall not be denied or abridged by the United States or any State by reason of failure to pay any poll tax or other tax."	This amendment prohibited states from requiring the payment of poll taxes in federal elections. Poll taxes had been used by Southern states to prevent African Americans from voting.
Twenty-sixth Amendment (1971)	"The right of citizens of the United States, who are eighteen years of age or older, to vote shall not be denied or abridged by the United States or by any State on account of age."	This amendment gave people eighteen years and older the right to vote. Before that, eighteen-year-old men were being drafted to fight in Vietnam and other wars but were not considered old enough to vote.

The Historian's Apprentice

1. Do you think Reconstruction was a success or failure? Discuss your answer with a partner and share your views with the class.
2. Make an illustrated timeline showing the expansion of voting rights in the United States.
3. Describe three things that you learned about early American history this year that surprised you. Write your answer in your journal or on a separate piece of paper.
4. Does knowledge of early American history make us better citizens? Explain your answer.

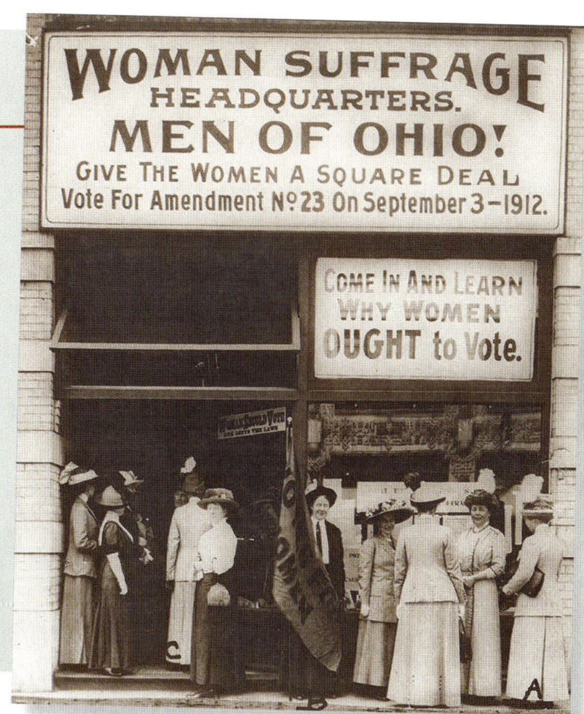

Chapter Review Cards

The Challenges of Reconstruction

- To "reconstruct" is to rebuild. Following the Civil War, Americans had to rebuild their country, especially the South.
- They faced many challenges:
  - How should Southern states be readmitted into the Union?
  - Should former Confederate leaders be punished or be permitted to participate in public life?
  - How to help the freedmen (*former slaves*) adjust to freedom? How would they earn their livings? How could they learn to read and other skills? How could they be prepared to vote and participate in public life?
  - How could the economy of the South be rebuilt? How could it be organized without slavery?

The Thirteenth Amendment (1865)

- This constitutional amendment abolished slavery in all states. The **Freedmen's Bureau, a federal agency**, was set up to help the freedmen (*freed slaves*).

Presidential Reconstruction

- Should the President or Congress decide on the terms for readmitting the Southern states into the Union?
- **Lincoln**: In his Second Inaugural Address, Lincoln told Americans he wanted to act without "malice" (bitterness or spite). He planned to readmit Southern states into the Union as soon as 10% of the voters in a state pledged allegiance to the Union and recognized the end of slavery.
- **Johnson**: Lincoln was assassinated in April 1865. The new President, Andrew Johnson, came from Tennessee—a state that had sided with the Confederacy. Johnson insisted that Confederate leaders seek personal pardons from him. Once they asked, however, Johnson would always pardon them.
- **State Governments and the "Black Codes"**: New Southern state governments, led by former Confederate leaders, passed "**Black Codes**." These were state laws like older "Slave Codes." They limited the rights and movement of the freedmen.

Congressional Reconstruction

- **Radical Republicans** were an influential group of Republicans in Congress. They wanted to increase African-American rights.
- Shocked at the Black Codes and the election of Confederate leaders, Radical Republicans refused to seat Southerners in Congress.
- The Radical Republicans passed the **Civil Rights Act**. This law was passed over President Johnson's veto. The new law granted freedmen the rights of citizenship, overturning the Black Codes.
- The Radical Republicans were afraid that the Supreme Court might overturn this law. Congress rewrote the Civil Rights Act as the **14th Amendment**. This important amendment defined citizenship and the rights of citizens. The 14th Amendment protects citizens from unfair acts by state governments.
- The amendment defines a **citizen** of the United States as anyone who is born in the United States or naturalized. (Thus, Dred Scott would have been considered a citizen.) **Naturalization** is the process that a foreign resident must go through to become a U.S. citizen.
- "**Due process of law**": This is a person's right to fair procedures before a state government takes away his or her property or freedom.
- "**Equal protection of the laws**": This is the requirement that state governments treat everyone as equals under the law. We should all enjoy the same basic rights.
- In 1870, **Susan B. Anthony** tried to vote on the basis of the 14th Amendment. She was arrested and lost her case.
- The **Reconstruction Act** (1867) divided the South into military occupation zones. The South was occupied by the Union army.
- The **Fifteenth Amendment** was ratified in 1870. It guaranteed men of all races the right to vote.

The Impeachment of President Andrew Johnson

- The Radical Republicans passed the "Tenure of Office Act." (Tenure refers to the holding of office by a person.) This law stated that the President needed the consent of the Senate to remove any Cabinet member.
- President Johnson felt this new law violated his rights as President. He removed the Secretary of War without the permission of the Senate.
- Johnson was **impeached** for violating the Tenure of Office Act. He became the first President to be impeached. When an officeholder is impeached, he or she is accused of wrongdoing that may cause the person to lose his or her office.
- In the U.S. Constitution, the President is impeached in the House of Representatives and tried in the Senate. To remove the President requires a two-thirds vote.
- When tried in the Senate, Johnson was saved from removal by only one vote. His term ended soon afterward, and Ulysses S. Grant was elected President.

Reconstruction Governments

- Carpetbaggers, scalawags and freedmen participated in Reconstruction governments in the South.
- **Carpetbaggers** were people from the North who came to live in the South during Reconstruction. Some came to help and others came for economic opportunities.
- African Americans voted and served in government for the first time. They filled positions in state government and some were elected to Congress.
- Reconstruction governments banned racial discrimination, established public schools, and encouraged railroad construction. They were also guilty of corruption (such as accepting bribes).

The Economics of Reconstruction

- Southern governments had to rebuild their economies.
- **Sharecroppers and Tenants**: White Southern landowners needed a work force. The former slaves needed work. The freedmen often became workers for their former masters. Many became **sharecroppers**. They used a landowner's land and at the end of the harvest paid the landowner a share of the crop. Other freedmen became **tenants**, renting land from the landlord.

The End of Reconstruction

- Reconstruction ended in 1877.
- **Rutherford B. Hayes** won disputed votes from Southern states by promising to withdraw Northern troops from the South.
- By this time, most Northerners had lost interest in Reconstruction.
- White Southerners quickly took back control of their state governments and took away many of the rights gained by African Americans during Reconstruction.

The "Jim Crow" Laws

- Southern state governments took steps to stop African Americans from voting. They required that they pass **literacy tests**, pay **poll taxes**, and meet special residency requirements. Poor whites were excused from these requirements by "**grandfather clauses**." These clauses said that if their grandfathers had voted earlier, they would be allowed to vote.
- African Americans were also threatened by violence. White Southerners dressed up in disguise as members of the **Ku Klux Klan.** They beat up or murdered African Americans who tried to exercise their right to vote and other rights.
- African Americans in the South also remained dependent on the white community for work.
- Finally, Southern state governments passed **"Jim Crow" laws**. These required **racial segregation**, or the separation of whites and blacks, in schools, railroads, restaurants and other public places.
- The "Jim Crow" laws were upheld by the U.S. Supreme Court in *Plessy v. Ferguson* (1896). The Court said separation by race was lawful so long as the facilities were "separate but equal."

The Expansion of Voting Rights

- The United States has gradually enlarged its democracy through constitutional amendments:
  - The 19th Amendment (1920) guaranteed women the right to vote.
  - The 24th Amendment (1964) prohibited poll taxes to vote in federal elections.
  - The 26th Amendment (1971) guaranteed the right to vote to those 18 years old and older.

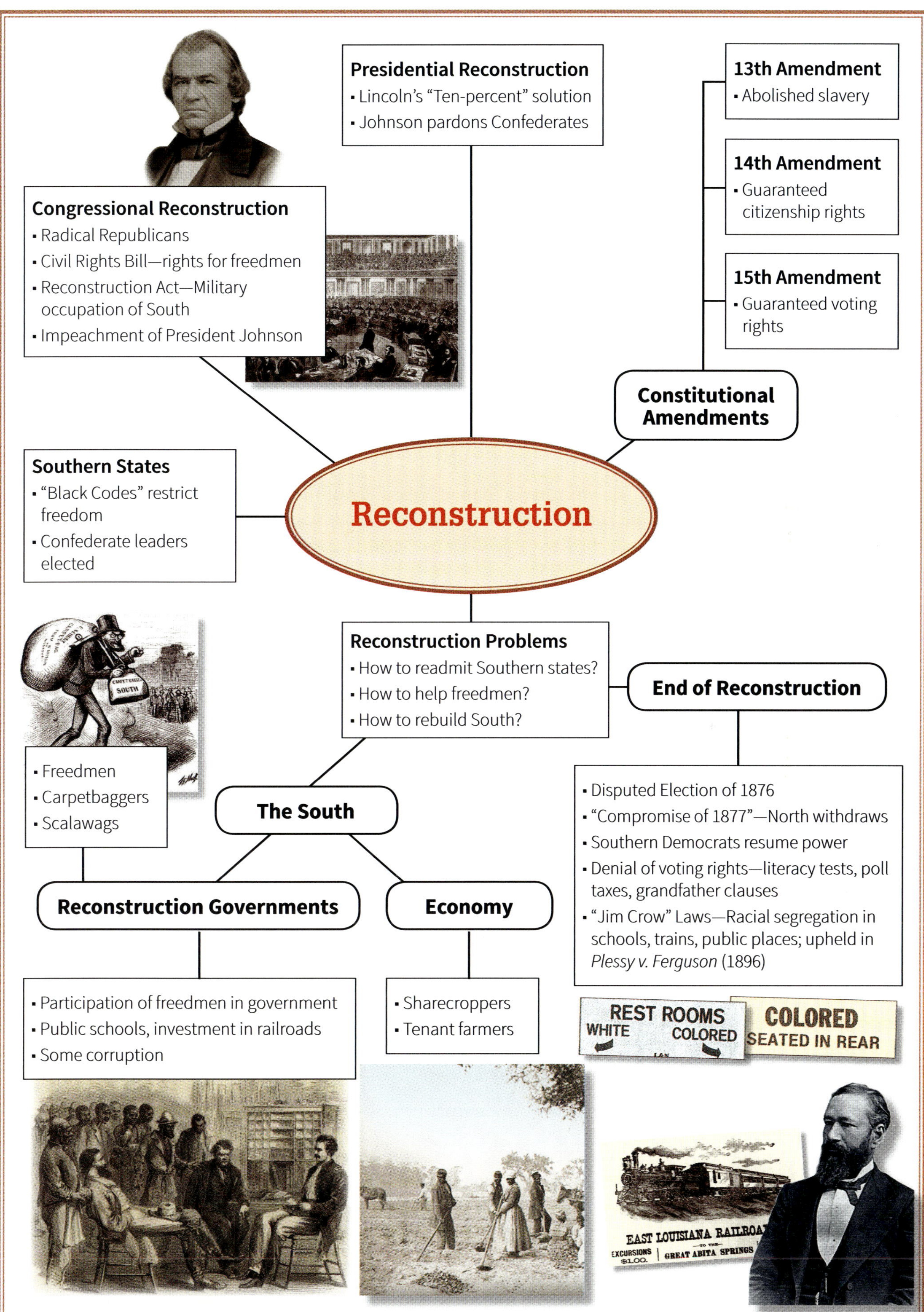
Presidential Reconstruction
• Lincoln's "Ten-percent" solution
• Johnson pardons Confederates
13th Amendment
• Abolished slavery
14th Amendment
• Guaranteed citizenship rights
15th Amendment
• Guaranteed voting rights
Congressional Reconstruction
• Radical Republicans
• Civil Rights Bill—rights for freedmen
• Reconstruction Act—Military occupation of South
• Impeachment of President Johnson
Constitutional Amendments
Southern States
• "Black Codes" restrict freedom
• Confederate leaders elected
Reconstruction
Reconstruction Problems
• How to readmit Southern states?
• How to help freedmen?
• How to rebuild South?
End of Reconstruction
• Freedmen
• Carpetbaggers
• Scalawags
The South
• Disputed Election of 1876
• "Compromise of 1877"—North withdraws
• Southern Democrats resume power
• Denial of voting rights—literacy tests, poll taxes, grandfather clauses
• "Jim Crow" Laws—Racial segregation in schools, trains, public places; upheld in *Plessy v. Ferguson* (1896)
Reconstruction Governments
Economy
• Participation of freedmen in government
• Public schools, investment in railroads
• Some corruption
• Sharecroppers
• Tenant farmers
REST ROOMS
WHITE
COLORED
COLORED
SEATED IN REAR

What do you know?

SS.6.A.5.8

1. Which was an important challenge of Reconstruction?
   A. how to restore slavery in Southern states
   B. how to reduce immigration from Latin America
   C. how to educate the freedmen to participate in public life
   D. how to improve conditions for workers in New England factories

SS.6.A.5.8

2. How were Abraham Lincoln and Andrew Johnson similar?
   A. They were both impeached.
   B. They were once slave owners.
   C. Their election resulted in a Civil War.
   D. They favored a lenient treatment of the South.

SS.6.A.5.8

3. Why were many Northerners upset when Southern legislatures passed "Black Codes"?
   A. They preferred a restoration of slavery.
   B. They wanted to pass similar codes in the North.
   C. They feared African Americans might move out of the South.
   D. They felt white Southerners were ignoring the outcome of the war.

SS.6.A.5.8

4. How did the Radical Republicans in Congress threaten the separation of powers?
   A. by proposing three constitutional amendments
   B. by giving the full rights of citizenship to former slaves
   C. by interfering with the actions of Southern state governments
   D. by limiting the President's power to dismiss Cabinet members

SS.6.A.5.8

5. Which amendment abolished slavery?
   A. Thirteenth Amendment
   B. Fourteenth Amendment
   C. Fifteenth Amendment
   D. Nineteenth Amendment

SS.6.A.5.8

6. The information below lists two events of the early Reconstruction Era.

- State governments passed Black Codes.
- Southern states elected former Confederate leaders.

How did the Radical Republicans in Congress respond to these events?

A. They welcomed former Confederate leaders back into Congress.

B. They voted to give extra federal money to help rebuild the South.

C. They passed the Civil Rights Act of 1866 and imposed martial law.

D. They gave extraordinary powers to President Johnson to deal with Southern leaders.

SS.6.A.5.8

7. The statement below is from an interview recorded by the Freedmen's Bureau.

I work on my former master's land. He gives us our tools and seeds to plant. We give him a share of our crop.

Who is being interviewed?

A. a scalawag

B. a carpetbagger

C. a sharecropper

D. a tenant farmer

SS.6.A.5.8

8. What was the main purpose of the Ku Klux Klan?

A. to make freedmen afraid to exercise their rights

B. to create a new political party in the South

C. to teach the freedmen how to read and write

D. to assist Southerners who had lost their savings in the war

SS.6.C.1.6

9. Which amendment to the Constitution guaranteed the right to vote to American women in 1920?

A. Fifteenth Amendment

B. Nineteenth Amendment

C. Twenty-fourth Amendment

D. Twenty-sixth Amendment

SS.6.A.5.8

10. The passage below is from Abraham Lincoln's Second Inaugural Address in 1865.

> *With malice [resentment, bad feeling] toward none, with charity for all, . . . let us strive on [make efforts] to finish the work we are in, to bind up the nation's wounds . . to do all which may achieve and cherish a just and lasting peace among ourselves and with all nations.*

How did the Radical Republicans disagree with the views expressed in this passage?

A. They wanted former Confederate leaders to return to local public office.

B. They believed the South should be severely punished for causing the war.

C. They thought Southern states should be immediately readmitted to the Union.

D. They did not think the freedmen were able to exercise full civil and political rights.

SS.6.A.5.8

11. The information below describes conditions in the South in 1865.

- Former plantation owners were without workers.
- Former slaves were without land, farm animals, or tools.

How did Southerners deal with these problems?

A. Most freedmen moved to Northern cities.

B. Southern landowners sold small pieces of land to the freedmen.

C. The freedmen bought inexpensive land from the federal government.

D. Most freedmen became sharecroppers or tenant farmers on the land of their former masters.

SS.6.A.5.8

12. What did the Supreme Court decide in the case of *Plessy v. Ferguson* (1896)?

A. Racial segregation in public places violates the equal protection clause.

B. Racial segregation in public places was lawful if due process was provided.

C. Racial segregation is lawful in some public places but not in public schools.

D. Racial segregation in public places was lawful if equal facilities were provided.

SS.6.A.5.8

13. The illustration below shows citizens in the South during Reconstruction.

Which consequence of Reconstruction is shown in this drawing?

A. Freedmen left farming to find work in industry.

B. For the first time freedmen exercised political rights.

C. Northerners took control of Southern life for more than ten years.

D. Southern whites and African Americans mixed freely without prejudice.

SS.6.C.1.1

14. The passage below is from the 14th Amendment.

> *All persons born or naturalized in the United States, and subject to the jurisdiction [legal authority] thereof, are citizens of the United States and of the State wherein they reside [live]. No State shall . . . deny to any person within its jurisdiction the equal protection of the laws...*

Based on the passage, which conclusion can be drawn about the 14th Amendment?

A. It gave citizenship to former slaves born in the United States.

B. It denied citizenship to the freedmen but gave it to their children.

C. It only permitted people born in the United States to become citizens.

D. It gave different rights to citizens born in the United States and naturalized citizens.

INDEX

Abolitionist, 272, 273, 275, 276, 330, 334, 335, 336, 359, 365
Adams-Onís Treaty, 241, 304
Adams, Abigail, 122
Adams, John, 89, 104, 106, 110, 114, 119,120, 122, 136, 195, 210–212
Adams, John Quincy, 237, 241, 244, 246, 247
Adams, Samuel, 104, 106
Albany Congress, 80
Alien and Sedition Acts, 210, 211, 212,
Annapolis Convention, 143
Anti-Federalists, 170
Antietam, Battle of, 364–365
Appomattox, 370
Articles of Confederation, 136, 137, 138, 139, 140, 156, 159, 167

Baltimore, Lord, 33, 65
Banneker, Benjamin, 121
Beecher, Lyman, 355,
Bill of Rights, 171, 172,173, 212
Black Codes, 384
Bonaparte, Napoleon, 213, 214, 218, 219
Boston Massacre, 89, 90
Boston Tea Party, 90, 174
Bradford, William, 30
Brown, John, 359
Bull Run, 363
Bunker Hill, 106, 107

Cabinet, 188, 189
Calhoun, John C., 233, 240, 269, 270
California Gold Rush, 301, 302
Calvert, George, 33
Carpetbagger, 392
Champlain, Samuel, 10, 11
Charles II, 33, 34, 35
Checks and Balances, 167, 168, 169, 170
Cherokee, 265, 266, 267
Cherokee Nation v. Georgia, 266
Civic virtue, 174, 188
Civil disobedience, 277
Civil Rights Act of 1866, 388
Clay, Henry, 233, 237, 244, 246, 260, 263, 267, 270, 296, 356
Clay's "American System," 239, 240, 241, 247
Coercive Acts, 91, 104
Columbus, Christopher, 5, 6, 7, 8
Common Sense, 103, 110
Compromise of 1850, 356–357
Confederacy, 360–371, 387, 392
Conscription, 362
Constitutional Convention, 156, 158, 162, 163, 167, 188

Daughters of Liberty, 87
Davis, Jefferson, 360, 370
Declaration of Independence, 91, 110, 111, 112, 114, 120, 121, 136, 156
Declaration of Sentiments, 276
Declaratory Act, 87
Democratic-Republican, 194, 195, 218
Dix, Dorothea, 274
Douglass, Frederick, 272, 276, 330, 335, 359
Dred Scott v. Sandford, 358, 389

Edwards, Jonathan, 65
Electoral College, 161, 188, 218, 247, 394
Emancipation Proclamation, 365–366, 386–387
Embargo of 1807, 219–220, 232, 239
Emerson, Ralph Waldo, 105, 276–279
English Bill of Rights, 62, 121, 171
Enlightenment, 91–92, 110, 168, 195
Era of Good Feelings, 239, 241, 243, 245–247, 263, 356
Erie Canal, 272, 324, 327

Federalism, 167, 170
Federalist Papers, 170–171
Federalists, 170–172, 189, 194–195, 210, 213, 216, 221, 238
Fifteenth Amendment, 392, 395
Finney, Charles Grandison, 272, 278–279
First Amendment, 172, 211
First Continental Congress, 104, 144
Fitch, John, 324–325, 328
Force Bill, 270, 279
Fort Duquesne, 78–80, 82, 93
Fort McHenry, 235–236
Fort Sumter, 360–361, 365
Fort Ticonderoga, 107–108, 115, 118, 121, 189
Fourteenth Amendment, 388–390
Frame of Government (Pennsylvania), 33, 59–60
Franklin, Benjamin, 80–81, 109–110, 116, 119–120, 122–123, 144, 160
Freedman, 388, 393
Freedmen's Bureau, 386
French and Indian War, 78–80, 83, 85, 94, 144, 213
French Revolution, 195–196, 210, 214, 221, 244
Fugitive Slave Act, 335, 355, 357
Fulton, Robert, 325, 328
Fundamental Orders of Connecticut, 33, 35, 59

Gadsden Purchase, 300, 305
Garrison, William Lloyd, 272–273, 275, 279, 335
Genêt, Citizen, 195
George III, 84, 85, 87, 104, 106, 109, 114, 144
Gettysburg Address, 367
Gettysburg, Battle of, 366–367
Gibbons v. Ogden, 325–326
Grant, Ulysses S., 299, 367–368, 370, 391–392
Great Awakening, 65–67, 271
Great Compromise, 160, 162

Haiti, 7, 214
Hamilton, Alexander, 116, 123, 158, 170, 189–196, 210, 218, 242
Hancock, John, 104–105, 123
Hartford Convention, 238, 240
Haynes, Lemuel, 121, 123
Henry, Patrick, 86, 104, 110, 170
House of Burgesses, 28–29, 59, 62, 67, 86
House of Representatives, 158–159, 164, 218, 246, 261, 391
Hudson River School, 277
Hudson, Henry, 12
Hutchinson, Anne, 33, 35, 37, 64

Impeachment, 165, 390–392
Impressment, 219, 233, 237
Indentured servant, 54, 56–57, 59
Indian Removal Act, 263, 265, 279
Industrial Revolution, 320, 322, 328–329
Interchangeable parts, 323, 328

Jackson, Andrew, 237–238, 241, 246–247, 260–263, 265–271, 273, 279, 304, 326, 336
Jacksonian Democracy, 261, 263
Jamestown, 25–32, 38, 62, 79, 82–83, 320
Jay Treaty, 196, 210
Jefferson, Thomas, 106, 110–111, 121–123, 136, 189, 190–192, 194–196, 210, 212–216, 218–221, 232, 240, 246–247, 269, 279, 332
Jim Crow laws, 396
Johnson, Andrew, 387–388, 390–392
Judicial Review, 216–217
Judiciary Act of 1789, 216–217

Kansas-Nebraska Act, 357, 359
Kentucky and Virginia Resolutions, 212
Key, Francis Scott, 236
King Philip's War, 36
Ku Klux Klan, 395

La Salle, Robert de, 11
Lafayette, Marquis de, 107,117, 119, 123
Lake Erie, Battle of, 235
Lee, Richard Henry, 110–112, 123, 170
Lee, Robert E., 362, 364–368, 370–371
Legislature, 61, 91, 112, 136, 138, 158–159, 164, 212, 214, 274–275, 324–325, 328, 393

Lewis and Clark Expedition, 214–216, 303
Lexington and Concord, Battles of, 104–106, 109, 120–121
Lincoln-Douglas Debates, 359
Lincoln, Abraham, 355, 359-368, 370, 386–387
Locke, John, 63, 92
Long Island, Battle of, 108
Loose constructionist, 192
Louisiana Purchase, 213–215, 238, 243, 300, 303, 357
Lowell, Francis Cabot, 322, 328
Loyalists, 108–109, 118, 121–122

Madison, Dolley, 235
Madison, James, 110, 123, 157, 160–162, 168, 170–171, 190–192, 194, 212, 216–217, 232–233, 235, 240, 246
Magna Carta, 58–59, 62, 67, 92
Manifest Destiny, 296–297
Mann, Horace, 274–275, 279
Marbury v. Madison, 216–217
Marshall, John, 216, 242, 266
Mason, George, 110, 123
Massachusetts Bay, 30–33, 53, 59, 63–64
Mayflower Compact, 29–30, 59
McCulloch v. Maryland, 242–243, 267
McClellan, George, 363–366, 368
Mercantilism, 85
Mexican-American War, 298, 301, 303
Missouri Compromise, 243–244, 356–358
Monroe Doctrine, 244–246
Monroe, James, 240, 244–246
Mormons, 303
Mott, Lucretia, 275

National Road, 239–240, 299
Natural Bridge, Battle of, 371
New Amsterdam, 12, 34
New France, 10
New Jersey Plan, 159–160
New Netherland, 11–12, 34–35
New Orleans, Battle of, 237–238
Non-Intercourse Act of 1809, 232
Northwest Ordinance, 140–142, 244
Northwest Passage, 10
Nullification, 268–270, 279

Oglethorpe, James, 35, 37
Ohio River Valley, 78, 80, 83–84, 91, 93, 294
Olive Branch Petition, 106
Olustee, Battle of, 366, 371
Ordinance of Nullification, 270, 279
Oregon Territory, 296–298

Paine, Thomas, 110, 123
Party nominating conventions, 261–262
Patriot, 104–110, 119, 121–122, 161, 170, 174, 261
Penn, William, 33, 37–38, 54, 59–61, 63–65
Perry, Oliver, 235
Pilgrims, 28–31, 36, 59, 64
Pinckney's Treaty, 196, 214
Pizarro, Francisco, 9–10
Plantation, 34, 52, 55, 57, 62, 67, 86, 162, 243, 261, 304, 328–333, 337–338, 354, 388, 393–394
Plattsburgh, Battle of, 236–237
Plessy vs. Ferguson, 396
Plymouth, 28–32, 38, 63–64
Political party, 109, 193, 212, 232, 267–268
Polk, James, 296–299
Poll taxes, 391, 393
Preamble, 163, 307, 355
Precedent, 188–189
Princeton, Battle of, 108
Proclamation Line of 1763, 84, 122
Proclamation of Neutrality, 195
Protective tariff, 192–193, 240, 247, 355
Protestants, 10–11, 24, 28, 30, 32, 33, 54, 65, 271, 276, 305, 355
Puritans, 28–33, 53, 59, 64, 277

Quakers, 33, 54, 64, 272, 334
Quartering Act of, 1765, 87–88, 91
Quebec Act, 91

Radical Republicans, 388, 390–391
Ratification, 166, 170–171, 388
Reconstruction, 386–388, 391–397
Religious toleration, 32, 64–65, 67
Republican Party, 357, 359–360
Revolution of 1800, 212

Sacajawea, 215–216
Santa Anna, 295–296, 300
Saratoga, Battle of, 115, 119
Scalawag, 393
Scott, Winfield, 299–300, 362
Secession, 238, 360, 371
Second Continental Congress, 105, 110, 114, 136, 139, 144
Second Great Awakening, 271–272
Sectionalism, 354
Segregation, 396
Seneca Falls Convention, 276, 279
Separation of Powers, 167–170, 390
Sharecropping, 393
Shays, Daniel, 143
Shays' Rebellion, 143, 145
Sherman, William Tecumseh, 368
Slater, Samuel, 322, 328
Slave culture, 333
Slave trade, 12, 55, 162, 333
Smith, John, 27, 37, 320
Social contract, 63, 92, 111
Sons of Liberty, 86, 87, 174
Southern colonies, 52, 54–61
Spoils system, 261–263
Stamp Act, 85–87,94, 120
Stamp Act Congress, 86–87, 144
Stanton, Elizabeth Cady, 275–276, 386
Star Spangled Banner, 236
Steam engine, 321, 324–326, 328, 361
Strict constructionist, 192
Subsistence farming, 56
Suffrage, 276
Supreme Court, 61, 165, 167–169, 188–189, 216–217, 239, 242–243, 261, 266, 267, 269, 325, 358–359, 388, 396
Suspension of *habeas corpus,* 362

Tariff of 1816, 240, 269
Tariff of Abominations, 268–269, 279
Tea Act, 90, 94
Tecumseh, 232–235
Temperance Movement, 272, 275
Thirteenth Amendment, 366, 387
Thoreau, Henry David, 277
Three-fifths Compromise, 161–162, 238
Tocqueville, Alexis de, 263, 274
Town meetings, 59–60, 67
Townshend duties, 87, 90
Transcendentalists, 277
Treaty of Ghent, 237
Treaty of Guadalupe Hidalgo, 300–301
Treaty of Paris (1763), 83
Treaty of Paris (1783), 119–120, 140, 144
Trenton, Battle of, 108–109, 240
Triangular trades, 52
Tubman, Harriet, 335–336, 359

Unalienable rights, 111, 112
Underground Railroad, 334–336

Valley Forge, 109, 116–117,
Vicksburg, Battle of, 367–368
Virginia Plan, 159–160

War hawks, 233
War of 1812, 232–234, 238–241, 261
Washington, George, 78–80, 86, 104, 106–109, 114, 116–117, 119–123, 136, 142, 144, 156, 188–198, 210, 232, 260, 320, 332
Webster-Hayne Debate, 269, 355
Whiskey Rebellion, 196–197
Whitney, Eli, 323, 328–329
Williams, Roger, 32–33, 35, 37–38, 64, 67
Winthrop, John, 31, 37–38, 64
Wolfe, James, 82, 86
Women's rights, 87, 121, 122, 272, 275–276, 279, 336, 390, 397
Worcester v. Georgia, 266, 279
Yorktown, Battle of, 119–120

Zenger, John Peter, 63–64

The United States in 1877
CANADA
Alaska
Minnesota
Michigan
Wisconsin
Michigan
New Hampshire
Vermont
Maine
Massachusetts
New York
Rhode Island
Connecticut
Pennsylvania
New Jersey
Delaware
Maryland
Oregon
Nevada
California
Colorado
Nebraska
Kansas
Iowa
Illinois
Indiana
Ohio
West Virginia
Virginia
Missouri
Kentucky
North Carolina
Tennessee
South Carolina
Arkansas
Mississippi
Alabama
Georgia
Louisiana
Texas
Florida
Atlantic Ocean
Gulf of Mexico
MEXICO
CUBA
Pacific Ocean
Caribbean Sea
0
500 miles
0
1000 km